"Be Kind to the poor"

The Life Story of

ROBERT
TAYLOR
BURTON

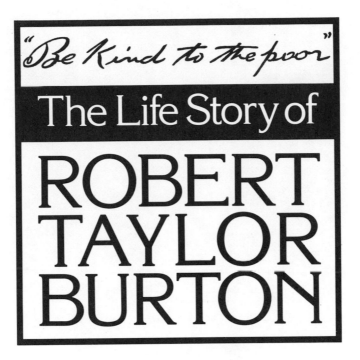

"Be Kind to the poor"

The Life Story of

ROBERT TAYLOR BURTON

Janet Burton Seegmiller
for the
Robert Taylor Burton Family Organization

To my many cousins,
the posterity of
Robert Taylor Burton

This book uses an author-date system rather than footnotes or endnotes for documentation of sources. The author, date of writing or publication, and pages are shown in the text in parentheses and keyed to the bibliography on pages 455 to 463. For example, "(R. T. Burton 1843–69, 1–3)" refers to pages 1–3 of a journal kept from 1843–69 and described under Burton, R. T. in the bibliography (see p. 456). If the author is mentioned in the text, only date and page are in parentheses; ie. "(1843–59, 3–4)" refers to same journal, pages 3–4. Several items by Robert T. Burton and William S. Burton were not dated and are shown in the bibliography as "n.d." with an alphabetical superscript, ie. "n.d.[a]" refers to Robert T. Burtons undated autobiography (see p. 456).

Contents

Preface

This book has its roots in a family meeting held in the year 1885. It was in the fall of the year, on his sixty-fourth birthday, that Robert Taylor Burton called together fifty-eight family members and friends at his Haven Villa residence to organize the family into a "Burton Family Association."

Robert Taylor Burton was, in his words, "on the underground" at the time. He had been away most of this year of 1885 and was planning to be gone again. (He left twenty-five days later to begin his longest period of self-exile from his home and family.) But he stayed long enough to launch the family association.

Not only did Robert T. Burton organize his family, he became the first president of the Burton Family Association and remained so for twenty-three years, long enough to assure the perpetuation of the family as an organized unit. At the twenty-third annual meeting, held October 25, 1908 at the Burton farm, William S. Burton became the new president. One hundred three years later at the publication of this book, the family association remains intact. It continues to meet regularly.

This biography, written by Janet Burton Seegmiller, is published by the Robert Taylor Burton Family Organization. It is precisely because the family was organized and continued as a unit from its inception to the present time (1988) that this book was made possible.

At that first family meeting in 1885, grandpa Burton said to his children: "I may meet you many times in gatherings the same as the present but we can not tell what a day may bring forth; still, I trust I may have the opportunity of being present in my family circle many, many times on occasions like the present."

He has indeed been with us in spirit at the hundred annual meetings of the family. I have felt that in these many family gatherings Robert Taylor Burton has had that "opportunity of being present" in his family circle to witness what his example has wrought.

I believe the spirit of his life has been captured by Janet B. Seegmiller in this biography. It has been a labor of love for her. (She hasn't received a dollar for her thousands of hours on this book.) All the "cousins," all of the descendants of Robert Taylor Burton join with me in thanking Janet for this dedicated work.

Robert Taylor Burton was a good man who led a most interesting life. When you read this book and ultimately close the cover of grandfather's biography—much before you turn that last page on the life of grandpa Burton—you will have come to the powerful conviction that here was a man to remember! Here was a noble man, one of the great ones among all the sons and daughters of God who walked upon this earth.

> —Rulon T. Burton, chairman of the book publication committee and a former president of the Robert Taylor Burton Family Organization

Acknowledgements

One of the rewards of writing my great-great-grandfather's biography has been getting to know many cousins who share his parentage. This book could not have been written without their assistance. It's purpose is not just to tell the history of a great man and wonderful father, but to nurture the family ties of his descendants, filling his request to "keep the family together." In many ways, even the process has helped accomplish this goal, as friendship and love have grown among the family members who have contributed to this project.

I have been inspired by a note written by one of Robert's granddaughters, Theresa Burton Brown, who found a collection of old family letters in a small trunk in her attic. "To me they are all precious and so closely connected with history of country and church and family. . . . I wish I had the ability to write an interesting story," she lamented. "The people of my family all seem so real and I can see the reason for their characters and actions all so plainly."

Thanks to family members like Theresa, many letters, memoirs, and documents have been preserved, along with the dream of publishing the family's "interesting story."

From the day in 1975 when he called me as "biography specialist," Rulon T. Burton has been my mainstay. As president of the family organization for over ten years and chairman of the book publication committee, he has been generous in his encouragement, personal dedication, and patience. His prompt responses to requests for direction and for financial and technical support have kept the project going and his experience with writing and publishing have been vital in producing a quality book. The entire family is indebted to the leadership and vision of Rulon T. Burton.

I also wish to acknowledge and thank the following cousins whose contributions have been significant:

Theodore M. Burton began research for this biography in the 1950s. He has generously opened his files to me, shared insights from his knowledge of the family, reviewed individual chapters and the completed manuscript, and continually encouraged me. I have drawn strength and peace from a priesthood blessing he gave me in August 1981.

Rebecca Upham spent many days copying by hand the entries from Robert T. Burton's journals at the LDS Historical Department Archives so that this resource would be available for my constant use. She made my task so much easier. Rebecca died not too long after the biography was begun, but her sacrifice and spirit have been a guide to me. I recognize and appreciate her major contribution.

My uncle, Robert H. Burton, collected and copied many family papers and was the first to express confidence in my ability to undertake this project.

Helen B. Raybould and Mildred C. Cram, daughter and granddaughter of William S. Burton, have preserved many valuable family records of both William and his mother Maria. I appreciate their willingness to provide copies of these records and to read parts of the manuscript. Helen shared her memories of Robert and Maria in a lengthy interview and has answered many questions over the years. I also pay tribute to William S. Burton for writing his memoirs and compiling a history of five generations of Burtons.

Douglas B. Cutler, Geneve C. Walker, Lenore C. Gunderson, Alice May Cutler, and Theodore C. Walker, who are children and grandchild of Virginia Burton Cutler, have been generous with family resources and their time. They have done original research, shared personal genealogical and historical records, and reviewed the manuscript. Their history of Ralph and Virginia Cutler, published in 1976, has been a valuable resource and set a standard for this biography.

Betty Burton Stohl, great-granddaughter of Susan McBride Burton, gathered information from family and Church resources for Appendix D on Susan's life and the McBride family. I also appreciate the McBride family in Arizona, descendants of Susan's brother James Andrew McBride, who have shared their family records through Philis McBride Bryce.

Faun (Mrs. Lawrence) Burton of Kamas located the land records for the "Weber Ranch" near Peoa in the Summit County records.

Lillian B. Andrew searched the Relief Society records of the Fifteenth Ward for information on Robert, his wives, and Sarah M. Kimball, and shared a special letter written from Robert to his children.

The various members of the family organization board of trustees have been very supportive and patient over the thirteen years of this project.

My parents William G. and Zella S. Burton have solved several different research problems and have tended my children on many occasions while I was researching and writing. My brothers and sisters and their spouses and my aunts and uncles have helped in a variety of ways in addition to giving me constant encouragement. My love and appreciation to them is unfailing.

In addition, a number of historians have been interested in this pioneer biography and I am indebted to them for assistance and encouragement. Leonard J. Arrington urged me to write Robert's history, suggested sources and research problems, and finally reviewed the manuscript. William G. Hartley has shared his own research and sources, especially on the role of the Presiding Bishopric, has reviewed several chapters, and answered many questions. Richard E. Bennett researched the Canadian, Michigan, and Ohio property and church records for Chapters 1 and 2. John Peterson added information about Robert's military service and items on Robert from his personal research. Steven Heath and Susan E. Black have reviewed the chapters on the early history of the Church through the Nauvoo period, and Mark Stuart commented on the history of the Morrisites.

I thank the staff at the LDS Historical Department Archives and Library for their cooperation and assistance. Linda Haslam has been especially helpful and has promptly responded to several urgent requests for materials from the Journal History.

I also appreciate the help of my friends at Southern Utah State College Library and Cedar City Public Library who have gone the second mile in ordering books through inter-library loan, locating materials and original information in their special collections, and in cheering me on as the manuscript neared completion.

Lavina Fielding Anderson has patiently and carefully edited the manuscript to enhance the writing and resource documentation. Her expertise in LDS resources and style has added significantly to the scholarly aspects of the book. I also greatly appreciate her caring attitude and enthusiasm for this project.

During the past thirteen years, my family has lived in Brigham City, Utah; Albany, Georgia; Sparks, Nevada; and Cedar City, Utah. I am grateful that there were special friends in each community who made my family, church, and community tasks easier while I was working on this book.

Finally, I acknowledge the support and sacrifice of my husband, Keith, and my children, Harmony, Mercy, Adam, Enoch, and Joy Genevieve. They have permitted me to live in the nineteenth century during my spare moments for the past thirteen years. They can hardly remember when Mom wasn't working on "the book" and believe that mothers are supposed to spend all vacations in libraries and visiting with cousins. I appreciate them; I love them; I am pleased I can help my children and my loved ones to honor their Burton heritage.

Janet Burton Seegmiller
Cedar City, Utah

Introduction

"Never disgrace the name of Burton. Be faithful to the Church. Keep the family together. Be kind to the poor."

It was November, 1907. An eighty-six-year-old Robert Taylor Burton, weak and aware that death was near, called his sons William S., Henry F., and Willard C. to his bedside. To them, the eldest sons of each of his three wives, he gave those instructions as parting counsel to his posterity. His admonitions summarized the principles he lived, particularly the plea, "Be kind to the poor."

This venerable Utah pioneer, whose name was frequently prefaced with a number of titles, including general and bishop, spent his life taking care of the poor—the poor in spirit as well as the physically poor. His great desire was to see his descendants carry on his work.

From the day he left Nauvoo in June 1843 as a twenty-two-year-old Mormon missionary preaching the gospel of Jesus Christ in the humble villages of Illinois, Ohio, and Michigan, through the rescue of the handcart pioneers in 1856, the days of caring for seasick immigrants crossing the stormy Atlantic in 1875, and the building of a railroad in 1880 to lower the price of coal for impoverished Salt Lake City residents, to nights he personally tended a sick child or comforted a son or daughter upon a child's death, Robert T. Burton was kind to the poor.

He chose to align his life with an unpopular religion and to live its most misunderstood principle—plural marriage—thereby introducing struggle, persecution, disappointment, and controversy into his life's work. His story is intertwined with the history of the people he loved and the land he pioneered.

The Family of Samuel and Hannah Burton

Robert Taylor Burton was the son of English immigrants Samuel Burton Jr. and Hannah Shipley Burton, who came to North America in 1817 seeking a more prosperous life. He was born in Canada in 1821 but moved with his family to America and back again to Canada before he was nine years old. One of fourteen children, Robert was influenced by strong family ties.

On the morning of May 4, 1817, a sailing ship weighed anchor at Liverpool, England, embarking on an Atlantic voyage to Quebec, British America. Among the hundreds of passengers soberly leaving their homeland were Samuel and Hannah Burton and their four children.

Samuel was a youngish thirty-four years old, slight of build and dressed in common clothes, that indicated neither wealth, nor poverty. Hannah Shipley Burton was just thirty years old, but already the mother of seven children, three of whom lay buried near their former homes in Lincolnshire. The four children accompanying them were Jane, age eleven, William, seven, Betsy, five, and eighteen-month old Ann.[1]

Surely excitement mingled with sadness as this young couple left England. There had been three earlier moves in the thirteen years since their marriage June 12, 1804. The Luddington marriage records note: "Samuel Burton, bachelor and cordwainer, and Hannah Shipley, spinster, both of this parish, married by banns June 12." Hannah was born and raised in Gilberdyke, Eastrington Parish, just across the Ouse River in Yorkshire. Samuel and Hannah lived first at Luddington, but moved about 1807 to the village of Garthorpe, which had been Samuel's birthplace.[2] Eastrington, Gilberdyke, Luddington, and Garthorpe are villages in north-east England near the confluence of the Old Don, Ouse, and Trent rivers about twenty miles inland from the North Sea (see map, p. 113).

In 1815, they moved down river to the much larger city of Hull, a Yorkshire port. Each move was made so that Samuel would have better employment, but instead the struggle to provide for his family became more difficult.

Great Britain had been at war with Napoleonic France throughout those years. In addition, the United States declared war on England in 1812, a war which ended in 1814, bringing desperate postwar conditions. Unemployment reached unprecedented heights, wages went steadily down, and the plight of the poor intensified. Fear gripped the people as they heard rumors that the population was outgrowing the food supply. The government began encouraging the exodus of the "suffering masses" (Craig 1963, 124–25). Samuel and Hannah Burton and their counterparts who immigrated before 1820 were the vanguard of the greatest migration of modern times.

Although Samuel's father (Samuel Burton, 1744–89) died when he was six years old, leaving his mother, Mary Johnson Burton (1745–1809) to provide for the family, Samuel somehow was able to attend school and learn to read and write before apprenticing as a shoemaker, or cordwainer as the trade was called in England. These skills had a great influence on his children and on the pattern of their family life. Although the shoemaking trade did not provide a good income and security in nineteenth century England, it was an asset in the frontier communities of the New World. Samuel taught his children to read and write or saw to it that they attended school whenever possible.

As Samuel struggled to provide for his family during the 1804–17 period, he heard of great opportunities in the new United States and in Upper Canada, as Ontario and Quebec were then known. Books were circulating throughout England authored by earlier English immigrants describing the vastness of the fertile western prairies, the unclaimed land, and abundant opportunities for all. Letters probably came from Hannah's brother, William Shipley, who had immigrated in 1816, urging them to immigrate also.

Perhaps it was the promise of owning land and finding both prosperity and security in a new country that led Samuel and Hannah to the point of departure. They found neither. Instead of monetary prosperity, the New World gave them spiritual wealth in the restored gospel of Jesus Christ, and it was their posterity who found temporal and spiritual abundance.

They left family members, including Hannah's aged father, William Shipley (1755–1818). Her mother, Jane Taylor (born 1757), had died in 1792. But relatives were also waiting to greet them, and others either accompanied them or followed soon after. Samuel and Hannah lived near relatives in both New York and Canada, and their children kept contact with cousins through letters and visits into the twentieth century. Family ties were important to the posterity of Samuel and Hannah Burton.

From May 4 to July 4—sixty long days and nights—the Burtons sailed the Atlantic. Although seasickness, crowded quarters, limited rations, and occasional illnesses were common on such a voyage, none of these "expected" hardships were overwhelming. They probably kept busy attending to family needs and helping fellow passengers. Perhaps Samuel used the hours to teach his children. Seven-year-old William, writing about the trip many years later, would only remember that it took sixty days and that they landed in Quebec where they remained but "a short time" (W. Burton n.d.).

By boat the Burtons traveled up the St. Lawrence River and across Lake Ontario, landing in Ontario County, New York (perhaps at Rochester) where they were welcomed by Hannah's brother and sister-in-law, William and Elizabeth Waters Shipley. They made their first home near the Shipleys in a small village on the borders of Lake Ontario, near the town of Pultneyville (sometimes Putneyville or Poultneville), in the immediate vicinity of the Shipley family (R. T. Burton 1898). Just over a year later on August 31, 1818, Hannah delivered her eighth child, a daughter named Mary Hannah. She was the first of seven children born in the United States and Canada.

At the time Samuel and Hannah left England there was much controversy over whether British subjects should immigrate to America—so recently the country's enemy—or to Upper Canada where they could remain British subjects and strengthen one of the colonies. Many articles proclaimed the advantages of settling the wilderness west of Montreal and Quebec north of the Great Lakes. Actually few immigrants were swayed by these arguments, but the Burtons were among the minority who moved into Canada. Their decision was probably influenced by the availability of land near relatives and friends. Two years after arriving in Pultneyville, the Samuel Burtons moved to Essex County, Canada West (also known as the Western District of Upper Canada).

Essex is the western-most county along the north shore of Lake Erie. Since the wilderness roads were few and often impassable, the Great Lakes provided passage deep into the continent. The Burtons probably traveled by boat through Lakes Ontario and Erie to the Detroit River, finally arriving at the settlements opposite Detroit known as Windsor, Sandwich, and Amherstburg (see map, p. 115).

This area had been settled late in the 1700s. When Michigan became a U.S. territory, the loyal British living there moved directly across the river. Richard Pollard, a priest of the Church of England, became the first rector of the parish of Sandwich in 1802, assuming missionary jurisdiction for the church in the Western District. He was therefore chaplain to the British forces at Fort Malden, prominent in the War of 1812. After the war, the area near the fort was renamed Amherstburg (Neal 1909, 179).

In 1819, Samuel, Hannah, and their five children settled near Amherstburg. Reverend Pollard was now minister at Christ's Church, Amherstburg, where the Burton family was welcomed into the congregation. Samuel began making shoes and waited to obtain a land grant. Life was pleasant; the community was growing and busy. On August 21, 1820, a son was born, but the family's joy was short-lived as tiny John Shipley Burton died at the age of three months.

A year later on October 25, 1821, another son was born, one who would live to provide protection and support to his parents in their old age and who would be patriarch to the Burton family for over sixty years. He was named Robert Taylor Burton, for his maternal great-grandfather. On January 7, 1822, the first Sunday in a new year, Samuel and Hannah had their new son baptized by Reverend Pollard at Christ's Church, Amherstburg[3] (see photograph, p. 116).

While Robert was young, Samuel apparently obtained the land grant he had been waiting for and the family moved from the relatively settled area around Amherstburg into the unbroken wilderness of Mersea township, thirty miles eastward. No land records have been located for Samuel Burton in Mersea; but Robert, in an 1897 "abridged account of my progenitors," wrote that his father owned land in Canada.[4] It is possible that he did not have clear title to the land he claimed in Mersea, but the family lived on that farm from 1823 to 1828 and from 1830 to 1837 (Burton Family Association 1885–1953, 33–34).

Rural Mersea was the least populated of any area where the Burtons had been. Communication was difficult; religious and educational opportunities existed only in the larger settlements. In general, it was a primitive society with few of the amenities of civilization (Craig 1963, 131). The Samuel Burtons, familiar with village and city life, were suddenly on their own land—an uncleared forest—and living in a roughly built home. The wilderness did not yield easily to the plow and Samuel was not an experienced farmer. The long hours he and his children spent working the land brought little return.

Hannah faced the challenge of making a home and caring for her children with the barest of necessities. She must have been a remarkable woman, a strong and supportive wife, a resourceful mother. She did not know how to write even her own name and may never have attended school, but she taught her children the importance of learning to read and write, always encouraging them to attend school and teach each other. The letters and journals written by her children in later years reveal a command of language uncommon to frontier families.[5] According to family tradition, Hannah taught her children to sing and love music. Not only did Robert learn to play violin, piccolo and bugle, but family gatherings up to the third generation always included singing and instrumental music. Because the isolation of Mersea made it impossible for the family to attend church, the responsibility of religious instruction fell upon Samuel and, as he grew older, William. William's autobiography indicates that he felt he was reared to be moral and temperate in his dealings with mankind; he had serious thoughts about future existence and was prayerful (W. Burton n.d.).

Living in Mersea township were two English families who became good friends and, eventually, relatives by marriage to the Samuel Burtons. They were William and Ann Oats Leybourn, formerly of Staindrop, Durham County, England, and William (Ann's brother) and Elizabeth Jefferson Oats, from Bowling Green, Yorkshire. Shortly after the move to Mersea, Samuel and Hannah's oldest daughter, Jane, married John Leybourn, eldest son of William and Ann, on September 30, 1823.

Three daughters were born to Samuel and Hannah in Mersea: Sarah, born November 16, 1823; Rebecca Maria, February 16, 1826; and Melissa, March 2, 1828. They now had nine living children. With the birth of Jane and John Leybourn's first son, William, on July 19, 1824, in Mersea, they also became grandparents.

Before their baby was a year old, Jane and John decided to locate in a new settlement being developed at the mouth of the

Maumee River directly across the west end of Lake Ontario in U.S. territory. John rowed his family in a small boat across the lake, now and then taking advantage of the wind by using Jane's shawl as a sail. The boat was not very seaworthy, for William Leybourn related the family story that Jane held him in one arm and continuously bailed with the other during the long trip. They rowed into Maumee Bay and up Ten Mile Creek to the settlement of Tremainsville ("Eighty years ago . . . " 1905).

The area had great potential as a Great Lakes port, but the undeveloped land was swampy with almost impenetrable marshes edging the river and its several tributary streams. Above the marshes, the ridgelands were covered with giant oaks and dense forests. Wild swans, geese, and ducks were abundant in season; beaver, otter, and muskrat thrived in the bayous while bear, deer, and elk roamed the deep forests (Von Tassel 1929, 1230). Not too far from Tremainsville, at the confluence of Swan Creek and the Maumee River, was a "paper city" called Port Lawrence. Six years earlier in 1817, a group of investors had formed the Port Lawrence company, arranged purchase of 974 acres, and platted a city. After the company defaulted on its 1818 payment, ten years of legal controversy ensued which was apparently settled by 1827 when a new plat was approved although it was not recorded until 1832. In the meantime, several families, like the Leybourns, moved into the area and waited for the lots to be sold. The village of Tremainsville was a little better organized and claims to have had a church and postal services, the first in the area by 1825 (Von Tassel 1929, 1239–51).

John and Jane could not immediately buy land in Port Lawrence, but arranged to farm forty acres which they finally purchased in 1829 for $100. John Leybourn made his farmland productive and added more acreage in 1833 and 1835. Their letters to Jane's parents encouraged them to move there also.

After farming at Mersea for five years, Samuel evidently was very discouraged. Clearing and working land was difficult; the winters were harsh; his family missed the comforts of city life; economic conditions were not good and it was difficult to pay the taxes levied by the English parliament. Samuel was ready to move, and it appeared the Leybourns had found a place with potential. At some time after Melissa's birth in the spring of 1828, the Burtons crossed Lake Ontario and arrived in Port Lawrence. They may have been somewhat surprised to see that the settlement still consisted of a few dwellings, a warehouse, chills and fever, frogs, swamp and yellow scum ("Eighty years ago . . . ," 1905; Burton Family Association 1885–1953, 33).

Although the Leybourns were prospering, Samuel Burton and his family did not. Robert believed his father "owned a quarter section of land on which a part of the city [Toledo] now stands," but no land records in Samuel's name in the area have been found. It may be that the legal problems of the Port Lawrence Company kept him from completing purchase of the land he claimed. Samuel stayed for only two years. The land owners were not pursuing the development with much energy, and other companies were developing competing settlements in an effort to become the major port city. In 1833, the city of Toledo was formed by uniting Port Lawrence with the new town of Vistula and the older Tremainsville, but the Burtons had already moved in the spring of 1830, to Adrian, thirty-five miles northwest, on the Rosin River in Lenawee County, Michigan Territory (Burton Family Association 1885–1953, 33).

Samuel and Hannah reluctantly left behind them not only Jane, but another married daughter. Betsy, at seventeen, had married young landowner Joseph Roop, one of Port Lawrence's earliest settlers,[6] on September 8, 1829. They were expecting their first child. John and Jane by then had two sons and a baby daughter. These two Burton daughters lived out their lives and raised large families in Toledo (W. S. Burton n.d.[a], 3–5)

Arriving in Adrian, Samuel and Hannah were pleased with the decision to move. They found a town divided into nineteen village lots, with streets, a grist mill, a post office, a dry goods store, a cabinet shop, a brickyard, and a good frame school house (Knapp and Bonner 1903). They were grateful to be away from the fever and chills common to the swampy Maumee River settlements.

Shortly after their arrival, Hannah delivered a son, her fourteenth and last child, named Charles Edward, on June 4, 1830. When the census was taken in September 1830, Samuel Burton and his household of ten were among the 1,431 residents of Lenawee County (1830 Michigan census, Adrian District).

Samuel Burton was anxious to purchase land in the promising area but did not have enough money. Robert believed that his father tried to dispose of his property in Canada and, when he could not find a buyer, was forced to return to Canada. The move was made after the census was taken September 27 and before October 19. The Burtons had not really traveled far from Essex County and probably were able to get back to their farm in a few days travel by wagon.

At the time of their return, Robert Burton was nearing his ninth birthday. Samuel and Hannah were in their mid-forties, yet they had a very large and young family to care for. The move back to their Mersea farm put them near their friends and relatives just before Essex County entered a period of religious and political turmoil.

Notes

1. For complete genealogical information on the family of Samuel and Hannah Burton, see Appendix A.

2. Many family genealogical records incorrectly show this as Garth*rope*. According to his mother's certificate of burial and his parents' marriage certificate (copies in possession of Geneve Cutler Walker), he was born at Garthorpe, a parish and village in north Lincolnshire, six and a half miles northeast of Crowle (*Gazetteer of the British Isles* 1966, 280).

3. Ontario Church Records, Sandwich, Anglican Church, 2:136. This record states that Robert T. Burton was born on the "twenty-sixth of October." All family records and his personal writings give the October 25 date which is that accepted by the family. Family members have visited Christ's Church, Amherstburg, built in the early 1800s as recently as 1979.

4. At the author's request, Richard E. Bennett, a professional researcher, searched the land deed records in Windsor and Mersea and found record of William Burton owning land, but none of Samuel Burton owning land in Canada.

5. The best examples are the journals of William and Robert, the holographs of which are in the Historical Department Archives. Typescripts and a few holographs of many letters written by William, Robert, Ann, Sarah, and Rebecca are kept in the Robert Taylor Burton Family Association files, photocopies in my possession. The location of most of the holographs is unknown.

6. *General Index to Deeds*, nos. 1 and 2, Lucas County, Ohio; also *Record of Deeds*, 8:71 and 15:319, contain information about land holdings for Joseph Roop and John Leybourn.

Student, Reluctant Investigator, Convert, 1830–38

Returning to Canada in 1830 was the first step the Samuel Burton family took which led to membership in The Church of Jesus Christ of Latter-day Saints. In Western Canada, the years between 1834 and 1838 were filled with religious and political turmoil. During this explosive period, sixteen-year-old Robert persuaded his father to shelter two strange American preachers in their home. A year later, his family had to convince him to consider their message of a "restored gospel." His conversion "by unmistakable evidence" followed.

It was good to be home in Canada. The Burtons discovered that many more people had settled in Essex County and the roads were much improved. Neighbors and relatives welcomed them, especially Mary Shipley Harsine, Hannah's sister, her husband Charles, and their children, who were long-time residents in Essex County.

The Burtons had not been involved in an Anglican congregation since 1821. However, on one of the first Sundays after their return to Mersea, they presented their four youngest children, Sarah, Rebecca, Melissa, and Charles, for baptism at Christ's Church in Amherstburg. The Reverend Romaine Ralph, priest from 1819 to 1836, baptized the children. He recorded their birthplaces as Mersea, which is incorrect for Charles Edward. Samuel gave his occupation as "shoemaker," indicating that he did not think of himself as a farmer or landowner. William Burton is listed with Charles and Mary Harsine, and their children Thomas and Hannah, as "sponsors" ("Register" 1829–72, October 19, 1830).

From this time, the Burtons began a period of frequent church attendance and activity. During the next four years, Christ's Church records list at least six occasions when they were sponsors at baptisms and marriages, an indication that they had a wide circle of Anglican friends. William Burton's name appears particularly often, although in his autobiography, he wrote he had not joined any religious society before his conversion ("Register" 1829–72, October 1830 to September 1834; W. Burton n.d.)

The last entry referring to one of the Burtons is in September 1834, yet they remained in the area until 1838. The sudden break with the Anglican Church is puzzling. Three years later, Samuel and William became embroiled in a local political crisis known as the Rebellion of 1837, which stirred up anti-American sentiments. They were considered pro-American. It may have been during the very beginnings of this "rebellion" the family stopped attending a pro-British church and began meeting with other religious societies. Although William was listed as a witness at the March 17, 1832, marriage of John Oats, his own marriage to John Oats' cousin on July 28, 1834, and the September 7, 1834, marriage of his sister, Ann, are not recorded in Christ's Church parish records.

William's wife was Elizabeth Oats Lawrence, widow of Prosper Lawrence and daughter of William and Elizabeth Jefferson Oats. Elizabeth was born in England April 11, 1804, and had immigrated with her parents to Canada. She was thirty years of age at the time of the marriage; William was five years younger.

Eighteen-year-old Ann Burton married her cousin, Waters Shipley, son of William and Elizabeth Shipley of Pultneyville, New York.

Robert wrote nothing of his life from 1830 until 1837, when the family decided to send him to Toledo, Ohio, to board with the Leybourns and attend school— "opportunities for obtaining an education being very meager where my parents lived in Canada owing to the unsettled condition of the country and my fathers limited means" (R. T. Burton n.d.ª, 2). Apparently there were schools in Amherstburg or Windsor, but no money to pay board and room. The decision to send him to Toledo indicates the depth of commitment Samuel and Hannah had to their children's education.

Before Robert left for Toledo in the fall of 1837, two Americans came into the community. Family tradition says that Robert met them on the street, and when they asked if he knew of a place they could stay, he offered his father's home. He described this meeting in an address to the family association in 1903:

> When but a boy of sixteen, two strangers came to my home, and they were indeed strangers, and very unwelcome ones in that section of the country as the prejudice of the people was great against them. They sought the privilege of holding meetings, to present their strange doctrine. We were indeed entire strangers and none of our neighbors would give shelter to these men. I prevailed upon my father to invite them to our home, and to give them an opportunity to be heard. He did so, and they held meetings in the place. (1903, 1)

These "strangers" were elders of The Church of Jesus Christ of Latter-day Saints, sent into Canada from Church headquarters in Kirtland, Ohio. One was Zerah Pulsipher, who would be called in 1841 as one of the first presidents of the First Quorum of the Seventy (D&C 124:138). The other was Jesse Baker. Zerah Pulsipher wrote of this mission:

> I took a mission to Canada. There I found the Roman Catholicks and Methodists. I commenced preaching among them. I soon found that I was followed by the Circuit Preacher. . . . He followed me up till we came in contact one Evening as I had met a congregation. I arose to speak but hearing footsteps at the door I paused when the Methodist Preacher came in with about twentyfive of his society. We got them seated altho the house was crowded before. . . . After he sat down I arose and said to him as he had made Nine Propositions

to prove my discourse wrong I should take them all up and if I should forget any of them I wish him to remind me of the same but I took up every one of them and opened them till I knew that the congregation were satisfied that I was right. As soon as I sat down he arose and began to spat against Joseph Smith and the Book of Mormon. I immediately called him to order as I had not spoke upon Joseph nor the Book of Mormon and at that late period he had no right to bring up subjects that not been on to the Carpet that night, but said I will Preach Tomorrow evening if you pleas. I will meet with you and we will discuss these subjects but he said there would not be time. I then said you Preach at the meeting house on Sunday and we can have time and realm to investigate according good order, but he declined. I told him I did not wish to hold any man by the button and if he could not be with me I should be under the Necisity of spaking on them in his absence. He finally said none, but retired and afterwards said to his Methodist breathren to let me alone as he did not know what it might amount too. I immediately took up the character of Joseph Smith and the Book of Mormon and laid them open to the people and soon began to Baptise till I found a branch of twenty-nine members, many of them Methodist. I set them in order, ordained elders, returned to Kirtland around the head of Lake Erie (Pulsipher n.d., 9).

This meeting was likely held in the home of Samuel and Hannah Burton, with the younger children, plus William and Elizabeth Burton, and her parents in the congregation. William described his first encounter with Mormonism: "In the fall of 1837 I heard the first Latter Day Saint Elder preach the 'Everlasting Gospel' which was strangely new and different from any other preaching I had ever heard and it appeared to change my mind altogether. I was lead to embrace the Gospel of Jesus Christ with all my heart" (W. Burton n.d.).

William Burton's papers show that his in-laws, William and Elizabeth Oats, were the first LDS converts in Mersea. With John Hampton, they were baptized November 29, 1837. Samuel and Hannah Burton were baptized on December 4, William and Elizabeth Burton on December 9, Rebecca and Melissa Burton on December 23, and Mary Burton on May 7 (W. Burton 1837–51, 4).

Robert heard Pulsipher and Baker preach only a few times before he left for Toledo where he boarded with John and Jane Leybourn and their six children, attended school, and helped on the farm to pay for his keep. John Leybourn had acquired several sections of land by this time. Robert also visited his sisters, Betsy and Ann. Betsy and Joseph Roop had a large, successful farm and a family of four children. Ann and her husband, Waters Shipley, who had moved to Toledo in 1835 when he received a land patent, had two small sons.[1]

Robert attended school during the winter, but on March 4, 1838, John Leybourn died leaving Jane "with a large family of children to care for and educate." Robert recalled, "Soon after the death of my brother-in-law it became necessary for me to quit school and assist my sister and her family on the farm, being thus engaged untill the early part of September 1838" (R. T. Burton n.d.[a], 2).

Toledo was about 150 miles from Kirtland. Even though members of The Church of Jesus Christ of Latter-day Saints were in the process of moving to Missouri, the problems of the Church in Kirtland and the bitterness of the first apostates created great prejudice as vicious rumors of financial wrongdoing reverberated through Ohio and the Midwest. Robert and his sisters absorbed these prejudices. Thus, they were dismayed when Hannah came to Toledo in September 1838 with news of the family having embraced the Mormon religion. At his mother's request, Robert returned home "to aid in the support of the family, my father being engaged in what was known as the Patriot War on the Canadian line and on this account he was necessarily away from home" (R. T. Burton 1903, 1). However, Robert planned to return to Ohio as soon as possible and not associate with the Latter-day Saints. "I was much opposed to this people in consequence of the many damaging rumors in circulation against them in the State of Ohio, and other states" (R. T. Burton n.d.[a], 3).

The timing was crucial. The establishment of Mersea Branch the previous fall coincided with the open outbreak of hostilities known as the Rebellion of 1837. Dissatisfied with the aristocratic, pro-Anglican Tory government of Upper Canada, political opposition began in the Detroit-Essex area, abetted by Americans who conducted border raids and generally stirred up the peace along the U.S.-Canadian border. Rumors raged that Canadian refugees were gathering in Detroit, soon to be joined by hordes of unemployed, "cut-throat" Yankees, who would march against Windsor and Sandwich and wrench the entire western peninsula from the British. Vindictive Tory editorials denounced "unbridled democracy," accused Americans of fostering "mob" authority, and ridiculed the "land of the free" where only anarchy could result from a philosophy that each and every man was equal. American editors of Detroit newspapers reciprocated by attacking the subservience of the majority of Upper Canadians to the British Crown: "The inhabitants of Upper Canada are neither morally nor physically prepared 'to make the sacrifices necessary to achieve and maintain their independence,' " they sneered (Eady 1969, 5).

Elders Pulsipher and Baker, preaching the strange doctrines of an American religion, had walked right into the center of this controversy late in 1837. After establishing the branch of twenty-nine converts and ordaining William Burton as presiding elder, they had returned to Kirtland in January leaving their converts the targets of persecution by Essex's pro-British residents. It is not clear whether the political situation sparked the persecution of these converts as American or rebel sympathizers, or whether their enemies took advantage of the political situation to attack their Mormon neighbors without reprisal. The men were dragged from their beds in the night, some were tarred and feathered, and rock-throwing mobs broke up Latter-day Saint meetings.

William Burton subscribed to the second theory:

About this time a rebellion broke out in Canada and this gave our friends a good opportunity to persecute us. We were called rebels and some of the members including my father were carried to prison. All these things were conducted against us by our old neighbors.

> What a change this doctrine had made in our friends. They were almost ready to take my life simply because I had started to serve the "God of My Fathers" (W. Burton n.d.).

In Mersea, Robert was astonished to find a new spirit in his father's home, a sense of peace and direction in spite of the attacks and threats. One night, a mob gathered near the Burton home and, at a given signal, smashed in all the windows at one time. Robert naturally resented the persecution, and he also knew it to be unjust. "This state of affairs caused me to reflect, as I knew these people had broken no law nor had they in any way trespassed upon or interfered with the other religious sects around them" (R. T. Burton n.d.ᵃ, 3–4). No one tried to force their new beliefs on him.

> My brother and my sisters . . . very kindly urged me to read some of the books and investigate their doctrines. I thought I knew about all that I cared to of these people, as I had heard damaging reports from Kirtland. I was finally persuaded to read some of their books, such as the Voice of Warning and other works of this kind and finally attended their meetings and this is where I was first privileged to hear the doctrine of the Latter Day Saints. I had read some and was soon satisfied that my conclusions were wrong, that I knew nothing of the people whom I had so misjudged (R. T. Burton 1903, 1–2).

One Saturday night he fell asleep pondering the new doctrines, and experienced the following:

> I dreamed I was in a Latter Day Saints meeting; during the service and while we were quietly seated listning to the Elders, we were attracted by the entrance into the room of what appeared to be Seventeen large black snakes, that immediately attacked the people assembled there, and in the struggle which followed, one of these snakes bit me on the side of the head and another on the right side of my body. Although the serpents appeared to be very venomous it did not appear to me that I received any injury from either of them. (R. T. Burton n.d.ᵃ, 4–5)

The next evening, Robert attended an LDS meeting in a home. The meeting was opened and an elder stood to speak when a loud knock was heard at the door. When it was not answered immediately, the door was broken open.

> A mob appeared and began to throw tar into the room on chips or strips of wood; they finally pushed their way into the house and engaged in a general fight or struggle with the Saints. The mob consisted of Seventeen Men (?) with their faces blackened and themselves otherwise disguised in a hideous manner.
>
> In the struggle which ensued I came to the aid of one of the "Mormons" (so called) who was attacked by two mobbers. I was in the act of wrenching a club from one of them when a third one came to their aid and struck me with his club with much violence on the side of my head just where (in my dream) the snake had bitten me. Continuing the struggle with these men for some little time, another mobber came up and struck me with his club on the right side with much force; but strange to say neither of these blows hurt me in the least. (The mob was armed with heavy clubs.) The dream and its almost literal fulfillment came to my mind as soon as order was restored, and has had a lasting impression on me during my life (R. T. Burton n.d.ª, 5–6).

Sixty-five years later, Robert Taylor Burton told his family that "the Lord showed me by unmistakable evidence that this doctrine taught by the Latter Day Saints was correct, and so sure was my conversion that it has never left me to this day" (R. T. Burton 1903, 2).

A few days after the dream and its literal fulfillment, Robert was baptized by Elder Henry Cook and confirmed by Elder John Landers, missionaries to Canada from the States. The baptismal date is usually shown as October 23, 1838, although William Burton's Mersea Branch records and Robert's "High Priest's Genealogy" duplicate certificate dated April 1892 show the date as September 23, 1838.

As so many nineteenth century converts to Mormonism discovered, it was impossible to live the new religion and remain in their home communities. The members of Mersea Branch endured the persecutions for nearly a year, all the while preparing to move to the new gathering place in Missouri. William sold 200 acres for 162 pounds, 10 shillings to help finance the trip for the Burtons. There is no record that Samuel sold any property. Perhaps it was William's land that Robert remembered as his father's or perhaps they owned it jointly.[2]

Robert's baptism made a great difference in his plans for the future. He now fully shared his family's anxiety to leave Mersea and gather with the Saints. Instead of returning to Ohio, he joined the family in preparing for the long trip, the eighth move for Hannah and Samuel. However, Hannah approached the packing for this trip with a different spirit because she expected the move to Missouri to be her last. She expected to live the remainder of her life among spiritual brothers and sisters, guided by their prophet-leader, Joseph Smith. The grand promises of life in Zion must have made Hannah's heart light as she directed her children where to stow each box, barrel, chair, pot, and pan. Her six children still unmarried were more help than ever. Mary was a young woman of twenty years; Robert was seventeen; Sarah was fifteen, Rebecca, twelve, Melissa, ten, and Charles was eight. All but Charles were baptized. Although Charles would share the fortunes of his family and the Saints for many years, he would be forty-two years old before finally accepting church membership.

Late in October 1838, a party of horse-drawn wagons left Mersea. William Burton headed the company, which included the membership of the Mersea Branch, with the notable exception of his in-laws, William and Elizabeth Oats. The company traveled to Windsor, crossed the river into Detroit on November 1, and moved on toward Far West, Missouri, "the general gathering place of the Saints" (W. Burton n.d.).

Notes

1. There are many references to land transactions for John Leybourn and Joseph Roop in *General Index to Deeds*, Lucas County, Ohio, 1825–50. Waters Shipley received eighty acres on October 1, 1835, *Record of Deeds*, Lucas County, Ohio, 1825–50, Vol. 10, p. 61.

2. Deeds of Essex County, Ontario, Book H. no. 29. William's land was described as Lot #232, north on Talbot Road West, Mersea Township. Six years later, he was given or purchased Lot #230, from his father-in-law. He sold this land in 1847 to finance his move to the Salt Lake Valley.

3

Refuge
in Illinois,
1838–42

The Burtons made a temporary home in Knox County, Illinois, during the expulsion of the Latter-day Saints from Missouri and the imprisonment of the Prophet Joseph Smith in Liberty Jail. Robert grew to manhood during this interlude, finding it, despite the turmoil, a "pleasant time" in his life.

As they were being ferried across the Detroit River, the small party of Canadian Saints could not have known of the violence falling upon the members of the Church in Missouri.

During the week before the departure from Mersea, even as Robert helped load the wagons and while branch members sold property and excess possessions, the Missouri Saints were fleeing ugly mobs, their belongings mostly left on farms they would never be permitted to sell. Caldwell County was a battlefield. Once considered a haven for more than 12,000 Mormons, Caldwell and nearby Daviess and Carroll counties succumbed to the vicious rumors and political plots of the non-Mormon opposition. Harassment escalated into burnings, beatings, rapes, and assaults. When word reached the Missouri state leaders that the Mormons were "rioting" and arming themselves, the state militia was sent under command of Captain Samuel Bogart, becoming just one more mob with which the Saints had to contend. On October 25, Robert Burton's seventeen birthday, seventy-five Mormons, organized under David W. Patten, met Bogart's militia-mob at Crooked River. One Missourian and three Saints were killed. Exaggerated reports of the skirmish were carried to the new governor, Lilburn W. Boggs. Using this battle as his excuse, on October 27, Governor Boggs issued an infamous order: "The Mormons must be treated as enemies, and must be exterminated or driven from the state if necessary for the public peace—their outrages are beyond all description" (CHC 1:478–79; Arrington 1974, 59).

The day the Burtons left their Canadian homes, seventeen Mormons were killed and twelve wounded at Haun's Mill, and as the Burtons entered Michigan, Joseph Smith, Sidney Rigdon, Parley P. Pratt, Lyman Wight, and George W. Robinson were tricked into surrendering to General Lucas, while Charles C. Rich, Hosea Stout, Lorenzo D. Young, Samuel Smith, Phineas H. Young, and fifteen other men escaped from Far West ahead of the militia-mob which took control of the city (CHC 1:485–87; Arrington 1974, 60).

One cold November day after another, Samuel and William Burton urged their horses forward across Michigan, then Indiana, and Illinois. The journey was not easy, but they were prepared for cold weather and grateful that the poor roads were frozen rather than muddy. Robert was a great help, adept at handling the horses and caring for the stock. From the eastern border of Illinois, the Mersea Mormons headed for the Illinois River, following it down into the Peoria area (R. T. Burton n.d.[a], 6–7).[1]

Approaching Illinois from the west were the thousands of Saints fleeing the Missouri mobs. Robert described them in 1903 in relating his history to his children and grandchildren:

> The first of them that I met was in Quincy Illinois on the Mississippi River. They were poor, indeed, having been driven from their homes and farms in the inclement season of the year of 1838. Their suffering was indeed very great; it was truthfully said that

their trail as they travelled over the barren prairies of the State of Missouri could be traced by the blood from their feet (2).

Upon their arrival in Peoria, the Burtons heard the shocking news of the imprisoned prophet and fleeing Saints. Since they could not go on to Missouri, they stayed there a few weeks to rest their horses, replenish their supplies, and consider their future (R. T. Burton n.d.ª, 7).

In Canada, they had known only as much about the Church as they could learn from the traveling elders and a few pamphlets. They had never seen an apostle, attended a conference, or met more than a few Church members. In contrast, they were now welcomed by Saints who had joined the Church in the first years of its founding, 1830–32. Among them may have been Henry Cook, who had baptized Robert. Near Peoria, Charles C. Rich, Hosea Stout, and other leaders had been converted and built up branches before the move to Missouri (Arrington 1974, 14–17, 22–23, 45–49).

In Robert's seventeen years, he had not seen much prosperity, but apparently neither had he seen such poverty as he observed among the refugee Saints. He traveled with his brother William to Quincy, Adams County, Illinois, where the sight of these vagabonds was deeply impressed on his mind. The people of Adams County had sympathetically offered the Saints refuge in their neighborhoods, but still the masses of people were ill, hungry, poorly sheltered, and inadequately clothed. Many were in mourning for their dead loved ones and racked by fears for the prophet and other leaders imprisoned in Liberty, Missouri. Robert never forgot this time of "sorrow and suffering" (1903, 2).

Back in Peoria, information circulated among the Canadian Saints and other refugee families that Moses Smith, an elder in the Church originally from Burlington, Wisconsin, had purchased 160 acres in Walnut Grove, a township just being developed forty miles northwest. Smith was encouraging Saints to move with him to Walnut Grove until word came from the prophet about future gathering places, and the Burtons were among the first families to move. They rented land from Smith and lived in small houses near his frame home. When the Walnut Grove Branch was established, Moses Smith was chosen presiding elder.

The township had extensive groves of walnut trees for which it was named and was amply watered by Walnut Creek and its tributaries. The first permanent settlers came in 1836, so there were not too many non-Mormon neighbors to oppose the small community of Saints. Robert wrote that his last opportunity for schooling was in Walnut Grove in the winter of 1838–39 (n.d.[a], 7), probably in a home as the community's first school house was not built until 1841. His younger sisters and brother may have studied in the new 16 x 16 foot log schoolhouse, where Mary Frail and Eugene Gross were the first teachers (University of Illinois 1878, 502).

Walnut Grove was about 130 miles from Quincy where the majority of the Latter-day Saints took refuge. However, by the spring of 1839, Church members were purchasing land at Commerce, a village 50 miles upriver from Quincy on the Mississippi. The tract of land was surrounded on three sides by a sweeping curve of the river, and from the river banks the land rose gradually for nearly a mile. In the lowlands the soil was moist and miry, and malaria plagued the early residents. Robert described the area as "a very sickly place, or perhaps [the Saints] would not have had the privilege of stopping there" (1903, 2).

Commerce became the hub of Church activity and, in the spring of 1840, was officially renamed "Nauvoo." The early settlers labored long and hard to create a city which could be called "the beautiful" from the swampy land and low hills overlooking the Mississippi. William Burton visited the area in 1839 and again in 1842 between his second and third missions. When he returned in 1845, he was amazed at the changes wrought by the industrious Saints:

> My heart leaped with joy to behold my Brethren and friends . . .
> and also to see the progress of the Temple—the walls being nearly
> [up] and other improvements that were made in the City. My mind
> reflected back to the scenes that were past, when first the Saints

> began to build the Temple and City, in their afflictions and poverty.
> What a change had taken place! in the face of the country where it
> was a howling wilderness but a year or two back. It was now a part
> of the city (W. Burton 1839–51, May 1845)

Two years later, Robert would help his father's family move
to Hancock County, settling fifteen miles from Nauvoo; for the
time being, they stayed in Walnut Grove. The 1840 census
reported eight persons in the Samuel Burton household: obviously Samuel and Hannah, their two youngest sons and four
youngest daughters. One person, probably Robert, was engaged
in agriculture, while another, undoubtedly Samuel, was employed
in manufacturing and trades.

Robert wrote little about the temporal activities of his family because they were overshadowed by the great joy he was
experiencing within the thriving branch of 100 members which
the Burtons had helped to establish. Apparently Moses Smith
talked of building a temple in the area, which aroused the non-
Mormon neighbors who did not want Walnut Grove to become
a Church center (University of Illinois 1878, 501). Robert was
continuing his study of the scriptures and he listened attentively to William, who devoted most of his time to preaching
and missionary work.

The summer before Robert's twentieth birthday, Walnut
Grove was the site of a district conference. On July 10, 1841,
Church members gathered from Tolon, Richland Grove, and
Walnut Grove, most likely finding shelter from the heat and
humidity in a shady grove. William Burton, clerk of the con-
ference, recorded that ninety-two members were present from
Walnut Grove, including one high priest, ten elders, two priests,
two teachers, and two deacons "all in good standing" (c1837–51,
July 12, 1841).

The district conference was not only important for the instruction and spiritual strengthening of these new Saints, but was
also a significant social gathering. Robert and his sisters were
well known among the Mormon youth. When the day ended in
singing, dancing, and storytelling, Robert undoubtedly participated wholeheartedly.

His twenty-two-year-old sister, Mary, was courting. On October 24, 1841, she married Samuel Dennis White, son of John G. and Lucy Bailey White, also Walnut Grove Saints. Elder Moses Smith, who performed the ceremony and filed the marriage certificate, was a partner in land ownership with John White. Samuel and Mary would become the parents of ten children and eventually settle at Beaver, Utah.[2]

Within small farm communities like Walnut Grove many men often sought work for wages during the winter in larger towns and cities. Robert spent the winter of 1841–42 in Galesburg, Knox county seat, where he worked for the Fair Play Grant Company. In February, nineteen-year-old Sarah wrote her brother news of Church and family, a letter he must have cherished for he kept it all his life.

> Walnut Grove, Feb. 5th, 1842
>
> Dear Brother I gladly embrace the opportunity of addressing a few imperfect lines to you in answer to yours that I received the 3 of Feb. and was pleased to hear that you was well and also to inform you that we are well. I feel to thank my heavenly father that though you are seperated from your friends and from the Church of God that he is still mindful of you and that he still bestows upon you the blessing of health and I trust with many other blessings. We ware very anxious to hear from you and had almost give up the idea of ever hearing from you again. I should have wrote to you but was wating to hear from you as Mary had written to you and requested you to write. I received a letter from Mary and Samuel the same day that I received yours. They was well and stated that they had received a letter from you. Mary complains of being lonesam but I dare say she is not more so that we are for you must well know that the society of a kind sister and Brother must be misst and I can assure you that you are and particular at home. We do not have the company that we once did neather do we enjoy it as well as the absence of those we love oft cast a gloom over our minds but we look forward to the time when we shall enjoy each others company through a vast eternaty for if in this life only we have hope surely of all we would be most miserable and I can truly say that if in this life only I had hop I should be miserable and I persume you could say the same. Things here are not as I wish they were. There is considerable contention more than ever there has been before and perhaps it is not necesary for me to send the particulars but suffice it to say

that you know the stories about Rebeka and Brother Smith and many others have been brought up. We had a letter from Wm. last week. He said he should not return till spring. He was in Michigan. He visited our friends in Ohio and found them favourable to our doctrin all with the exception of Ann and she opposed him. I have written to Waters as William wanted us to. Now concerning going to Nauvoo our folks think of moving about the first of April and they think you had better return as soon as the first of March if you can. They do not know where they shall go but they think of going some where in that county. Your friends here often speak about you and perticular the girls. Lucretia thinks that still is as good intent as any. Brother Smith wishes to be remembered and says he often thinks of you. It is Saturday night and I must bring my letter to a close. Colen sends he compliments to you and all the rest of the folks. I must now close by suscribing my self your affectionate sister

Sarah Burton[3]

Robert would have been pleased with the report from William that their sisters, Jane and Betsy, had received him favorably as a missionary, and very concerned about the contention and rumors among the Mormons in Walnut Grove. He returned from Galesburg in March as requested to help his parents prepare for the move to Hancock County. In his autobiography, Robert summarizes the Walnut Grove interlude: "We had a very pleasant time and formed some very agreeable acquaintances in this vicinity" (n.d.[a], 7).

Notes

1. In his biography, Robert says they went to Peoria, but in his family history given to the Burton Family Association, October 25, 1897, he identifies the location as Canton. These two towns are not far apart, but Peoria is on the Illinois River.

2. Marriage Certificates, Knox County, Illinois, filed November 5, 1841. Photocopy in my possession.

3. Sarah Burton married Elijah Austin on March 16, 1843. They lived in Walnut Grove, Illinois, before settling in Sublette, Illinois, about 1850.

Missionary from Nauvoo, 1842–44

The events, triumphs, and trials of seven years in Nauvoo set the course of The Church of Jesus Christ of Latter-day Saints and established the pattern for development in the Great Salt Lake Valley. The name of Robert Taylor Burton does not appear in current histories of Nauvoo, but because of the events he witnessed, the decisions he made, and the alliances he developed during this period, he is part of the history of the Church and state in Utah.

At the outset of the Nauvoo period, Robert was a seventeen-year-old convert. Although young and impressionable, he was a deep thinker; he was hard-working but unskilled except at farming; he was unacquainted with the world outside the frontier settlements of Canada, Michigan, and Ohio. In contrast, at age twenty-four as he left in the vanguard of the Nauvoo exodus, he was a seasoned missionary and musician, an ordained Seventy, a new husband, and perhaps most crucially, a friend and protégé of Brigham Young. The achievements of a mature Robert were deeply rooted in his Nauvoo experiences.

In April 1839, when Joseph Smith selected Commerce as the new center for Mormonism, he vetoed proposals made by other Church leaders that the Saints live in scattered communities. Joseph Smith decided on concentration rather than fragmentation as the means of survival. When word went out in the fall of 1839 that the new Nauvoo was now the gathering place, the family of Samuel Burton did not immediately respond. At the time, their temporal needs were being met, and they felt they were "gathered" in the branch at Walnut Grove. However, two years later, with "considerable contention" dividing the Saints in Walnut Grove (Sarah Burton 1842), Samuel was ready to follow the prophets counsel. In the May 24, 1841, *Times and Seasons*, the Church's official organ, Joseph Smith had announced the discontinuance of all stakes outside Hancock County, Illinois, and Lee County, Iowa (directly across the river from Nauvoo), and called all Saints residing elsewhere were "to make preparations to come in without delay." The prophet wrote:

> This is important and should be attended to by all who feel an interest in the prosperity of this, the corner stone of Zion. Here the temple must be raised, the university be built, and other edifices erected which are necessary for the great work of the last days; and which can only be done by a concentration of energy and enterprise (in Whitney 1:187).

Several Church leaders, including Joseph Smith, had contracted for extensive and expensive land in the Nauvoo area, planning to pay off the notes by selling city lots. New settlers meant financial relief and skills to build the temple and other public buildings. Church members with property outside Nauvoo were urged to deed it to the Church in exchange for property in Nauvoo. This exchange of lands was one way of dealing with the financial burdens which plagued Church leaders during the earlier years in Nauvoo.

Although the city was rapidly growing, its economic base was neither agricultural nor industrial but speculation in real estate. Nauvoo had all the appearances of a prospering community, but could not support its increasing population. Concern for the poor consumed Joseph Smith. On June 13, 1842, he noted:

> Attended a general council in the lodge room to devise ways and means to furnish the poor with labor. Many of the English Saints

have gathered to Nauvoo, most of whom are unacquainted with any kind of labor, except spinning, weaving, &c.; and having no factories in this place, they are troubled to know what to do. Those who have funds have more generally neglected to gather, and left the poor to build up the city and kingdom of God in these last days (HC 5:25).

Although Samuel Burton wanted to move, perhaps he knew of these large numbers of poor immigrants, and not having any land to exchange for property in Nauvoo, he decided to live outside the city. According to Sarah's letter to Robert, they were planning "to go someware in that county." "Someware" turned out to be a farm near Camp Creek, in Hancock County, about fifteen miles northeast of Nauvoo. The family moved to the farm in the spring of 1842. On February 15, 1843, Samuel paid $80 to Jeremiah and Abigail Bingham for forty acres; the deed was recorded March 12, 1844 (Book of Deeds, Hancock County, Illinois, M:189).

This farm was located on a plateau between Camp Creek and a small tributary in the central and east side of Dallas Township. The soil was rich and black; water was nearby; the farm had great potential.[1]

Although much of the responsibility for the farm fell upon Robert's shoulders, he was close enough to ride into Nauvoo where he attended community celebrations and Sunday meetings. The Nauvoo Legion, pride of the city, was a year old, formed in the spring of 1841 after the Illinois Legislature accepted the Nauvoo City Charter. The legion was exceptionally well trained, evidence of mid-nineteenth century America's fascination with military display, and also evidence of wariness toward the "protection" Mormons had received in the past from state militia units. By May 1842, the legion numbered approximately 2,000 troops, nearly one-fifth of the population. The legion was also the center of Nauvoo social life. It had its own band and held frequent parties, drills, and parades (Flanders 1965, 56, 109–12).

Robert loved to join the spectators who turned out for these events. His admiration for and knowledge of military ways grew with each trip into the city. He also grew in devotion and respect for Joseph Smith, who he observed leading the troops as Lieutenant General of the Nauvoo Legion and addressing the Saints who met in the "Grove" each Sunday for worship. The influence of this prophet-mayor-general pervaded the entire community where he could be found assisting in his general store, meeting with the city council, leading an excursion on the Mississippi River in the *Maid of Iowa*, and welcoming the Saints who arrived by steamboat from up and down the Mississippi.

One day in May 1841, he greeted a party of four families which included Robert's future wife, Maria (pronounced Ma-RI-ah) Susan, then fifteen, her parents, John and Judith Temple Haven, Holliston, Massachusetts, and her twelve-year-old sister, Eliza Ann. John Haven was Brigham Young's uncle by marriage; his first wife, Elizabeth Howe, had been the sister of Brigham's mother. Brigham had converted them in Massachusetts and was with Joseph Smith at the wharf. Eliza Ann wrote of their arrival: "The first ones to greet us were the Prophet Joseph Smith and Brigham Young. After shaking hands and bidding us welcome, brother Joseph's first question was: Had we any place to go?" She also remembered "Brother Joseph was a great lover of children. I never met him but what he always gave me a bow and that wonderful smile. I used to love to hear him preach, although I was only a child, but he was always so interesting" (Westover 1918).

The Havens purchased a lot on Mulholland Street, three-quarters of a mile east of the temple site, where they built their home. (For more information on the family, see Appendix B.)

That summer of 1841 was darkened by the apostasy of John C. Bennett, former mayor of Nauvoo and Major General of the Nauvoo Legion. Following his excommunication, he used the Whig press to spread vicious rumors and the lecture podium to denounce Joseph Smith and the Latter-day Saint people as threats to civic order and public morality. So effective was his campaign that the Church leaders were spending the majority of their time in working to offset growing anti-Mormon sentiment.

Late in August 1842, news reached the Burtons at Camp Creek that through the Council of Twelve Apostles, the prophet had called a special conference to convene on August 29. William Burton had just completed his second mission and returned to his home in Walnut Grove. He stopped at his parents' home en route to the conference and invited Robert to accompany him into Nauvoo.

Joseph Smith had been hiding for most of the month in the homes of trusted friends to avoid arrest and extradition to Missouri for an alleged assault on the life of former Governor Boggs. It appeared impossible to obtain justice, so Joseph simply avoided arrest. As hundreds of elders gathered in the grove near the temple, Robert overheard rumors that the Prophet had disappeared from Nauvoo and was en route to Washington or Europe. At 10 o'clock, Hyrum Smith convened the conference which he said had been called because of public inquiries concerning the true nature of statements by John C. Bennett, "in consequence of which it is thought wisdom in God that every elder who can, should go forth to every part of the United States, and take proper documents with them, setting forth the truth as it is, and also preach the gospel" (HC 5:136). In other words, this was a mission call to change the public mind about the falsehoods spread by Bennett and other enemies of the church. Hyrum counseled the elders to "go wisely, humbly setting forth the truth as it is in God, and our persecutions, by which the tide of public opinion will be turned" (HC 5:136).

As Robert and William Burton listened intently, they were surprised to see Joseph Smith walk through the grove and take a seat on the stand to hear the conclusion of his brother's remarks. Electricity seemed to run through the congregation. Joseph felt the change in spirit and later wrote: "My sudden appearance on the stand, under the circumstances which surrounded us, caused great animation and cheerfulness in the assembly" (HC 5:137). He could not contain his own pleasure at having so astonished his brethren and lifted their spirits. He arose to speak and issue the call himself. He said he desired to send all the elders away, so that the mobs would be ashamed of coming against women and children.

> I don't want you to fight, but go and gather tens, hundreds, and thousands to fight for you. If oppression comes, I will then show them that there is a Moses and a Joshua amongst us; and I will fight them, if they don't take off oppression from me. I will do as I have done this time, I will run into the woods, I will fight them in my own way. I will send Brother Hyrum to call conferences everywhere throughout the states, and let documents be taken along and show to the world the corrupt and oppressive conduct of Boggs, Carlin, and others, that the public may have the truth laid before them.
>
> Let the Twelve send all who will support the character of the Prophet, the Lord's anointed; and if all who go will support my character, I prophesy in the name of the Lord Jesus, whose servant I am, that you will prosper in your missions (HC 5:138–39).

As the Prophet concluded, Robert thought his heart would burst with love for this man and he decided to answer the call. Joseph Smith felt "an indescribable transport of good feeling" manifested by the assembly, as Robert and William stood with some 380 elders, volunteering for this mission (HC 5:139).

Robert returned to Camp Creek, William went on to Walnut Grove, and both began preparing to fill the call. In his own words, Robert needed to "recruit my finances."

> In the fall of 1842 in consequence of 'means' being so scare in Nauvoo and vacinity I went to Galena Wisconsin [sic] to seek employment for the winter, and was quite successful in obtaining it, in galena mines, in taking contracts for cutting wood, etc." (R. T. Burton n.d.ᵃ, 8).

Galena was a port city north of Nauvoo on the Mississippi River almost at the Illinois/Wisconsin border. It was then the largest city in northwestern Illinois and a principal mining center for lead and zinc.

In the spring of 1843, he returned to Nauvoo where Hyrum Smith ordained him an elder. On June 19, 1843, he began his mission in company with Nathaniel Very Jones, a close friend and future husband of his sister, Rebecca. Robert carried a small valise containing his clothing and books or pamphlets, including a small brown leather New Testament given to him years earlier by his sister, Ann. The flyleaf is inscribed: "Ann Burton, January 1st, 1834," followed by "Robert Burton. His Book."[2]

At the commencement of this mission, Robert began keeping a journal, a practice he continued off and on until the 1870s when it became a daily habit. In his journal, he recorded daily travel and the location of meetings, but omitted the names of investigators, converts, and benefactors. While it lacks information and introspection that would be invaluable, the places and events of his mission are defined, and other information is available from William's journal for the time they were together.[3]

Robert and Nathaniel left Nauvoo on foot, walking eastward across the unsettled prairies, still covered with water and mud from the wet spring. Their destination was Toledo, Ohio, where Robert planned to teach friends and family members he left in the fall of 1838. Their journey across Illinois took them through LaHarpe, Macomb, Bernedoff, and Canton to Mackinaw where they held their first two meetings. They also held meetings in Liberty and Delevan, and then traveled by way of Bloomington to Indiana, arriving in Vermillion County in early July (R. T. Burton 1843–69, 1–3).

In this area, where they spent the next four weeks, they were befriended by the John Nebeker family, "who entertained us very kindly" (R. T. Burton 1843–69, 3–4). John's wife, Lurena Fitzgerald Nebeker, and mother, Susannah Meredith Nebeker, were already baptized; John and his brothers, George, Peter, and Henry converted about 1846 and came to Utah in 1847 (Jenson 2:177–78). During the years from 1842 to 1846, the Nebeker home was a haven for missionaries; Laurena was known to make or mend clothing for the missionaries while they taught in Vermillion County (Jenson 2:178–79). Robert's friendship with the Nebeker family lasted over fifty years. On February 10, 1898, Robert would speak of the family's hospitality at the funeral of Lurena F. Nebeker in Salt Lake City, and write that night in his journal, "I have never forgotten their kindness."

These two new elders were both young and completely inexperienced, yet their faith was strong and aided them in these first meetings, which included an encounter with a Campbellite minister at a public discussion before his congregation. Of their preaching, Robert wrote: "This was the first attempt of either my companion or myself at public speaking, both being quite young and with limited education, but we were blessed by the Lord with strength and wisdom equal to every emergency" (n.d.ª, 9).

The month of July was gone, and the missionaries resumed their travel, "being somewhat anxious to get to Ohio." They walked northeastward through Lafayette, Logansport, and Peru to Fort Wayne, all Indiana towns on the Wabash River. From Fort Wayne, they traveled by boat down the Wabash Canal and Maumee River into Toledo where Jane Burton Leybourn and her family welcomed them on August 13. Three years after Robert left Ohio in 1838, Jane married her husband's brother, Anthony Leybourn, October 1, 1841, and they lived in the suburb of Tremainsville. Robert was also reunited with his sister Betsy, her husband, Joseph Roop, and their children, who lived in nearby Sylvania. Anthony and Jane hosted the young missionaries, who commenced missionary labors "with greater earnestness," holding meetings in Tremainsville, Bedford, Sylvania, and Washington. Robert recalled their reception: "In persuing our labors here, expounding the first principles of the Gospel we met with much opposition, especially from Sectarian Ministers which of course did no hurt to the cause but on the contrary had the advantage of creating greater inquiry" (1843–69, 6).

In late October, they decided to leave Ohio for a while and go to Jackson County, Michigan, "to open up the gospel" there (R. T. Burton 1843–69, 6). Jackson County is just north of Lenawee County, where the Burtons lived in 1830; its central community of Jackson is about eighty miles northwest of Toledo. Their message was well received and they soon had "many persons inquiring into our principles" (R. T. Burton 1843–69, 7). After sixteen meetings in fifteen days, and one baptism, they walked back to Toledo, promising their Michigan investigators they would return.

Although Robert's journal generally reflects optimism and success, it also shows that traveling as a missionary without purse or script was not easy. Robert wrote, "Finding ourselves very destitute of clothing and our friends too poor to administer to our wants [we] sought to obtain some kind of labor which we accomplished and relieved ourselves of our more pressing wants. During this period of labor we continued our meetings as time and opportunity afforded. Working in day and preaching at night" (1843–69, 7–8).

Thus, they spent the month of December and the first three weeks of January 1844.

On January 21, they traveled about twenty miles to the western section of Lucas County and began holding meetings in the towns of Ritchfield and Washington. This was the first of several fruitful visits to this area. They returned again and again because of the urgent requests of the people. "The people [were] appearently interested and many professed to be believing" (1843–69, 9). They alternated their teaching every week or two between Tremainsville and Ritchfield for the rest of January and all of February.

Early in March, they kept their promise to the investigators in Michigan by returning to Jackson County. Robert's journal summarizes the next four weeks: "Arriving here we immediately commenced our labours, finding the people very anxious to investigate 'Mormonism' so called. Having no public opposition from Sectarian Ministers, baptizing four persons. On 25th [of March] we organised a branch of the church with eight members, three of whom had already been baptised on our arrival" (1843–69, 10–11). When they left Michigan at the end of March, they left behind an area fruitful for future missionaries and traveling Church leaders.

Back in Tremainsville, they held meetings on April 6 and 7 in the Houghton school house. "After this meeting, four more persons were added to the church by baptism" (1843–69, 12).

Meanwhile, William Burton had set off on his own mission in October 1843, taking his wife with him to make her last visit to her aged parents in Mersea, Ontario, where he planned to teach friends and relatives. William had promised to meet Robert in Ohio in the spring. When he did not come, Robert decided that he would travel to Canada "since I felt very anxious to learn of his welfare" (1843–69, 13). Traveling alone, Robert took a boat across Lake Erie on April 12, and arrived at Mersea on April 15. "I found my brother in the enjoyment of good health. I also found many other relatives and old friends here. Spending a few days here visiting friends and seens of early childhood" (1843–69, 13).

At the conclusion of Robert's visit, the two brothers left Mersea together, walking westward into Windsor, where they held a meeting on Sandwich Street, the main thoroughfare. After crossing into Detroit, they were entertained by a Brother Van Avery until they were able to obtain passage to Toledo. At the Leybourn home they rejoined Nathaniel Jones on April 22, and the three elders immediately resumed their labors.

William's journal describes a busy month of missionary successes.

> Friday, April 25th, 1844, Held a meeting in the Houghton School house. I preached; the congregation was very attentive, but small.
> Sunday, April 27th, 1844, Held a meeting in the Town of Ritchfield, about 20 miles west of Toledo. I addressed the assembly; the house was very much crowded. In the evening we held another meeting in the Town of Washington, Michigan. My brother spoke; I also made some remarks. The following evening we held a meeting in the same place; Brother N. Jones addressed the congregation. Numbers began to believe our testimony concerning the work of the Lord in these last days.
> The next day I preached on the "Coming Forth of the Book of Mormon." After meeting was out four persons were baptized.
> May 4th, I preached in the school house near Tremainsville. The next day being the Sabbath I preached there again, and in the afternoon in the Houghton school house. At this time the prospect appeared rather flattering relative to our labors being blessed by our Heavenly Father. The same day Brother Robert Burton baptized three more in Ritchfield (W. Burton 1839–51).

On Sunday, May 12, the three missionaries returned to Ritchfield, baptized two members, and organized a branch with twelve members "all in good standing." Andrew Scott was ordained as teacher to preside over the branch, with George Burnzy as a deacon (R. T. Burton 1843–69, 15–16).

Once again, Robert and Nathaniel "were compelled to obtain some labor," but Robert almost immediately received a letter from his parents "desiring me if consistent with my mission to return home. I accordingly made immediate preparations to comply with their request" (1843–69, 16).

Before leaving for home, Robert took William to visit Mr. and Mrs. Samuel Roach in Providence, Ohio. Roach had been one of their father's farm hands many years earlier in Canada. Robert and Nathaniel had been in Providence in the fall, and Mrs. Roach attended their missionary meetings. During William and Robert's visit, Mrs. Roach requested and received baptism. In addition, Robert wrote, "Mr. Roach helped me to $5 to help me with my mission. This is about the heaviest and only donation I received" (1843–69, 17).

In Tremainsville, Robert concluded his mission by baptizing three more converts. On May 28, the missionary brothers bid farewell to their relatives and to Elder Jones who was going to visit his own relatives in New York. William and Robert booked passage from Toledo to Detroit where they parted, William returning to Canada and Michigan where he preached for another year. Robert had an interesting and comfortable, but lonely journey home on the steamer *Madison* bound for Chicago via the Great Lakes.

On my trip through the Lakes we stoped for a short time at Michilinack. The next stoping place was Manitoo Island, and from thense to Milwakee and from here to South Port, from thense to Chicago where we arrived on the third [of June].

I now desired to make my way to Nauvoo, but there being no railway or other public convenience of travel, the only thing apparently was to procede on foot. I chanced, however, to fall in with a team that was going across to Henry Co. and the owner gave me a chance to ride part of the way, traveling by way of Naperville and Princeton and from here to Walnut Grove, Knox Co. in the same state, where our family had formally resided. Finding old friends here, tarried with them a day or two resting, and then proceded on foot to Hancock Co., arriving at my father's home on Camp Creek on the 13th of June. Found our family all well (1843–69, 19–21).

Robert was very pleased with the results of this mission, which had lasted almost a year. Over and over, he gave credit in his journal to the Lord for blessing him and his companions at times when inexperience and limited education left them vulnerable in a situation. He helped organize branches in Ritchfield, Ohio, and Jackson County, Michigan, baptized twenty-four, and left many others investigating. According to family records, his sister Jane Burton Leybourn was baptized in 1843. Robert does not mention her baptism, but perhaps the baptisms or serious investigation of the gospel by some family members were the highlight of this missionary year.

Notes

Principal sources on Nauvoo and this period include: Robert B. Flanders, *Nauvoo: Kingdom on the Mississippi*, Urbana: University of Illinois Press, 1965; David E. and Della S. Miller, *Nauvoo: The City of Joseph*, Santa Barbara and Salt Lake City: Peregrine Smith, Inc., 1974; and Leonard J. Arrington, *Brigham Young: American Moses*, New York: Alfred A.Knopf, 1985, Chapters 7 and 8.

1. The farm site is located by driving northeast from Nauvoo on Illinois Highway 96 to Dallas City. At Dallas City, turn south on Illinois 9/94 and drive 2.5 miles. The farm was located 2500 feet to the left of Illinois 9/94. The legal description reads: Begin 40 rods north of the SW corner of the S. E. Quarter of Section 13 in T7N, R7W, thence East to Section quarter line, North 40 rods of East Section quarter line and south to beginning.

2. This New Testament is kept in the files of the Robert Taylor Burton Family Association. It is two and three-fourths by four and one-fourth inches in size.

3. The journal used as resource for this chapter is not the original written during Robert's mission. Late in the 1890s, he either dictated his mission journal to Ada M. Burton, using the original (which may have been disintegrating) as a source or allowed Ada to copy the original.

Defending Nauvoo, 1844–46

Two weeks after Robert's return from the mission field, Joseph Smith was assassinated at Carthage Jail. Robert was on duty with the Nauvoo Legion and spent most of the next eighteen months defending the Saints at Nauvoo. By witnessing the "transfiguration" of Brigham Young as "the mantle of Joseph" fell on him, Robert gained a testimony of who should succeed Joseph Smith. Robert was endowed in the Nauvoo Temple and married to Maria Haven just weeks before the Saints fled from Nauvoo.

Robert Burton walked back into a county and a people in turmoil.

Three days prior to his return, the Nauvoo city marshall and a contingent of the Nauvoo Legion destroyed the press of *The Nauvoo Expositor*, spilled the type into the street, and burned every printed sheet in the building. In a moment of questionable judgment, Joseph Smith and the city council defied the American concept of freedom of the press by declaring the *Expositor* a public nuisance and ordering its destruction for printing matter they deemed libelous. The publishers of the *Expositor* fled Nauvoo. Among them were Robert Foster, William Law, and Wilson Law, excommunicated Church members who created a "reformed" church with William Law as leader.

The *Expositor's* one and only issue on June 7 had charged Joseph Smith with "exercising illegal authority, both in ecclesiastical and civil affairs; with the introduction of the plural wife system, and other supposed doctrinal heresies; with gross immoralities; and malfeasance in the administration of the affairs of the church" (CHC 2:228). The paper caused an immediate furor among Church members who had been taught the principles of plural marriage, as well as among those who still believed that polygamy was a false rumor.

Beyond Nauvoo, the destruction of the *Expositor* gave gentile neighbors increased reason to rise against Joseph Smith under pretext of avenging wrongs done to Foster and the Law brothers. John C. Bennett renewed his attacks, supplying newspapers in Warsaw, Sangamo, and Alton with evidence of Mormon political strength and aspirations, warning against the Nauvoo Legion and the prophet-leader who reportedly planned to set up a military and religious empire with himself as "emperor and pope" (HC 5:80n; Flanders 1965, 278–79).

Issues of the *Warsaw Signal* of June 12, 18 and 19 kindled the public anger, urging "CITIZENS ARISE, ONE AND ALL!!!" "You will be doing your God and your country service, in aiding us to rid earth of a most heaven-daring wretch." "Let their be no cowards in the camp . . . but upon every man's countenance let there be written, the desperate determination . . . to strike the tyrant to the dust . . . Strike then! for the time has fully come."

Public reaction was immediate and intense. Although all Hancock County residents were not anti-Mormon, thousands responded to emotional mass meetings and rousing editorials. Mobs began to demonstrate, and the state militia was called out. It appeared that civil war was imminent.

Robert would have heard these reports and rumors about Joseph Smith as he journeyed southward from Chicago. Perhaps he observed the militia drilling or read the inflammatory newspaper editorials. But his loyalties were clearly defined and his faith in his leaders remained strong despite the accusations spread by their enemies. From the day of his return, he observed the rapidly worsening state of affairs. In his biography, he describes a "great excitement among the people here, mobs were gathering in different places, burning houses, destroying property and life and in various ways persecuting the Saints almost beyond endurance." His reaction was to enlist in the Nauvoo Legion's First Cavalry Company, under Captain Gleason (n.d.ᵃ, 10–11).

In Nauvoo and the surrounding Mormon settlements, residents feverishly prepared their defenses. On June 18, Joseph Smith called out the Nauvoo Legion and placed the city under martial law. The troops pitched their tents in a campground east of Nauvoo, then dug trenches around the city from which they expected to guard the citizens and their homes against the mobs.

Early in the evening of June 27, Robert rode to his guard post north of Nauvoo. The night was hot and sticky, the air almost as oppressive as the spirit which blanketed the town. It was Wednesday. Since Monday, Joseph and Hyrum Smith had been in Carthage, and were now in jail, under the pledged protection of Thomas Ford, governor of Illinois.

But Governor Ford was not at Carthage. He spent June 27 in Nauvoo, intimidating the citizens with threats of holding them responsible if "anything of a serious character should befall the lives or property of the persons who are prosecuting your leaders" (HC 6:623). Ford left before sundown and was met two miles out of Nauvoo by two men who reported the assassinations of Joseph and Hyrum Smith at Carthage Jail. He forced the messengers to return with him to Carthage to postpone Mormon knowledge of the atrocity long enough for him to reach safety.

Late that night, the news reached Nauvoo. Robert was still on guard duty as the seemingly impossible reports of the martyrdom spread through the community. The soldiers stayed at their posts, not knowing what further attacks might come upon the people.

While the gentiles awaited the avenging retaliation of the legion, the citizens and soldiers of Nauvoo received the news subdued in grief. By two o'clock on the afternoon of June 28, they began to gather along Mulholland Street to watch for the wagons bearing the bodies of Joseph and Hyrum. As Mormons from the outlying settlements joined the throngs, their numbers grew to ten thousand. Robert may have waited with his cavalry company, or perhaps he rode out to Camp Creek to get his parents and younger brother and sisters, and he stood with them in the sweltering heat. When word came that the cortege was near, the people walked out to meet the wagons, their piercing lamentations preceding them across the plain (Hill 1977, 4).

Willard Richards and Samuel Smith drove the wagons through town to the Mansion House where Richards spoke, mildly asking the people to keep the peace. He explained that he had pledged his life on the good conduct of the Mormons and reminded them that John Taylor, who was seriously wounded at the jail, lay helpless in Carthage. Still in shock and consumed with sorrow, the Mormon people agreed to leave vengeance to God.

Many years later, Robert explained the overwhelming loss which the Saints felt knowing their prophet was gone:

> The Latter-day Saints universally had such an abiding faith in the protecting care of the Lord over His Prophet, who had been so many times arrested upon frivolous charges trumped up by evil designing persons, actuated solely by the spirit of persecution; and from all of these our Heavenly Father had delivered him; until the Latter-day Saints, including myself, almost were led to believe that he had a charmed life, that mobs would not have the power to destroy him. (1905, 2)

Although the people of Illinois and Missouri expected first vengeance, then the Church's disintegration, they were mistaken. While a few members seemed to think that without their prophet there was no church, most of Joseph Smith's followers responded with increased zeal and unity in memory of his martyrdom. Missionaries like William Burton continued to preach and baptize; and thousands of converts from the Eastern states, Canada and England continued to arrive in Nauvoo, swelling the population to 15,000. Once the anti-Mormon citizens of Illinois realized that the Mormons were not scattering, harassment and persecution resumed. During July 1844 and for several months thereafter, Robert remained on duty with the Nauvoo Legion in the city and nearby vicinity, endeavoring to protect the lives and the property of the Saints from mob violence and robbery (W. S. Burton, n.d.[b], 2).

During the many hours of guard duty, his thoughts and conversations must have turned often to the question of leadership for the Church. There was no easily apparent line of succession. The Council of Fifty had assumed civic and religious leadership, but no one felt this was a permanent solution. The fifty included most of the apostles and other leading men which meant that this body was lacking some of its most illustrious members at this time. Joseph Smith created this council in March 1844 as a semi-secret leadership group which served as a shadow government for Nauvoo and which might have played a major role in the "political kingdom of God" if Joseph Smith's plans had come to fruition. Council members had been studying the foundation and principles of all governments, had prepared memorials to Congress for redress of grievances, and had undertaken missions in support of Joseph Smith's candidacy for president of the United States (Arrington 1985, 109–11).[1]

At the time of Joseph Smith's martyrdom, most of the members of the Quorum of Twelve Apostles were in the states on such political missions. Willard Richards and John Taylor sent letters to Brigham Young, Wilford Woodruff, Heber C. Kimball, Orson Pratt, George A. Smith, Charles C. Rich, Orson Hyde, and Lyman Wight asking the quorum members and other Church leaders to return from their missions.

A number of men stepped forward to claim the position as head of the Church. Sidney Rigdon, counselor to Joseph Smith, came from Pittsburgh and offered himself as a "guardian" to the people. James J. Strang claimed to have a letter from Joseph Smith appointing him successor and naming Moses and Aaron Smith to assist him (Russell 1973, 236, 252–54). Some people thought the presidency should remain in Joseph Smith's family, although it was many years before his sons claimed the right of succession (Quinn 1967, 222–232). In his "Statement on Succession," written in the Presiding Bishop's Office, July 28, 1905, Robert T. Burton said: "A number of persons claimed the legal succession, and to have this authority, among them Sidney Rigdon, James J. Strang, Aaron and Moses Smith and others."[2]

For days, the succession crisis grew. On August 4, Sidney Rigdon told a large Sunday gathering that on the day of Joseph's death, the Lord had shown him in a vision that the Church must be built up to Joseph, the martyr, and that he should be guardian for the Church. In the hope of having his position ratified, Rigdon called for a meeting on Thursday, August 8. Apostles Parley P. Pratt and Willard Richards thought Rigdon was hurrying too fast and that the people should not act before the apostles returned. On Tuesday night, August 6, Brigham Young, president of the Quorum of the Twelve, returned with Wilford Woodruff, Heber C. Kimball, Orson Hyde, Orson Pratt and Lyman Wight. All the apostles were now in Nauvoo excepting William Smith, brother of the Prophet, John E. Page, and Orson Hyde (CHC 2:412).

On August 7, Rigdon made his proposal in a meeting of the apostles, the Nauvoo Stake High Council, and all high priests.

> The object of my mission is to visit the saints and offer myself to them as a guardian. . . . I have been ordained a spokesman to Joseph, and I must come to Nauvoo and see that the church is governed in a proper manner. Joseph sustains the same relationship to this church as he has always done. No man can be the successor of Joseph" (HC 7:229).

Next, Brigham Young stood to speak for the leadership resting on the Twelve Apostles. He said he did not care who led the Church, but "one thing I must know, and that is what God says about it. I have the keys and the means of obtaining the mind of God on the subject" (HC 7:230).

Among the many accounts which describe the great assemblies which took place the next day is a 1905 testimonial by Robert T. Burton. Sidney Rigdon and Brigham Young addressed the special conference which Rigdon had called. Rigdon spoke first, discoursing for an hour and thirty minutes without stirring much emotion nor rallying the people to his claim. Brigham Young followed with a brief message during which some of the congregation saw in his appearance and manner the person and voice of Joseph Smith, a phenomenon described as the "mantle of Joseph" resting on Brigham. Young's diary suggests that this event occurred in the morning session (Arrington 1985, 455n7). Many other accounts, including Robert's, place it at the opening of the afternoon session. Although it was written over sixty years later, Robert's account is significant for the obvious effect it had on his life and his loyalty to Brigham Young.

> The occasion that I now refer to was a general meeting of the Latter-day Saints, soon after the return to Nauvoo of President Brigham Young and other members of the Quorum of the Twelve Apostles, from their missions. The meeting had been called to order, and after the usual opening exercises President Brigham Young arose to address the assembly.
>
> At that time I was not acquainted with President Young, but his voice, manner, expression, and in fact, his personal appearance was so strikingly that of the martyred Prophet, that I rose from my seat, as did hundreds of others, to look at the Prophet Joseph Smith Jr. The likeness was so marked that I could hardly make myself believe that the Prophet had not himself returned; not that there was a resemblance between the two men. I am not going to say why this was other than I received it, as an evidence to the people that God had chosen Brigham Young as successor to the Prophet Joseph Smith Jr. There were dozens, even hundreds of others, who were impressed just the same as I was at that time, and I have heard many, many who are now gone make similar statements or expressions to that I am here making.
>
> Now I will repeat that it was a positive indication to me where the succession had fallen, and from that time, until the death of President Brigham Young, I never had one doubt, never thought that I was deceived. I believed, still believe, and know that he was the legitimate successor to the Prophet Joseph Smith.
>
> (signed) R. T. Burton

Another interesting account of this event was written by his sister-in-law, Eliza Ann Haven Westover, who sat in the conference with her sister, Maria, and other family members. The Havens had first heard the gospel preached by Brigham Young, their father's nephew, so they were intimately acquainted with him. In 1918, when she was in her late eighties, she wrote to her son:

> The question was a general one: "What shall we do without our Prophet?" I was then 15 years of age and we all felt so sad. I was at the meeting when Sidney Rigdon arose and declared himself our true Prophet and leader. Very few responded to his declaration. I am happy to say that not one of my fathers family felt he was the right one. Soon after Pres. Brigham Young came home from the East, where he had been on a mission. I was at the meeting when the mantle of Bro. Joseph encircled him . . . When he spoke, it was in Bro. Joseph's voice. I arose to my feet and said to my mother: "Our prophet has come to life, mother we have Bro. Joseph back", for there he stood as plain as I ever saw him in life; and his voice and features were truly those of our beloved Prophet. Shortly a mist seemed to pass from Bro. Brigham's face and there stood brother Young talking in his natural voice, but we knew he was to be our leader. Hundreds witnessed the same thing, but not all that were there had that privilege (Westover 1918).

Those who could not be reconciled to the leadership of Brigham Young eventually left the Church; numerous small splinter groups formed, each claiming to have the true authority. For a period of time, leaders and followers of these groups traveled throughout the branches of the Church trying to pull away converts to their congregations. In 1846, the Leybourns in Ohio were visited by Moses Smith who tried to convert them to Strangism, using "a great deal of eloquence and perhaps told some strange stories about Spiritual Affairs" (W. and E. Burton 1847). Those who accepted the leadership of Brigham Young rededicated themselves to building Nauvoo and completing the temple.

Robert continued his service in the Nauvoo Legion, "as the Saints were compelled to defend ourselves more or less all the time from the violence of mobs, who continued to harass and annoy us" (R. T. Burton n.d.[a], 12). He also joined the Nauvoo Choir and the Nauvoo Brass Band, also known as Pitt's Brass Band.

On October 8, 1844, he was ordained a Seventy by George A. Smith and made a member of the Seventh Quorum, organized the same day. Shortly thereafter, in January 1845 the Twelve called missionaries to labor in the surrounding counties to allay prejudice. This second mission was short, but Robert considered it successful: "I labored with Samuel W. Richards in the adjacent countys to Nauvoo, indevoring to lay prejudice that was groing to an alarming extent in consequence of falsehoods circulated by apostates and other enemies to the people. Had a very pleasant time and was successful to a great extent and in a few weeks returned to Nauvoo" (R. T. Burton 1843–69, 24).

In spite of this effort, a general feeling of anti-Mormonism swept the state. The Illinois Legislature repealed the Nauvoo charter in January 1845 in an effort to undermine the military and judicial independence of the Latter-day Saint people. Without the charter, the police force and the legion had no legal right to preserve public order, but they continued to respond to the need for protection of Church members still living outside the city and to guard Church leaders. The apostles were plagued with various writs and summons and frequently stayed in hiding to avoid arrest and trial (Arrington 1974, 83–85).

Like many families seeking protection, the Samuel Burtons moved into Nauvoo, living on a small corner lot at the intersection of Ripley and Green Streets.[3] During the spring of 1845, the family celebrated the marriage of nineteen-year-old Rebecca Maria to Nathaniel V. Jones, Robert's first missionary companion, March 13, 1845. Not long afterward, William and Betsy Burton returned from Canada. They arrived in time to witness the laying of the temple capstone, May 24, 1845.

The Burtons joined thousands of Saints to see the capstone put in place at a 6 A.M. ceremony, the apostles leaving hiding to officiate at the ceremony. Robert took his place with the brass band, which played the "Capstone March," composed for the occasion by William Pitt. Once the capstone was laid, Brigham Young stood on top and spoke to the assembled Saints. His words implied what many already knew—they would soon be leaving their homes again: "The last stone is now laid upon the Temple and I pray the Almighty in the name of Jesus Christ to defend us in this place and sustain us until the Temple is finished and we have all got our endowments" (HC 7:417–18).

On the streets and in the homes and businesses of Nauvoo and throughout Hancock and neighboring counties, everyone discussed the fact that the Latter-day Saints were being forced to leave the state. The Council of Fifty and the Quorum of the Twelve had been deliberating where the Saints might move, even before Governor Ford candidly wrote Brigham Young on April 8, 1845:

> Your religion is new, and it surprises the people as any great novelty in religion generally does. They cannot rise above the prejudices excited by such novelty. . . . If you can get off by yourselves you may enjoy peace; but surrounded by such neighbors I confess I do not foresee the time when you will be permitted to enjoy quiet. . . .
>
> I would suggest a matter in confidence. California now offers a field for the prettiest enterprise that has been undertaken in modern time. It is but sparsely populated by none but the Indian or imbecile Mexican Spaniard. . . . Why would it not be a pretty operation for your people to go out there? (HC 7:398).

The leaders read accounts of fur trappers, the reports of government exploring parties, and newspaper articles about Western travels; they also talked with people who had spent time in the Rocky Mountains and learned that there were at least two contiguous unsettled areas, both of which they might occupy— the valley of the Great Salt Lake and the Utah Valley. As early as the summer of 1845, the Salt Lake Valley was considered the most suitable site for settlement (Arrington 1985, 122–124). Although the move was now inevitable, there seemed to be no definite plan to leave until the anti-Mormon mobs increased their persecution early in September. A mob of 300 began systematically burning outlying Mormon homes; and by mid-September, forty-four buildings had been destroyed. Brigham

Young sent men from Nauvoo with their teams and wagons to bring the persecuted into the city (HC 7:439–43).

On September 9, the Council of Fifty resolved to send 1,500 men to the Great Salt Lake Valley, and late in September, the Quorum of the Twelve promised that if the Saints could dispose of personal and private property, they would leave the following spring. A week later, in response to a commission sent by Governor Ford headed by General John J. Hardin, Brigham Young promised that the Mormon leaders and a thousand families would leave in the spring regardless of whether their property was sold. He asked the gentile citizens to aid them in disposing of their lands and houses and also outlined what steps the Saints were taking to prepare for prompt departure (HC 7:439–55; Miller and Miller 1974, 189–94).

Immediately the Saints began organizing. The Council of Fifty oversaw the formation of companies and appointment of captains. Each family of five would need a good wagon, three yoke of cattle, two cows, two beef cattle, three sheep, 1000 pounds of flour, a tent and tent poles, and numerous other items of food, tools, cooking utensils and bedding. Social Hall was turned into a carpenter shop where the wagons were built. Individual families worked on their tents and clothing, while trying to trade their homes and property for wagons, teams, and whatever else they could get (HC 7:454–55; M. Burton n.d.)

The Saints also continued to labor day and night on the still unfinished Nauvoo Temple, as they were determined not to leave without the promised temple blessings. The first meeting in the temple was a four-day conference beginning Sunday, October 5, when 5,000 Saints sat on temporary seats placed on temporary flooring, and leaders spoke from unfinished pulpits. It was a time of rejoicing in spite of the dark clouds that overshadowed their future. Seven weeks later on November 30, the attic story was dedicated for use (HC 7:456–77, 534).

The fall of 1845 was as busy a time as twenty-four-year-old Robert could ever remember. He had assumed much of the responsibility for his father's family and continued to serve with the remnant of the Nauvoo Legion. He may have served, as did his brother William, on a posse called by the county sheriff to help suppress mob violence against the saints. He and William had been called on a mission to Europe, but were later asked to defer their missions until they had accompanied the Saints to the West (R. T. Burton 1843–69, 27).

Robert also found time for one more activity—courting Maria Susan Haven.

Since 1841, John and Judith Haven and their daughters, Maria and Eliza, had been living comfortably in the Nauvoo Third Ward in a home on Mulholland Street, near John's daughter and son-in-law, Elizabeth and Israel Barlow (Barlow 1968, 180–186). It is thought that John Haven may have been a merchant in Nauvoo, while his wife and daughters made straw hats and ladies' millinery for his customers (Raybould 1978). In the fall of 1845, Maria was nineteen years old. She had fine features, dark hair, and soft dark eyes.

The Haven home and Burton property were only a few blocks apart. Whether Maria and Robert met at a church meeting, at a social, or through mutual friends is not recorded, nor did they write about their courtship in later diaries and biographies. But Maria liked to tell her grandchildren about one of their "dates." They were out on a buggy ride when Robert turned to Maria and said, " 'I've half a mind to put my arm around you.' " "I was so bold," responded Maria, "I said, 'Never change a good mind!' " (Raybould 1978). They decided to be married in December.

The Prophet Joseph had initiated a few Church leaders and their wives into the full temple endowment in improvised quarters in 1842 and 1843. This sacred ceremony includes instructions that "illuminate the plan of Christian life and salvation" and covenants to live chaste, obedient, Christian lives (Arrington 1985, 102). These ordinances were not available to large numbers of faithful Saints until the completion of the Nauvoo Temple. On December 10, the first of these ordinances were performed in special rooms in the attic story. Robert Taylor Burton was one of sixty-four persons to be endowed on December 15.

Officiating was President Young, assisted by other members of the Quorum of the Twelve (R. T. Burton n.d.ᵃ, 12; HC 7:547).

Those serving in the temple worked from early in the morning to late at night; Brigham Young recorded in his journal on January 12 1846, that he had given himself "entirely to the work of the Lord in the Temple" often serving twenty hours in a day and seldom going home even to rest (in Arrington 1985, 126). However, on Thursday, December 18, 1845, Brigham left the temple to go to the home of John Haven, where he performed the wedding ceremony for Robert and Maria, two young people whom he liked and whose union he approved. Their sealing would wait until the March 1856 after the Endowment House was completed in Salt Lake City.

When the 32nd Quorum of Seventies was organized during a Seventies Meeting in the Music Hall the next Sunday, December 21, Robert was sustained and set apart of one of the seven presidents (R. T. Burton 1843–69, 25; HC 7:549). His qualities of faith, missionary zeal, dependability, and leadership were already being recognized.

On Christmas day, Maria Susan Haven Burton was one of 107 persons to receive the temple endowment. On February 6, Samuel Burton received his endowment and was sealed to Hannah, who had been endowed on December 24. Five hundred and twelve were endowed that day and upwards of 600 the next day, Saturday, February 7. Then, on Monday afternoon, a stovepipe in the temple's upper story overheated and fire raged for half an hour. The damage was not extensive, but the temple had served its purpose, and President Young declared that "if it is the will of the Lord that the temple be burned, instead of being defiled by the Gentiles, Amen to it" (HC 7:581).

It had been supposed that the removal from Nauvoo would take place in April; but toward the end of January, two threats prompted an earlier exist. One was an indictment against Brigham Young and eight other apostles accused of harboring counterfeiters in Nauvoo. Second, rumors were circulated that federal troops from St. Louis were coming up the river as soon as it thawed to prevent the Mormon migration (Miller, 1974;

197–98). Brigham believed these threats, although his biographer, Leonard Arrington says, "It now seems that the rumors were circulated precisely in order to induce the Mormons to leave sooner than they had planned" (Arrington 1985, 127).

Church leaders decided on February 2 to let those who were ready begin crossing the frozen Mississippi River, the first step of the exodus from Nauvoo.

Notes

1. Robert T. Burton became a member of the Council of Fifty in Utah. Further information on the council is found in Klaus J. Hansen, *Quest for Empire: The Political Kingdom of God and the Council of Fifty in Mormon History*, East Lansing, Mich.: Michigan State University Press, 1967; and D. Michael Quinn, "The Council of Fifty and Its Members, 1844 to 1945," *BYU Studies* 20 (Winter Quarter): 163–97.

2. Moses Smith was the presiding elder in Walnut Grove and at one time was highly respected by Samuel, William, and Robert T. Burton. His brother, Aaron, lived in Burlington, Wisconsin, and associated with James Strang in the Mormon community there. Moses Smith was a brother-in-law to James Strang (their wives were sisters) and probably Strang's first contact with The Church of Jesus Christ of Latter-day Saints. Both Moses and Aaron initially followed Strang; Aaron served as his first counselor from 1844 to 1846 when he became disaffected and established a rival church (Russell 1973, 235–40).

3. Dr. T. Edgar Lyon told Ivan and Beth Cutler (A. Cutler to Janet B. Seegmiller, 1977), that Samuel Burton owned 1/16th of an acre on the Northwest Quarter of the Kimball Lot #1, which is on the corner of Green and Ripley streets, about four blocks east and one block south of the Nauvoo Temple. Extensive research has not uncovered a deed to this property, nor a record of property tax payment. It is likely that Samuel purchased this land under the bonding law, which permitted him to bond to the owner of the property that he would pay for it in a certain length of time. Because of the exodus from Nauvoo, he probably did not complete the purchase and receive the deed. Samuel's farm near Camp Creek was sold on April 6, 1846, and he left Nauvoo before May 1. There is a white frame church standing on the Nauvoo property today.

6

"Wedding Tour" Across Iowa, 1846

Maria Burton always called the trek across Iowa from Nauvoo to the Missouri River her "wedding tour." She and Robert forded the Mississippi River in the bitter cold of February 11, 1846, and spent five very difficult months crossing Iowa. In July, they were homeless in Council Bluffs, facing an uncertain future.

Day after day, heavily laden wagons crawled slowly down frozen, rutted roads to the Mississippi River landing where they were just as slowly ferried across the icy, partly frozen river. The exodus from Nauvoo began as a trickle when a few families crossed on February 4, then became a day-and-night flood as families hastily completed their preparations and moved to the Sugar Creek Camp, staging point for the so-called "Camp of Israel."

Some 400 families crossed on February 11, the day Robert and Maria bade loved ones farewell, urging them to follow soon. In a borrowed wagon, they joined the procession to the river and the ferry. Robert recalled this wedding trip.

> In the month of February when the thermometer was several degrees below zero, we crossed the Mississippi River, camped in the snow and pitched our tents as best we could. . . . I had a friend who lent

me his team and I was requested to accompany President Young west. I took my present wife, Aunt Maria as so many of you call her, packed up our duds and got into the wagon. It did not require many baggage wagons to hold them; we had about what we stood up in (R. T. Burton 1903, 2–3).

Maria remembered the kind neighbor of the Burton's from Camp Creek who offered his wagon so they could obey President Young's request: "Bro. Erastus Bingham let Mr. Burton have a Wagon and a Span of beautiful Sorrel Horses and his son Calvin Bingham to drive and care for the horses. Mr. Burton belonged to the Nauvoo Brass Band; he played the Trumpet. The Band kept in a Company by itself" (M. Burton n.d.)

So it was Robert's membership in the Nauvoo Brass Band which led to the invitation from Brigham Young that he and his wife travel with the advance company out of Nauvoo. The trip was not easy for any of the companies, but the first was least prepared for the terrible conditions it encountered. Robert wrote:

At this time the river was froze over and we crossed back and forth to and from Nauvoo on the ice [to obtain supplies for our journey]. During our encampment the weather was intensely cold, snow part of the time a foot deep in our camp, with scanty supply of food and clothing, so there was necessarily much suffering among the people; but we preferred rather to endure cold and hunger, to face all the danger consequent upon traveling over more than 1500 miles, most of which was at that time an unexplored desert, rather than endure the continued oppression, robbing, plundering, which the Latter-day Saints had been forced to endure almost the entire time since the martyrdom of Joseph and Hyrum Smith (R. T. Burton n.d.[a], 13–14).

Huddled around log fires and sheltered by a single tent, Robert and Maria waited with their impoverished companions through the month of February. The thermometer dropped as low as twelve below zero and rarely climbed above freezing. Brigham brought his wagons across on February 15, and the exodus continued until there were about 500 wagons and approximately 5,000 Saints crowding the site (Kimball 1972).

Advance parties finally left Sugar Creek on February 25, but the main company, which included William Pitt and his band members, left on March 1. After crossing Sugar Creek and moving northwest five miles along the river bank, they stopped and camped in several inches of snow. The second day's march brought them within four miles of the village of Farmington. It might have been expected that at the end of such days, the travelers would be exhausted and hurry off to their tents with solemn faces and sore bodies. But such was not the case in the early days of the trip.

> After encampment was made and the toils of the day were over, the snow would be scraped away, a huge fire or several of them kindled within the wagon enclosure, and there to the inspiring music of Pitt's band, song and dance often beguiled the exiles into forgetfulness of their trials and discomforts . . . The men of Iowa, it is said, looked on with amazement, when witnessing such scenes and were told that these were the exiled "Mormons" from Nauvoo, "bound they knew not wither, 'except where God should lead them by the hand of his servant' " (CHC 3:47).

A number of Farmington citizens visited the camp. After witnessing the festivities, they invited the band to entertain in their village. So the next evening found Robert and the other band members giving a concert at Farmington, Iowa, the first of several along the route from the Mississippi to Council Bluffs (CHC 3:47). Farmington was the first community of any size along the path and it afforded opportunity for some men to work a day or two. Both the band and the laborers were paid in much-needed money and goods, a confirmation of Brigham's foresight in asking the band to accompany the advance party (Kimball 1972, 41).

Travel conditions deteriorated instead of improved as days passed, but many preferred to remember the cheerful spirit and musical uplift in the evening camps. The intense cold had been a terrible hardship, but thawing during the day and freezing at night only made traveling more difficult for the huge band of outcasts. There were few roads to follow, and they made their own way as best they could. Robert Burton was understating the situation when he wrote in his journal, "Our journey is indeed a weary and toilsome one" (1843–69, 31). He later recounted conditions in more detail.

> As snow and frost gave way, then came mud and water; the streams were so swollen by the melting of the winter snow that they overflowed their banks untill whole sections of the pararie [sic] were covered with water. Sometimes we were compelled to camp where the water was several inches deep. Improvising beds by throwing down willows and brush enough to raise the bedding above the surrounding floods, and so diffacult was the traveling that in some instances we could only make three miles per day. During this slow and tedious march we were obliged to go to the settlements of Missouri and work for food for ourselves and animals, and what made it still more unpleasant for me my wife, being young and at that time delicate in consequence of these exposures, was attacked with chills and fever and would shake untill the bows of the wagon would rattle and but little could be done for her comfort. Thus we continued our weary journey to the west (n.d.[a], 14–15).

After seven days of travel, the main party was only thirty-six miles from Sugar Creek, camped at Richardson's Point. Robert wrote in his journal: "The weather being so bad and the rain falling almost constantly we remained here till 19th. During this time, the Band held several concerts in the settlements of Misouri"[1] (1843–69, 32).

Although the leaders had decided in Nauvoo how to organize the trek, the actual working of the plan brought out the need for restructuring and reorganization which began at the headquarters camp at Richardson's Point. As the realities of the march settled in, the leaders stopped looking to the far-off colonization of Upper California and decided to find a temporary stopping place at the Missouri River where the saints could raise crops and work for additional supplies. The pioneers were advised to eat their provisions as needed, thus lightening their loads, since they would be able to get other provisions for the journey over the mountains (Nibley 1937, 73).

It was also decided that an advance company of "pioneers" would blaze a trail for the wagons by building bridges, clearing away underbrush, selecting campsites, and making trading expeditions to exchange cash and household goods for food and grain. But when the march resumed, some were not content to follow and pushed ahead into the advance company's encampments; a few small groups moved ahead independently. From March 27 to April 1, the terrible condition of the roads once again forced a long encampment at the Chariton River, and during this delay Brigham Young called a meeting to restore order to the camp and rebuke the "independent spirits." At this meeting, Brigham was unanimously elected president over the whole Camp of Israel, while three men were elected as captains of hundreds (meaning hundreds of families), and six as captains of fifties. The fifties were subdivided into tens, each with its own captain, guards, herdsmen, etc. Willard Richards was sustained as the historian of the Church and the camp, and William Clayton was appointed as clerk for the whole camp, with other clerks appointed for each fifty. Commissars were also appointed, with a commissary general for the camp (CHC 3:52–53).

These reorganizations increased efficiency and unity, although road conditions continued to plague the companies and, in some cases, scattered the camps. Robert's narrative of the journey from the Chariton River to the interim settlement at Mount Pisgah illustrates their plight:

> Our next prominent stop Charldon River where we arrived on the 22nd. Here in consequence of the terrible conditions of the road we were compelled to stop until April 1st when we resumed our journey and arrived at Shole Creek [Locust Creek] on the same night. Traveled 7 miles. Here we remained until 3rd and obtained corn and supplies from Misouri. Moved on 3rd to Shole Creek, and roads and weather were so bad we remained untill the 9th when we again resumed our journey. The roads were so bad and water so bad, Mrs. Burton and I were compelled to camp on pararie in mud and water, having only traveled three miles today. The balance of the company, however, reached a point three miles in advance of our wagon.
>
> On the next morning, we were helped to six yoke of cattle, with this help we succed [succeeded] camping in little point of timber before mentioned. Here we were compelled to remain till the 13th in consequence of the terrible condition of the roads. We then resumed the journey and traveled 4 miles and camped with Heber C. Kimball's

company. Moving on the next [day] succeded in getting 3 mi and reached Pres. Young's company (1843–69, 32–34).

Their progress in two weeks' time totaled a mere thirty-two miles. The last camp mentioned was named Locust Creek Camp Number 2. Here on April 15, William Clayton wrote the words of "Come, Come, Ye Saints." As his journal records, "This morning I composed a new song—'all is well' " (in Kimball 1972, 42). Brigham Young's history also identifies this as site of a council which determined that the first temporary settlement, later named Garden Grove, would be on the Grand River, although Robert Burton apparently learned of this decision a week later at Pleasant Point, a camp sixteen miles farther on.

A council was held here at which it was determined a portion of the company should remain on Grand River, where we arrived on 23rd and commenced erecting houses, plowing and fencing, preparing for raising crops of grain etc. Here many of the Saints remained more perhaps from necessity than choice. The council determined to make another farm on the west fork of the Grand River. On May 13 we started for this point, the brethren of the Nauvoo Brass Band except myself were compelled to remain here [Garden Grove] having not the means of transportation to persue their journey farther at present.

We arrived at the point of destenation at the West Fork of Grand River 35 miles in a most violent rain storm and commenced making some preperations for settlement, plowing, fencing etc. (1843–69, 37–39).

These two settlements followed Brigham Young's plan that the Saints should build shelters, fence fields, then plow and plant crops for later companies to harvest. The first was called Garden Grove, or sometimes the "Magic City of the Woods" (Kimball 1972, 43). The second was named Mount Pisgah by Parley P. Pratt, who had led the advance party in search of a suitable site. Moses had viewed the Promised Land from Mount Pisgah (Deut. 3:27). Pratt's autobiography describes his first sight of the area:

Riding about three or four miles through beautiful prairies, I came suddenly to some round and sloping hills, grassy and crowned with beautiful groves of timber; while alternate open groves and forests seemed blended in all the beauty and harmony of an English park. While beneath and beyond, on the west, rolled a main branch of Grand river, with its rich bottoms of alternate forest and prairie. . . . Being pleased and excited at the varied beauty before me, I cried out, "this is Mount Pisgah" (1968, 342).

While Robert and Maria were crossing Iowa with Brigham Young and the Camp of Israel, other Nauvoo residents were in various stages of following. Some leaders of the advance party came only far enough to get the exodus started, then returned to Nauvoo for their families. As they moved from camp to camp and others returned to Nauvoo for supplies, they formed a postal system, exchanging letters between the pioneers and their families in Nauvoo. On the evening of May 2, a Brother Staley stopped at John Haven's home, offering to carry a letter to the Camp of Israel for them. A concerned mother quickly began filling a page with news and encouragement for Maria.

Nauvoo, May 3, 1846

Dear Child:

I received a letter from you last week. I felt very sorry to hear you are so unwell. I hope you will keep up with good courage and will gain your health soon. I saw your Father Burton today. They have gone over Miss. River but cannot go further on account of the going. They think they shall start in two or three days. Sister F. Young was here Friday last. She told us they had a letter from Brother Brigham, which informed them that those that were appointed to go to England last fall must now fulfill their mission. He (Brother Brigham) says the Brothers Burton will go as soon as they can leave their families. Sis. Young says she don't know why they should thus be singled out, but thinks they are not going at present. Be that as it may, whenever Robert goes, I shall depend upon your promise, that is, to live with us. Nothing short of that will make us happy Maria. Make no other calculation we are making all possible speed to come. We intend to make our tent this week. Whenever we can exchange our house and lot for a team and a little clothing, we shall come. There is a great many in to bye. They call on us often. Their people have not met our prices yet. We may sell within 24 hours.

Maria, I have sold your bonnet. I shall get you a dress. I have not sold Robert's hat yet but think I shall, and your other bonnet. You must write as soon as you receive this and let me know what you want. Joseph and Jene have sold for 26 dollars a piece. Israel has not sold yet. Elizabeth has a fine son. She is smart. Chauncey West and Mary Houghlin were married today. We went into the Temple to meeting today. Brother Hyde preacht. It was very interesting. Porter Rockwell is in Quincy; sail Judith Morey May 5.

At this point, Eliza began writing, her lines running crosswise on the page so that they crossed her mother's writing at right angles, a nineteenth century custom to get more information on a page:

> Sister & Bro. Staley was here last night. He said he was going directly to the Camp and I could send a letter and I embrace the opportunity. Mother has wrote in her letter that Chauncey and Mary were married. They expect to start for the west in a few days. I was to meeting Friday. We had a good one. The house was not near full as all had to pay. I sat with the singers. We had no meeting Saturday. It was free for everyone on Sunday. I was there all day. Bro Hyde preached in the forenoon. He preached excellent. I presume you will have the particulars in the Camp. Mellissa and Bro. Burton were over to meeting Sunday. They have been across the river about a week waiting for the roads. Cass [Charles] is very sick. . . . He felt very bad when he heard that you were sick.
>
> Mother began her letter wrong and I don't know as you can read this. . . . We have sold our house and lot but have not got much for it. We got two yoke of cattle, a wagon and twenty dollars in money. We cannot get many clothes. If you want anything in particular send word or write what you want. We shall start in about two weeks. Father and Mother have been down and got us a tent and wagon cover.

Eliza continues her letter with bits of news and messages of greeting to and from friends and relatives, mentioning only first names. She concludes by sending her love and expressing dismay at the way they had to write to cover the paper, "Let no one see this but yourself, it looks so bad. I don't know as you can read this." There is also a note at the bottom written again by her mother, "E. filled my letter whilst I was gone so I can write no more. My love to Robert and I hope I shall see you soon. Mother"

Wherever Brother Staley caught up with the Camp of Israel, he was warmly welcomed. Nothing could have lifted the spirits of these homeless exiles more than a letter from their loved ones; and this letter contained the promises Maria and Robert wanted most to hear—that their families would soon be on their way to join them. Sitting by the campfire, Maria must have read the letter again and again, turning it to figure out the crossing lines. Then she would have shared its messages with the many persons it mentioned.

Maria and Robert were left without even a tent for shelter when young Calvin Bingham returned to Nauvoo, where his father's family was waiting for the wagon to begin their journey. They found temporary quarters in the tent of friends but anxiously awaited the arrival of their families. Both the Burtons and the Havens reached Mount Pisgah in June. Although their traveling was somewhat easier because of the improved roads and ferries, they still suffered from exposure to the elements and the discomfort of trail life. Hannah Burton, who was nearly sixty, was in particularly poor health and never fully recovered from the exhausting trip across Iowa.

Mount Pisgah became a thriving community of 2,000 as refugees from Nauvoo arrived at the rate of twenty to thirty wagons a day throughout the summer of 1846. However, Brigham Young left June 1, and two weeks later established his headquarters camp at Kanesville (later Council Bluffs), on the Missouri River, where the pattern of plowing, planting, and building began again.

At Mount Pisgah, Robert's youngest sister, Melissa, married her sweetheart, William Coray, June 22, 1846, and Robert traded Samuel's team of horses for three yoke of work cattle, a large cow, and a two-year-old heifer. Robert and Maria, Samuel and Hannah Burton, with fifteen-year-old Charles, and John and Judith Haven, with seventeen-year-old Eliza, traveled on together from Mount Pisgah, early in July. They found great numbers of Saints gathered on both sides of the Missouri River, preparing to spend the winter. Many were camped on the lands of the Pottawattamie Indians who permitted the exiles to live on their unoccupied land, to cut and use timber, and make improvements.

At Kanesville, the Burtons heard confirmation of a rumor first heard on the trail: the United Stated had declared war on Mexico and was recruiting a battalion of Mormons to march to California and claim it for the United States.

Five months had passed since that bitter cold morning when the exodus had begun at Nauvoo. Robert, Maria, and their families had crossed the muddy prairies and endured exposure to cold and rain, but still they had no place to go. Like the thousands who waited on the banks of the Missouri, their future was no more certain than when they left Nauvoo. July 1846 was to be another month of decisions.

Notes

A new study of the trek across Iowa and wintering on the Missouri is Richard E. Bennett's *Mormons at the Missouri, 1846–52*, Norman and London: University of Oklahoma Press, 1987.

1. The settlements were actually in present-day Iowa. The border between Iowa and Missouri was under dispute, and in 1846 the boundary was ten miles north of the present line. On April 2, the camp was quite close to Missouri and Brigham Young decided to bear more to the north. In spite of their previous experience in Missouri, the Mormons did work and trade in nearby Missouri communities (Kimball 1972, 42).

Missouri Interlude, 1846–47

After the enlistment of the Mormon Battalion, the remaining Saints were counseled to makes homes for the winter and plan to continue the journey westward the next summer. Robert and Maria went to Missouri with their parents where they thought work opportunities would be better. In a small log cabin Hannah Burton died and Robert and Maria's first child was born. Maria, remarkably, chose to remember "many happy hours" about their eighteen-month stay in Missouri.

The farewells and "God bless you's" were over; the families of Council Bluffs pulled back from the road to allow their husbands, fathers, brothers, and even sisters to form into companies and march out of camp. They waved as long as someone might be able to turn and still see them, then kept their watch until the procession was swallowed up by the prairie and only the rising dust in the distance marked their course.

Five hundred men—described by Robert as the "flower of the colony"—were en route to Fort Leavenworth, Kansas, as soldiers in the U.S. Army, and with them were a few young, strong women. Robert and Maria stood at the road's edge with Samuel and Hannah, his sister Rebecca, a baby in her arms, and his youngest brother, Charles. Their hearts were almost breaking at the realization of another separation from loved ones.

Marching away was Nathaniel Jones, Rebecca's husband, William Coray, their new brother-in-law, and Melissa, their youngest sister. She was eighteen years old and a month-old bride when Brigham himself came to Mount Pisgah to encourage volunteering by the young and able bodied men of the camp. William had enlisted as a sergeant for $14 a month; and Melissa, who hired on as a cook and washerwoman, expected to earn just as much during the 1,000-mile march to California. She was one of only four women who made the complete march (Whitney 1:269). Nathaniel Jones, a first sergeant, kept a journal which has proved to be a valuable record of a feat unequaled in American history.

It may have seemed unusual to the thousands of homeless followers that Brigham Young deliberated only a few hours on the proposal that 500 of his best men volunteer to aid the government which had so recently neglected their rights. Captain James Allen had hardly been in camp a day when Young met with him and promised to raise a battalion for service in the Mexican War. Very few Saints knew that Brigham Young had instructed his nephew, Jesse C. Little, representative of the Church in the East, to "take every honorable advantage of the times you can" to get government assistance for the Saints' migration west. Little's letter of appointment urged: "If our government shall offer any facilities for emigrating to the western coast, embrace those facilities, if possible" (in CHC 3:67).

Captain Allen's appearance in Council Bluffs on June 29, 1846, was the result of Little's appeal to President James K. Polk. Brigham quickly recognized many benefits in the proposal, including the cash income from army pay which would help many impoverished families buy outfits. Young also negotiated permission from Allen to winter those left behind and their stock on Indian lands beyond Council Bluffs. At noon on June 30, Captain Allen read his orders to the Saints:

I have come among you, instructed by Col. S. F. Kearney of the United States Army, now commanding the Army of the west, to visit the Mormon camp, and to accept the service for twelve months of four or five companies of Mormon men who may be willing to serve their country for that period in our present war with Mexico; this force to unite with the army of the west at Santa Fe, and be marched thence to California, where they will be discharged.

They will receive pay and rations, and other allowances, such as other volunteers or regular soldiers receive, from the day they shall be mustered into the service, and will be entitled to all comforts and benefits of regular soldiers of the army, and when discharged, as contemplated, at California, they will be given gratis their arms and accoutrements, with which they will be fully equipped at Leavenworth. This is offered to the Mormon people now. This year an opportunity of sending a portion of their young and intelligent men to the ultimate destination of the whole people, and entirely at the expense of the United States, and this advanced party can thus pave the way and look out the land for their brethren to come after them (CHC 3:86).

President Young followed Captain Allen with a speech of loyalty for the U. S. government, a remarkable position in light of the treatment his people had received from that government. His journal reports that speech:

I said, the question might be asked, "Is it prudent for us to enlist to defend our country? If we answer in the affirmative, all are ready to go.

Suppose we were admitted into the union as a state and the government did not call on us, we would feel ourselves neglected. Let the "Mormons" be the first to set their feet on the soil of California. Captain Allen has assumed the responsibility of saying that we may locate on Grand Island, until we can prosecute our journey. This is the first offer we have ever had from the government to benefit us.

I proposed that the five hundred volunteers be mustered and I would do my best to see all their families brought forward, as far as my influence extended, and feed them when I had anything to eat myself (in CHC 3:79).

One of the first Burton family decisions made during July 1846 was that Robert would not volunteer. Although he possessed every quality sought in the enlistees, he wrote in his journal simply, "I remained to take care of my aged parents" (1843–69, 41).

Because of the great loss of manpower and the almost destitute condition of the Saints, the Church leaders decided to establish a "permanent" camp and wait until 1847 to go west. After considering several sites on the west side of the Missouri River, they finally laid out a location north of Council Bluffs and named it Winter Quarters.

Samuel Burton, however, determined in late July or early August that the thousands left behind could not support themselves around Council Bluffs and he moved his family to a Missouri settlement about forty miles southeast. Robert recalled the circumstances of their decision and the removal to Missouri in his journal:

> We thought it would be better for our family—that we could obtain the outfit for our journey quicker by moving down into the state of Missouri.
>
> Accordingly leaving the Bluffs and traveling down the Missouri River arriving at Atchinson [sic] Co., about the middle of August [1846].
>
> In our little company were my father and family and my father-in-law (John Haven) and family. I purchased a claim near the mouth of the Nishbotna River. Here we erected cabins, cultivated land and I obtained labor, part of [the] time in Missouri (1843–69, 41–43).

In November, Samuel Burton began wondering about his ten children. "Whilst musing on Sun. Morning," November 29, he began a lengthy letter to his eldest daughter, Jane, and her husband, Anthony Leybourn. Betsy lived close to Jane, Ann had moved back to Pultneyville, New York, while William, Mary, and Sarah were scattered among Mormon settlements in Illinois and Iowa. Melissa was with the Battalion, and Rebecca, Robert, and Charles were with their parents in Atchison County, Missouri. In his letter, Samuel described their journey from Nauvoo, their move to Missouri, the formation of the Mormon Battalion, and the children's circumstances:

Dear Son & Daughter.

Whilst musing on Sun. Morning over my fore side it came to mind to drop a few lines to you once more perhaps the last the Lord only knows, but at the present I have no reason to complain as to my health. I with the rest of my family have great reason to praise my Heavenly Father for the good health we all enjoy at the present time. . . . Well my children we left Nauvoo the last week in April & crossed the Mississippi river. There by the side of the river we staid two weeks & then took our journey for Mt. Pisgah, which we found to be very tedious owing to the wet spring, it made the road very bad as it had never been traveled before by the whites. There was no bridges over the rivers or streams of water. Our brethren that went on first found hard labor. We found Robert & his wife & staid at Pisgah about one week & then left acrost the grand river & pitched our tents two miles from Pisgah. . . . Bro. Young & the Twelve with a great number more crosst the Missouri River and pitched their tents and building houses, but everyone to his notion. I thought it best to go where there was a settlement and something to live on and some employment to earn something so we left Council Bluffs & returned back about forty miles where we found a settlement and a very good range for our stock and built up a log house and are quite comfortable at this time as we think. I work at my trade and so Robert and Charles work some at such as they can get to do.

Corn is worth 25c per bu., trade wheat 37 1/2c. Pork $2.00 per cwt. Good beef the same. Yet some of our poor brethern that acrost the river with the Twelve I think will find a hard winter. There is not anything to earn to live on nothing but rough Indians. Near to them our settlement for 30 miles is full of Mormons everywhere. . . . I expect you heard of our brethern entering in the United States service. . . . Nathaniel Jones has gone but Rebecca is with us. Jones is 1st Sergant in the 4th Company. Jones wrote a letter Wed. on the road to Santa Fe. He had bought a pony to ride & a mule to carry his luggage on. Wm. Corry that married Melissa has gone with her husband is Sergant has $14.00 per mo. & Melissa if she has her health will make as much. . . . I cannot say anything about Wm. Burton. He had not got back from Michigan when we left Nauvoo. We left Billy there but I say he is back to Nauvoo for he wrote a letter to me when I was at Mt. Pisgah, he then said he should be for starting by the middle of the month, but heard nothing from him since. Samuel & Mary while can't say where they are but I do think in the neighborhood of Roney, part of the DeMoine River about 40 miles from Nauvoo, in the Territory of Iowa. Elijah Austin & Sarah I think is on their way, but have not reached us at this time. I do wish they were all with us for we feel uneasy about them. Since commencing my letter we have bought a place of a man a quarter section 23 acres improved & 4 horses on it for $150.00. We shall try & break up 20 acres more & put in corn in the spring, if the Lord be willing. We make a home somewhere so as to live whilst the Church found a place to satisfy themselves for a season. My son, it is a hard tug for our people, for my part I don't like it moving about so much, but I will assure you it's trying work for the Saints such suffering & persecution they have to endure, but the Lord will carry His work through in His own due time. Your Mother's health is better than it has been for some years back. Thank the Lord for it. I do assure you we've wished to see you all with us. My love to Wm. & Samuel Leybourn likewise to Eliza & Verline & Steven & Mary Hannah, your two youngest. I cannot name my kindest love to Joseph & Betsy & all their children also to Waters & Ann Shipley & their child. I do long to see you all once more if it could be so. We are far parted in body but are near to me in thoughts.

Resuming his letter at a later date, Samuel is able to send recent news from Rebecca's husband and Melissa.

At time of writing Rebecca Jones was at Brigham's Camp to receive some money. Jones sent $20.00; in another letter from Jones $45.00 more. They were at Santa Fe in Mexico. Arrived there on the 9th day of Oct. . . .

Santa Fe lays in a valley betwixt two mountains. The houses are built of unburnt bricks but richly furnished inside. Melissa says there is plenty of fruit such as apples, peaches & the largest grapes she ever saw, as large as great plums. . . . Melissa says the city is very rich. More wealth than all Missouri. They have about five thousand Mexican troops in Santa Fe, but the 500 of the Mormon Battalion is going to leave the rest of the troops in Santa Fe & follow after Gen. Carney & when they overtake Carney, he takes the command of them. They go to foot of Rocky Mts. which is nigh 600 miles. There they will have to leave their wagons and will have to take all their luggage on mules right to the Pacific Ocean to the bay of San Francisco. There they are going to build a fort & then to take shipping for California. Its 800 miles for them to go on mules, after they leave their wagons. Melissa will be surely tired of riding on mules so far. She says her health is good but she says she could wish to have the society of her father & mother, brothers & sisters which would be the greatest consolation on earth. Jones feels bad he has not received none of Rebecca's letters & he has rote ten to her, which fills him with grief. Melissa says their is plenty of game such as buffaloes & antelope & wolves as plentiful as they ever saw dogs. Melissa says she could if with her tell of a great many curiosities. There is not any chance for her to send letters any more. I cannot say for certain whether we shall go after them this spring or not. Brigham has altered his mind & says all may go that can get ready, but he may alter his mind half dozen times before spring. We cannot say what will be done whilst spring comes. Whilst Rebecca was at headquarters she heard of your brother Wm. Burton, he was in Nauvoo, but where he is at this time I can not say. Rebecca also heard of Samuel & Mary White. They are on their way to here but stopt some where on the road to winter. Mary buried one of her children on the road which would make her feel very bad. . . . Well my dear children I must come to close with my scribbling & do sincerely desire the welfare of all my children & grandchildren temporal & spiritual. My children your aged parents desire all your prayers for you have ours. So the Lord bless you all is the prayer of your father & mother, brothers & sisters in the Lord Jesus Christ, even so Amen.

A postscript indicated that Sarah had written and that her family, still at Walnut Grove, expected to join with the saints "in the spring." That promise was never fulfilled as the Austins separated themselves from the Church and remained in Illinois for the remainder of their lives.

Samuel Burton painstakingly wrote his letter over a period of days, writing first across the paper, then lengthwise, hoping to include as much news as possible on one sheet. The Leybourns, thrilled to receive the letter and share it with family and friends in Ohio, preserved it and it was brought to Salt Lake sometime late in the nineteenth century.

Even with many travelers passing through the scattered settlements between Winter Quarters and Nauvoo, it was eight long months before Samuel learned about his eldest son, William, whom he had thought was in Nauvoo. Planning to obtain a team and outfit for the trek by selling his property in Canada, William was headed north while most Saints were crossing Iowa. In Michigan, after some difficulty he finally got a wagon and harness from a Brother Jinks Bagley in return for the power of attorney to sell his land in Mersea, Essex County. When William returned to Nauvoo, Betsy's poor health and other problems kept him from following his father's family across Iowa.

Over 16,000 Saints crossed the Mississippi River from Nauvoo between February and May of 1846, but 1,000 still remained, many too poor or sick to begin the journey. William recorded in his journal how he kept busy throughout the summer caring for this remnant of the Latter-day Saint people. He served with a quasi-posse or guard which protected the Saints against the mobs who harassed them. He also helped with the harvest and attended prayer meetings in the temple, which had been completed and dedicated (1839–51, June-September 1846).

The anti-Mormons of Hancock and surrounding counties continued to threaten this pitifully weak group of Saints, even calling for their "extermination" if they did not leave. The threats and attacks increased, even though Governor Ford had stationed a small military force in Nauvoo ostensibly to "protect" the Mormons. As the summer of 1846 drew to a close, 800 men, acting as a posse under the constable at Carthage and led by "General" Thomas S. Brockman, set up six cannons on the south side of Mulholland Street about a mile east of the city and threatened to destroy Nauvoo. The governor's representative tried to negotiate a sixty-day truce to give the remaining Saints time to get out of the city, but the mob countered with its "terms of peace": surrender the city and stack all arms (CHC 3:12).

Neither the Mormons nor the new Nauvoo residents intended to allow Brockman's forces to enter the city unopposed. Although they numbered at the most 300 and were armed with only steamboat shafts turned into cannons and individual weapons, the Nauvoo force, which included William Burton, fought back from fortifications built north of Mulholland Street. Shots were exchanged September 10, 11, and 12, without either side gaining the advantage. However on the thirteenth, Brockman's forces made a desperate advance to cross Mulholland Street. The Nauvoo defenders mounted a "spirited" resistance and drove the mob back to their field encampment. Three Mormons died in this "Battle of Nauvoo," among them Captain William

Anderson and his fifteen-year-old son, August. When Samuel Burton heard of the battle, he said, "The Mormons lost but three men, one by name of Anderson & he was worth more than all the 50 of the mobecrats put together. Anderson's son was killed the day after his father. Wm. Burton baptized him, the father of the boy, and Anderson was not to [be] frightened By man but he is gone" (Samuel Burton 1846). Peace negotiations resumed. Realizing that state authorities would give them no assistance, the Nauvoo residents finally submitted to a treaty of surrender which allowed Brockman's troops to take possession of the city on September 17. A Mr. Brayman, special representative of Governor Ford, described the complete defiance of both the terms of the treaty and the supposed order of "General" Brockman, as the "victors" entered Nauvoo on September 18:

> Bands of armed men traversed the city, entering the houses of citizens, robbing them of arms, throwing their household goods out of doors, insulting them, and threatening their lives. Many were seized, and marched to the camp, and after a military examination, sent across the river, for the crime of sympathizing with the Mormons, or the still more heinous offense of fighting in defense of the city, under command of officers commissioned by you [Gov. Ford] and instructed to make that defense (CHC 3:18).

The Mormons were given one or two hours, or at most a day to leave. The drunken conquerors robbed the citizens, and desecrated the temple which they made their headquarters. Approximately 650 frightened, destitute Saints took refuge on the banks of the Mississippi River, some in the open, some crowded into the homes of members or kind benefactors. William and Betsy Burton went down to the river on September 18 and found shelter with Hiram Kimball; on the twenty-sixth they crossed over to Montrose, Iowa. Betsy, already frail, suffered from exposure and within a few days took sick and appeared near death. After many priesthood administrations and conscientious care, William could write to Robert nine months later, "Through the mercy of our Heavenly Father, she is getting well" (W. Burton July 2 1847).

Most of these last exiles found their way into the Iowa settlements and remained there, having neither the means nor strength to follow the Saints. William still hoped to join the pioneer companies, but found it difficult to achieve. In February 1847, he wrote a letter encouraging his sister Sarah and her husband Elijah Austin to join him "all ready to roll on."

> We were sorry to hear of you and the Children being sick. But we hope that your health has got good, and also your family. I am happy to inform you that we are all tolerably well. Elizabeth has not got entirely well, but upon the whole, I think her health is improving. We feel thankful to our Heavenly Father for His goodness unto us.
>
> I have been able to get employment so that we have not suffered for anything and have had a comfortable house to live in, while numbers of our brethren have suffered much in various ways. I hope that you have been favoured in your temporal concerns.
>
> I want to go West in the spring if I possibly can but I lack a considerable of those things that are actually necessary, yet I hope that I shall be able, by the help of God, to succeed in this matter. Relative to the time when I shall start I cannot positively say, But I would like to get ready about the middle of April, and I should like to see you here before that time all ready to roll on. We have got some good news from the Bluffs. . . . They intend to send a large company on in the Spring who will go about 700 miles and put in a crop. The Lord has given a revelation respecting the gathering of the Saints and other Matters. The council is for all to go that can consistently. (A word to the wise is sufficient.)
>
> I received a letter from Bro. Anthony Leybourn about the first of Jany. They were all well and all others of our relatives in that part of the land. Moses Smith had called to see them and tryed to convert them to Strangism. He, no doubt, had used a great deal of eloquence and perhaps told some strange stories about Spiritual Affairs from what Anthony wrote.
>
> If you have received any intelligence from Father's Folks, let us know when you write. I want to know what your prospects are about going West in the Spring (W. and E. Burton 1847).

Neither William nor Sarah's family went west in the spring of 1846. As late as July, William wrote Robert that he would come to Council Bluffs in the fall "if it be the will of God."

Instead, he spent the winter of 1846–47 driving freight or "teaming" between the Mississippi River towns.

This same winter, about the middle of December, Robert was forced to leave home and look for work in the bigger cities along the Missouri River. He and a Brother Coons searched for almost two weeks before they found a job in Weston, Missouri, about 110 miles downriver from Austen Township. On January 3, filled with homesickness and concern for his family, Robert wrote to his beloved Maria:

> With pleasure I resume my seat to drop a few lines to you hoping they may find you in the enjoyment of as good [health] as I enjoy myself and better spirits being surrounded with home and all its joys, friends, etc.
>
> We passed down the river hearing of a job here and there but when we came to trace them out there was no work there or we was a day too late for the work and so on until we arrived here and got a job of chopping at 37 1/2 cents per cord for steam wood, and commenced work Christmas afternoon. We are not certain as to the punctuality or the qualifications of our employer to pay us according to our agreement.
>
> Business is very dull in this place at present to what it generally is—the fact is we're a little too late in the season. Such contracts as we would like to have taken were all gone.
>
> Today I have attended the Presbyterian Church in Weston where there was a very fashionable audience and speaker also, but believe me I would much rather have been at home, but I will say no more about home or you will really think that I am homesick. I confess that I came nearer at this time than ever before; perhaps it is because I am getting older and more childish in my mind and not so strong.
>
> I will not intrude on your time much more at present. I wish you to write to me immediately on the receipt of this letter and give me the particulars of the domestic concerns of the family, as well as that of the community to which we belong and then I must make my calculations accordingly.
>
> Let me know if Rebecca has received her money or not. Give my love to all the members of our family and friends also.
>
> > With feelings of the greatest respect and esteem, I remain your affectionate and constant Husband until death,
> > Robert T. Burton

By spring, Robert was back in Austen Township, cultivating the land on his homestead and planting crops. He also obtained a contract from the U.S. government to furnish a certain tonnage of wild hay for a detachment of cavalry quartered south to the south. He hired men to help him and spent the late summer months cutting and stacking hay. He received $300, a sizeable sum in those days, which in time helped purchase an outfit for the journey to the Rocky Mountains (M. Burton n.d.; W. S. Burton n.d.[b], 2–3). The residents of this sparsely settled corner of Missouri did not mind Mormon families in their midst. Robert wrote that he found employment among the local residents "who treated us as a rule very kindly and we were enable to accumulate some means toward getting teams etc for the Journey westward" (R. T. Burton n.d.[a], 16) Maria recalled many years later that there were "a great many happy hours" in the log house in Atchison County (M. Burton 1881, 1). Her sister Eliza remembered, "We raised fine crops, watermellons that I couldn't lift. Everyone there was so kind and friendly. We used to have quilting parties, and we Mormon girls were made much of. There were four other Mormon families besides us" (Westover 1918).

Samuel Burton continued to worry about his children who had not joined the Saints. On July 11, 1847, he wrote to Sarah and Elijah Austin, who were now in Princeton, Bureau County, Illinois, evidently planning to stay there. The letter mentions the unexpected death of Betsy Burton Roop, at Sylvania, Ohio, on March 6, 1847.

> My dear children,
>
> I received your letter dated May 12 and was glad to hear from you, my dear child, that you was all well but felt some disappointed at not having your society this summer amongst us. It makes me sometimes think that you don't mean to come amongst us and to gather with the Saints of God. I feel for your neglect in not gathering with the Saints. No wonder things seemes dark to you and they will still be darker for I am afraid the God of this world hath blinded your Eyes and you are to be not had in rembrance with the people of God. My children, don't let John Landers lead you to hell. It's a serious matter. The things of God are not to be trifled with. Its for

those who Endure to the end are to be saved and enter the kingdom of God. Neglect not the things of God for the trifling things of this world. My dear Sarah we grieve for you. We are well and in health and sperits too at this time. Thank God for his fatherly care over us. Your sister Mary and her three children is with me and has been this month back. Mary Elizabeth White was born at Garden Grove Nov. 2, 1846. They live 40 miles from me and old Father White is with them. . . . We have not got William as yet but is looking for him all the time. Our corn looks well. It's just tasting out. It's a great country of land the best I ever saw. We have the Best Garden I ever had in all my life. As respects the Church we have heard nothing positive from Brigham since he and his Company left. Brother Taylor and P. P. Prat is gone after with a large company but Taylor and Prat left their familey behind. We all expect to go next spring. . . . We received a letter from Anthoney Leybourn and poor Betsy's dead. But I do live in hope if I am faithful to have her companey on this Earth in a little time. She only sleeps for a little Season. She rests from her labour. She will be a mist woman by her familey and friends. My dear children I fancey I shall se you no more. If Elijah don't mean to come, say so and then we shall know. My Dear Sarah, you know your father and poor aged Mother longs to se you. So I shall say the Lord add his blessing to you and all your family and crown you with salvation in his Kingdom is the prayer of aged parents.

Samuel & Hannah Burton

Robert added his thoughts to Samuel's at the bottom of the page.

Dear sister and brother, as father has been writing to you and left space for me to write a little, I seat myself to do so. . . . It is now more than two years since I have seen you. Since that time how many changes have taken place in the world. How many thousands have lingered and died in our own country. How many thousands have fallin on the field of battle; how many thousands have been deprived of frinds, of home & all things dear to them but why need I look at the world to discover changes of times & changes of fortune. At the time we last met a long journey in the west to seek a new home was not so soon expected; a totle banishment of the Saints from the butifull City of Nauvoo and the Temple which they taken so much pains to arect was not so soon looked for and in fact we did not think that our familey would be part of them in the State of Ohio & part in Ill. part in Missouri and part in Iowa, and part in the Pacific coast and last of all the death of our much beloved sister;

all these changes in the short space of two years then in the future by us were not meditated. But I must stop for want of room. We would like to see you hear before fall to start with us in the spring. I remain your affectionate Brother, Robert T. Burton

Neither Robert nor his father could anticipate that Hannah Burton would die just two weeks later. Thirty years had passed since the Burtons sailed into Quebec and down the St. Lawrence River to a new homeland. Hannah faithfully followed her husband through ten moves between frontier settlements in America and Canada. Hannah and Samuel spent the first twenty years seeking a home, a farm, and some comforts of life. They spent the next ten years in quest of "Zion," hoping to find peace and safety near a prophet, a temple, and their children and grandchildren. The flight from Nauvoo was an unexpected chapter in this quest. Sixty-year-old Hannah suffered greatly while they were encamped at Sugar Creek and crossing muddy Iowa. She never completely regained her health and died on July 26, unaware that two days earlier Brigham Young's company had entered the Great Salt Lake Valley, finding at last a sanctuary for the Saints. Hannah's family mourned that she was buried in a lonely grave while they resumed the journey she longed to complete. Robert wrote of his mother's passing:

> Here in this our temporery, lonely home on the banks of the Missouri, my dear old mother departed this life on the 26th of July 1847. Where, at this period in the history of the west, none of the delicacies and but few of the actual comforts of life could be obtained.
>
> It was therefore impossible for us to render her such aid and comfort as her age and condition in life required. She therefore fell an easy prey to desease superinduced by her great exposure consequent upon our expulsion from comfortable homes in the state of Ill.
>
> We placed her remains in a lonely grave near our humble dwelling. Thus freed from suffering and care is this good, patient, gentle Saint quietly laid to rest to await the call of the Angel to come forth in the morning of the Resurection of the Just. None felt this loss more keen than did my father for she had truly been his faithful helpmate, monitor, and guide in all their married life (R. T. Burton n.d.[a], 16–17).

Within weeks Robert and Maria learned that she had conceived, and eight months later, on March 26, 1848, Maria delivered their first child, a daughter named Theresa Hannah.[1]

Following the baby's birth, Robert wrote: "We are now very busy indeed, preparing for our contemplated journey" (1843-69, 44). He purchased a "wide track" wagon, whose four-feet-wide wagon box allowed a bed to be placed across the rear and trunks to be stowed under the bed. Robert recalled:

> On the 17th of May we started from our home in Misouri with a team composed of two yoke of cattle and two cows and a fairly good wagon. My father and his family consisting of his second wife (Widow Smith married to him Sept. preceeding) her daughter Julia and my youngest brother Charles Edward had an outfit similar to mine.
>
> My father-in-law John Haven and family consisting of wife and daughter Eliza Ann also accompanied, [to] the starting place for the west, where we arrived on the 21st of the month (n.d.[a], 18).

The waiting was over, and the trip to "Zion" was underway. Robert and Maria were in high spirits and traveling in relative comfort as they arrived back at Winter Quarters where from every direction the saints were regathering.

Notes

1. Family records indicate that Theresa (pronounced Thres-sa) was born in Hamburg, Iowa, but she was actually born in the log house in Austen Township, Atchison County, Missouri, a few miles south of Hamburg (see M. Burton to her granddaughters, March 13, 1881).

Across the Plains, 1848

Robert and Maria and her parents were organized into Brigham Young's company which departed June 1 for the westward trek. Nearly four months later, the "tedious journey" ended at the pioneer fort, in the valley of the Great Salt Lake.

The Burton and Haven families' arrival at Winter Quarters on May 21, was a remarkable contrast to their dreary and tragic departure from Nauvoo some twenty-seven months earlier. The prairie air was alive with the colors and fragrances of spring and brimming with expectation as friends and family members met on the roads leading into the settlement.

At Winter Quarters, Brigham Young was in command. He had remained in the Salt Lake Valley only long enough to set in motion the plans for a settlement. By August 26, 1847, he was leading 107 men—some from his pioneer company and some Mormon Battalion veterans—back to Winter Quarters to get their families. The returning party passed the second, third, and fourth companies of immigrants, led by Daniel Spencer, Parley P. Pratt, and John Taylor, respectively. These 1,700 travelers would swell the valley population to 2,000 and endure many hardships through the winter of 1847–48. At Winter Quarters, Brigham Young had his own business affairs to put in order and his own families to make ready, in addition to superintending the preparations of about 2,500 immigrants. This was to be Brigham's last journey across the plains. His destiny was to lead the Church and govern the gathering Saints from the Rocky Mountains, leaving the world-wide traveling to others.

During December, Brigham Young was finally sustained as prophet, seer, and revelator as well as president of the Church. The Twelve had discussed the need for sustaining a prophet during a series of lengthy discussions and prayer meetings between mid-November and December 5, when they unanimously decided to organize a First Presidency under Brigham Young. President Young and his counselors, Heber C. Kimball and Willard C. Richards, were formally sustained in a general conference held December 27 in a huge log tabernacle erected especially for the occasion (Arrington 1985, 153; CHC 3:315–16).

Soon after their arrival at Council Bluffs, Robert and Samuel were reunited with William and Betsy Burton. Their meeting was both joyful and sad as they felt the loss of their mother keenly. Though they were grateful to be ready for the journey, they were sorrowful that other family members were not.

Nathaniel Jones returned from his service with the Mormon Battalion in the fall of 1847 after serving as an escort to General S. F. Kearney to Fort Leavenworth, where he was discharged. Nathaniel and Rebecca made the trip west in 1849. Mary and Samuel White, who were still living in Iowa, came to Utah in 1850.

Sarah and Elijah Austin settled in Sublette, Illinois, confirming her father's fears that they would not "gather with the saints of God." Sarah died in 1859, but Robert kept in close contact with his brother-in-law, and often stayed at the Austin home during his cattle-buying trips and while fleeing from federal marshals during the 1870s and 1880s.

The Burtons and Havens drove their wagons to the Elkhorn River ferry, twenty-three miles west of Winter Quarters, which served as the rendezvous point for the companies about to depart.

When Brigham Young arrived at the ferry on May 28, he organized the wagon parties into traveling groups of hundreds, fifties, and tens, a pattern revealed to him the previous spring (D&C 136). There were 623 wagons and nearly 1,900 Saints divided into two great companies. Brigham Young would lead 397 wagons and Heber C. Kimball 226. Willard C. Richards and Amasa Lyman would bring a third company from the same place in July. John Haven's wagon and Robert and Maria's were included in Brigham Young's company. Robert's wagon was in the second ten, and he was appointed camp bugler. "It therefore became my duty," he recalled, "to call the camp which was usually about 4 o'clock" (1843–69, 46). Samuel and William Burton's wagons were organized into Heber C. Kimball's company, which followed three or four days behind the first company. William was assigned to keep the company journal.

As the departure date neared, Brigham Young called the pioneers together to give them instructions for maintaining order during the trek. Robert and Maria stood close to Brigham's carriage, which served as his rostrum. He cautioned them not to abuse their cattle or oxen, not to make noises or be up at night, and to attend to prayers, go to bed at nine o'clock, and put out the fires. They were to tie their cattle outside of the corral with their horses inside; dogs should either be tied up or shot, and other animals should not be permitted to run loose. June 1 dawned bright and clear; the first wagons were ferried across the Elkhorn and moved out onto the prairie. In all, 397 wagons, 1,229 Saints, 74 horses, 19 mules, 1,275 oxen, 699 cows, 184 cattle, 411 sheep, 141 pigs, 605 chickens, 37 cats, 82 dogs, 3 goats, 10 geese, 2 beehives, 8 doves and a crow, began their journey to the "promised land" (in Nibley 1937, 118–19).

Spirits were high. Thomas Bullock, clerk of the Camp of Israel, wrote to Levi Richards:

> On the 1st day of June, Lorenzo Snow's company (one hundred wagons) moved off the ground to the "Liberty Pole" on the Platte, in order to make room for other wagons that came pouring in from Winter Quarters. If any person inquire "Is Mormonism down?" he ought to have been in the neighborhood of the Elkhorn this day,

and he would have seen such a host of wagons that would have
satisfied him in an instant that it lives, and flourishes like a tree by a
fountain of waters; he would have seen merry faces, and heard the
song of rejoicing that the day of deliverance had surely come (in
CHC 3:319).

Robert's journal entries during the march were brief and
infrequent. The few problems he mentioned were minor compared to the struggle he and Maria had endured while crossing
Iowa. "We are now on our journey to Great Salt Lake, traveling up the Platt River towards the Mountains with ox teams
and wagons. The journey was necessarily tedious and slow. To
add to our discomfort we lost some cattle, materially reducing
the strength of our teams" (1843–69, 45–46).

The marches of 1847 had proven that "oxen, unless horses
and mules were grain-fed en route, made the better team for
crossing the plains, as they would make from 15 to 25 miles per
day and often gain in strength with no other feed than the grass
of the plains and the brouse and grass of the hills" (CHC 3:293).
But the large number of oxen in Young's company, coupled
with the large number of immigrants, made this trip even slower
and more exhausting than the trips of 1847. Robert explained,
"The teams of these companies were principally oxen and cows
there being but very few horses and mules. Our march therefore was necessarily slow and tedious, having to travel in large
companies for protection against Indians. Up the Platt River we
traveled much of the way four teams abreast. Some difficulty
was also experienced from the vast herds [of] Buffalo stampeding the cattle" (n.d.[a], 18).

The dusty, soft ground along the Platte River limited their
progress to fewer than ten miles in a day. Wood was scarce and
the only alternative was damp buffalo chips, which Maria and
the other women found distasteful as cooking fuel. But neither
Robert nor Maria recorded many complaints; their health was
excellent, and they enjoyed the Havens' companionship throughout the trip. Maria's sister Eliza said of the trek, "I had a pleasant time, was young, blessed with good health and had no
cares" (Westover 1918).

Brigham's company reached Fort Laramie, halfway between Winter Quarters and the Salt Lake Valley, on July 20, fifty days after their departure. They crossed the Platte, leaving flat and "easy" stretches behind, and headed into the mountains. Brigham Young was constantly busy; he rode ahead in his carriage looking for good campsites; he directed the fording of creeks, warned of dangers in descending steep ravines, cautioned drivers about feed and water for the animals; he bore the personal burdens of his people and grew impatient with their grumblings when all did not go smoothly or the trip seemed too long and too difficult. His daughter, Susa Young Gates, related this illustration of his methods of keeping the pioneers moving:

> When the company halted at Sweetwater, women were tired, men were discouraged. Day after day passed, and the discontent of the party grew with every passing hour. Among any other people there would have been mutiny and a sharp turn backward to the shelter of civilization. Always alert to the pressure of influences about him, President Young felt the resistance that manifested itself in silence, rather than in words. One afternoon he hitched up his coach and with the terse statement that he was "going to the valley; if anybody wants to follow, the road is open," the President put the whip to his horses and gave not a glance behind (in Nibley 1937, 121).

Reportedly, he drove on alone eighteen miles, and then waited for the wagon train to catch up to him, hoping that the Saints had learned that he was going to go to the valley regardless of the difficulties.

The ascent to the continental divide up the east slope of the Rockies along the North Platte and Sweetwater rivers provided the greatest challenge to the three companies of 1848. The soil and water were saturated with alkali, causing discomfort to the people who inhaled it in the dust, but bringing death to the cattle and oxen who drank it from pools and streams. Robert, whose losses here were great, appeared stranded at this point in the trip. He wrote:

> On arriveing at the North Platt and up the Sweet Water not knowing how to take advantage of mountain travel selecting feed

ground, etc. my cattle died by drinking poisonous or alkali water. So much so that my team and many others was so reduced that we could not travel until aid was sent us from Salt Lake Valley by those who had emigrated the previous year (R. T. Burton n.d.[a], 19).

Arriving at the upper part of the Sweetwater River, we were compelled to remain some two weeks in consequence of loss of cattle. During our encampment here we had very severe snowstorm which—of course—made it very hard for our already weakened animals (1843–69, 46–47).

During July, Brigham wrote Parley P. Pratt and John Taylor in Salt Lake, requesting that a wagonload of salt and as many wagons and oxen teams as could be spared be sent to meet the company at the Green River by August 20. Accordingly, when forty-seven wagons and 124 yoke of oxen came into sight on the afternoon of August 28, led by Brigham's brother Lorenzo and Abraham O. Smoot, cheers resounded in the camp. Saints in the valley had sacrificed teams and wagons to help these companies over the mountains. Many of the outfits in the Young company were borrowed from families still waiting at the Missouri River who had sent their wagons on "to help out the poor." With the arrival of the fresh teams and wagons from the valley, Young discharged a number of wagons to return to Council Bluffs. He also sent a letter to Orson Hyde, now the leader of the Saints in Kanesville, reporting "We have been sixty-three days in traveling from the Elkhorn to the last crossing of the Sweetwater at an average of 12 miles a day, resting 22, including Sundays to recruit and strengthen our cattle. The very dry season, the scarcity of grass, the heavy dragging roads, and inhaling so much of the alkali by breathing, eating and drinking has been the cause of our losing many of our cattle" (in Nibley 1937, 122).

After harnessing animals brought by Albert P. Dewey, Robert and Maria resumed their journey, traveling three days behind Brigham Young and the first stage of the company. They remained indebted to Dewey for his assistance all their lives.

From the top of the pass at Big Mountain, which would come to be known as Pratt's Pass, Robert first viewed the valley; it was a long and humbling look. He had come so far and there was so little that seemed inviting. During the descent of East and Emigration Canyons, the tree-lined stream banks brightened his hopes that some part of their new home would be green and fertile. As they approached the valley, the small fort community and acres of tilled land came into view. A fence enclosed some 5,000 acres, more than half of which was already tilled and much was planted. Robert could not keep from comparing what he saw with what he had left behind. But he believed that this valley had been selected by the Lord as a sanctuary for His people and he was dedicated to making it "home." He was young, a month away from his twenty-seventh birthday, and physically very strong. He had a gentle, loving wife and a healthy baby daughter. As he surveyed the valley and pondered the years ahead, he decided that he would not be found ungrateful nor unsuccessful in this sanctuary for the Saints.

> Of course it can readily be understood that the mountain region (Salt Lake Valley) on the arrival of the L. D. Saints was anything but inviting so desert so much unlike the prairies of Ill. Mo and Iowa interspersed as they were with nice groves of timber and rich fertile lands, but we had been driven from our homes there. Had been compelled at the point of Bayonet [to find] a new one and had but little choice.
>
> We are at least free for a time from the hate and violence of mobs and now must depend for the next year mostly on the scanty supply of provisions brought with us from the States but little has yet been produced in the country (R. T. Burton n.d.[a], 19–20).

Robert and Maria had spent 116 days on the trail. On Saturday, September 23, 1848, weary but rejoicing, they rode down into the valley of the Great Salt Lake.

Notes

The 1848 crossing of the plains, led by Brigham Young, is treated in Chapter 10 of Leonard J. Arrington's *Brigham Young: American Moses*, New York: Alfred A. Knopf, 1985.

Early Years in the Valley, 1848–56

The first few years in the Great Salt Lake Valley were simple ones for Robert and Maria Burton. In the harsh frontier environment, they paid dearly for their food, home, security, and entertainment. They built their first home in 1849, began farming, and added sons to their family while Robert continued his associations with Brigham Young, William Pitt's band, and the military leaders who had come to trust him. Robert's disappointment with the region did not affect his commitment to his people.

The immigrants of 1847 had been anything but idle during their fourteen months in the valley. Leaders John Smith, Charles C. Rich, and John Young organized the settlers into efficient work groups. They enlarged the one-block square stockade to enclose three blocks by adding a block on the north and another on the south. They built 450 log cabins and erected a fence around the city to control the livestock. They began a network of roads, prepared the "big field" of 5,133 acres for planting, and planted some 3–4,000 acres in the spring of 1848. Despite their labor, these first valley residents nearly starved. The stake presidency, acting as a municipal council, had to control the price of food staples and institute voluntary rationing of one-half pound of flour per person per day. Settlers supplemented meager food supplies with crows, thistle tops, bark, sego lily bulbs, and similar items.

The pioneers had expected to see the hand of providence in the 1848 harvest, vindicating their leaders' judgment in settling them in the Great Salt Lake Valley and proving that the desert could support them and the thousands of Church members yet to come. Unfortunately, late frosts slowed the development of winter wheat and garden vegetables. When it finally looked as though they might have a harvest, hordes of ravenous crickets descended on their fields and devoured the crops. The plague of crickets was not an overnight drama as it is so often depicted. For weeks the Saints—men, women, and children—used every available method to repulse the invaders. They encompassed their fields with ditches and fire, knocked the crickets off plants with ropes and flails, and tried to bury them in holes or drown them in streams, all to no avail. Late in June, when it appeared to the distraught settlers that the disaster was complete, sea gulls native to Great Salt Lake began devouring the crickets in large quantities. Between the continued efforts of the pioneers and the aid of the gulls, some crops were saved and abandonment of the valley was averted (Arrington 1974, 128; CHC 3:332–33).

In September, as Robert Burton entered the valley along the road skirting the fields to the north, he looked over the sparse crops and wondered how they would all make it through the approaching winter. He and Maria did not have much food left from their journey, and he knew that most others were in the same situation. By evening, their wagon was secure in what was now called the "Old Fort." As they prepared to retire, they were overwhelmed with gratitude and offered up prayers of thanksgiving for the safe arrival of their family and their loved ones.

The next day being the Sabbath, Robert attended worship services in the bowery on Temple Square, an open air meeting place covered with limbs and leaves. Brigham Young spoke at the morning meeting, and Heber C. Kimball, who had just arrived, spoke at the afternoon meeting. At the latter meeting, these two men were appointed to apportion off the city lots in a kind of lottery. It seemed safe now to leave the forts and build individual homes. Lots were free except for a $1.50 surveying and filing fee. Only married men were given land allotments, and polygamists were allowed one for each family. Each family head drew a slip of paper with the number of the lot on it.

The original pioneer company had surveyed and laid out the city on July 28, 1847. After exploring various parts of the valley, President Young and the seven apostles with him designated the site of the temple block between the forks of City Creek, and decided to lay out the city in blocks of ten acres with streets eight rods wide running at right angles. Twenty feet on each side of the street was reserved for sidewalks. With much foresight, they also established detailed plans for this "City of Great Salt Lake," as it was officially named on August 14, 1847: "The blocks were to be divided into lots containing one and one quarter acres in each. It was decided also to build but one house on a [lot], and that twenty feet back from the line and in the center of the lot—'That there might be uniformity throughout the city' " (CHC 3:280).

Robert Burton drew Lot 8, Block 66, the northeast corner lot of the block at the intersection of First South and Second West [now Third West]. He was not prepared to begin building a home, however, and resided with his family for the first four months in a "good sized log cabin" which he and his father-in-law built in the South Fort (R. T. Burton 1843–69, 47–48; Westover 1918).

In December, Robert's younger sister, Melissa, and her husband, William Coray arrived in Salt Lake from California where they had been since being discharged from the Mormon Battalion. While living at Monterey in September of 1847, Melissa had delivered their first child, a son named William, Jr., but he only lived through the winter and died in May 1848. Apparently there had been some communication between Robert and his sister and brother-in-law because he had been busy erecting a house for them on their lot which was directly northwest of the Old Fort. The Coray home was probably built first because they had money from their earnings with the battalion and from employment in California.

On January 20, 1849, William and Melissa Coray and Robert, Maria, and ten-month-old Theresa moved into the Coray home. Just about two weeks later, on February 6, Melissa delivered a baby girl, but the joy in this pioneer home was short-lived. Weakened by the hardships of his battalion experiences, William became seriously ill in the severe cold of the winter. On March 5, President Young came to their home and sealed William and Melissa for all eternity with William too ill to leave his bed. Two days later, he died.

The winter of 1848–49 proved to be a great test to all 4,000 residents of the valley. Food supplies were meager and the hastily built houses did not protect the settlers from a particularly harsh "upper New York" kind of winter. A letter from the Twelve to Orson Pratt, living in England, reported that "snow covered the ground to some depth, for nearly three months, and finally disappeared, from parts of the valley, the latter end of February; since that time cold winds have prevailed and light snows are frequent" (in CHC 3:337n).

The reformed Council of Fifty tried to help the Saints make it through the winter. During the fall of 1848, some of the members of the original council regrouped and began exercising most governmental authority although it often acted through the ecclesiastical organizations of the high council and the nineteen wards. The high council had acted as the municipal government up to this time. When food staples became scarce, the Council of Fifty used its influence to control prices for wheat and corn and to equitably distribute the surplus thus preventing exploitation and starvation of the poor. A rationing system was established within the wards whereby each bishop provided for the needy of his ward by asking anyone with a surplus to turn it over to him for distribution. Many of the more well-to-do Saints did not like the plan, but President Young preferred to "reason" with them rather than regulate the price of food by law. He declared, "If those that have do not sell to those that have not, we will just take it and distribute it among the Poors" (in Arrington 1958, 60).

By spring, most settlers were subsisting on less than three-quarters of a pound of flour or breadstuffs per day, and many were supplementing their diet with sego roots, thistles, cowhide soup, and small game as had been done the previous winter.

The Burtons stayed with Melissa and her infant daughter, also named Melissa, through the spring and early summer. Robert obtained a ten-acre plat in the Big Field and began working it. "My first attempt at cultivating the ground in the city and in the ten acre platte was in 1849. I succeded in raising some grain" (1843–69, 50).

On August 20, Robert and Maria moved their wagon onto their lot and together commenced building their first home in the valley. After driving the wagon off the road, they lifted the wagon box off the running gear and placed it on logs on the ground with the front end gate removed. Maria recalled this memorable event, "When this was done I thought I was in a palace, having lived, most of the time, for the past three years 'on Wheels' so to speak—having to climb up and down over that front end gate every time I wanted to get in or out. Being fixed so that I could step from 'the floor' to the ground was almost a luxery" (in W. S. Burton n.d.[b], 3).

During the next four months, Robert and Maria worked on their home. Robert hauled rock for the basement and foundation from the east bench and brought logs from Mill Creek Canyon which were sawed into lumber at Neff's Mill, paid for with half of the logs. He also made his own adobe bricks at the adobe yard. According to his journal, "I was enabled with the assistance of my wife to build quite a comfortable house which we moved into Dec. 18, the [fourth] anniversary of our wedding day. It had four rooms, in one and a half stories, two up and two down, plus a basement" (1843–69, 49–50). (See drawing, p. 117.)

During these early years in the valley, the pioneers may have gotten long without some physical comforts of life, but they did not live without the social extras—music, drama, picnics, outings, and dancing parties. The members of Nauvoo Brass Band—including Robert Burton—reunited in the fall of 1848 to play for October General Conference and took a leading role in the twenty-fourth of July celebration in 1849. On September 1, 1849, the band accompanied Brigham Young and his party north to Brownsville, a settlement on the Weber River.

> At 8 o'clock A.M., the brethren who were going to visit the Brownsville settlement (later Ogden) on the Weber, commenced to gather at the Council House, Great Salt Lake City, and when President Young's two carriages and coach, Willard Richards' carriage, Jedediah M. Grant's carriage, and Seth Taft's vehicle, (carrying the band) were filled, the band commenced playing some lively and animated airs. About nine A.M., President Young, Willard Richards, Jedediah M. Grant, and ladies . . . and the band left Great Salt Lake City and started for Brownsville. While driving down the street toward the Warm Springs the band continued playing. . . . We arrived at Captain Brown's at six-thirty P.M., where supper was provided for the whole company. After supper the band played and two or three cotillions were danced" (in Nibley 1937, 136–37).

Undoubtedly Robert was included on this trip with his instruments; he could play trumpet, flute, piccolo, and violin. He wrote in his journal "In the winter of 1849–50 much of my time was occupied with the Nauvoo Brass Band also in playing the violin evenings for dancing parties" (1843–69, 51). In April of 1850, the band members met at the Burton home to formally reorganize. Nineteen members of the original band William Pitt led out of Nauvoo were present. They voted to accept four new members and to work on two major projects: a band carriage and straw hats, white dress coats, white pantaloons, sky blue sashes, and white muslin cravats to outfit each player for the celebrations on July 4 and 24. Times must have been getting better for the impoverished pioneers because they were successful on both counts. Hosea Stout, who rode in the band carriage on its first run, left this description: "This carriage is drawn by 14 horses and is 9 feet wide & 29 feet long with a suitable flag waving, and is altogether a beautiful and magnificent sight" (Brooks 1964, 375).

Throughout the 1850s, the band gave concerts, performed at holiday celebrations, and helped welcome pioneer companies entering the valley at the mouth of Emigration Canyon. In 1853, the band played for the dedication of the Salt Lake Temple grounds and later performed for the laying of the temple cornerstone on April 6. Band members were also known for their support of theatrical activities and Robert was one of the members who formed the Musical and Dramatic Company, "the original Thespian organization of the Rocky Mountains," and also the Deseret Dramatic Association and Salt Lake Dramatic Association (R. T. Burton 1843–69, 62,68; Whitney 1:502–03; Purdy 1980, 23).

> Utah's first dramatic company was organized at the house of William Clayton in the Seventeenth Ward, Salt Lake City. Robert Campbell was its President, and A. M. Musser, Secretary. The *corps dramatique*, a portion of whom appeared in the initial performance at the Bowery, were: Hiram B. Clawson, James Ferguson, Philip Margetts, John Kay, Horace K. Whitney, Robert Campbell, Robert T. Burton, George D. Grant, Edmund Ellsworth, Henry Margetts, Edward Martin, William Glover, and William Clayton. The ladies were Miss Orum, Miss [M.] Judd, and Miss Mary Badlam. The orchestra consisted of William Pitt, violin and flute; Jacob F. Hutchinson, violin and clarionette; James Smithies, cello, and others. Messrs. Kay, Burton, Clayton and Whitney when not taking part upon the stage, also assisted in the orchestra. The Musical and Dramatic Company was succeeded by the Deseret Dramatic Association, organized in 1851 with A. H. Raleigh as president. For it the Social Hall was erected in 1852 (Whitney 1:502–03).

Dancing parties were sometimes held in the Burton home, which Maria called "Cotillion dances," even though only a few could dance at a time in the fourteen-foot square parlor. Robert's oldest son William remembered these early parties and claimed that "his music would make one want to dance even if he was lame" (W. S. Burton n.d.ᶜ, 16).

Robert wrote about these activities, "We were compelled to furnish our own amusements or be without them." He did not choose to live without them and gave them this credit: "Thus in our new homes we indeed made ourselves comfortable and happy" (n.d.ᵃ, 25). The Nauvoo Brass Band gradually dissolved as members were called to military service, to missions, to positions of authority in Church councils, and to the great colonization effort. Notes in Robert's journals indicate, however, that he continued to support cultural arts in the city by attending performances in the Social Hall and Salt Lake Theatre for fifty years and through his children's music activities.

During the first years of settlement in the Great Basin, the relationship between the Mormon settlers and the neighboring Indian tribes was delicate, difficult, and sometimes disastrous. The Salt Lake region had long been a kind of neutral site where generations of Utes and Shoshones met to settle their differences. The territory of the Shoshones extended north and west of the Salt Lake valley, while the Utes roamed the area south and westward even to California. The first white trappers and traders who came lived among the Indians, often intermarrying. Brigham Young had a different policy. Although he urged his people to feed the Indians rather than fight them, he often warned against becoming unduly familiar with them. He explained this policy in an October 18, 1849 letter of instruction and reproof to the first colonists at Fort Utah (now Provo):

> Stockade your fort and attend to your own affairs, and let the Indians take care of theirs. Let your women and children stay in the fort, and the Indians stay out; but, while you mix with them promiscuously, you must continue to receive such treatment from them which they please to give. This is what we have told you continually, and you will find it true.
>
> Let any man, or company of men, be familiar with Indians, and they will be more familiar; and the more familiar, you will find the less influence you will have with them. If you would have dominion over them, for their good, which is the duty of the elders, you must not treat them as your equals. You cannot exalt them by this process. If they [consider that they] are your equals, you cannot raise them up to you.
>
> You have been too familiar with them, your children have mixed promiscuously with them, they have been free in your houses, and some of the brethren have spent too much time in smoking and chatting with them; and instead of teaching them to labor, such a

course has encouraged them in idleness and ignorance, the effects of which you begin to feel (in CHC 3:458–59).

According to B. H. Roberts, Brigham Young's policy of aloofness from the Indians may have led to alienation, to depredations on their part against those whom they regarded as intruders, and eventually to a series of engagements between the Indians and the pioneer militia known as the Indian Wars. The militia had barely been organized in March 1849 when it was called upon to pursue a band of Indians who had stolen horses and cattle in the Tooele and Utah valleys. The standing general order to the soldiers was "Shed no blood," yet Captain John Scott's troops killed five Indians (CHC 3:459–60).

The legislature for the State of Deseret planned for an extensive military organization to be named after the Nauvoo Legion. It was organized in March 1849 with plans for forty companies, though only eleven functioned during the 1850s—six horse companies and five foot companies. The first company of cavalry became known as the "Minute Men" or "Life Guards." Solomon F. Kimball explained the role of the "minute men" companies: "They were expert horsemen, and almost lived in their saddles. They were first class marksmen, and always kept their powder dry and firearms in good condition. These young heroes, called 'minute men,' were organized into companies of sixty. . . . Within twenty-four hours from the time they were notified to be ready, they had their supplies lashed to their pack animals, and were in their saddles and off" (S. F. Kimball 1908, 671–72). This select unit attracted the attention of Robert Burton, and he enrolled in it in the fall of 1849. He was assigned the position of bugler, to serve under the command of Captain George D. Grant (R. T. Burton n.d.[a], 21).

The second engagement of the so-called Indian Wars was Robert's first expedition with the "Life Guards" during the cold winter months of 1850. A band of Utes led by chiefs Old Elk and Opecarry had been harassing the colonists at Fort Utah. The Indians first pestered the camp of Captain Howard Stansbury who was leading a survey party from the U.S. Corps of Engineers in Utah Valley during the fall of 1849. Indians hung around the camp begging scraps of food, stealing small items, and generally annoying the officers and men. Their herdsmen accused the Indians of scattering the cattle and of killing stock for meat. The Indians grew bolder as the winter progressed, killing cattle of the Mormon settlers and boasting about it to them, frightening women and children inside their cabins, and taking provisions by force. Toward the end of January, all the colonists took refuge in the fort and appealed to Brigham Young for assistance (CHC 3:467–68).

President Young was reluctant to send the Nauvoo Legion. He finally agreed after Isaac Higbee, leader of the Fort Utah settlers, sent a letter, dated January 31, stating that the Indians had threatened to get help to kill all settlers and after Captain Stansbury testified that "the contemplated expedition against these savage marauders was a measure not only of good policy, but one of absolute necessity and self-preservation" (in CHC 3:467–68).

Captain George D. Grant and his "Life Guards" were called up first when President Young asked for a force of 100 men. Robert Burton hurriedly packed his saddle bags, put on his warmest clothing, and reported for duty. It was bitter cold, and snow covered the valley. Hoping to take the Indians by surprise and secure an advantageous position, Captain Grant took the first fifty men who reported and rode at night over the crusted snow from Salt Lake to the banks of the Provo River. Major Andrew Lytle with fifty more men and Lieutenant Howland from Captain Stansbury's mounted riflemen followed a few hours behind.

The settlers' fort was on the south side of the river. The Indians were strongly entrenched in the willows and timber of the river bottom a mile or two away. Besides their barricade of cottonwoods, the Indians had taken over the double cabin of James A. Bean; and from its windows and shelter, they kept up continuous fire.

The main force of militia assumed a position about a half mile from the cabin. For two days the militia attacked, and the Indians successfully defended themselves.

The afternoon of the second day, Captain Grant determined to take the log house at any cost and ordered William H. Kimball to pick fifteen men and lead a charge. Robert Burton and Lot Smith were two of those men.

On horseback the men advanced up the river until they were directly opposite the log house which was between them and the river. They turned to the left, facing the rear of the house, and Kimball gave the word to charge. Robert was on the right flank. Using a ravine that momentarily hid the charge from view, the sixteen horsemen emerged upon the flat within a few rods of the house and were immediately met with a roaring volley. Indians fired from both the cabin and the river banks. Fourteen men pulled up, temporarily repulsed and unsure; two men—Robert Burton and Lot Smith—spurred their horses onward, ignoring the bullets whistling past them, and rode directly to the front of the cabin and into the passageway between the two cabins, firing as they rode. Their bullets sent the Indians in quick retreat to the river banks.

Moments later, the other troopers gathered to the rear of the house. The Indians recovered and increased their fire upon the cavalry and the captured building. One trooper was wounded and seven of the best horses killed. The battle continued until Lieutenant Howland devised a movable battery, a barricade of planks in the shape of a "V", covered with brush, boughs, and blankets, allowing the militia to attack from close range. Frightened by the mysterious object and discouraged because Chief Old Elk was seriously wounded, the Indians retreated during the night to the foothills. Old Elk eventually died from these wounds (Whitney, 1:429–30).

Robert Burton stayed with the force, now commanded by General Daniel H. Wells, which tracked some of the warriors to the south end of Utah Lake. There they fought and defeated the Indians, battling on the ice of the frozen lake. After the victory, they were forced to spend a bitterly cold night in vermin-infested Indian wickiups on the bleak mountain side. Sleep was impossible and in the morning they returned to Fort Utah with relief. The militia killed forty Indians, over half of Old Elk's warriors. Joseph Higbee, son of Isaac, was the only white casualty (Whitney, 1:427, 430).

After several weeks in Utah Valley, Robert and the other militia members returned to their homes in Salt Lake City, where they mustered out on March 8.

There is a postscript to this expedition. In June 1854, President Young learned from James A. Bean, one of the Utah Valley settlers, that the Indian aggression had apparently not been unwarranted. It had been caused in part by

> the cowardly murder of a somewhat noted Indian called "Old Bishop," so-called, it is said, on account of his resemblance in looks and gestures to Bishop N. K. Whitney. Three men from Fort Utah met "Old Bishop" some distance from the fort wearing a shirt which one of the men claimed to be his and he demanded it. The Indian refused to give it up saying he had bought it. Whereupon a struggle ensued between the white men and the Indian for possession of the shirt, and the latter to defend himself in the unequal struggle of three against one, drew his bow, when one of the white men shot him to death and his body was disemboweled, the cavity filled with stones, sown up and thrown into the Provo River (CHC 3:466).

When an Indian search party discovered the body, they began aggressive plundering. When Brigham Young learned in 1854 of the incident, he commented "These facts which were kept hid at the time, explain to me why my feelings were opposed to going to war with the Indians" (in CHC 3:466).

Robert and William Burton's missions to England had been postponed since Nauvoo. Once the Saints were established in the Salt Lake Valley, however, William left with a number of other missionaries in April 1850, traveling back along the pioneer trail toward Kanesville, passing Mormon immigrant companies and camps. Robert was not held to his call at this time. Three of William's letters from this journey to England survive, each a chronicle of endurance and submission to the hand of Providence. Parts are excerpted here to illustrate the feelings and experiences which he desired to share with his loved ones. The first was written to his wife, Betsy, in Salt Lake Valley. The others were written to his sisters' families in the Midwest who had not followed the main body of the Church.

> Pottawatame Co Musqueto Creek, July 5th 1850
>
> My Dear Elizabeth
>
> Through the blessing of a kind Providence, I have got safely over the Missouri River. I arrived here yesterday in good health within ten miles of Kanesville, having met Elder Hyde & others who had started for the Valley. I gladly improve the opportunity of conversing with you by letter to let you know my situation. I realize that it is by the hand of God our Father, that my live [life] has been preserved unto the present moment, and those of my Brethren who have come through with me. You are aware that we have had a perilous Journey, attended with dangers on every hand. But notwithstanding, here we are all well and in good spirits. Thank the Lord for his goodness and Mercy Manifested unto Me. I wrote to you on the other side of Kearney, bearing date June 25th, which I hope you will receive. In that letter I mentioned a sever attack of sickness that I had a few days previous but by the administration of the Elders, I was healed so that I was able to ride in the waggon the next day. I am aware it is marvelous how I have passed through disease and death and those who are with me. Nothing but the power of God could sustain us. The Cholera has been verey fatal among the Emigrants. It is almost like a grave yard on each side of the road for several hundred miles. I think I also stated the report had reached us that the Cholera was in the Camps of the Saints which I am sorry to say is true. . . . All those camps in which Cholera raged appeared to be cast down. We comfort[ed] them all we could whenever we had an opportunity. There is a large Emigration of Saints to the Valley this year. We have met about eight hundred waggons. Perhaps you may not get my last letter. Therefore I say that I met sister Mary [and] Samuel White about 40 miles the other side of Kearney. Mary's health was rather delicate. She had to drive a span of horses which I am afraid will be to hard for her. I advised them to get some help. The family were all well. I also met Howard Corey with his Mother & family. I have met a number of our old acquaintance[s] on the way to the Valley. Many of them have promised me to call upon you & comfort you all they could which I hope they will. . . . I cannot positively say which route from here we shall take. Our horses are not fit to travel any further. . . . I do not know as yet what means I shall have to start with. If we have good luck in selling our Waggon & horses, I may have near enough. But the Lord will provide a way for us to get along. If I had the means,

I would send you some fruit, but there is no chance to send anything at present.

Samuel [White] removed Mother's remains to a Burying on the Bluffs which will do as well perhaps as to be brought to Kanesville. I think I will not try to remove her from where she now rests. . . .

May the Lord bless & comfort you and provide for your every want is my prayer . . . I remain your Affectionate Husband, Wm. Burton

To Anthony and Jane Leybourn, Washington, Ohio:

New York City, Aug. 13th, 1850

Dear Brother & Sister:

I am once more permitted to take my pen in hand to address a few lines to you which I hope will reach you & yours, enjoying good health. My health is good. I suppose you will be some what surprized at receiving a letter from me bearing date from this City. I will tell you the truth. I always thought of coming myself to bring you the news. But I have failed. I left the Valley the 20th of last April. I was appointed to take a Mission to England. There were several others appointed at the April Conference to go to England & Scotland. Some part of the way we had considerable of a hard time of it. The snow was deep in the mountains. After we got out of the Valley we were 18 days in coming 113 miles. . . . I left Elizabeth enjoying only tolerable health. The air in the place is to pure for her lungs. The remainder of our folks were well that are there. Father, I expect, has gone to California to get rich. His wife, I think, is the principle mover in the affair. I was very sorry to have him go. I did all I could to persuade him otherwise. He was in the valley when I left. Charles went last fall by the southern route. He had a hard time of it I think. I did not want him to go then. I saw a Brother in this city yesterday who told Me that Charles had got through safe. . . . A great many more went last fall to the Mines and more were going this spring, Many without Council and will ruin themselves by following there own vain imagination. Gold is very attractive to man. But how many can bear to handle any quantity of it without being more or less inclined to worship it.

. . . I am thankful to God that I am here and that my life is spared for I have passed through a scene of death and decease [disease] since I started from home . . . May the Lord preserve our lives that we may meet again. I hope when I return that I shall be able to come to you. But I hope before that time you will be in the Valley. May the Lord bless you & yours is my prayers in the name of Jesus Christ, Amen. I remain your Brother, Wm. Burton

To Elijah & Sarah Austin:

Hull, Oct. 22nd, 1850

Dear Brother & Sister,

I again take my pen in hand to write to you to inform you of my safe arrival in England on the 14th of last month after a passage of 29 days in crossing the Ocean. We had a pleasant trip, but rather long, no very stormy weather or high winds. But we had a head wind for three weeks before reaching Liverpool. I thought sometimes that his Satanic Majesty, if he had control of the wind, was determined that we should not reach the land of our destination. . . . I can look back upon my Journey since I left home and see His Almighty hand that hath been over Me in providing for my wants. . . . A few lines from any of my Brothers & Sisters would be a great consolation to Me in this strange land. I often think of those that I have left behind. The Mighty Ocean rolls between us & perhaps some will pass within the vale before I return. The Saints in England are kind and warm hearted. They are willing to do all they can for the comfort of the Elders that come from America, but many of them are poor. I have been much blessed in their company. They are humble & enjoy the spirit. It would do you good to hear them sing the songs of Zion. Their hearts are all engaged in the work of the last days. It is certainly enough to stimulate us to action if we were lifeless in the cause. The work is increasing in all parts where the Elders are laboring. On the 5th of this month our General Conference commenced at Manchester. There was a large congregation, over two thousand, & a great many could not get into the room. A great many noble looking Elders were present. Elder Taylor was there from France. The work is beginning there and in other parts of Europe where the Elders are. . . . I am now going to the Edinburgh Conference in Scotland to labor with Elder Dunn who used to travel with Me in Michigan. . . .

Your Affectionate Brother,
William Burton

A few months later, William became seriously ill. Robert wrote: "His zeal in the missionary work and the severity of the climate proved too much for him as he was never very rugged. He was taken with a very violent cold which culminated in Pnewmonia and he died in the city of Eddingborough where he had gone to attend a conference March 17, 1851" (1843–69, 56–57). He was buried there, but a year later, Robert had the body brought to Salt Lake where he buried it in his lot in the city cemetery on September 5, 1852. Remarkably, his wife Elizabeth (Betsy), who nearly died several times during the early years and while fleeing from Nauvoo, lived to be ninety-one years old. She died in Salt Lake City on May 2, 1895.

As William reported in his letter to Anthony, Samuel's second wife, Louisa Maria Chapin Smith Burton, was unhappy in Salt Lake Valley and wanted to move on to California where life was reportedly easier and riches could be had by all. Robert and William each tried to persuade their father to remain with the main body of the Saints, stressing the rigors of the trip (Samuel was in his late sixties) and Brigham Young's counsel. Their arguments were in vain. Samuel and Louisa with their twenty-month-old daughter Louisa left in May 1850, traveled across the Sierra Nevadas, and settled near Sacramento. The family heard little, only that Samuel was very homesick and desired to return to the company of his older children. He died before he could return, on January 21, 1852, in Suttersville, Sacramento County, at age sixty-nine. His sixteenth child, Dixon P. Burton, was born posthumously the next summer, July 14, 1852. Louisa remarried and later moved to the Northwest. Robert contacted his brother, Dixon, in Oregon and corresponded with him during the 1890s.

Robert's early years in the valley were filled with military and civil service, cultural associations, and work to take care of his growing family. His journal and biography summarize the months after William's departure in April and his father's in May:

> In Sept. of this year (1950) the Cavelry company to which I belonged was ordered out on an expedition against the ShoShone Indians. During my absence on the expedition, my second child William Shipley Burton was born Sept. 27. I returned to Salt Lake on the 5th of Oct. and in November following went on another expedition against the Utah Indians, part of the same tribe with whom we had had an engagement in the February preceeding. This expedition was in Utah and Juab Co. While in the field at this time I was elected Lieutenant in Company B, Life Guards or Minute Men (1843-69, 57-58).
>
> Returning to the City for a few days and in Dec. was ordered west to Toole Valley. The weather this time was very severe snowing

most of the time. Went as far west as Skull Valley. Weather continued severe, no tents or shelter of any kind. Clothing and beding very limited. Returned to Salt Lake without accomplishing very much against the Indians (n.d.[a], 24).

In the spring following (1851) I went south with Pres. Brigham Young and party visiting southern settlements, messed with Gen. D. H. Wells and Geo. D. Grant, had a very pleasant time most of the way, however we did encounter one very sever snow storm as we were passing over the tops of Severe Mts., on our way to Parawin Valley. We returned to Salt Lake City the latter part of May.

In June of this year I went on another Indian expedition to Skull Valley against a band of Indians located on the edge of the desert west of this valley. These Indians were continually stealing stock from the settlements and had amassed a great quantity of dried beef. Our first day against these Indians after arriving in the vicinity was a failure as we had to cross a 20 or 25 mile desert and they could observe our movements from the tops of the mountains where they located, and made good their retreat to the fastnesses of the mountains. We were consequently compelled to return to the east side to obtain water for ourselves and animals. After resting in camp one day we made a night march (1843–69, 59–61).

His biography completes the account:

We managed to attack them just at the break of day. The surprise was complete. Most of the males of the tribe were killed and much of the stolen beef burned and their women and children brought into the settlements and cared for.

None of our company were killed by the Indians but many of them suffered very severly for the want of water. Some of them having to be caried into camp fainting from exhaustion, their tongues becoming so swollen they could not speak. There being no water known to us there for either men or animals.

This expedition however was eminently sucessful, settlers left in peace for years (n.d.[a], 24–25).

In May 1852 I started south with the mail and express to overtake Pres. Brigham Young who had started out some weeks previous to visit the southern settlement. I overtook the Presidents party at Corn Creek or (Kanosh) after two and a half days rapid driving. Continued with the party during their visits and returned to Salt Lake City the last of May, and in June following went south with an exploring party under Prof. Albert Carrington. After pretty thourally exploring the Severe River and Mountains returned to S.L.C. in

July and remained at home the balance of the summer attending to my farm (1843–69, 62–64).

Remained at home most of the time now until fall when I was appointed U. S. Deputy Marshal, also deputy sherif.[1] Served most of the papers for the U. S. District Court and also for the Probate Court of Salt Lake County. Was absent but a few days at a time.

Also served this winter as an Officer [foreman] in the first Legislative Assembly of Utah. Also had the contract in connection with William H. Kimball to supply the Legislative Assembly with wood and was kept very busy this winter (n.d.[a], 26).

My second son, Robert Taylor was born March 20, 1853. On May 23 of this year I started east to the vicinity of Fort Bridger, Green River to serve warrants issued from the district courts on certain lawless men who were in the vicinity of Green River. Was accompanied by a posse composed of Jas. Furgeson, Wm. Kimball. All the Streams between S. L. C. and Green River were very much swoolen. We returned to S. L. C. June 3 after serving the writs.

At home attending to farm most of time until Sept. following I was then ordered on another expedition to Fort Bridger and Green River to serve some processes of court and surpress lawlessness among Mountaineers and renegate Indians. On this expedition I was accompanied by a full company of Cavelry commanded by Jas. Furgeson. Left the main company at Ft. Bridger and with a detachment of the company went to Green River. On learning the actual situation there, I dispatched a messenger to Major Furgeson (at Fort Bridger) who came with reinforcements to my assistance. On arriving at the camp of the mountaineers and outlaws some of them (especially the ring leader) resisted arrest, had some difficulty, some shooting took place at which the leader of the party was killed; others submited to arrest and some fled and thus peace was restored on the border for the time (1843–69, 65–67).

Robert failed to state that one of the writs charged that James [Jim] Bridger, "unlawfully aided and abetted the Utah Indians and supplyed them with arms and amunition for the purposes of committing depredations upon and making war on the citizens of United States in [Utah] territory" (U.S. 1853). However, Bridger was not at Fort Bridger or at the camp on the Green River, reportedly having fled the country, and his writ was returned unserved. An attached muster roll shows that Ferguson's company included men closely associated with Robert in many dangerous assignments: Andrew Cunningham,

Lot Smith, Ephraim Hanks, Lewis Robison, George Nebeker, Phillip Margetts, Andrew Burt, William A. Hickman, Warren Snow, William H. Kimball, and Stephen Taylor.

Robert's brief journal entries show his own view of his activities. He never dwelled on the violence he encountered, even though it was an inevitable part of his responsibilities for the courts and the city. It is probable that his important law-enforcement service kept him in Salt Lake when many of his friends and loved ones were called to colonize away from the valley.

As Salt Lake grew, many building projects were undertaken. The cornerstones were laid for the heralded Salt Lake Temple in impressive ceremonies on April 6, 1853. The Nauvoo Brass Band assisted by Captain Rollo's band and the martial band played at the temple site, and four speeches and consecratory prayers given, one at each corner. Limited funds and building materials forced the work on the temple to proceed slowly during the 1850s, then come to a standstill. The bowery on the southwest corner of Temple Square was replaced by an adobe building which became known as the "Old Tabernacle" and was dedicated on April 6, 1852. In the 126 by 64 foot hall, two to three thousand Saints could assemble for Sunday services.

The Social Hall was also built in 1852 east of State Street between South Temple and First South. It became the home for the dramatic productions of the Deseret Dramatic Association and site of the early sessions of the Legislative Assembly. The hall was dedicated at a New Year's Eve social, December 31, 1852, and the first production held January 19, 1853. Robert Burton was not in the cast of *Pizarro* that night, although he wrote "Much of my time was occupied with the theatre this winter" (1843–69, 64). He also provided the wood for heating Social Hall during the legislative sessions and served as Sergeant at Arms during the 1854 session (1843–69, 68).

By 1854, the pattern of public service was firmly set in the life of Robert Burton. He had been elected a captain in the 1st Company of Cavalry and was advanced to major on April 27, 1854. He was described as "the ideal cavalryman, tall, slender, graceful, dashing" during these years when he commanded the "Life Guards" ("Our Gallery of Pioneers" n.d.)

In August 1854, he was elected sheriff of Salt Lake County, while still serving as an officer of the Territorial Legislature and deputy U. S. marshal (see copy of certificate, p. 120). As sheriff, he had to keep the prisoners and often used his basement as the jail. His wife and children assisted him, his daughter and sons learning young the value of hard work and dependability which characterized his own life. His oldest son William remembered keeping prisoners during 1855.

> When I was almost 5 years old a man was killed by 2 Indians, near the point of the mountain west of Great Salt Lake City. The Indians were caught. My father being Sheriff of Salt Lake County and there being at that time no jail, these Indians were confined in the Cellar of my fathers home for safe keeping.
>
> Guards were employed all the time to watch and care for the Indians as the cellar was not a safe place. They (the Indians) were locked in the cellar nights, but were generally brot out during the day to give them fresh air and more especially to ventilate the cellar. . . . As soon as possible they were given a jury trial, convicted and hanged from a bridge over the Jordan river on North Temple St., called the White Bridge.
>
> For many years after that to those of father's children old enough to understand and to others of that neighborhood, that cellar was "haunted" by the ghosts of those Indians and none of us could be induced to go there after dark alone although some one had to go there often as all our supplies were kept there (W. S. Burton n.d.ᶜ, 1).

In the spring of 1855, Robert Burton and Andrew Cunningham successfully obtained a contract to build a Salt Lake County court house with a jail in the basement on the northeast corner of Second South and Second West streets, across the street and less than a block south of the Burton home. Construction began on May 21 and continued throughout the summer. The Burtons kept the responsibility for feeding the prisoners after the court house and jail were completed in the fall. William wrote:

Father fed the prisoners. The cooking was done at father's home. It was often my job, after I was old enough to do so, to carry the food from our home to the prison 3 times per day. When there were many prisoners confined there the task was not light. Often there would be a "trusty" who could be depended on to help.

One of these was a man by the name of Williams, confined as insane; He soon appeared to be improving, was not dangerous but really silly. He called my mother Mrs. Quakingasp because she insisted on his bringing Quakingasp wood for the stove. . . . This man Williams fully recovered. The doctors said the altitude had affected him. He proved a fine and well educated man. Worked for father for a short time after his recovery. The family, especially mother and Aunt Sarah, respected him very much. As soon as he could get in communication with his people, he went on to California, his original destination (n.d.ᶜ, 2).

Other highlights of 1855 include the birth of Robert and Maria's third son, Charles Samuel, on May 18, and a call in October for Robert to take a posse of fifty men to the eastern part of the territory to suppress an Indian uprising and protect incoming emigrant wagon trains. Since the legislature met in Fillmore in 1856 and his services were not required, Robert enjoyed a winter at home with his family, "much engaged" in the theater activities at the Social Hall (1843–69, 70–71).

Notes

1. The letter of appointment in the Robert Taylor Burton Family Association files indicates Robert was appointed Assistant Deputy U.S. marshal on April 19, 1853, by Joseph L. Heywood, U.S. Marshal. He was also appointed constable of Salt Lake City by Brigham Young in 1852.

Maps,
Photographs
& Illustrations

England and Scotland.
Enlargement shows the Lincolnshire and Yorkshire villages
where the Burton and Shipley
families lived (see Chapter 1).
William and Robert Taylor
Burton served as missionaries in
the other cities on the map.

United States, Canada, and Mexico. Enlargement shows the towns where the Samuel Burtons lived between 1817 and 1838, including Robert's birthplace of Amherstburg, Ontario. Dashes indicate the Mormon pioneer trail, 1846-69.

Roger Cox

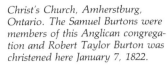

Christ's Church, Amherstburg, Ontario. The Samuel Burtons were members of this Anglican congregation and Robert Taylor Burton was christened here January 7, 1822.

Charles Edward Burton, Robert's brother. A pioneer of 1848, he went to California and back to Ohio in the 1850s, returned to Utah in 1870, and later settled in Mesa, Arizona.

(bottom, right) Jane Burton Leybourn at age fifty-nine. She and John Leybourn settled Tremainsville, now Toledo, Ohio, and Robert lived with them as a student and missionary.

(bottom, left) Ann Burton Shipley. She married a cousin, Waters Shipley, and Robert visited them in Pultneyville, N.Y., in 1870 and 1885.

116

52 feet long
Drawn by L. G. Burton.

a plan of the old home. we moved into the first two rooms Dec 18ᵗᴴ 1849,
The addition on the south, we moved into April 1855,—
The old home was taken down Mar 1878.

Mr. S. Burton for.
Flonce B. Wilcox

(bottom) *Earliest known photograph of Robert T. Burton, his wife Maria, three-year-old Theresa, and one-year-old William Shipley, taken about 1851. Robert, whose light blue eyes did not show up in early photographs, is thirty and Maria is twenty-five years old.*

117

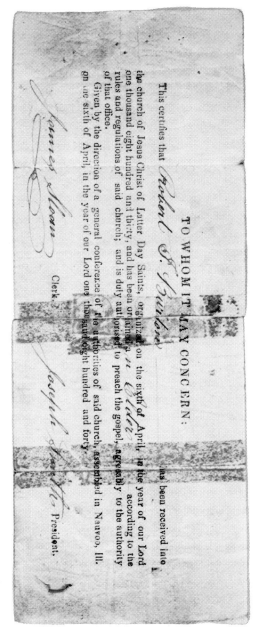

TO WHOM IT MAY CONCERN:

This certifies that *Robert B. Burton* has been received into the church of Jesus Christ of Latter Day Saints, organized on the sixth of April, in the year of our Lord one thousand eight hundred and thirty, and has been ordained *an Elder* according to the rules and regulations of said church; and is duly authorised to preach the gospel, agreeably to the authority of that office.

Given, by the direction of a general conference of the authorities of said church, assembled in Nauvoo, Ill., on the sixth of April, in the year of our Lord one thousand eight hundred and forty.

James Sloan
Clerk.

Joseph Smith
President.

Recorded, Book A page 111. — June 11th, 1843.

118

Kay Boulter, Utah Division of Parks and Recreation

Fielding Garr ranch house, Antelope Island. Sarah lived in this adobe home built by her father from 1850 to 1855. The ranch house (shown here in ca. 1979) was the oldest continuously occupied home in Utah when Antelope Island became a state park.

Sarah Anna Garr, second wife of Robert T. Burton, as a young woman. She is reportedly wearing the dress made for her wedding on February 7, 1856.

119

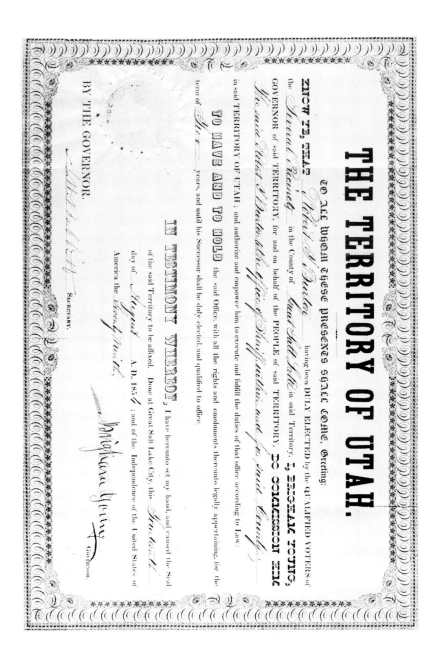

Robert and his sisters who were Utah pioneers, ca. 1855. Left to right, Mary Burton White, Robert T. Burton, Rebecca Burton Jones, and Melissa Burton Coray Kimball. Mary lived in Beaver; Rebecca lived on Second West; Melissa lived after 1860 at Kimball's Hotel.

Kimball's Hotel. William H. Kimball built this eleven-room sandstone structure about 1860 as an Overland Stage station. Robert stayed with Melissa and William many times and made the hotel his headquarters while building the Utah Eastern Railroad. The hotel can be seen east of Kimball's Junction on I-80, twenty-five miles east of Salt Lake City.

Utah State Historical Society

121

Abraham Lincoln,

President of the United States of America,

TO ALL TO WHOM THESE PRESENTS SHALL COME, GREETING:

Know ye, That, reposing special trust and confidence in the integrity, diligence, and discretion of Robert J. Walker, of Great Britain City,

I DO APPOINT HIM a Collector of Taxes for the Collection District of the Territory of Utah

and do authorize and empower him to execute and fulfil the duties of that office according to law; and to have and to hold the said office,

with all the rights and emoluments thereunto legally appertaining, unto him, the said Robert J. Walker

during the pleasure of the PRESIDENT OF THE UNITED STATES for the time being, and until the end of the next session of the Senate

of the United States, and no longer.

In testimony whereof, I have caused these Letters to be made Patent, and the Seal of the Treasury

Department of the United States to be hereunto affixed.

Given under my hand, at the CITY OF WASHINGTON, this twenty-sixth day of Sixty

in the year of Our Lord one thousand eight hundred and Sixty-two and of

the INDEPENDENCE OF THE UNITED STATES OF AMERICA the Eighty-seventh.

BY THE PRESIDENT:

Abraham Lincoln

Secretary of the Treasury.

RB

Robert Burton registered this brand June 13, 1850, in the Great Salt Lake City Brand Book. It was to be three inches tall, four and a half inches wide, and placed on the left shoulder of all livestock.

Salt Lake County courthouse, northeast corner of Second South and Second West. Andrew Cunningham and Robert Burton built this building in two phases in 1855 and 1858. As sheriff, U.S. deputy marshal, and county assessor, Robert had offices here and kept prisoners in the basement jail.

Utah State Historical Society

Utah State Historical Society

General Robert T. Burton and his staff of the First Military District, Nauvoo Legion, after his selection as major general in October 1865. Robert is on the far left on the light horse. He was once described as "the ideal cavalryman, tall, slender, graceful, dashing."

123

Robert T. Burton at age
forty-nine in 1864.

Sarah Garr Burton in her
twenties in the 1860s.

Deseret Woolen Mill, one of two mills operated by Robert T. Burton in partnership with
Abraham O. Smoot and John Sharp. They built nearby Wasatch Woolen Mill in 1866-68
and bought the Deseret Mill from Brigham Young in 1877.

124

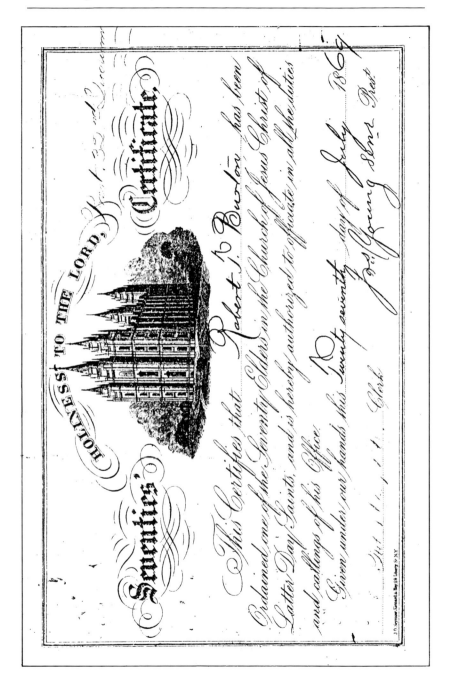

Maria and her children about 1869 when Robert was a missionary in New York. Front row: Theresa Burton Hills, Florence, William S., Maria, Mary, and LaFayette. Back row: John H., Charles S., and Robert T., Jr.

Robert T. Burton became bishop of the Fifteenth Ward in late 1867. Under his "fostering care," the first Relief Society hall was erected in the Fifteenth Ward in 1868-69 (right). Sarah M. Kimball was Relief Society president and his wives were members.

Bishop Burton had this photograph (below) taken February 26, 1870, on Bowery Street in New York City while serving a short-term mission the winter of 1869-70.

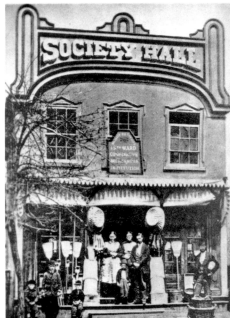

Utah State Historical Society

Utah State Historical Society

Fifteenth Ward, Salt Lake City, Utah.

Duplicate   April 18/92

High Priest's Genealogy.

Name in full, Robert Taylor Burton

Born on the 25th day of October 1821

Town, Amersburg

County, Canada West (Ontario)

Country, Canada

Father's Name, Samuel Burton

Mother's Maiden Name, Hannah Shipley

Baptized on the 23rd day of Sept 1838

By Henry Cook

Confirmed on the ___ day of Sept 1838

By John Landes

Ordained a High Priest on the 2nd day of Sept, 1875

By President Brigham Young

At at his Office —

Residence in full 106 South 2nd West

S L City

128

Robert T. Burton, London, 1875

Maria S. Haven Burton, Eliza Ann Haven
Westover, and Judith T. Haven.

Presiding Bishopric's General Tithing Office and yard.

Utah State Historical Society

129

Utah State Historical Society

Territorial Insane Asylum, Provo, dedicated July 1885. Robert T. Burton was president of the asylum board of directors from 1880 to 1885 and was actively involved in selecting the site and establishing an institution embracing all the improvements and conveniences of a modern asylum.

Utah State Historical Society

University Hall of the University of Deseret, Union Square (now site of West High School), completed 1891. Robert T. Burton was a regent serving on the building committee when construction began in 1881. Governor Eli H. Murray vetoed university building appropriations in 1882 and 1884, but the regents finished the walls, roof, and two floors with public subscriptions including Robert's contribution of $500.

130

Robert T. Burton, 1885

Maria S. Burton

Sarah G. Burton

Susan M. Burton

R. T. Burton Lot, *1880-1910*

The Burton neighborhood about 1880-1910 was the eastern half of the block along Second West between First and Second South streets. Haven Villa was built on Robert's original lot for Maria and her children. Susan's home, called the "redwood house," is the last home on the left. William S., LaFayette G., and Robert T., Jr., lived along Second West (although Robert, Jr., moved in 1895 to Fifth East and Thirteen South), and Florence and Heber lived west along First South. The barnyard and buildings were used by all.

"Redwood House" Susan McBride
Burton lived in the north side of this
double house

Robert T., Jr. & Rosalia Burton

coal & wood
sheds, outhouses

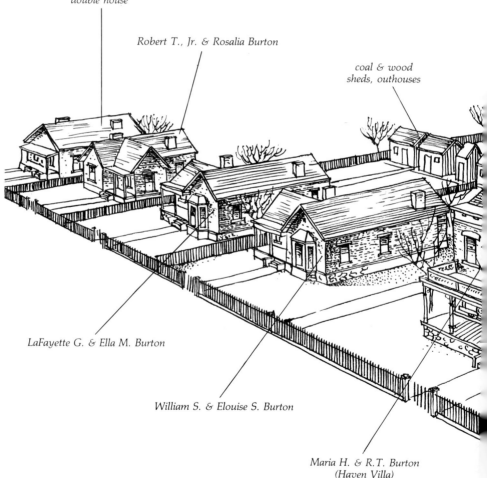

LaFayette G. & Ella M. Burton

William S. & Elouise S. Burton

Maria H. & R.T. Burton
(Haven Villa)

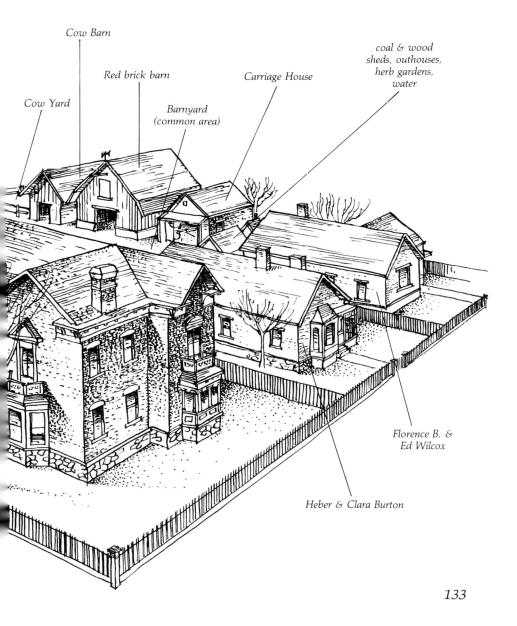

Cow Barn

coal & wood
sheds, outhouses,
herb gardens,
water

Red brick barn

Carriage House

Cow Yard

Barnyard
(common area)

Florence B. &
Ed Wilcox

Heber & Clara Burton

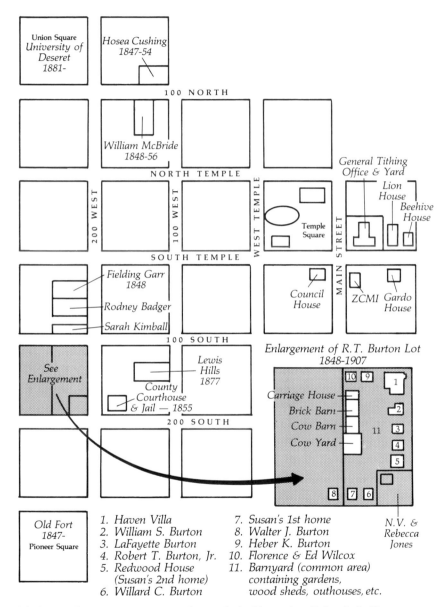

The Burton downtown property was close to the buildings where Robert had offices as sheriff, U.S. deputy marshal, assessor and tax collector, legislator, city councilman, and counselor in the Presiding Bishopric. Robert was one of very few pioneers whose main residence remained on their original lot given in 1849.

Haven Villa, about 1888 (above), and the Burton farm home (right), centers of family activity for three decades. Robert and Maria's original adobe home was replaced in 1879 by the two story brick home known as Haven Villa. The Burton Family Association was organized there in 1885, and it was the site of family reunions, holiday dinners, wedding parties, and other socials.

The original lath and plaster farm house was divided and moved away in 1889 so a modern home could be built for Sarah and her youngest children. The circular landscaped drive was preserved as well as the grove to the north where summer picnics and Sunday family visits took place. Henry, Willard, Alfred, Lyman, and Hardy built homes along State Street north of the farm house.

R. T. Burton Farm

*The boundaries of Robert T. Burton's farm are shown superimposed on present-day
(1988) South Salt Lake City. Sarah and her children moved to the farm in 1868.
Between 1885 and 1910, his sons Henry, Alfred, Lyman, Hardy, and Willard built homes
on State Street north of the farm house to the railroad tracks. A granddaughter and her
husband, Evadna and James W. Burt, lived in an adobe home north and west of the
farm house.*

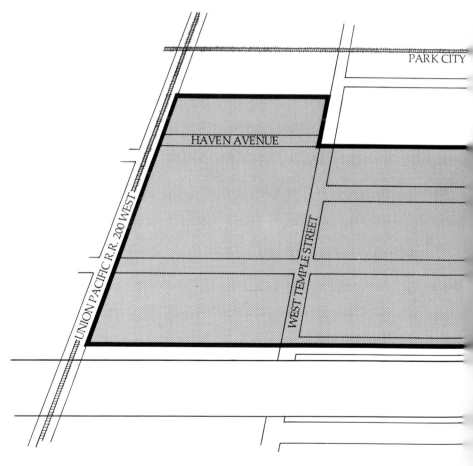

Robert T. Burton Family Portrait
October 25, 1891

Front Row

1. Alice Maria Burton
2. Sarah Laurette Burton
3. Carl Cushing Burton
4. Willard Gardner Burton
5. Arthur Taylor Burton
6. Theresa Louisa Burton
7. Charles Haven Burton
8. Theresa Burton
9. Phyllis Hardy Burton
10. Ivie Rosalia Burton
11. Harold Haven Hills
12. Evadna Burton

Second Row

13. Lucile Burton
14. Julia Burton
15. Charles Westover
16. Anna Gibby Burton
17. Eliza Ann Haven Westover
18. Margaret Mitchell Burton
19. Elizabeth L. Peart Burton
20. Franklin Lebron Burton
21. Hardy Garr Burton
22. Eloise Burton
23. Judith Temple Haven
24. Henry Fielding Burton, Jr.
25. Vernico Burton
26. Elizabeth Borum McBride
27. Mary Salisbury Burton
28. Maria Susan Haven Burton
29. Leone Burton
30. Ray Shipley Burton
31. Austin Garr Burton
32. John Franklin Burton
33. Lyman Wells Burton

Third Row

34. Walter James Burton
35. Alfred Jones Burton
36. Lucy Ellen Brown Burton
37. Hattie Westover
38. Clifford Peart Burton
39. Anna Eliza Gibby Burton
40. Susan Ellen McBride Burton
41. Mary Jane Gardner Burton
42. Ella Mitchell Burton
43. Melissa Burton Coray Kimball
44. Virginia Louise Burton
45. Melissa Westover
46. Eloise Crismon Burton

Fourth Row

47. Sarah Elizabeth Burton
48. Mary Amelia Burton

Fourth Row

49. Robert Taylor Burton, Jr.
50. Charles LaFayette Burton
51. Edgar S. Hills
52. Theresa Hannah Burton Hills
53. Charles Samuel Burton
54. Rosalia Salisbury Burton
55. Willard Cushing Burton
56. Prudence Brown
57. Henry Fielding Burton
58. Heber Kimball Burton

59. Louis Burton Hills
60. Florence May Burton
61. Theodore Taylor Burton
62. Eugene Temple Hills
63. ROBERT TAYLOR BURTON
64. Elbert Turner Burton
65. Ada May Burton
66. Edward Leon Burton
67. Maria Theresa Hills
68. LaFayette Grant Burton
69. Herbert Thayer Hills
70. William Shipley Burton
71. Robert Taylor Burton III

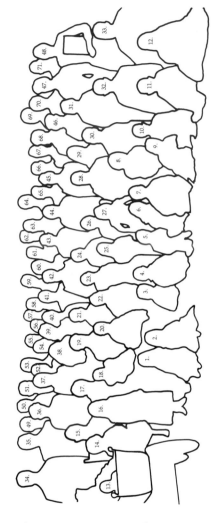

Young adults of the Burton family pose at Wasatch Resort in Little Cottonwood Canyon, probably July 24, 1892. A lattice fence enclosed several small tent cabins used for summer outings by the families of the Presiding Bishopric. This photograph includes Charles and Eliza Westover (left front); Lewis Hills, Florence Burton, Austin Burton, Maria (Rie) Hills, and Mary Burton (center front); Lafayette Burton holding Margaret (right front). Back row: (unidentified), Edgar Hills, (unidentified), Robert A. Fenton, Elizabeth (Lizzie) Burton, Clara Herman, Heber Burton, and Ella Mitchell Burton.

Robert Taylor Burton, marshal on Statehood Day, January 6, 1896. Virginia Burton Cutler remembered her father on that exciting day: "We were all proud of him — that he could sit up as straight as he did — because he was then what was considered an old man."

General Robert T. Burton. Robert recorded in his journal on October 23, 1901: "I came to Johnsons Photograph Galery [sic] to see if I could get a Military picture of myself at 80 years of age." He had more than thirty photographs made in two sizes and several poses and gave them to his children, other relatives, and colleagues.

Robert T. and Sarah Garr Burton Family Group

142

Robert T. and Maria Haven Burton Family Group

Robert T. and Susan McBride Burton Family Group

The three preceding family group pictures appeared in the 1935 "Fifty Year Anniversary Souvenir," of the Burton Family Association.

143

Robert Taylor Burton, 1905.

10

Tests
of Faith
and Courage,
1856

The year 1856 brought tests of faith, loyalty, courage, and endurance into the lives of Robert and Maria Burton and the two young women who became his plural wives, Sarah Anna Garr and Susan Ellen McBride. They had lived together as a family only a few months when Robert volunteered for a dangerous winter rescue mission to find and bring to the valley hundreds of handcart immigrants stranded in early snowstorms

A cold wind spun the light snow into patterns along the street and between the houses, but Maria was thinking of neither the snow nor the cold as she hurried up Second West Street with Robert on the afternoon of February 7, 1856.[1] Great changes were about to occur in their family. At First North, they turned right, passed a few homes, then entered into the small, but comfortable home of William McBride. They warmly greeted William, his wife Elizabeth, and members of the Garr family who were already gathered there. Shortly Heber C. Kimball, counselor to Brigham Young, arrived to perform marriage ceremonies which would unite these three families in the unique Latter-day Saint practice of celestial or plural marriage.

That afternoon Robert married Sarah Anna Garr, seventeen-year-old daughter of Fielding and Paulina Turner Garr, both deceased, and Susan Ellen McBride, nineteen-year-old daughter of William and Elizabeth Borum McBride, host and hostess. Robert wrote that their marriages were solemnized "according to the customs and usages of the L. D. Saints as revealed to Joseph Smith" (n.d.ᵃ, 28).

Although plural marriage had been revealed as early as 1831 and Church leaders close to Joseph Smith were living this order in Nauvoo, the doctrine was not publicly announced for a sustaining vote of the membership until August 1852. Apostle Orson Pratt preached the first authorized sermon on plural marriage the morning of August 29, 1852, at a conference in the "Old Tabernacle." That afternoon, Brigham Young addressed the conference, saying, "Though that doctrine [polygamy] has not been preached by the elders, this people have believed in it for many years," and Thomas Bullock read the revelation of July 12, 1843, now Doctrine and Covenants, Section 132. After that, thousands of copies of the revelation were published for missionaries to circulate throughout the states and the world (Whitney 1:493; Larson 1971, 37n).

Much of the persecution during the last months of Joseph Smith's life can be traced to this doctrine, and that persecution resumed with a vengeance in the 1880s, but in 1852 loyal Church members sustained their leaders and defended the right of those who chose to live in plural marriage. The Saints considered it a sacrifice, not a call to ease and pleasure. Ideally, potential plural partners had to demonstrate good character and financial stability, and successful polygamous families showed genuine commitment to religious principles (See Larson 1971, 37–50). As part of the Reformation of 1856–57, righteous Church members were encouraged to recommit themselves to their faith through repentance, rebaptism, and increased sexual purity, which placed a renewed emphasis on plural marriage. Consequently, there were 65 percent more plural marriages during 1856–57 than in any other two years (Larson 1958, 48). However, Robert entered polygamy in February 1856; the reformation began the following September.

Undoubtedly, Maria Burton approved the young women her husband married. Her acceptance and love for Sarah and Susan combined with many acts of service freely given to them and their children over the next fifty years made these plural marriages successful by any standards. She took them into her home the day of the ceremonies and they lived together for several years. On his sixty-fourth birthday, October 25, 1885, Robert recalled these early years to his children: "In our early days, when you were all small, and we had not the comforts and conveniences of life that we have at the present time, we all lived as one family, and if there were any feelings that were not harmonious they were never known" (Burton Family Association 1885–1953, 5).

Sarah became acquainted with Robert and Maria while living with her widowed sister, Nancy Garr Badger, a half block north on Second West from the Burton home (see map p. 134), and attending the Fifteenth Ward. Until her father's death, her family lived on Antelope Island where Fielding Garr and his sons herded livestock. Sarah's mother Paulina died in 1840 near Nauvoo. After Fielding's death in 1855, Sarah and her sisters Caroline and Mary moved in with Nancy, widow of Rodney Badger. (For Sarah's history and information on the Garr family, see Appendix C.)

Susan had been betrothed to Hosea Cushing, a stalwart 1847 pioneer, who lived across the street from the McBrides on First North. However, he died on May 6, 1854. When Brigham Young approved Sarah and Robert's plural marriage, he asked Robert to marry Susan also, but only for time. Temple Index Bureau records indicate that Susan was sealed to Hosea Cushing at her father's home on February 7, 1856 (Stohl 1987, 1). (For Susan's history and information on the McBride family, see Appendix D).

Robert was sealed March 18, 1856, to Maria and Sarah by Brigham Young at the Endowment House (R. T. Burton 1843–69, 71–72).

In the spring and summer of 1856, Robert felt satisfied with his home, his farm, and his profession. He planted and harvested enough grain and vegetables to feed his growing family through the winter, added rooms to the adobe house to accommodate the new wives, and served as both sheriff and deputy U.S. marshal.

During the summer, three handcart companies of English Saints entered the valley, having walked the entire distance from Florence, Nebraska, pulling their possessions in small carts. They had made good time and the settlers were excited about this new, less expensive way to immigrate.

The first Sunday of October, unusually cold for so early in the fall, Robert hurried through his early morning chores. Later as he dressed for conference, he added extra clothing, remembering how difficult it was to keep the tabernacle warm. As he walked toward Temple Square, he heard startling news about emigrant trains, some with handcart companies, who were still on the trail trying to reach the valley.

Thirteen men had arrived in the valley the previous evening from missions in the East and England, and they had traveled some distance with the companies; in fact they had encouraged them to continue their journey from Nebraska instead of waiting until spring. Franklin D. Richards, George D. Grant, William H. Kimball, Joseph A. Young, Cyrus H. Wheelock, Chauncy G. Webb, James Ferguson, John D. T. McAllister, William C. Dunbar, Nathan H. Felt, John Van Cott, Dan Jones, and James McGraw were all to be at conference and people were anxious to hear their reports first hand.

As the congregation settled into its seats, President Young rose to address his people:

> I will now give this people the subject and the text for the Elders who may speak today and during the Conference. It is this. On the fifth day of October, 1856, many of our brethren and sisters are on the plains with handcarts, and probably many are now seven hundred miles from this place, and they must be brought here, we must send assistance to them. The text will be, 'to get them here.' I want the brethren who may speak to understand that their text is the

people on the plains. And the subject matter for this community is to send for them and bring them in before winter sets in.

That is my religion; that is the dictation of the Holy Ghost that I possess. It is to save the people. This is the salvation I am now seeking for. To save our brethren that would be apt to perish, or suffer extremely, if we do not send them assistance.

I shall call upon the Bishops this day. I shall not wait until tomorrow, nor until the next day, for 60 good mule teams and 12 or 15 wagons. I do not want to send oxen. I want good horses and mules. They are in this Territory, and we must have them. Also 12 tons of flour and 40 good teamsters, besides those that drive the teams. . . .

I will tell you all that your faith, religion, and profession of religion, will never save one soul of you in the Celestial Kingdom of our God, unless you carry out just such principles as I am now teaching you. *Go and bring in those people now on the plains* (in Hafen and Hafen 1960, 120–21).

Robert probably knew as he sat in the tabernacle that the rescue would need his cavalry unit, the Life Guards or Minute Men. This select corps of the Nauvoo Legion prided itself on being ready to ride at a minute's notice. Made up of boys born during the traumatic years of Mormonism, historians have described them as rugged and fearing nothing, "having crossed plains, tended herds, logged, plowed and irrigated, carried mail, and fought Indians" (Cornwall and Arrington 1981, 8). Although other volunteers were part of the rescue party, the core of the company was Robert and his Minute Men (S. F. Kimball 1908, 678). They respected Robert as their leader; he called them his "boys."

Immediately following the conference, the community began to gather its surpluses to send with the rescuers. From meager stores, the people gave all they could—shoes and boots, quilts, bales of hay, coffee, sugar, flour, salt, and beef, socks and stockings, petticoats, vests, hoods, comforters, oats and onions, even handkerchiefs, neckties, and mittens. Robert Burton kept a ledger, recording the donors and eventually the recipients. He was undoubtedly assigned to keep this record, and it remains as evidence of his personal commitment to the principle of accountability. He made detailed entries, even though he would have had no convenient time or place to write in the bitter cold of the snow-covered mountains.

Sixteen fully packed wagons each drawn by a good four-mule team were ready for departure early Tuesday morning, October 7. Of the twenty-seven volunteers[2] in the first relief party, six were from the missionaries just returned to the valley who had encouraged the handcart companies to leave Florence so late in the season. George D. Grant, captain of the party and Nauvoo Legion commander in Salt Lake, was one of these missionaries. Second in command was another missionary William H. Kimball, Robert's close friend and brother-in-law.[3] Robert was elected third in command. Each night after establishing camp, Robert took out his notebook and, by the light of the campfire, recorded a sentence or two in the camp journal.

> 7th Oct/56 Left Salt Lake City, going east to meet the Emmigrating Comp. Encamped tonight at the foot of the Big Mountain.
> 8th Passed over the Big Mountain and Camped in East Kanyion. Had a light snow storm.
> 9th Had good Roads. Camped in Echo Kanyion.
> 12th Arrived at Fort Bridger. Left some of our flour, feed etc at this place.

As the rescue party climbed higher into the mountains, the temperatures dropped. On October 14, they sent scouts—Cyrus H. Wheelock, Joseph A. Young, Stephen Taylor, and Abel Garr, brother of Sarah—ahead to locate the first company and report back their situation. The first company, captained by James G. Willie, had left Florence on August 19 with 500 members. It was followed by the Edward Martin company which left August 25 with 576 members, and two independent wagon companies under John A. Hunt and W. Benjamin Hodgetts, with 200 and 185 emigrants respectively (Hafen and Hafen 1960, 93).

The relief train pushed on toward the continental divide. While camping on the "Big Sandy" on the fifteenth, more teams and men from the valley joined them. Storms threatened each day, but held off until South Pass was behind them, then struck with force while the rescuers were traveling along the Sweetwater River. Robert later recalled:

> At one time while we were traveling down the Sweet Water about 300 or 400 miles east of Salt Lake City, the snow was so deep that the axle-trees of our wagons dragged and we were compelled to remain camped at the same place for one or two days in consequence of the severity of the storms, but with no idea other than resuming our journey when the weather would permit, until we found the companies we were sent to relieve (R. T. Burton 1907, 1–2).

While they were thus camped on the night of October 20, Captain Willie and Joseph Elder of the Willie company emerged from the storm riding two worn-out mules. They had been sent back by the scouts who were now riding even further east searching for the Martin, Hunt, and Hodgetts companies.

Willie and Elder reported suffering and imminent death for members of their party if they could not be rescued the next day. Rations had been reduced to ten ounces of flour per day since the company passed Independence Rock. As they traveled up the Sweetwater and the nights grew colder, even the hardiest found little comfort in the seventeen pounds of clothing and bedding they carried. Instead of rising each morning strong and refreshed ready for another day, the beleaguered travelers would crawl out from their tents haggard and benumbed, with insufficient energy to make a good day's journey (Hafen and Hafen 1960, 101–02).

Until this time only the old, the infirm, or the very young had perished, but now the young and naturally strong were also dying. The day came when John Chislett, captain of the fourth hundred, could not raise enough men to pitch a tent, and he had to carry the sick in his group from their wagons to the fire at night and back to the wagons in the morning. He also had to dig the graves for those who died and offer the prayers at the graves—prayers which were pleas for help for those yet living. Chislett wrote about the rescue:

> We travelled on in misery and sorrow day after day. Sometimes we made a pretty good distance, but at other times we were only able to make a few miles' progress. Finally we were overtaken by a snow-storm which the shrill wind blew furiously about us. The snow fell several inches deep as we travelled along, but we dared not stop,

for we had a sixteen-mile journey to make, and short of it we could not get wood and water.

As we were resting for a short time at noon a light wagon was driven into our camp from the west. Its occupants were Joseph A. Young and Stephen Taylor. They informed us that a train of supplies was on the way, and we might expect to meet it in a day or two. More welcome messengers never came from the courts of glory than those two young men were to us. They lost no time after encouraging us all they could to press forward, but sped on further east to convey their glad news to Edward Martin and the fifth handcart company who left Florence about two weeks after us, and who it was feared were even worse off than we were. As they went from our view, many a hearty "God bless you" followed them.

We pursued our journey with renewed hope and after untold toil and fatigue, doubling teams frequently, going back to fetch up the straggling carts, and encouraging those who had dropped by the way to a little more exertion in view of our soon-to-be improved condition, we finally, late at night, got all to camp—the wind howling frightfully and the snow eddying around us in fitful gusts. But we found a good camp among the willows, and after warming and partially drying ourselves before good fires, we ate our scanty fare, paid our usual devotions to the Deity and retired to rest with hopes of coming aid.

In the morning the snow was over a foot deep. Our cattle strayed widely during the storm, and some of them died. But what was worse to us than all this was the fact that five persons of both sexes lay in the cold embrace of death. . . .

The morning before the storm, or, rather, the morning of the day on which it came, we issued the last ration of flour. On this fatal morning, therefore, we had none to issue. We had, however, a barrel or two of hard bread which Captain Willie had procured at Fort Laramie in view of our destitution. This was equally and fairly divided among all the company. Two of our poor broken-down cattle were killed and their carcasses issued for beef. With this we were informed that we would have to subsist until the coming supplies reached us. . . .

Being surrounded by snow a foot deep, out of provisions, many of our people sick, and our cattle dying, it was decided that we should remain in our present camp [called St. Mary's Station] until the supply-train reached us. It was also resolved in council that Captain Willie with one man should go in search of the supply-train and apprise its leader of our condition, and hasten him to our help. When this was done we settled down and made our camp as comfortable as we could. As Captain Willie and his companion left for the West, many a heart was lifted in prayer for their success and speedy return. They were absent three days—three days which I shall never forget. The scanty allowance of hard bread and poor beef, distributed as described, was mostly eaten the first day by the hungry, ravenous, famished souls.

We killed more cattle and issued the meat; but, eating it without bread, did not satisfy hunger, and to those who were suffering from dysentry it did more harm than good. This terrible disease increased rapidly amongst us during these three days, and several died from exhaustion. . . . During that time I visited the sick, the widows whose husbands died in serving them, and the aged who could not help themselves, to know for myself where to dispense the few articles that had been placed in my charge for distribution. Such craving hunger I never saw before, and may God in his mercy spare me the sight again (in Stenhouse 1873, 322–24).

Captain Willie's report alarmed the relief party who had no way of knowing that the companies were totally without flour and provisions. The men from the valley waited only until first light to break camp and in one long day covered the miles which had taken Willie and Elder two days to ride. Just at sundown on October 21, they sighted the pitiful camp and were overcome seeing so many feeble and underclothed Saints gathered in front of their camp, shouting with joy through their tears. Children danced; everyone who could stand rejoiced although the temperatures were below freezing and no one in camp had eaten all day (Stenhouse 1873, 325).

Immediately Robert Burton set about distributing food and clothing while other men mounted mules, ax in hand, and rode to the hills to bring back enough wood to get the fires roaring. They hastily prepared a stew of flour, potatoes, and onions. Years later, one handcart pioneer told her grandchildren that her very favorite food was potatoes and onions cooked together because it had saved her life and that of many others in the handcart companies (Clive 1980).

When the meal was over, the songs of Zion were heard in camp for the first time in many days. Overwhelmed with gratitude to their Father in Heaven and to the men from the valley, the entire camp united in prayer before retiring to their tents. In spite of the rejoicing, the fires, and the food, help had come too late for some. Nine died that night (Hafen and Hafen 1960, 106)

The next morning, Captain Grant ordered William H. Kimball and almost half of the relief party to stay with the Willie company and get them safely to the valley. He and Robert took the remaining men in search of the Martin company and the two rear wagon trains, somewhere east of Independence Rock. They knew nothing about their situation, but feared the worst.

From St. Mary's Station, the party rode seventeen miles; the snow growing deeper and deeper all the way. They camped on October 22 and 23 under Independence Rock with the snow so deep they could neither travel, nor find much feed for their animals. Robert's journal records seven more days of deep snow, some traveling, poor feed, and disappointment in not finding the companies.

> 24th Clear and fair. Some warmer. Started on. Camped tonight below the crossing of Sweet Water. Snow still deep. Seen a large herd of buffalow 3 miles distant.
> 25th Wind blowed hard. Camped tonight below the Wallhualleah Rock. Snow going away slowly. Weather some warmer.
> 26th Travelled 19 miles. Encamped near the Devil's Gate. Found the Express that had been sent on at this place waiting further orders. Heard nothing from the Co. behind.
> 27th Remained at the same place. Feed tolorable good. From this point sent on another express to the Bridge on Platt River, J. A. Young, A. Garr, Dan Jones to find Co. if possible & report back their situation, whereabouts, etc.
> 28th Remained in the same Camp. Weather fine, snow going away. At night clowdy. Snow began to fall fast. After Prayer ceased snowing.
> 29th In the same camp. Fine warm morning. Continued thru the day.
> 30th Good weather. Snow going away slowly. Remained in the same camp. Express returned tonight 7 o'clock reported the companies on the Platt River had been encamped three days not far apart.

Young, Jones, and Garr finally returned with tragic news of the remaining companies. The Martin handcart company was completely snowbound about a day's journey east.

After leaving Florence on August 25, the company made good time and reached Fort Laramie on October 8. They traded watches and jewelry for a little food at the fort, but still the ration of flour was cut from one pound daily to three-fourths, then one-half. Growing weaker, the emigrants reduced their baggage to ten pounds per adult at Deer Creek by piling and burning "excess" bedding and clothing. Two days later, October 19, they were hit with the fury of winter's first storm at the crossing of the icy Platte River. Here, the Hunt and Hodgett wagon trains caught up with the Martin company and helped the emigrants cross although many still had to wade waist deep, dodging blocks of mushy snow and ice. The company traveled only twelve miles the next six days, and had been stalled for three days with the Hodgett train nearby. Along that twelve-mile stretch were scattered the common graves of fifty-six emigrants, victims of exhaustion, exposure, and starvation.

Those who greeted the express—Young, Jones, and Garr—as "angels from heaven" were barely better off than the loved ones they had buried, yet they gathered to welcome the first rescuers with "cheers and tears and smiles and laughter" (Whitney 1:562). Young, Jones, and Garr urged the exhausted emigrants of the Martin and Hodgett companies forward toward Devil's Gate where the relief party waited in the abandoned houses of an old trading fort. They went ten miles farther back and found the Hunt wagon train almost at the Platte crossing. These emigrants were not yet suffering from starvation, though their cattle were dying in the deep snow and they had hardly moved since the storms' onset nine days earlier. Joseph Young stayed with Hunt's train, while Jones and Garr turned back to the west and overtook the Martin company slowly ascending a long muddy hill. Dan Jones wrote:

> A condition of distress here met my eyes that I never saw before
> or since. The train was strung out for three or four miles. There
> were old men pulling and tugging their carts, sometimes loaded with

a sick wife or children—women pulling along sick husbands—little children six to eight years old struggling through the mud and snow. As night came on the mud would freeze on their clothes and feet. There were two of us and hundreds needing help. What could we do? We gathered on to some of the most helpless with our riatas [lassos] tied to the carts, and helped as many as we could into camp on Avenue hill.

This was a bitter, cold night and we had no fuel except very small sage brush. Several died that night.

Next morning [October 30], Brother [Joseph] Young having come up, we three started for our camp near Devil's Gate (Jones 1960, 67–68).

On October 31, Captain Grant and Robert Burton left Devil's Gate with some supplies under "fine, clear skies" and met the handcart company at Greasewood Creek. Once again, Robert distributed the precious life-saving food and clothing, faithfully recording the items given out in his relief camp journal. He dispersed:

     25 pairs mans shoes
      7 pairs mans boots
     27 pairs womens shoes
     43 pairs boys boots & shoes
    157 pairs socks & stockings
     12 quilts
     27 womens undergarments
     18 quilts & comforts
      8 pairs mittens
     23 childrens dresses
     24 petticoats
     39 pairs of pants
      7 mens vests
     45 dress & frock coats
      7 jackets
     18 woolen dresses
     20 womens capes & mantels
      9 womens dresses
     10 boys coats
     36 hoods
     18 shawls
     21 handkerchiefs & 14 neckties
     29 womens petticoats

19 cotton shirts
8 womens sacks (p.1)

During the first three days in November, he gave out nearly 4,000 pounds of flour and two bushels of onions—a diet which offered little more than hope to the hundreds of emigrants.

After he had distributed all the clothing, Robert noticed a mother whose newborn baby did not have sufficient clothing to keep it warm, so he took off his own homespun shirt and gave it to the mother to cover the baby (Gunderson 1956, 3).

On the morning of November 1, after getting the Martin company moving again, Grant and Robert rode four or five miles east and met Hodgett's train. They camped with them one night in a snowstorm near Independence Rock, then returned to Devil's Gate and held a council on wintering all the emigrants at Devil's Gate. They decided to push on to the valley. Captain Grant prepared a dispatch for Brigham Young, which Joseph Young and Abel Garr carried to Salt Lake.

> It is not much use for me to attempt to give a description of the situation of these people, for this you will learn from your son Joseph A. and br. Garr, who are the bearers of the express; but you can imagine between five and six hundred men, women and children, worn down by drawing handcarts through snow and mud; fainting by the wayside; falling, chilled by the cold; children crying, their limbs stiffened by cold, their feet bleeding and some of them bare to snow and frost. The sight is almost too much for the stoutest of us; but we go on doing all we can, not doubting or despairing.
>
> Our company is too small to help much, it is only a drop to a bucket, as it were, in comparison, to what is needed. I think that not over one-third of Mr. Martin's company is able to walk. This you may think is extravagant, but it is nevertheless true. Some of them have good courage and are in good spirits; but a great many are like children and do not help themselves much more, nor realize what is before them.
>
> I never felt so much interest in any mission that I have been sent on, and all the brethren who came out with me feel the same. We have prayer without ceasing, and the blessing of God has been with us. . . .
>
> We will move every day toward the valley, if we shovel snow to do it, the Lord helping us (Grant 1856).

Numerous accounts of the experiences of both the emigrants and the rescuers mention the unwavering faith of their leaders who never doubted the Lord's blessing, nor doubted that more help would come from the valley. Yet, that faith was sorely tested during the encampment at Devil's Gate when they had no way of knowing that hundreds of wagons were on the trail from the valley.

For the first nine days of November, a savage storm assailed the campsites and supply station. It took the Hunt train five days to reach Devil's Gate. Its arrival swelled the camp population to over 1,200. There was simply not enough shelter in the area, so the Martin company, with help from the rescue party and some wagons, moved on to find another sheltered place where wood was available. They selected a depression later to be known as Martin's Cove, across the Sweetwater and only two and a half miles from Devil's Gate.

When the handcart company reached the Sweetwater, it was filled with floating ice. Elder John Jacques reported that this passage was almost beyond the ability of the people:

> It was the last ford that the emigrants waded over. The water was not less than two feet deep . . . but it was intensely cold. The ice was three or four inches thick and the bottom of the river muddy or sandy. I forget exactly how wide the stream was there, but I think thirty or forty yards. It seemed a good deal wider than that to those who pulled their handcarts through it (in Whitney 1:562).

As women shrank back and men wept at the prospect, four eighteen-year-old boys from the valley, C. Allen Huntington, George W. Grant, Stephen Taylor, and David P. Kimball, stepped forward and picked up women and children and even some of the men, and carried them one by one across the snow-bound river, crossing it many times late in the afternoon. Solomon F. Kimball reports that the strain was so terrible, and exposure so great that in later years these boys died from the effects of carrying the emigrants through the icy water (S. F. Kimball 1914, 288).[4]

By nightfall, the handcart company was encamped in the cove against a granite mountain, a place offering some shelter through the coldest days which were yet to come.

Robert Burton noted in the relief camp journal of November 9 that "During our stay in this place we had a meeting every evening to Counsel together and ask the Lord to turn away the Cold and storm so that the People might live." Yet, his brief daily entries note: "Snow deep and very cold. . . . So cold that the Co. could not move. . . . Cold continued very severe. . . . Colder than ever. Thermometer 11 degs. below Zero. . . . So cold the people could not travel" (November 1–6).

On November 7, Robert recorded a day spent in "trying to save the people and the stock." Finally on the eighth, the wind calmed and it was "some warmer." Parties were detailed to hunt up the cattle and horses "to move on the morrow."

During this time, all unnecessary freight from the wagon trains was cached, and on November 9, Dan Jones, plus two men from the valley and seventeen from the wagon train were appointed to remain at Devil's Gate until spring and guard the freight. They endured six weeks of virtual isolation and subsisted on flour, lean cattle, and finally rawhide (Jones 1890, 70–98).

The meager loads from the handcarts and all the emigrants possible were packed into the empty wagons of the Hunt and Hodgett trains. Those strong enough still had to walk, but no one pulled a handcart past Martin's Cove. Captain George D. Grant, Cyrus Wheelock, Stephen Taylor, and Robert Burton were the last to leave the campsite at 3 P.M. on November 10. When they reached the company the next day, Ephraim Hanks was with them, having come alone from the valley to assist the rescue. Although he had abandoned his wagon load of supplies, he had pushed on with a saddle horse and pack animal. Providentially, the night before he reached the first emigrants, he encountered a buffalo and killed it. After skinning and dressing it out, he loaded his horses with meat cut in long strips.

Thereupon I resumed my journey, and traveled on till towards evening. I think the sun was about an hour high in the west when I spied something in the distance that looked like a black streak in the snow. As I got near to it, I perceived it moved; then I was satisfied that this was the long looked for hand-cart company, led by Captain Edward Martin. I reached the ill-fated train just as the immigrants were camping for the night. The sight that met my gaze as I entered their camp can never be erased from my memory. The starved forms and haggard countenances of the poor sufferers, as they moved about slowly, shivering with cold, to prepare their scanty evening meal was enough to touch the stoutest heart. When they saw me coming, they hailed me with joy inexpressible, and when they further beheld the supply of fresh meat I brought into camp, their gratitude knew no bounds. . . . At first I tried to wait on them and handed out the meat as they called for it; but finally I told them to help themselves. Five minutes later both my horses had been released of their burden—the meat was all gone, and the next few hours found the people in camp busily engaged in cooking and eating it, with thankful hearts (Hanks and Hanks 1946, 135–36).

Hanks did as much emergency doctoring as he could: "Many of the immigrants whose extremities were frozen, lost their limbs, either whole or in part. Many such I washed with water and castile soap, until the frozen parts would fall off, after which I would sever the shreds of flesh from the remaining portions of the limbs with my scissors" (Hanks and Hanks 1946, 140).

Ephraim Hanks' arrival was visible proof to the rescue team and the emigrants that the Salt Lake Saints were still bent on rescue. Hanks said that while some of the more than 200 rescue teams sent out from the valley had turned back at South Pass, others were waiting there, and more help was on the way.

Robert, recording Hanks' arrival, quickly summarized the camp's feelings, "Br. E. Hanks . . . brought good news (1856–1907, November 11, 1856)

A messenger sent to South Pass on November 12 brought back four wagons loaded with flour. The weather and road conditions began to improve, and the company's spirits rose. Robert's journal entries reflected the better weather and raised hopes. "No deaths in Camp tonight," he recorded on November 14.

Wagons arrived from the valley nearly every other day, and Robert was kept busy recording both who gave and who received supplies. Meals improved vastly as his records show distribution of beef, coffee and sugar, oats and other feed for the stock, instead of just flour and onions. William H. Kimball returned with teams and supplies on November 18 after having guided the Willie company safely into the valley on November 9. On November 19, it began snowing again, but now there were enough wagons for all to ride and they crossed South Pass safely, even comfortably by comparison. Feeling confident now of success, the rescue party leaders gave Robert Burton charge over the wagons carrying the companies and Grant and Kimball went ahead to the valley.

As the wagon train moved slowly toward the Salt Lake Valley, the men from Salt Lake and Ogden disagreed about the best route through the snow-covered mountains east of Salt Lake. Robert wrote for Brigham Young's advice and received a reply at their camp on the Weber River late in the evening of November 27:

G. S. L. City, Nov. 26, 1856

Major Robert T. Burton:
Dear Brother:

Brs. Wheelock and Bullock arrived with your letter to me, dated at Muddy, Nov. 24, at a few minutes past 9 p.m. of date; and I was truly rejoiced to learn from them and by your letter of your whereabouts, welfare, prosperity and good spirits.

From the best information I can obtain, I deem it to be decidedly impolitic, unwise and hazardous for any teams to go down through Weber river Canyon; I therefore counsel you and all the companies to travel on the main traveled route to this city crossing the Big Mountain; and I hereby direct and empower you to bring every man, woman, child, horse, mule, wagon and everything pertaining to the immigration by the route named above. In that track you will find safety and meet with constant aid; whereas, upon the Weber river Canyon route you will meet difficulty and be out of the line of assistance. Say to the Ogden and other northern brethren to back up this counsel without gainsaying or murmuring, for it is for their good as well as for the benefit of all concerned.

161

Judging by a remark in your letter that you will be scant of rations, I have taken steps to furnish you with the requisite supplies; and you will meet them on the route you are counseled to travel, and by the time you will be apt to need them.

> Praying our Father in Heaven
> to bless, prosper and sustain you as
> hitherto, I remain Your Brother in the
> Gospel, (signed) Brigham Young

President Young was true to his word. Robert praised the efforts of the men sent out from the valley to assist them across Big Mountain:

We met with no difficulties that were not easily overcome until we arrived at East Canyon on November 28th. We found the road there sideling [steeply inclined to one side], but were enabled to get all the wagons over safely, thanks to the foresight of President Brigham Young, who had kept ox teams constantly traveling up and down the big mountain to keep the road open for us. We succeeded in getting over that part of our journey without serious difficulty, although the walls of snow on each side were as high as the bows of the wagons, and those who witnessed this sight can never forget it, as those 104 wagons freighted with human beings who had been so miraculously saved, wended their way up this mountain. It was indeed to us a great sight, as we were now near our homes (R. T. Burton 1907, 3).

As the immigrants passed over Big and Little Mountains, snow began falling again, and they camped the last night in the storm at the head of Emigration Canyon where they received food from the valley. They began their final descent early the next morning, Sunday, November 30.

At services in the tabernacle that morning, Brigham Young offered another practical sermon:

As soon as this meeting is dismissed I want the brethren and sisters to repair to their homes, where their Bishops will call on them to take in some of this company; the Bishops will distribute them as the people can receive them. . . .

The afternoon meeting will be omitted, for I wish the sisters to go home and prepare to give those who have just arrived a mouthful of something to eat, and to wash them and nurse them up. You know that I would give more for a dish of pudding and milk, or a baked potato and salt, were I in the situation of those persons who have just come in, than I would for all your prayers, though you were to stay here all the afternoon and pray. Prayer is good, but when baked potatoes and pudding and milk are needed, prayer will not supply their place on this occasion; give every duty its proper time and place. . . .

Some you will find with their feet frozen to their ankles; some are frozen to their knees and some have their hands frosted. . . . We want you to receive them as your own children, and to have the same feeling for them. We are their temporal saviors, for we have saved them from death (in Hafen and Hafen 1960, 139)

Although the long and tragic journey was over, the suffering for many handcart immigrants was not. Some died within a week of their arrival. Others lived long lives on the stumps of frozen feet and legs and yet rejoiced to be alive in "Zion."

In recent years the tragedy of these two handcart companies and accompanying wagon trains has been compared to the disastrous Donner Party in the Sierra Nevadas in 1846 and the John Fremont expedition in 1849 which lost one-third of its party in blizzards in the San Juan Mountains of Colorado. Proportionately these parties' losses were greater; but in sheer numbers the handcart pioneers still constituted the worst disaster in the history of western migration. Over two hundred died, and hundreds more faced life permanently maimed. As western historian Wallace Stegner has observed,

Perhaps their suffering seems less dramatic because the handcart pioneers bore it meekly, praising God, instead of fighting for life with the ferocity of animals and eating their dead to keep their own life beating, as the Fremont and Donner parties did. And assuredly the handcart pilgrims were less hardy, less skilled, less well equipped to be pioneers. But if courage and endurance make a story, if human kindness and helpfulness and brotherly love in the midst of raw horror are worth recording, this half-forgotten episode of the Mormon migration is one of the great tales of the West and of America (Stegner 1956, 85).

Robert T. Burton's accounts of the episode noticeably play down the horror and the suffering. In later life he rarely described the scenes he witnessed. His handwritten biography calls this the "most critical campaign of my life" but concludes, "The hardships and sufferings of this company of people can never be told" (n.d.[a], 30). His oldest son, William S. Burton, wrote, "Father could seldom be induced to talk of this trip, saying it was too sad and heartrending to even recall to memory, let alone tell it" (1931, 3). Similarly, Robert wrote to the handcart association in 1907 that "in spite of all that we could do many were laid to rest by the wayside. These matters I do not desire to dwell upon. I would rather forget them and look [at] the brighter side, and thank the Lord for his kind providence in saving those whom he did spare."

Francis Webster, one of those survivors who settled in Cedar City, many years later heard a Sunday School class sharply criticize the Church leaders who allowed crossing the plains by handcart. Webster responded in substance:

> I ask you to stop this criticism. You are discussing a matter you know nothing about. Cold historical facts mean nothing here for they give no proper interpretation of the questions involved. Mistake to send the Hand Cart Company out so late in the season? Yes. But I was in that Company and my wife was in it. . . . We suffered beyond anything you can imagine and many died of exposure and starvation, but did you ever hear a survivor of that Company utter a word of criticism? . . . every one of us came through with the absolute knowledge that God lives for we became acquainted with him in our extremities.
>
> I have pulled my hand cart when I was so weak and weary from illness and lack of food that I could hardly put one foot ahead of the other. I have looked ahead and seen a patch of sand or a hill slope and I have said I can go only that far and there I must give up for I cannot pull the load through it. I have gone on to that sand and when I reached it the cart began pushing me. I have looked back many times to see who was pushing my cart but my eyes saw no one. I knew then that the Angels of God were there.
>
> Was I sorry that I chose to come by hand cart? No. Neither then nor any minute of my life since. The price we paid to become acquainted with God was a privilege to pay and I am thankful that I was privileged to come in the Martin Hand Cart Company (Palmer 1943).

The return of the company was not a day too soon for Robert. The next day, December 1, Susan delivered their first child, Willard Cushing Burton, his middle name given in remembrance of Hosea Cushing. On the same day Jedediah M. Grant, mayor of Salt Lake City, major-general in the Nauvoo Legion, and first counselor to Brigham Young, died. He had devoted himself day and night to the reformation of 1856, preaching, baptizing, and exhorting the Saints to repent and renew their covenants. Weak and overworked, he succumbed to illness. So Robert mourned the passing of his leader and friend, yet rejoiced in his own bountiful blessings as the year 1856 drew to a close.

Notes

There are many interesting histories of the handcart pioneer companies: LeRoy R. and Ann W. Hafen, *Handcarts to Zion*, Glendale, California: Arthur H. Clark Company, 1958; Rebecca Cornwall and Leonard J. Arrington, *Rescue of the 1856 Handcart Companies*, Charles Redd Monographs in Western History No. 11, Provo: BYU Press, 1981; Solomon F. Kimball, "Belated Emigrants of 1856," 4 pts., *Improvement Era* 17 (November 1913–February 1914); Wallace Stegner, "Ordeal by Handcart," *Collier's* 138 (July 6, 1956), 78–85; T. B. H. Stenhouse, *The Rocky Mountain Saints*, New York: D. Appleton and Company, 1878, 313–329; CHC 4:83–107, and Orson F. Whitney, *History of Utah*, 1:555–564.

1. Although the date of marriage to Sarah and Susan is shown on some family records as February 6, 1856, the date of February 7, 1856, is recorded in Robert Taylor Burton's autobiography (n.d.ª) and journal (1843–69).

2. They were George D. Grant, William H. Kimball, Joseph A. Young, Cyrus H. Wheelock, James Ferguson, Chauncey Webb, Robert T. Burton, Charles F. Decker, Benjamin Hampton, Heber P. Kimball, Harvey H. Cluff, Thomas Alexander, Reddick N. Allred, Ira Nebeker, Thomas Ricks, Edward Peck, William Broomhead, Abel Garr, C. Allen Huntington, George W. Grant, David P. Kimball, Stephen Taylor, Joel Parrish, Charles Grey, Amos Fairbanks, Daniel W. Jones, and Thomas Bankhead (Hafen and Hafen 1960, 124n).

3. William H. Kimball married Melissa Burton Coray, widow of William Coray, on December 24, 1851.

4. S. F. Kimball (1914) mentions only three boys—Huntington, Grant, and Kimball—but John Jacques's record adds Taylor to the list (in Whitney 1:562)

Resisting
the Invasion
of Utah,
1857–58

Although 1857 began peacefully, a storm was brewing which would place Robert right back in the mountain passes when winter came again. Relations between Utah Territory and the federal government had deteriorated throughout the 1850s as appointed officials tried to wrest territorial control from Brigham Young. Robert's prominence in the Utah militia gave him a major role in the "Utah War" and sent his family south to Provo while he watched Johnston's army march through Salt Lake City.

In the spring of 1857, General Daniel H. Wells, commander of the Nauvoo Legion, divided the entire territory into military districts, each led by a local commandant. This increased the effectiveness of the Saints' military arm as regular musters and drills were now conducted in the major communities. A new election of officers was called for and on April 20, Robert T. Burton was elected colonel and appointed commander of his cavalry unit, the Life Guards.

This election occurred as he was preparing to accompany Brigham Young and 141 other Church and community leaders on a month-long trip into the Oregon Territory. They left on the afternoon of April 24, some in 56 wagons and carriages and some on horseback. Robert kept a journal, but unfortunately his notes are brief and uninteresting, listing departure times and distances traveled rather than his impressions of this new country. Lot Smith was his traveling companion. His later biography describes this as a "splendid trip" during which he traveled 800 miles, "and of this distance I had only ridden one half day out of the saddle" (n.d.ᵃ, 30).

The company's ultimate destination was Fort Lemhi, a Mormon colony on the Salmon River, but they traveled through areas which were being considered for new colonies. Following the common wagon trails, they went north through the Box Elder settlements to Malad, and then into the Bannock Creek Valley following the creek to the Portneuf River where they camped at Fort Hall, a prominent stop on the Oregon Trail. At Fort Hall, the Portneuf joins the Snake River, which they followed for three days before turning northwest to go up over the mountains and down into the Lemhi River Valley. Fourteen days from Salt Lake City, they reached Fort Lemhi in a snowstorm. Robert's horse had become lame and, after failing to respond to treatment, was left at the fort. From May 9–13, the party held meetings, built roads, and in general encouraged and uplifted the families colonizing the area.

Two weeks later, the party returned to Salt Lake in good spirits in spite of traveling through late spring storms in the mountains of eastern Idaho. Once again, Robert returned just in time for the birth of a child, on May 28, his sixth and Maria's fourth boy in a row. He was named John Haven Burton.

Although this trip was billed as a tour of the Latter-day Saint settlements on the Snake and Salmon rivers, Brigham Young revealed his real purpose upon his return by quipping in a Sunday sermon:

> I have accomplished what I designed to accomplish and I believe the brethren will join with me, at least on one point, namely, that we started from here to rest the mind and weary the body; and so far as the body is concerned, I believe all parties will agree with me in saying that we have done that most effectively. . . .

> I rested my mind. . . . My mind was so taken from the cares
> that surrounded me here, that it was perfectly relaxed into an easy
> state of rest, and I had no anxiety, not in the least, about one care
> that had formerly been upon me (in Nibley 1937, 280).

What cares was Brigham Young fleeing? Besides the challenges of taming a desert and colonizing a vast territory, Young
and his people were also under verbal attack in the "States"
where rumors and accusations started by Utah's federal officials were in every newspaper. Relations between most feder-
ally appointed officials and Church leaders had been fragile
since 1851–52. During the early months of 1857, all the important "gentile" territorial officers—and most especially associate
justice, Judge W. W. Drummond—were in the East circulating
their complaints against the Mormons. Some were in Washington, D.C., urging the government to curb the "insurrection" in
Utah; others lectured and wrote letters to the press in the major
cities, decrying their treatment at the hands of the Mormons.
No one knew what was really going on in Utah Territory, but
the papers printed the worst scandals as their readers clamored
to know all about this "degenerate and defiant" people.

The summer of 1857 marked the tenth anniversary of the
arrival of the pioneers in the Salt Lake valley; a "grand
celebration" was planned for the Saints to be held at the head
of Big Cottonwood Canyon, now known as Brighton. As military units led the pioneer processions, Robert received special
orders on July 15, 1857, appointing him "Officer of the Guard."

He and his wives and children traveled with 2,600 other
Saints on July 22 to the canyon entrance where the procession
was formed. Early on the morning of July 23, Brigham Young's
carriage led the way up the "stairs" of the lower canyon and
onto a new road constructed in 1856 by the Big Cottonwood
Lumber Company, which had three saw mills in the canyon.
Five miles of road were constructed above the last mill to permit travel to the top for outings. In his *History of Utah*, Orson
F. Whitney recorded:

> It was a motley yet merry sight to see them come; wagons loaded
> with camping outfits, bedding, provisions and human beings of all
> sizes and ages, from the tottering, silver-haired veteran to the tod-
> dling or nursing child; wending their way by different routes toward
> the place of gathering, greeting with glad faces and happy hearts
> friends and kindred along the way, or good naturedly jostling against
> them at the general camp-ground (1:601).

The military escort included a detachment of Robert's Life
Guards and a platoon of lancers. For this celebration there were
several bands: Captain Balloo's Band, the Nauvoo Brass Band,
Springville and Ogden City brass bands, and the Salt Lake City
and Ogden martial bands. Five hundred vehicles and 1,500 animals transported the Saints to the banks of Silver Lake, where
the lumber company had built three spacious boweries with
plank floors. The trip up the canyon took five to six hours, and
the Saints spent the first afternoon pitching tents and preparing
for the next day's celebration.

At sunset, a bugle call summoned the campers to the center
of the grounds where Brigham Young addressed them. He
recounted to them the Lord's mercies in delivering them from
their enemies in the past and in bounteously blessing them in
this isolated home for ten years. He concluded with a remarkable prayer in which he prayed for "Israel and Israel's enemies"
and then dedicated anew the spot upon which they were assembled (Whitney 1:603). While many retired to their campsites
after prayer, the majority spent the evening dancing to the tunes
of the bands.

The Twenty-fourth's festivities began early when two United
States' flags were unfurled from the tops of the two tallest trees
on the summits overlooking the encampment. Prayer was offered,
the choir sang, the cannon roared, bands played, and the military units performed drills. Once the formalities were over, the
Saints were free to enjoy games, dancing, boating, picnicking,
hiking, and visiting for the rest of the morning and afternoon.

Most people were so busy having fun that they scarcely
noticed the arrival about noon of four men, three of them dust-
stained as though they had traveled a long distance. Abraham

O. Smoot, Judson Stoddard, and Orrin Porter Rockwell, accompanied by the Salt Lake postmaster Elias Smith, immediately sought private council with Brigham Young. They had ridden over 500 miles in five days and three hours to report that President Buchanan had ordered army troops to accompany a new governor to Utah where he believed that the citizens and the civil government were "in a state of substantial rebellion against the laws and authority of the United States" (in Arrington 1974, 217). President Young called for a council of the leading elders and gave them the news. That evening he told the rest of the people as they gathered for evening prayer. Robert Burton wrote later that the people had difficulty understanding the military movement, for they knew little of the misrepresentations made in Washington. However, Brigham Young was aware long before July 24 of impending trouble, for he had written to Colonel Thomas Kane in June of the possibility of armed intervention in Utah (Furniss 1960, 61; Young 1857, 49–53n). Brigham Young's diary of 1857 records the actions of the council and his feelings on July 24:

> Found that Bros Smoot and Stoddard were from fort Leavenworth 20 days. They informed [me] that a new Governor and entire set of officers had been appointed, 2500 troops with 15 months provisions. Sup[p]osed that General [William S.] Harney would command—to support the officials in their position. I Said if General Harney came here, I Should then know the intention of [the] Gover[n]ment; And it was carried unanimously that if Harney crossed the *South Pass* the *buz[z]ards* Should *pick his bones.* The feeling of Mobocracy is rife in the "States" the constant cry is kill the Mormons. *Let them try it.* The Utah mail contract had been taken from us—on the pretext of the unsettled state of things in this Territory.
>
> The news helped the people to enjoy themselves. Dancing and mirth continued until a late hour.

Much has been written attempting to explain this episode in the history of America and the Latter-day Saint people. It has been called "Buchanan's Blunder," the "Invasion of Utah," "Johnston's Army," the "Utah Expedition," and simply the "Utah War."[1] There were misunderstandings and miscommunication on both sides. President Buchanan acted without determining whether the accusations against Brigham Young and the people of Utah Territory were true and without examining the character of the federal officer who was his major source of information. He also failed to officially inform Brigham Young that he was no longer governor. On the other hand, Brigham Young did not recognize the approaching government force as merely a military guard for a new governor and stirred up his people by announcing on August 5, "Citizens of Utah— We are invaded by a hostile force who are evidently assailing us to accomplish our overthrow and destruction."

Thirty years later, Orson F. Whitney wrote:

> It has doubtless been noted by the reader that the avowed purpose of the Government in sending troops to Utah was to give the new civil officials a *posse comitatus* to secure and maintain for them the offices to which they had been appointed, and not, as the Mormons maintained, to make war upon the people, destroy or drive them from their homes. This was indeed the Government's claim. . . . But it is none the less true that throughout the nation at that time a sentiment prevailed and found expression in the newspapers and upon the lips of many public men, to the effect that the real object of the expedition was to take possession of the cities of the Saints, kill their men, confiscate their wives and daughters, delivering them to the soldiers as a spoil, and superseding the Mormon by a Gentile population, forever end the problem of polygamy. . . . Though indignant at having been misrepresented at Washington, tried, condemned and officially executed without a hearing and disgusted at the thought of more men like Judge Drummond being "dragooned upon" him and his people as officers, these considerations alone would never have induced Brigham Young to take up arms and resist the installation of his successor as Governor of Utah. . . . It was the coming of the troops that he objected to; it was the army, and the army alone that he opposed (1:606–7).

Brigham Young's proclamation of August 5 declared martial law, forbade all armed forces from coming into the territory, and ordered the Utah militia on alert.

From the council of elders in Brigham's tent at Silver Lake, Robert was totally involved in the preparations to defend his home, his wives and children, and his community. Undoubtedly he worried about obtaining help to work in his fields and harvest his bounteous crops that year. Both Maria and Susan had young babies, and Sarah was pregnant with her first child. The oldest children were only seven and eight years. He had much to think about and many decisions to make.

On August 1, the first orders to the Nauvoo Legion went to commanders of the military districts on August 1 from Lieutenant General Daniel H. Wells. "You are instructed to hold your command in readiness to march at the shortest possible notice to any part of the Territory. See that the law is strictly enforced in regard to arms and ammunition, and as far as practicable that each Ten be provided with a good wagon and four horses or mules, as well as the necessary clothing, etc., for a winter campaign. Particularly let your influence be used for the preservation of the grain. Avoid all excitement, but be ready" (in Whitney 1:620–21).

The Nauvoo Legion officers for this campaign included: Lieutenant General Daniel H. Wells, who answered to commander in chief Brigham Young, Generals George D. Grant, William H. Kimball, James Ferguson, and Hiram Clawson as the staff, with Colonels Robert T. Burton, Nathaniel Jones, James Cummings, Chauncey West, Thomas Callister, William Pace, Warren Snow, Joseph A. Young, and Albert Rockwood heading field operations. Major Lot Smith, O. Porter Rockwell, and William Hickman were chosen as captains of a cavalry guerrilla force accountable directly to President Young and General Wells. Their companies were sometimes called the "Mormon Raiders" (Arrington 1985, 255).

Robert's troops received the first orders to leave the valley. On August 13, Robert was instructed to "forthwith raise from your regiment One hundred and Sixty mounted men with thirty days rations to go back on the road to protect our Emigration now en route to this City" (W. H. Kimball 1857). What the orders did not say, but which Robert recorded in his biography, was that under the guise of protecting the immigrants, he and his men were a reconnaissance force "to move East until I met this regiment of soldiers now marching to Utah and carefully inspect all their movements, to know their mode of travelling and to report to the General commanding as often as in my judgement my information would be of value. Also to give such aid and protection to our emigrant company as in my power" (n.d.[a], 31).

He left the valley two days later, with 75 men instead of 160. A company from Provo came later.

Aided by fine weather and his experience on this road between the valley and the mountain passes, Colonel Burton and his cavalry made excellent time, reaching Fort Bridger August 21. Five days later they met the first Mormon immigrant company at Pacific Springs. The next day they encountered several large government supply trains traveling without military escort. Robert noted their size and makeup but had orders not to interrupt them (n.d.[a], 32). When he reached the Sweetwater, he left half of his command with their wagons while he and the other half went on by pack train to Devil's Gate which they reached on August 30. There were 1,200 Mormon immigrants on the trail in 1857, and their wagon trains passed almost daily, but none had been disturbed by the army.

While camping in the vicinity of Devil's Gate, Robert ordered his men to cache considerable provisions for future use and also sent several expresses (scouting parties) eastward. Such an express returned on September 12 and reported sighting the first U.S. troops, which included the 5th and 10th U.S. Infantry Regiments and two batteries of artillery, under command of Colonel E. B. Alexander. From this time on, Robert and his men closely observed the army's movement and scouting operations and sent back reports to Wells who was now with other legion units building fortifications in Echo Canyon. Robert and three companions were camped only a half mile away from the expedition when it reached Devil's Gate on September 22. He barely avoided contact, as Alexander had issued orders for forced marches to catch up with the unprotected supply trains (Furniss 1960, 139).

Posing as California immigrants, two of Robert's men— Charles Decker and Jesse Earl—infiltrated the camps of the Utah Expedition. They mingled freely with the soldiers, asking questions about the intent of the army, and answering inquiries from the soldiers about conditions in Salt Lake Valley. Since people in the states believed that Brigham Young ruled as a tyrant and his people would look upon the expedition soldiers as "heavenly messenger[s] sent to bring deliverance from 'Mormon' degradation, wretchedness and despair," the soldiers were somewhat surprised to hear from Decker and Earl that the Mormon people were loyal to Brigham Young and conditions were much different than publicized in the east. Many soldiers deserted the expedition—reportedly as many as 500—when the going became rough in the mountains and the true conditions in the Mormon stronghold became known (CHC 4:250).

A second, important exchange of information occurred when Captain Stewart Van Vliet, assistant quartermaster for the U.S. Army was escorted into the valley by Briant Stringham and Nathaniel V. Jones, also from Robert's command (and incidentally, two of his brothers-in-law). Brigham Young courteously received him, though his efforts to secure supplies and arrange for an encampment amounted to nothing. He learned the feelings and plans of the Mormons and hurried back to the advance companies of the expedition to urge them to camp at Ham's Fork and avoid conflict which might lead to bloodshed if they pressed forward to the valley. Nathaniel Jones returned with Van Vliet to the regiments and brought back the report that younger, brasher officers of the 10th regiment had vowed to fight their way into the valley and had forced their men to march thirty miles the next day instead of the usual fifteen to enforce their point (CHC 4:263–72).

On October 3, Fort Bridger was the site for a "council of war" for the leaders of the resistance. Colonel Burton and General Lewis Robinson were asked to bring from the field reports of the army's latest movements, present locations, and probable intentions. General Wells arrived on October 2 with two ecclesiastical advisors, John Taylor and George A. Smith. Generals Ferguson and Clawson, Briant Stringham, Porter Rockwell, and Judson Stoddard also attended. Nathaniel Jones's report was the only information the council had about the intentions of the expedition. All they could do was speculate (CHC 4:278). What they did not realize was that even Colonel Alexander did not know the purpose of the mission. General Harney had been appointed governor of Kansas, and no communication had come from the new commander. On October 8, Alexander wrote to the officers of his regiments: "I am in utter ignorance of the object of the government in sending troops here or the instructions given for their conduct after reaching here."

Fearing that young military hotheads might persuade Colonel Alexander to force his way into the valley before winter and hoping to delay actual conflict with the troops as long as possible, the council at Fort Bridger decided to begin actively harassing the expedition. The raiders led by Smith, Rockwell, and Hickman were to slow down or stop the expedition's march so that it would not enter Utah Territory before spring. Copies of the orders explaining the harassment were taken from Joseph Taylor when he was captured by the army and copied by Elizabeth Cumming into a letter to her sister-in-law Ann Cumming Smith in New York City:

> Head Quarters Eastern Exped.
> Camp near Cache Cave, 4 Octr 1857
> Mjr Taylor
>   You will proceed with all possible dispatch, without injuring your animals, to the Oregon road, near the bend of Bear R. n. by E. of this place. . . . When you approach the road, send Scouts ahead to ascertain if the invading troops have passed that way. Should they have passed, take a concealed route & get ahead of them. Express to Col. Burton, who is now on that road, & in vicinity of the troops & affect a junction with him, so as to operate in concert. On ascertaining the locality or route of the troops, proceed at once to annoy them in every possible way. Use every exertion to stampede their animals, & set fire to their trains. Burn the whole country before them & on their flanks. Keep them from sleeping, by night surprises. Blockade the road by felling trees, or destroying river fords, where you can. Watch for opportunities to set fire to the grass on their windward, so as, if possible, to envelope their trains. Leave no grass before them that can be burned. Keep your men concealed as much as possible, and guard against surprises. Keep scouts out at all times, & communicate open with Col Burton, Major McAllister,

and O.P. Rockwell, who are operating in the same way. Keep me advised daily of your movements, & every step the troops take, & in which direction. God bless you & give you success—

> Your Brother in Christ,
> Danl H. Wells
> Lieut. Gen. Nauvoo Legion,
> Commanding

P.S. If the troops have *not* passed, or have turned in this direction, follow in their rear & continue to annoy them, burning anything they may have. Take no *life*, but destroy their trains, & stampede or drive away their animals, at every opportunity (in Canning and Beeton 1977, 29–31).

Robert and his men received similar orders to break camp and "cooperate in these maneuvers, annoying the 'Expedition' in all the ways in his power 'without risking his men' " (CHC 4:278).

The policy of defensive action began at Fort Bridger and Fort Supply, which the federal troops could have occupied as winter quarters. Before nightfall on October 3, General Robinson, assisted by Robert, applied the torch to Fort Bridger, burning it to the ground. Robert rode back to Fort Supply where his command was encamped, spent two or three days caching the grain and supplies stored there, then burned it. The property loss at Fort Bridger amounted to only about $2,000, but the mills, buildings, and other property burned at Fort Supply were worth about $50,000 (CHC 4:278–79).

With five associates, Porter Rockwell led the first strike right into the heart of Alexander's camp at Pacific Springs. They entered the bivouac about 2 A.M., fired their revolvers into the air, rang cowbells, and led off the stampeding mules.

> Colonel Alexander rushed from his tent and called the regimental bugler to sound Stable Call hoping the stampeding animals would turn. At the moment the gesture seemed futile, but a single stroke of bad luck cost the Mormons their victory, and ironically a cowbell turned the tide of fortune. . . . Minutes after the stampede: "The bell mule by the merest accident got caught by the picket rope in a wild sage bush, stopping him and with him most of the herd stopped."

When Stable Call came blaring through the night, the mules
wheeled and headed full speed back to camp to an expected bag of
oats (Schindler 1966, 256–57).

Ironically, with hundreds of Mormons in the mountains at
different times, under various orders, all trying to thwart the
same enemy, on several occasions legion posses surrounded and
captured their comrades on similar missions. There were also
times when they rode into a camp expecting to be among friends,
only to discover they had ridden into the midst of the enemy
(Furniss 1960, 138, 142–43).

Robert positioned his troops where they could watch
Alexander's regiment struggle fruitlessly up Ham's Fork searching for an easier and unguarded passage into the Salt Lake Valley. He was pleased to receive fifty additional men sent from
General Wells at headquarters camp in Echo Canyon as well as
praise for his decisions: "I like your position so far as I can
learn it, being near the army, not requiring so much travel, but
still able to watch and report their movements" (Wells to Burton,
October 5, 1857).

Alexander moved up Ham's Fork for fourteen or fifteen days,
but had to return to Camp Winfield by order of General Albert
Sidney Johnston, who replaced General Harney as commander
of the Utah Expedition. Johnston feared that Alexander's men
would soon be stranded in the deep snow of the Bear River
Valley beyond the assistance of the other troops.

In the meantime, Lot Smith's cavalry turned back one large
supply train and set fire to three others, encountering no opposition from the civilian teamsters who preferred to surrender
rather than risk their lives against what they thought was 100
men but was actually only twenty-two. The army lost 300,000
pounds of food in these raids, most of it flour and bacon. Join-
ing forces with Rockwell, Lot Smith's raiders burned the grass
ahead of the army on Ham's Fork and stole 1,400 head of cattle
while startled guards watched without interfering. Thus, the
army was left quite unprepared for wintering in the mountains.

The first storms arrived on October 17. Alexander and his troops were still milling around on Ham's Fork, but Wells ordered Robert on October 8 to return to the valley:

> You had better take such of your men as you have with you (those who have been out the longest) with Capt. Kimball and the men that went down with him, and march to the City. . . . The probability at present is that the enemy will either go to Fort Hall or take the Northern route to the Settlement, in the latter event it will be necessary for you to be on hand for a march north to meet them.

General Wells wanted them to refit their supplies, wagons, and ammunition and be ready for a march north if needed. The men were stationed at Union Square at First North and Second West where roll call was held night and morning, but they enjoyed brief reunions with their families and friends (R. T. Burton 1856–1907, October 21, 1857).

They prepared to repel the enemy if needed, but the Mormon leaders were beginning to realize that a sustained campaign against the army would be impossible. Ammunition and guns were in short supply, even though Saints called home from California and other distant colonies brought as many arms as they could. Lead had been discovered in the territory, but the manufacture of ammunition was poorly developed. Maria Burton, like many other wives, learned to make lead bullets. Seven-year-old William stood at his mother's side as she poured the hot lead into molds, then he trimmed off the "neck" that adhered to the opening through which the lead was poured. He remembered: "I thought I was doing big things, helping to make ammunition to repel the troops" (1931, 3–4).

After three days in the valley, Robert and his "boys," as he affectionately described them in his diary, returned to the front after hearing that Alexander's command was returning to Camp Winfield. During the next few days, Robert was rarely out of the saddle as he rode from camp to camp, receiving and conveying messages from the scouts still trailing the army, conferring with other military leaders, and superintending the work of his troops. On October 29, they were ordered to reestablish camp at the site of Fort Supply. Occasionally a prisoner was brought to this camp; other days they received cattle and sometimes horses taken from the expedition. Ephraim Hanks had thirty men concealed near the army camp, some of whom noticed great activity about November 6. An express warned that the expedition was "on the move" and Robert quickly sent word to Brigham Young who ordered an additional 1,300 men to be ready for an "expected invasion."

But the U.S. Army was not preparing an assault on the valley. General Johnston had finally assumed command of the entire expedition. He saw the exhausted troops, who had been up and down Ham's Fork, and the cavalry, which had been force-marched across the mountains, and recognized some obvious facts: winter was upon them, they were short of supplies, and their campsite was inadequate. He quickly ordered a rendezvous at Fort Bridger, the only favorable spot for a winter camp.

> On November 6 began the desperate race to that sheltered valley before the animals failed completely. Intense cold froze the feet of the Dragoons on patrol and congealed the grease on the caissons' axles. Captain Gove wrote his wife that in the sub-zero weather outpost duty had become almost unbearable, that he himself almost perished from the cold one night. Savage snowstorms at times forced the men to huddle under any natural protection available. The animals, already weakened by the cold, had little to eat beside cottonwood bark and sage. . . . The stock accordingly died in such great numbers along the road that a soldier who followed the trail of the army in the summer of 1858 found carcasses of mules and oxen at every hundred steps. . . . With Johnston occasionally leading his men on foot, the troops bore the ordeal in good spirits, and their hardness, the result of several months' labors, stood them in good stead. Yet Johnston was not melodramatically enlarging upon the facts when he later wrote: "The army under my command took the last possible step forward at Bridger, in the condition of the animals then alive" (Furniss 1960, 115–16).

The Mormon troops, uncertain for over two weeks whether they should return to the valley or prepare for an attack, also suffered in the snow. The weather alternated from snow and high winds to cold and clear, causing Robert to frequently report in his journal the difficulties of scouting the expedition and preparing to move their camps which became necessary as the enemy approached closer. Patiently, he waited each day for a report from the scouts. On Monday, November 23, he wrote in his diary from their camp on the Bear River: "Still waiting the movements of the Enemy," followed the next day by: "The Enemy preparing to store their supplies at Fort Bridger. Did not know if they would winter there."

But the snow continued to fall, and it soon became apparent that the Utah Expedition was going nowhere until spring. Robert called in his scouts and sent some of his men back to Echo Canyon where 2,500 more troops waited.

He was somewhat surprised to receive at his camp on November 28 a letter which was a proclamation from Governor Alfred Cumming to the "People of Utah Territory." Cumming was in the army's winter camp on Black's Fork near Fort Bridger, called Camp Scott. He announced:

> On the 11th of July, 1857, the President appointed me to preside over the executive department of the government of this Territory. I arrived at this point on the 19th of this month, and shall probably be detained some time in consequence of the loss of animals during the recent snow-storm. I will proceed at this point to make the preliminary arrangements for the temporary organization of the Territorial Government.
>
> Many treasonable acts of violence have recently been committed by lawless individuals supposed to have been commanded by the late Executive [Brigham Young]. Such persons are in a state of rebellion. Proceedings will be instituted against them in a court organized by Chief Justice Eckels held in this County. . . .
>
> It is my duty to enforce unconditional obedience to the Constitution, to the Organic law of this Territory, and to all the other laws of Congress, applicable to you. . . . I come among you with no prejudices or enmities, and by the exercise of a just and firm administration, I hope to command your confidence. Freedom of conscience and the use of your own peculiar mode of serving God, are sacred rights, the exercise of which is guaranteed by the Constitution and with which it is not the province of the Government or the disposition of its representatives in this Territory to interfere.

> In virtue of my authority as commander in chief of the militia
> of this Territory, I hereby command all armed bodies of individuals
> by whomsoever organized, to disband and return to their respective
> homes. The penalty of disobedience to this command will subject
> the offenders to the punishment due to traitors (in Whitney 1:655–56).

Frederick Kesler described the response of Robert's troops:
"After hereing the New Gov orders, we gave 3 Cheers For Gov
Brigham Young which made the Kanyon ring" (Arrington 1985,
261). Cumming's proclamation was forwarded to General Wells
in Echo Canyon.

Church and military leaders finally concluded by December 4 that all but forty men could return to the valley. They
were left in Echo Canyon with orders to watch the enemy through
the winter without further interference or harassment (R. T.
Burton 1856–1907, November 28–December 4, 1857).

On December 5, Robert T. Burton led his cavalry command through deep snow past Big and Little Mountains almost
one year from the time he had superintended the rescue of the
handcart companies along the same road. His characteristic journal entry of December 5 which concludes this episode tells what
was most important to him: "Arrived in the city 7 1/2 P.M.
Found my family all well."

Church leaders had hoped that if they could prevent the
outbreak of war while emotions were high, somehow during
the long winter their difficulties with the government could be
peaceably settled. While this settlement did not come easy, and
it should be noted that some high Washington officials did not
want to negotiate an end to the Mormon "insubordination," it
did occur. One modern historian notes:

> It is to be observed, then, that the Saints' resistance to the army,
> a public opinion divided on the merits of the campaign, and the
> other considerations reportedly working to soften the President's Mormon Policy did not materially influence Buchanan. Yet it remains
> true that during the winter he began to ponder the desirability of
> convincing the Mormons that they were not obliged to fight the
> United States in order to preserve their lives and their religious freedom. Although he did not go so far as to authorize [Colonel Thomas]
> Kane and the peace commissioners to negotiate with the Church, he

now permitted these men to examine with the Mormons the issues existing between them and the Government. Perhaps this change, slight as it was, came from a realization that, having failed to investigate the situation in Utah before he sent an army to correct it, he should now remedy this omission, lest he be charged with having needlessly precipitated a civil war. . . .

Despite their later assurances to the contrary, the members of Buchanan's Administration had obviously underestimated both the cost of an expedition against Utah and the number of troops necessary to stifle any resistance offered by the Mormons. Thus during the winter, when his army was huddled along Black's Fork instead of parading in triumphal possession of the Territory, the President found himself required to ask Congress for assistance, first to end the financial embarrassment into which the Government was plunged by the Utah War and the Panic of 1857, and second to bring the army to a strength adequate to meet any opposition from the Saints. When both the Senate and the House of Representatives delayed action on these requests for several months, Buchanan saw the desirability of seeking a peaceful end to his difficulties (Furniss 1960, 174).

The winter of 1857-58 is noted frequently in Utah territory history as a time of gaiety and innocent merry-making, "an agreeable winter" (CHC 4:301). It is difficult to imagine that the Saints were so little concerned about the army waiting to invade their valley that they spent the winter enjoying themselves, but Robert's diary shows that they did. True, he spent many days in military councils and often was away from home searching for horses, organizing the standing army, and otherwise attending to military business, but he also enjoyed many dinners with the legion officers, military parties in the Social Hall, ward parties in the newly dedicated Fifteenth Ward Store House, and evenings at the homes of his sisters and friends. He seemed particularly to enjoy the company of Lot Smith, Howard Egan, and his two brothers-in-law, Nathaniel V. Jones and William H. Kimball.

He also reports in his diary of days spent husking corn from the harvest and then carrying his "tithing corn" to the storehouse on New Year's Eve. He assessed all the property in the city for taxes, met with the tax collector, and attended ses-

sions of the county court. He frequently attended evening seventies quorum meetings and referred for the first time to "circle
meetings," where the ordinance of washing of feet was performed within the brotherhood of the quorum.

On February 21, Sarah delivered her first child, a healthy
boy who was named Henry Fielding. The next fast day, Robert
proudly took his entire family to meeting in the Fifteenth Ward
where he blessed this baby and Maria's son, John Haven. He
loved being home with his family and recorded the days he
spent at home in his journals just as he accounted for his time
in tax assessing and military operations.

Because he was a military leader, Robert Burton was one of
the few Salt Lake citizens who knew the correct identity of a
distinguished "Dr. Osbourne" who arrived from California on
February 25 and announced himself as "an ambassador from
the chief executive of our nation." The "ambassador" was the
old friend of the Mormons, Colonel Thomas L. Kane, quickly
recognized by Brigham Young and others who had known him
while he convalesced in Nauvoo in the early 1840s. He carried
a letter from President Buchanan which announced: "As you
have been impelled by your own sense of duty to visit Utah,
and having informed me that nothing can divert you from this
purpose, it affords me pleasure to commend you to the favorable regard of all officers of the United States whom you meet
in the course of your travels" (Furniss 1960, 177).

Colonel Kane had chosen to come, but the arduous trip
from New York to Los Angeles by boat with a wagon crossing
of the Isthmus of Panama, and then by wagon across the desert
to Salt Lake had left him in very poor health. Brigham Young
had sent Samuel W. Richards to see Kane at home in Pennsylvania during the summer of 1857, hoping that he could explain
the true state of affairs to President Buchanan before the expedition reached Utah. Finding the President disposed to believe
what he wished, the most Kane could get was the grudging letter, but with that letter he intended to mediate the differences
between Brigham Young and the new governor, Alfred Cumming. First, he tried to convince Brigham Young to allow the

army to enter the valley and enjoy the assistance and hospitality of the Saints. While Brigham Young preferred to wait the direction of the Lord in the matter, he did encourage Colonel Kane to "go to the army and do as the Spirit of the Lord led him, and all would be right" (CHC 4:349).

Kane left the valley on March 8, escorted by Robert Burton and other military leaders. Robert rode with them for one day, turning back at the home of Judson Stoddard in Weber Canyon. Others went as far as the Little Muddy where they camped while Kane traveled the twelve miles to Camp Scott alone (CHC 4:349).

While Colonel Kane was gone, a new chapter in the Mormon resistance began. At a military council on March 18, Brigham Young, apparently influenced by Kane's suggestion to allow the army peacefully into the valley, convinced the majority of the council that the best plan of action was to lead the Saints "into the desert and not war with the people [i.e of the United States], but let them destroy themselves" (CHC 4:360). President Young presented the plan to the Saints at a special conference the following Sunday in the Tabernacle. Such a different spirit was evident in the sermons of the day as the policy of flight, not fight, was presented. President Young announced that he intended to "remove the grain and the women and children from the city and then, if needs be, burn it and lay the country waste" (CHC 4:360).

Though the conference accepted the policy, many Saints were opposed, unconvinced that they should leave their homes without first trying to turn back the enemy. But Robert, fully aware of the legion's thin lines of defense and limited ammunition, was a stalwart supporter of Brigham Young. He began putting his affairs in order at the clerk's office and then spent long hours preparing "to move my family south." All Salt Lake families were going to move to Utah Valley first, then proceed to an unspecified refuge which Brigham Young had described as a "country of alternating desert and fertile valley, . . . capable of sustaining a population of 500,000" but completely isolated and defensible. Parties were sent to the southwest to search for this ultimate "paradise", but of course they never found it, although they did locate many smaller areas for settlement (CHC 4:365–64).

William S. Burton remembered that it took more than one wagon trip to carry the belongings and household supplies of his father, his mother, the two "aunts" and seven children. He thought they used the same wagon which had brought Robert, Maria, and Theresa to the valley, and it housed part of the family for the duration of their exile in Provo (n.d.^{c}, 2–3).

The Saints who were determined to go did so quickly. Thirteen days after the announcement Susan and her child left Salt Lake with the first load of goods. Robert did not drive the wagon this trip because he was busy refitting the military for whatever might happen. He received orders on March 30 to send more troops to watch the mountain passes, in case the enemy tried to surprise the Saints before they could flee. Then on April 9, Robert, as county sheriff, was assigned supervision and protection of the prisoners of war, to house and feed them, and keep them from communicating with their comrades (Wells, April 9, 1858). Robert devoted every day in April and May to either moving the family, refitting the military, or supplying the troops in the mountains. He traveled back and forth to Provo several times. Sarah and her baby moved on April 22, and the rest of the family joined her and Susan near the end of May. They left on the morning of May 25, encountered rain along the way, and stopped to wait out the storm at the home of Maria's sister Eliza and her husband, Charles Westover, who lived in Draper. Upon reaching Provo, Robert worked a day and a half on what he called "a shed," which was a one-room adobe house owned by a Mr. Conover which Robert had arranged to use. The wagon was parked nearby as a bedroom for the children.

Across the street from the house ran a canal about eight to ten feet wide with water in it twelve to fifteen inches deep. The water was a constant source of worry to Maria whose young boys were lured to wade and play, trying to catch the occasional fish which made its way from the Provo River. William often caught a fish, only to have it slip out of his hands.

> Mother several times whipped us for wading and playing in this stream, but the whipping did little good. I would go out, see other boys trying to catch the fish and in I would go. One day she called to me. I was in the stream, wet all over. I ran home. She did not scold me, but speaking kindly told me to go into the wagon box and take all my clothes off. I thought, "Is she going to whip me without any clothes on?" She followed me in carrying one of my sister Theresa's dresses. This she made me put on, then said, "Now you can go out and wade. You can hold that up high enough to keep it out of the water." I was cured of wading. Although soon some of my playmates called for me, I would not answer and did not leave my sleeping place until mother brought back to me my own clothes and allowed me to discard the dress and put my own clothes on (W. S. Burton 1931, 4).

During his three weeks at Camp Scott, Colonel Kane persuaded Governor Cumming to visit the valley ahead of the army. The governor agreed to the plan, not so much because he believed Kane's explanations about the Mormon people, but because he wanted to assert the authority of the federal government (Furniss 1960, 182). Leaving Johnston and his army in their snowbound camp, Cumming left Camp Scott on April 5 with Colonel Kane and two attendants, but no army escort. They met the first Mormon militia at Quaking Asp Hill, who escorted them across the snowy Wasatch Mountains and down through Echo Canyon.

> In order to make as impressive an appearance of their forces as possible, as also, doubtless, to keep concealed the location and nature of their 'fortifications' in the canon, the journey of the governor's party was made in the night. After the militia at the first campfire halt had been drawn up in form and solemnly addressed by his excellency, they were dismissed and hurried down to the second encampment to again solemnly received the governor in military array, and again hear his speech; again to cheer what he had to say about returning peace; and so again at the third encampment this performance was repeated (CHC 4:378–79)

Deep snow covered Big Mountain, so Governor Cumming was brought through Weber Canyon via Farmington into Salt Lake Valley. Governor Cumming had not been told that the Saints had abandoned every community north of the valley, in effect leaving him governor of nobody. He began to realize this as he journeyed through Davis County along a road thronged with people moving south, their wagons loaded with provisions and household goods, their animals moving in droves before them (CHC 4:380).

Although he had not entered the valley feeling sympathetic toward the Church leaders, within three days Governor Cumming wrote to Johnston: "I have been everywhere recognized as the governor of Utah; and so far from having insults and indignities, I am gratified in being able to state to you that in passing through the settlements, I have been universally greeted with such respectful attention as are due to the representative of the executive authority of the United States in the territory" (CHC 4:384). After meeting with Church and civic leaders, Cumming personally inspected the supreme and district court records and found them perfect and unimpaired, contrary to the reports which had prompted President Buchanan to conclude the Mormons were in a state of rebellion. When Cumming offered assistance to all who "considered themselves unlawfully restrained of their liberties," only fifty-six men, thirty-three women, and seventy-one children responded. Of these, the majority had no complaints against the Church leadership but wanted to leave the territory because they were not economically successful (CHC 4:392).

Early in May, Cumming returned to Camp Scott to persuade the difficult General Johnston to delay his march to the valley until the arrival of a peace commission from President Buchanan, then en route from Fort Leavenworth. Johnston did not like what was happening but promised to await word from the commission before beginning his march, although he would be prepared to begin about June 15 when new supplies arrived from the states.

Despite personal appeals from Governor Cumming expressed in the Tabernacle and to the exiles in Provo, the citizens of northern Utah continued to prepare their homes to be burned and migrated to central and southern settlements. When the governor returned from Camp Scott again in May with his wife, they found Salt Lake City almost deserted. Gardens were filled with bundles of straw and other combustible material, ready for the torch if the militia found it necessary.

Robert T. Burton was in command of the guard over the city. During April, May, and early June, he kept his detachment in constant readiness. Some of his regiment went into the mountains; the remainder met morning and night for roll call, inspection of arms, and an occasional drill. During the day he worked at home or in his fields, keeping his own horses groomed and ready for instant service.

Robert had been absent from his family most of the past ten months, including the time spent in the mountains and on various military trips throughout the settlements. Never once had he expressed loneliness or regret about the sacrifices and demands of his position in anything he wrote. Instead he expressed his faith that the Lord's will would prevail and that the prophet and others leaders were called of the Lord. Saturday evening, May 29, he returned after checking the guard to his humble adobe home, now stripped of most of its furnishings and missing the wives and children which filled it with love and life. He took from his pocket the little journal where he habitually recorded the day's events, detailed his trip to Provo, the work on the "shed," his trip back, and his afternoon military drills. Then, he ended the day's entry: "My house was now empty & if ever I felt lonesome in my life this was the time—a home & not a home."

The next day he was busy with military and home duties even though it was Sunday. But in the evening, he again had to return to his empty house and he wrote: "Family gone. Lonesome."

He noted a week later that he had dinner with his mother-in-law, "Mother Haven." Some residents did stay in the city, mostly elderly Saints and gentiles. One of his duties during June was to ride throughout the city with General George Grant and Colonel H. S. Beatie encouraging remaining families to move south. The ones who did not go stayed inside when the troops came through.

The very evening Robert dined at Mother Haven's, an express arrived from the East bearing a "Proclamation to the People of Utah" from President Buchanan. Among other things, it listed forty-two separate charges against the Saints and offered them "a free pardon for the seditions and treason heretofore by the committed." Of course, the Saints believed the charges were false, but the Church leaders agreed to meet with the peace commission, which Brigham Young said was not sent to "investigate the past, but to inquire if we will submit to the Constitution and laws of the United States." He added: "We always have and always expect to" (CHC 4:433).

Brigham Young, Daniel H. Wells, and other Church leaders met in long sessions on June 11 and 12 with L. W. Powell, senator-elect from Kentucky, Major Ben McCulloch of Texas, and Governor Cumming. Because President Young wanted the commissioners to understand the Saints' fear of troops in their city, he spent much time reviewing the history of their treatment in Missouri, Illinois, and the West. The commissioners wanted to know only that the territorial residents would support the Constitution in the future. No formal action was taken during the meetings, but there was general understanding which allowed the commissioners to write the Secretary of War Floyd: "We have settled the unfortunate difficulties existing between the government of the United States and the People of Utah. . . . They will cheerfully yield obedience to the Constitution and laws of the United States" (CHC 4:434).

The minutes of the meeting call Brigham Young's address on June 12 "the finest effort of his life," and Robert noted in his journal its effect on the concerned church members: "9 AM Council of the day previous met. Several persons spoke. Also Pres. B. Young & cheered the people mutch. Concluded to let the Troops in upon Condition that they do not Quarter [in] the settlements" (June 12, 1858).

Two weeks later, June 26, Robert watched from a secluded vantage point, as the Utah Expedition marched down South Temple from the mouth of Emigration Canyon. At his order, his men waited in their quarters, and only a small party of non-Mormon citizens gathered to greet the troops. The soldiers marched through the deserted city streets, crossed the Jordan River, and camped west of the river, thus avoiding setting up camp even once within the city limits. Except for the expedition's bands which played at interval's, the march was undemonstrative, quiet, and orderly, as the general had promised (CHC 4:445). Robert counted the troops, wagons, and animals as they passed him and reported that night a total of 3,000 men, 6,000 wagons, and 6,000 animals (1856–1907, June 26, 1858). Then he returned to his boarded-up home and knelt to thank the Lord that he and his guard were unnecessary.

The next day he rode out with other military officers to keep watch on the army encampment. His letter to Maria and the family the next day expressed both loneliness and continued caution.

> GSL City, June 28th/58
> St. Joneses House 7 1/2 AM
>
> Dear Maria & Family,
>
> Yesterday a report reached here & seemed to be well authenticated that the famileyes would return this week. This morning however, it is contradicted. I must say that I am glad of it not but I would be glad to have my family back if it were peace to me. The Cloud has not passed in the least yet. The Troops are encamped within a mile of my house across Jorden.
>
> Let Jence return as soon as he can for I am too lazy to keep the weeds out of the garden. If the report of yesterday had been correct he could have brought a load back with him.
>
> Staines is in a hurry. You can enquire of him for the news.
>
> Yours as ever
> R. T. Burton

P.S. James will be in today. Wm maire has not yet got a colt. Them hens of Roberts have got no chickens. Charleyes bushes have plenty currants. Theresas cat has one Kitten.

When word came July 1 from President Young that the people could return home, Robert was busy with the city council to which he had been appointed June 28, 1858 (Campbell 1858). He concluded his business at 7 P.M. and immediately set out for Provo. He rode through the night, arriving in Provo at 4 A.M. He spent July 2 packing and loading his wagon and the third driving the entire distance home, leaving at 4:30 A.M. and arriving in Salt Lake at 7 P.M. He had room for only part of the family, but returned the next week with two teams for the other members. William recalled this second trip:

> We were 2 days on the way camping at night near the town of Draper. When father hitched up the team to the wagon in which mother and her children were riding, one of the horses balked. . . . Father did not strike him, but unhitching the tugs, ran the team up and down the road a few times. Hitching them to the wagon again there was no further trouble. We arrived home early the next afternoon and what rejoicing there was among us (W. S. Burton 1931, 4).

The Fourth of July was celebrated that year on Monday, July 5. All of the city's residents were not back in their homes, but that did not keep the ones who had returned from their activities. The morning roll call at 6 A.M. included the disbanding of the legion regiments which Robert had kept in order for so many weeks. As bands played, military leaders socialized, and families picnicked, it was evident that Salt Lake citizens that day were celebrating more than their nation's independence.

Notes

1. For further information, see CHC 4:181–471; Whitney, 1:600–88; LeRoy R. and Ann W. Hafen, *The Utah Expedition, 1857–58*, Glendale, California: Arthur H. Clark Company, 1958; Norman F. Furniss, *The Mormon Conflict, 1850–59*, New Haven: Yale University Press, 1960; Richard Vetterli, *Mormonism, Americanism and Politics*, Salt Lake City: Ensign Publications, 1961, 381–457; *Diary of Brigham Young, 1857*, Ed. Everett L. Cooley, Salt Lake

City: University of Utah Library, 1980, and Leonard J. Arrington, *Brigham Young: American Moses*, New York: Alfred A. Knopf, 1985, Chapter 15, plus his bibliographical notes on 474–75.

Keeping the Peace, 1858–62

From 1858 until the mid-1860s, the Latter-day Saints shared their once isolated valley with soldiers of the U.S. Army and its camp followers, teamsters, and other parasites. Although Johnston's Army was gone by 1861, Colonel Patrick Connor's California Volunteers were sent in 1862 to establish a permanent military post. Robert T. Burton spent this time in peace-keeping activities: guarding the mail route at the start of the Civil War and serving as Salt Lake County sheriff, constable of the Salt Lake City police force, and deputy U.S. territorial marshal. He was also a city councilman, county assessor, and federal tax collector. His reputation for getting a job done put his name first whenever Brigham Young or one of several governors and judges had a difficult assignment. His part in the "Morrisite War" was such an assignment.

Their exile ended, valley residents quickly returned to their homes and farms. Robert had managed to plant his garden and some crops between military assignments in May and June, and during July and August, he recorded in his journal that he worked "at home," "down to my farm," "watering my lot," and "in the field."

Life in the valley, however, did not return to normal, nor would it ever be quite the same. With 3,000 soldiers and unnumbered camp followers and teamsters camped on the west side of Utah Lake, constant watchfulness and anxiety replaced peace and security. Brigham Young decided that the Saints would hold no public meetings, not even worship services in the Tabernacle, apparently not wishing to arouse the troops and create a confrontation. For weeks, he remained in seclusion, the entrances to his homes locked, bolted, and guarded constantly by trusted friends, including Robert Burton who stood guard almost every Friday night (CHC 4:452–53; R. T. Burton 1856–1907, July-December 1858).

Twice during the summer heat, Brigham Young "escaped" to the canyon. Aware that his life was constantly in danger, he never travelled without a trusted bodyguard and during this period it was either Robert Burton, Lot Smith or Porter Rockwell. Robert accompanied him on both canyon excursions. The first included only his counselors, the Twelve, and a few other brethren. Robert's journal entry of July 26 mentions leaving for Big Cottonwood Canyon with President Young, then traveling, camping, and having "a fine time" for the next three days.

On the second, more festive outing, Brigham Young sent special invitations to the elite of the valley. Guests included the now-friendly Governor Cumming and his wife, Elizabeth. Mrs. Cumming had come to the valley "with an ardent desire to see the country, & become acquainted with Mormon homes (& hearts) if possible" (Canning and Beeton 1977, 99). Brigham's invitation is proof that she succeeded.

Maria and Sarah Burton, who accompanied Robert to the canyon, found the outgoing Mrs. Cumming a striking figure as she rode her spirited pony alongside the wagon train, sometimes trotting off with her escort, General James Ferguson, to see parts of the canyon hidden from the trail. At the Big Cottonwood Lumber Company bowery at Silver Lake, the party enjoyed music, dancing, singing, prayer services, and cool mountain air. The *Deseret News* reported on September 8 that no one seemed to enjoy themselves more than the governor and his lady.

Robert noted in his journal for August 26–27 that they spent the days and evenings in camp "very pleasantly." He felt comfortable with these leading citizens, most of whom had been his military companions during the councils of war and strategy. He now sat with some of them on the Salt Lake City Council. He had earned their trust and respect through dedicated military and community service. Indeed, many stopped to congratulate him on his recent reelection as county sheriff and to discuss the growing problem of crime in the city.

The rest of the country viewed the Utah Expedition as an attempt at the "moral regeneration" of the Latter-day Saints. But in fact, the army and its followers brought drunkenness, street brawls, gambling, murder, prostitution, and other public crimes into a valley which had been peaceful for eleven years. As sheriff, deputy U.S. marshal, and constable of the 250-man police force, Robert had few work-free days from August 1858 until the army left the valley in 1861. He regularly met with the city council to discuss controlling street mobs, solving problems between the merchants, the police, and the camp followers, financing law enforcement, and supporting paupers. He also stood guard many nights and helped quell riots, described by B. H. Roberts as "street 'imbroglios' among gamblers and other camp followers and teamsters of the 'Expedition.' . . . There were also frequent armed conflicts between these elements and the police; and worse yet, in some cases, prominent merchants and some army officers sided with the rowdies against the police" (CHC 4:460).

Robert not only attended the police meetings and court sessions, he also led the posses that trailed fleeing criminals. On October 12, policeman William Cook was killed. Robert gathered a posse and spent the next ten days pursuing the murderer, a renegade known as McDonald. They rode as far as Salt Creek (now Nephi) two separate times, but could not apprehend him (R. T. Burton 1956–1907, October 13–20, 1858; *Deseret News*, October 20, 1858).

In September 1858 construction resumed on the second phase of the county courthouse. When Robert was not enforcing the law, he worked on the courthouse, hauling trees and rock from the canyon and taking the trees to the mill to be split into lumber. He bought iron, hauled sand and clay, supervised and worked alongside the laborers, and kept the accounts of the project (1856–1907, September 13–November 30, 1858).

During these busy weeks, Robert did not often mention religious activities. Sabbath meetings were still cancelled, and it was a time of spiritual depression. The people were left to endure or give in to temptations according to their own strength. Many settlers found that they preferred the pleasures of the world which were once again within reach (CHC 4:465). But the apostles were not content to let Satan have his way with the people and in July the Twelve began special, private "prayer circles" to counter the influences of evil and exhort the brethren to righteousness. The First Presidency asked each apostle to organize a number of their close and personal friends into groups, patterned after the temple prayer circles and pray in behalf of the cause of God (CHC 4:466n). Robert was invited to attend Wilford Woodruff's circle of eighteen men which met in the Endowment Room (WW, 5:202–03) and Robert attended as often as he could through the fall and winter, meeting first on Wednesday evenings, then on Sunday mornings. Woodruff was particularly upset about the frequent street fights and murders. One involved two prominent Church members on August 27 and he recorded in his journal on September 1 his "exertation to the brethren" at that evening's circle meeting:

> I told them we were surrounded by the wicked Gentiles who were filled with wickedness and sought our destruction[;] that we were much exposed & should be on our guard & magnify our Calling and maintain our Dignity before all men as Saints of God & Elders in Israel & not mingle or drink with the wicked. If we have business with them let us do it & go our way. I feel ashamed before the Lord that any man that holds a station like Br George D. Grant should stoop so low as to create a fight with Thomas William as he did and to mingle and drink with the wicked. There is silence in Zion. No warning voice in the streets or in the tabernacle of the Lord. Evry

one is left to go his own way, and many are turning away from the Lord. And in this hour of temptation and darkness it is our duty to live our religin & to set a good example before all men & watch & pray that we enter not into temptation (WW 5:215).

On September 8, Woodruff recorded that Robert opened their circle with prayer (WW 5:217). Two days later, after hearing of a fatal fight between two gamblers and the murder of a soldier, he commented:

> Thus we have the fruits of Christianity & Civilization as manifest in the world introduced into our Territory. Untill the armey and its attendants arived here we had no such scenes manifest in our midst. The priests and people & the whole Government of the United States have tried hard to introduce those evils in our midst which are so common in almost evry City throughout the Gentile world & they have now accomplished it for a season & their is hardly a day passes but their is drunken[ess?] Gambling, swearing fighting & murder in the midst of the Gentiles in our streets (WW 5:217).

The ban on public meetings was lifted for the semi-annual conference in October and there were "two days of spirited discourses before crowded assemblies" even though Brigham Young was ill and unable to attend (Nibley 1937, 346). Robert attended a special meeting for the presidents of the quorums of seventy on Wednesday, October 6, and other sessions until Thursday afternoon, when he was called home for the birth of Susan's second child. It was Robert's seventh son in a row, and he and Susan named him Hosea McBride Burton (1856–1907, October 7, 1858).

As 1858 was drawing to a close, Robert's duties as deputy marshal of the district court took precedent. Charles E. Sinclair, newly appointed associate justice for Utah, arrived in July, but did not open district court in Salt Lake City until November. He promptly shocked the valley by attempting to have Brigham Young and other prominent Mormons indicted for treason for their part in opposing the Utah Expedition. However, Alexander Wilson, U.S. attorney for the territory, refused to allow the sitting grand jury to consider such charges because of President

Buchanan's pardon accepted by the people on June 14, 1858, and the matter was dropped (CHC 4:474–76).

During December, Robert was required to spend many days in court. He recorded in his journal of December 9 that he observed (he may have also testified in) the case of Burr vs. Ferguson. James Ferguson, Robert's friend and military leader, was tried and eventually acquitted on charges dating back to February 1857, that he and two other lawyers burst into the court of federal judge George P. Stiles and "by boisterous conduct and threats intimidated the judge, who quickly adjourned his court" (CHC 4:198–99, 476–78). As court business dragged into January, George A. Smith wrote sarcastically to Colonel Thomas L. Kane:

> The United States court in this district closed its first case on the 11th inst. after a session of thirty-eight sitting days, and occupying the time of one hundred days. The court is authorized to expend six days of its session, or so much of it as may be necessary, to accomplish United States business; but by prolongation, the marshal is enabled to deplete the treasury, and to sustain some of the strangers who are in the country. However correct legal men may regard this course of wasting time, the citizens look upon it as a species of ridiculous loaferism. . . . With a single exception, the Hon. Z. Snow, all the judges who have been sitting in this territory, have pursued a similar course, saddling upon the federal treasuries claims to the amount of nearly half a million. Rich and proverbially liberal as Uncle Sam is acknowledged to be, he has refused to pay these court expenses, and the paper certified by the judges as necessary and reasonable in amount is not worth three per cent. If Judge Sinclair and his drunken clique expect the counties to furnish at the ratio on which the federal funds have been expended since he opened court, they will find themselves drawing upon an empty box. . . .
>
> It is very annoying to a community to feel sensible that every act of the court that has jurisdiction over them, is a step towards placing them in an unfavorable position before their fellow countrymen. But while whiskey presides in our judicial halls, we expect the streets will be "icy," and the reports unfavorable (in CHC 4:481–82).

Although Governor Cumming made honest efforts at conciliation with Church leaders and Utah citizens, the federal judges would not cooperate. Instead they persisted in their efforts to restrict self-government for the Saints and to enlarge the powers of federal officers in the territory. The confrontation would continue for the next forty years. Directly or indirectly, Robert Burton would be involved. He did not write of his problems and grievances in his journal, so it is sometimes difficult to pinpoint his role in the various episodes. Nonetheless, he and his wives and children endured separations, embarrassment, and hardship because of federal meddling in territorial and Church affairs.

During 1859, however, the national leaders overlooked the Mormon problem and instead focused their attention on states' rights and slavery, with all sides represented in the presidential campaign.

During this year, Robert was called to serve in the Fifteenth Ward as a counselor to Bishop Andrew Cunningham, a long-time friend and partner in constructing the courthouse,[1] and he continued serving as assessor and tax collector for Salt Lake County, following reappointment by the County Court on December 10, 1858. Three years later, on July 28, 1862, he was appointed the first federal Collector of Taxes for the Territory of Utah by President Abraham Lincoln (see copy of certificate, p. 122). The first federal income tax was devised to raise revenue to fight the Civil War and signed by Lincoln on July 1, 1862 (Arrington 1956, 21). Robert prided himself over the years in keeping accurate records. During a trip to Washington, D.C., in December 1869, he checked his accounts with the Department of Treasury and found the match to be "quite satisfactory" (R. T. Burton n.d.[a], 44–45).

Getting news from the states to Utah Territory was usually slow and difficult. However, the advent of the Pony Express in April 1860 brought more regular issues of the eastern papers, and the news topic of greatest interest was the widening breach between the northern and southern states. Abraham Lincoln's election in November 1860 was followed shortly by the secession first of South Carolina, and then of six other states. The people of Utah regarded Lincoln as their friend; as a member of the Illinois Legislature during the Nauvoo period, he had been influential in securing the Nauvoo Charter. As for the issue of secession, when Brigham Young and the Twelve discussed it on March 10, 1961, President Young said "he did not wish Utah mixed up with the secession movement" (in Nibley 1937, 369). At April Conference, he expressed gratitude that the Saints were safely gathered in the mountain valleys: "We are not now mingling in the turmoils of strife, warring, and contention, that we would have been obliged to have mingled in, had not the Lord have suffered us to have been driven to these mountains—one of the greatest blessings that could have been visited upon us" (in Nibley 1937, 370).

Utah Saints kept aloof from secession and the ensuing Civil War, only grateful that the impending conflict ended the Camp Floyd period. General Johnston left in February 1860, leaving Colonel Charles F. Smith in command. When Colonel Phillip St. George Cooke returned from the East, he was assigned as commander. Meanwhile, a number of the army companies were pulled out of the camp in May, and much to the relief of the Saints, many of the camp followers left with these detachments.

An news item in the May 29, 1860, *Deseret News* exulted:

> *Moving Off*: Since the scarcity of money in this territory began to be felt by the riff-raff, that followed the army to Utah, they have been leaving slowly, and before it was generally known that a large portion of the troops were to be removed, the number of that class of beings had been greatly reduced in this and other cities in this part of the country, to the great joy of the citizens. The recent marching of troops has given a new impetus to their emigrating inclinations, and they have, during the last few weeks, been leaving the territory by scores; and gamblers, blacklegs, thieves, and murderers are not so plenty hereabouts by half as they were two weeks ago, with a fair and increasing prospect that their numbers will continue to grow less, till there will be but few, or none of them, left in the land.

In February 1861, Colonel Cooke changed the name of Camp Floyd to Camp Crittenden, apparently because Secretary of War John B. Floyd was out of favor. Floyd was later found guilty of manifest treason to the government during the Civil War. The people, however, hardly had time to become used to the new name before a directive in the summer of 1861 ordered the camp abandoned and all government property that could not be conveniently carried away by the troops sold at public auction. It was estimated that $4 million worth of property was sold for $100,000; Brigham Young purchased about $40,000 worth through an agent for the Church. The arms, however, were exploded, except for a few pieces of ordnance that could not be wrecked. These pieces were thrown into deep wells but afterward recovered by the citizens and used to arm the Nauvoo Legion (CHC 4:540–42).

Years before the Civil War broke out, southern leaders had been planning to extend slavery into the western states to increase their political power in Congress and add the tremendous wealth of western mineral resources to the labor and land resources of the Southeast. Once the Confederate States of America became a reality, they lobbied Utah, New Mexico, Arizona, Colorado, California, and even parts of Mexico to join the southern cause (Vetterli 1961, 503–07). Evidence suggests that "the peculiar aspects of the Utah War were indeed planned by some of the nation's leading Slavocrats, and effectively executed by Secretary of War John Floyd in concordance with preconceived plans concerning the annexation of the western territories into the Southern bloc" (Vetterli 1961, 508). Confederate leaders, assuming that the Mormons were bitter over their treatment at the hand of their government and on "the eve of a revolution" (Waldroup 1953, 167), hoped it would be relatively easy to enlist their aid in the Confederate cause. After all, Governor Cumming was a southerner from Georgia and both the Mormons and southerners were staunch advocates of "popular sovereignty," which protected the institutions of slavery and polygamy as domestic issues to be decided by the people themselves (Vetterli 1961, 516).

But the Confederates totally misjudged the attitude of the Latter-day Saints. Not only did Brigham Young decline to help the Confederacy whose representatives had promised polygamy would be safe under a Confederate government (Whitney 2:93; Vetterli 1961, 517), when the Overland Telegraph Line was completed to Salt Lake City on October 18, 1861, he stated in his first message: "Utah has not seceded, but is firm for the Constitution and the laws of our once happy country" (Whitney 2:30) The telegraph line was completed to the Pacific Coast the next week, thus linking the country from coast to coast at a critical time. As the Confederates continued to agitate in the western territories and California, both the overland mail and telegraph service, so vital to the Union war effort, were attacked. It appeared that Indians were raiding the mail stations, cutting the telegraph wires, and scattering the sacks of mail, but it soon became evident that white men, maybe southerners, were also involved (Vetterli 1961, 519).

In late April 1862, the Utah militia received two requests to protect the mail route until regular troops could get to the area. The first, from the superintendent of the Overland Mail Route to acting-governor Frank Fuller, asked for military protection of mail, passengers, and company property. The second, a week or so later, was from President Lincoln through Adjutant General L. Thomas of the War Department to Brigham Young, asking him to call up a "company of Utah volunteer cavalry, to arm and equip them immediately and send them east for the protection of the mail and telegraph lines extending from North Platte River below Independence Rock on the old Mormon pioneer trail to Fort Bridger" (Fisher 1929, 21). The first orders were given to Robert T. Burton and his Life Guards, while the second company was raised under Lot Smith.

Robert Burton actually received two sets of orders, one from Brigham Young on April 24 and another from General Wells of the Nauvoo Legion on April 25. In little more than twenty-four hours, Colonel Burton's company of twenty-two militia and teamsters left the valley, a day ahead of the mail coach and passengers which they were to escort east to the Platte River. His company included Heber P. Kimball, Brigham Young, Jr., John W. Woolley, R. J. Golden, Stephen Taylor, George Thatcher, John W. Young, Orson P. Wiles, S. D. Serrine, Henry Heath, James F. Allred, William J. Harris, Richard Margotts, Lewis Grant, Adam Sharp, James Woods,

Joshua Terry, J. M. Simmons, Mark Crocksell, William Carlos, George Spencer, and Lewis Neeley (R. T. Burton 1856–1907, April 26, 1862).

General Wells authorized the company to guard the route, mails, passengers, and property of the Overland Stage Company, but Brigham Young's letter of April 24, 1862, counseled them as a concerned leader:

> Col. Robert T. Burton
>
> and the detachment to guard the Mail Stage, under your charge— You are detailed for this special service and will proceed from this place in company with Col. Hooper, General C. W. West, Judge Kinney and probably other passengers in the Mail Coach for the eastern states as a guard to protect them against Indian depredations who are said to be hostile and continue in their company on the route so far as it may be deemed necessary by yourself and Col. Hooper for their safety. . . . In traveling be constant and vigilant and keep together and allow no straggling from Camp either night or day. There must be not any drinking of spirituous liquors, neither swearing or abusive language of any kind, and treat every body with courtesy and prove there is no necessity of trouble with the Indians when white men act with propriety. If you can get to speak with Indians treat them kindly showing them that you are their friends and so far as you are able, investigate the cause and origin of the present difficulties.
>
> You had better have one or two friendly Indians to accompany you through whose agency you may be able to communicate with others and thus become apprized of their intentions.
>
> When you meet the troops from the east said to be on their way you can return, but you will remain in the vicinity of the threatened difficulties until so relieved or so long as it may be necessary.
>
> In traveling favor your animals as much as possible by taking good care of them and by walking and leading them up hill and over rough or bad places.
>
> Keep a journal of every days proceedings and a strict account of every business transaction as well as of the causes leading to the disturbances if obtainable.
>
> Send by telegraph to President Young from every station giving us (in short) the current news and prospects of Indians, state of the roads and weather and any other matter of interest.

The company was hardly out of the valley on April 26 before Robert discovered that traversing the mountain trail in the spring was more difficult than it had been during the fall snow storms of 1856 and 1857. He later wrote: "The year 1862 will be remembered as the season of the highest water ever experienced in the mountains; as a consequence travel (over the mountains) was almost impossible" (in Whitney 2:44). They were first slowed by high water in Emigration Canyon, and the first day, one of the wide-track wagons became stuck a mile and a half from camp at Hanks Station (site of present-day Mountain Dell State Park). Robert had to leave the teamster with the wagon overnight. That evening the company was joined by William H. Hooper, Utah territorial delegate to Congress, and Chauncey W. West, traveling in the mail coach. Hooper was carrying papers presenting Utah's claim for statehood to Washington, D. C. The timing was critical since it would show Utah's "loyalty by trying to get in, while others are trying to get out" (Whitney 2:36).

After leaving Hanks Station the second day, the men struggled for eight hours through mud and snow and finally made camp in the road at 3 P.M. The snow was now so deep that they had to borrow a sled from the mail company at Hanks Station to carry the grain across the summit to their campsite. The third day, they broke camp at 4:40 A.M. so they could travel more quickly on frozen snow. With much effort, they reached Kimball's Station at 8:30 that evening.

Kimball's Station was a large stone hotel built by William H. Kimball, son of Heber C. Kimball and husband of Robert's sister, Melissa. The massive, eleven-room sandstone structure both housed and supported Melissa and her family for many years. As hostess, Melissa established her hotel as one of the finest stage stops along the Overland Stage route, famous for dinners of fresh trout, wild duck, sage hen, beef, or mutton. Numbered among its famous guests were Samuel Clemens, Horace Greeley, and Walt Whitman. Robert's family members were frequent guests between the 1860s and 1890s, as they drove cattle up and down Parley's Canyon, and Robert used the hotel as his headquarters during construction of the Utah Eastern Railroad in November and December 1880 (see photograph on p. 121).[2]

Other mail stations between Salt Lake City and Laramie were not so elaborate. Most had been built by the B. Y. Express Company during the summer of 1857 before its contract was annulled and the expedition sent. They provided a source of supplies and allowed a relay of horses and mules along the line (Hafen 1926, 62).

At Kimball's Station, Robert learned that there was no hay or grain until Fort Bridger. A lone rider coming from the east also warned him that the road ahead was very bad, so the company broke camp again early the next day hoping once again for a frozen road. But Robert recorded in his journal that travel on April 29 was even harder.

> At 5 o'clock broke camp and travelled until ten o'clock and by very hard labor in lifting waggons out of the snow, mules out of the mud, succeeded in making 6 miles and camped. At the head of Silver Creek Kanyon were three large land slides that made the road almost impassable. The first one we came to we got round it very well by taking the bed of the creek for a short distance. The other two had to be passed over which, after much labor, was accomplished without any serious accidents. . . . At half past 12 rolled out again and traveled until half after 5 and camped 1/2 mile up Echo. Found the road down Weber very good but Silver Creek Kanyon could not be worse and got over it at all.

That night while camped at Chalk Creek, they telegraphed to Brigham Young and received the report that, pursuant to President Lincoln's request, a company of Utah militia cavalry led by Lot Smith would patrol the road between Fort Bridger and Fort Laramie to protect the property of the telegraph and overland mail service for ninety days or until relieved by U.S. troops. Robert noted in his journal that "difficulties on the road [were] occasioned by the mail employees instead of the Indians" (R. T. Burton 1956–1907, April 29, 1862).

Once again the next morning camp was broken before dawn and the company worked "very hard" from 4 A.M. until 3:30

P.M. In traveling eleven miles, Robert recorded that they "crossed the creek four times which we found very high indeed. Had to swim the animals, haul the waggons across with ropes and then make foot bridges and carry over baggage. All hands very tired this evening and many of them wet through" (April 30, 1862).

After another day during which the wagons were submerged up to their beds in the creek at one crossing and nearly all the baggage soaked, they decided to abandon the wide-track wagons and pack their supplies onto one smaller wagon and their animals. They left Brigham Young, Jr.'s wagon at Yellow Creek Station, and sent Heber P. Kimball's wagon back to the city pulled by three span of mules.

Without a thought of returning to the valley, Robert urged his party on up into the mountains, meeting swollen streams and terrible conditions at every turn in the road. In his journal for May 2, he described,

> both men and animals working as hard as ever men and beasts did before. Eleven hours and a half made 5 miles, half a mile east of Yellow Creek. We were three hours getting through a drift of Snow west of Yellow Creek, twenty rods long by as many feet deep. Five hours getting across Yellow Creek bottom, the men in the cold snow water most of the time. I never saw men work more freely, although the water was so cold that their legs would be perfectly numb. The mail station we found as reported yesterday [submerged in three feet of water]. . . . The men were very tired and wet having done today what the Mail Co. could not do, and what they swore we could not. This is the 7th day from the City and we are now 70 miles, 10 miles per day and I think no other set of men could do better under the circumstances.

When they reached Fort Bridger on May 4, they found six wounded employees of the mail company recovering in the hospital. Fort Bridger had been a U.S. military post since the Utah War, and the officers stationed there provided Burton's company with oats, flour, 1,000 rounds of ammunition, tents, and camp equipment, which they loaded on pack animals.

East of Fort Bridger, they were in hostile Indian country and had to be constantly on guard. The mail stations beyond Fort Bridger were deserted with paper mail littered about. "All the stations this side of Green River look as though they were deserted in a hurry," Robert wrote in his journal May 8. That day, Robert's horse gave out and he sent it back to Lewis Robinson's ranch near Fort Bridger. On Sunday, May 11, he recorded reaching Ice Springs Station, about twenty-two miles east of South Pass, which had been robbed two weeks earlier.

> Found this station in a terrible state, mail bags cut open and their contents scattered about the premises, many letters tore open which evidently contained money. There was 22 sacks of U.S. locked mail, 8 of them cut open and rifled of their contents, 4 bags of Wells Fargo mail, 3 cut open and 27 sacks paper mail.
>
> Gathered up all the letters that we could find and secured them in leather sacks and sewed up the rents. Could not find any letters tore open that did not contain some evidence of money being enclosed. . . . This happened on Sunday, the 27th of April. Robert Kipernick, Station Keeper, says the Indians came in the evening about 10 o'clock and were carousing around the premises until after daylight. They chopped out some logs at back end of Stable, where they took out the stock. The mail was piled up in one corner of the stable. Also the trunks and clothing of the two passengers and the Station Keepers bedding. . . . The German on his way to California [was] a theatrical player. His loss was considerable having much custume, several wigs and a variety of trappings which were mostly taken or destroyed.

As most of the sacked mail was headed east, Robert's party brought it along with them, making detours to avoid fording rivers where the water was dangerously high. East of Split Rock Station, they found mail coaches still standing upon the road, riddled with bullet holes from attacks in which had drivers and passengers were killed, mail sacks burned, and harnesses cut to steal the team. All along the trail, evidence accumulated that white men were involved as well as Indians since the attackers always seemed to know which bags contained money. Robert telegraphed Fuller on May 16, 1862, that he suspected some of the depredations were the work of 30 Snakes and Bannocks, led by the Snake Pashago, but it appeared that the Indians were stealing stock while masquerading whites were stealing money from the mail stations. One station keeper was attacked by

"Indians" who spoke plain English and one even spoke German (Fisher 1929, 134).

But Robert Burton and his men were surprised to discover that someone was accusing them of the attacks. On the afternoon of May 13, they approached a camp of thirty-six very frightened men, who were traveling from Denver to the Salmon River. Having seen a note nailed to a telegraph pole at the junction of the Mormon and Oregon trails blaming the depredations on the Mormons and the Snake Indians, they expected to be taken captive by these Mormons (R. T. Burton 1856–1907, May 13, 1862). Much later in the journey, Robert saw a notice discovered by Lot Smith's command on the Three Crossings mail station which read: "The volunteer soldiers from Utah are out to make war on the Indians, the mountaineers, and squaw men, and are endeavoring to drive them out of the country and take possession of their lands" (in Fisher 1929, 45). The paper was signed by the principal mountaineers of the region including the Frenchman Plaunts and a rancher, Tim Goodell. Colonel Burton confronted Plaunts about the notice at the Platte Bridge Station, and he denied it said anything about the Mormons (R. T. Burton 1856–1903, May 14, 1862). Plaunts and other French traders all told of Pashago and his band stealing stock. A week later, Burton presided at the trial of Tim Goodell, who had been arrested and brought into the Lot Smith's camp. This old mountaineer was scared by the action taken against him but convinced Robert that he could not read or write, not even his own name, and that someone else had signed his name without his consent. He was set free and always after esteemed the Mormons for their fairness (Fisher 1929, 47–48).

At the Platte Bridge station (now Casper, Wyo.) on May 15, Robert turned over thirty-six sacks of locked mail to the mail agent, who provided a coach to carry Hooper, West and Brigham Young, Jr., on to the East. During the trip from Utah, Young decided to accompany Hooper to Washington, D. C. and received his father's permission by telegraph.

The Utah party began the return trip with two mail employees as passengers in the mail coach, a load of buffalo skins purchased from a French trader, and high hopes for an uneventful return trip. However, the first mail station they checked had been broken into by either Indians or white men; the stove, crockery and other stores were demolished. Upon reaching the Sweetwater Bridge Station, Robert recorded in his journal of May 20:

> Found that this place had been visited by some miserable rascals, since we were here in our downward trip. The telegraph batteries that were in good condition when we left, broken to pieces, tables smashed, best rooms made into stables for animals, taken away a large number of Antelope skins, a large tent, opened cache and took a large lot of harness, etc. The cache contained 45 sacks of locked mail, 35 for Cal. 10 for City. They had not harmed the mail otherwise than leaving the cache open to storms and we found the sacks very damp and mouldy. . . . This robbery is supposed to be done by some Pikes Peak Emigrants.

Two days later—after meeting with Lot Smith's company and the trial of Tim Goodell—they found the Three Crossings Stations broken into and the paper mail "shamefully used, every sack emptied and contents scattered about the premises and emigrants helping themselves to whatever they wish" (R. T. Burton 1856–1903, May 23, 1862).

Knowing that Lot Smith's volunteers were now responsible for peace-keeping, Robert was anxious to be called back to the city. His company traveled westward, picking up mail at each station (and sometimes out of the sagebrush nearby) and wiring ahead for orders. For several days no answer came, but finally on May 28 at Fort Bridger, Robert recorded they had the answer they wanted from Fuller, "Come ahead" (1856–1903, May 24–28, 1862).

The trail was much more passable now, and they met several Church wagon trains loaded with grain and supplies to replenish what they had borrowed the past thirty days. Still, to cross Yellow Creek they had to make a foot bridge out of two wagons and carry the baggage over, then swim the animals across, and haul the wagons by hand. They lunched May 31 at Kimball's Hotel and drove straight on to the valley, arriving at

8 P.M. Once again, Robert ended a hazardous and life-threatening assignment with the brief conclusion in his journal of May 31: "Safe. All well."

He was heartily welcomed home by his wives and children. In the evenings, his older boys gathered around him, begging for stories about the expedition. One story, retold to generations of Burton grandchildren, was recorded by William:

> One night they were camped in what they knew to be "Indian Country" and from signs which these frontiersmen could read they knew Indians were not far off although nothing could be seen of them. The officer in command had all animals in the center of the encampment while the men slept on the ground near them. Then double the usual number of sentries and guards were placed at near intervals about the camp.
>
> The commander made frequent trips around this sentry line urging each man to be very watchful for if one Indian with robe or blanket could get inside the guardline and between the men and their horses, the shaking of that blanket or a buffalo robe would stampede the horses and the command would be helpless. Father told me that he felt uneasy and did not lie down untill late. He had not been asleep long when some one or some thing took hold of his hair and gave it a hard pull. He sprang up and shouted Indians.
>
> As he shouted an Indian that had succeeded in crawling thru the sage brush between 2 of the sentries, jumped to his feet, dropped his robe and dashed out of the camp. The guards immediately fired at the retreating Indian. Whether in the darkness the Indian was hit they did not know. He got away.
>
> Who pulled father's hair? It was his own horse a very intelligent animal that hated the indians and had probably smelled the intruder as soon as he came near the camp and had among all those men found his own master.
>
> So the "old roan" saved the camp (W. S. Burton n.d.^{c}, 6–7)

The expeditions of Robert Burton and Lot Smith are credited with assisting the hard-pressed Union Army, keeping open an important line of communication, and demonstrating the loyalty of the Latter-day Saint people to the Union. These were the only direct operations by Utah troops during the Civil War, though not the only action in the western territories (see Vetterli 1961, 501–39).

212

Unfortunately, the Utah militia's service did not advance statehood. By the end of the summer, the U.S. Congress had rejected Utah's petition and added insult to injury by passing the Morrill Anti-bigamy Act, which President Lincoln signed July 8, 1962. Worse yet, seven companies of California volunteers under command of Colonel P. Edward Connor arrived to establish a permanent military post in the vicinity of Salt Lake City. While ostensibly the soldiers' purpose was to guard the mail routes and telegraph lines, the Saints were convinced that their real intent was surveillance of the people of Utah (CHC 5:15).

Robert's next task, however, dealt with internal dissent. While he had been on the trail between the Platte River and the Great Salt Lake Valley, an apostate group known as the Morrisites was defying both Church authority and the authority of the district court. Strong action seemed imminent, and not long after his return home, Robert was ordered, as deputy territorial U.S. marshal, to take that action.

Joseph Morris had joined the Church in England in 1847, emigrated to America with his first wife, Mary Thorpe, lived for two years in St. Louis, then for a short time in Pittsburgh where he was branch president. After his arrival in Utah in 1853, he became dissatisfied with his ward leadership and eventually turned against the Church. An enthusiastic, evangelical speaker, he was much involved with the Reformation of 1857, but seemed to preach his own brand of Latter-day Saint doctrine. He was especially opposed to polygamy. According to one of his disciples, J. R. Eardley, about that time Morris began "to declare the wonderful principles (of spiritual manifestations— especially visions and the gift of prophecy) and to denounce the errors and corruption which were destroying the spiritual life of the Church" (in Anderson and Halford 1974, 44).

Over the years until 1862, he claimed a number of revelations, some indicating that he had a divine commission as a prophet. In a series of letters written between 1857 and 1860, he directly challenged Brigham Young's leadership, asking him to "bring the matter before the people" and proposing that Young retain the office of president of the Church but relinquish the title of "prophet, seer and revelator" to him. Brigham Young ignored Morris's repeated requests (Anderson and Halford 1974, 46).

Among Morris's converts were several families from the Weber County community of Slaterville, who were reportedly experimenting with spiritualism and were receptive to a new religious experience, as well as some members of the South Weber Branch (Holley 1966, 21–41). When befriended by the South Weber bishop, Richard Cook, Morris moved his headquarters to Cook's home and began gathering followers to that area. In February 1861, Brigham Young sent Wilford Woodruff and John Taylor to a meeting of the South Weber Branch, where they excommunicated Morris and seventeen followers, including Bishop Cook and his brother John. On April 6, 1861, Morris formally organized "The Church of Jesus Christ of Saints of the Most High" (Anderson and Halford 1974, 46).

Morris gathered his followers to await the second coming of the Savior at an almost abandoned "fort" two miles west of the mouth of Weber Canyon and in the bottom lands south of the river. It was variously called Kington Fort, Kingston Fort, Morris Fort, Morris Town, and Weber Camp. This fragile collection of log houses, mud huts, covered wagons, and tents was arranged in a quadrangular area after the manner of a fort, but with open spaces between the structures and four streets entering, one from each side. A low crumbling adobe wall and a log corral partially surrounded the settlement, enclosing a bowery, a school house, and a tent used for a meeting place (Whitney 2:49).

Although the group did no proselyting, it had 507 members by the spring of 1862 (JH, June 12, 1862, 3). From the beginning, the Morrisite community came under fire from intolerant neighbors, some of them local rowdies who stole horses and stock and tried to provoke fights. The Morrisites usually endured their tormentors in silence, except for one instance when they chased several young intruders out of their settlement. The intruders swore out a complaint against eleven Morrisites and succeeded in convicting one of the eleven of assault in March 1862. Peter I. Moss was sentenced to forty days at hard labor and fined $50 plus court costs. The judgment convinced the Morrisites that they would not find justice in court, and from then on they refused warrants, writs, or other legal orders from the civil authorities. The judgment also strengthened the growing suspicion among Utahns that the Morrisites were religious fanatics who drew no distinction between right and wrong (Howard 1976, 122–23). As a result of these problems, the Morrisites formed their own militia of between 90 and 120 men with Peter Klemgard as leader (Klemgard 1977; Stuart to author, 1982). Whitney described the peculiarities he observed:

> A distinctive doctrine of the new creed was that the coming of the Savior was at hand, and that instead of sowing and reaping and following worldly pursuits, the elect people should hold themselves in daily readiness to receive Him. They were there to learn, not to labor . . . evident from their choice of a gathering place. There was scarcely any unoccupied farming land in the vicinity, and there is no intimation that any was wanted. The duties of the household were performed, and these, with occasional journeys to the canyon for wood, and to the surrounding settlements for breadstuffs comprised the sum of the temporal labors of the expectant community. . . . It was the leader's custom to receive revelations at least once a week, and his followers spent most of their time in attendance upon the meetings. All property was held in common, and though they could not but notice that their belongings were decreasing day by day through being sold or exchanged for the necessities of life, the zealous flock looked forward with contented joy to the day when the possessions of their enemies should all be given to them. It was charged that some of them, in anticipation of that day, had levied upon their neighbor's herds (Whitney 2:45).

The spiral of persecution from without and dissent from within, held in check by Joseph Morris's increasingly powerful appeals to faith, promises of the imminent millennium, and warnings of punishment to the disobedient, kept his people locked in place for the coming conflict. Between December 1861 and February 1862, he gave several specific dates for the Second Coming. His disciples would prepare for the day and gather in white robes to witness it, only to see it come and go uneventfully. Each time this happened a few more people would gather their belongings and quietly leave. As apostasies increased, Morris began receiving revelations about the treatment of apostates. First, he proclaimed that apostates could not reclaim property or goods turned over to the group. Later revelations set the penalty for apostasy at death—the only sure way to stop their wicked course (Stuart 1975, 11).

William C. Jones was a Slaterville convert who choose to leave. When he attempted to reclaim the property he had previously consecrated to the group, he was told of the new revelations. He left empty handed and bitter, vowing revenge. Not long afterward, he, John Jensen, and Louis C. Gurtson hijacked a wagon load of wheat being transported from Kingston Fort to Kaysville for milling. Morris dispatched twenty-five members of the Morrisite militia, led by Peter Klemgard, to apprehend the men and recover the wheat. They captured the men in Kaysville, brought them back in chains to the fort, and held them in a log chicken coop which was used as a jail (Howard 1976, 124; Stuart 1975, 11).

Gurtson managed to escape, but Jones and Jensen remained heavily shackled and guarded. When their wives and friends appealed to legal authorities for assistance, the stage was set for official intervention into the Morrisite community and affairs.

On May 22, 1862, while Robert Burton was recrossing Wyoming gathering mail from station ruins, deputy U.S. Marshal Judson Stoddard obtained a writ of *habeas corpus* from Territorial Chief Justice John J. Kinney, commanding Morris, John Banks, Richard Cook, and Peter Klemgard to bring the men held in custody before him. In spite of threats and warnings, Stoddard entered the Morrisite fort, obtained an audience with the leaders, and read the writ. Morris and his deputies refused the writ, letting the paper drop to the ground. A Morrisite poured a shovelful of live coals on the paper, burning it where it lay (Anderson and Halford 1974, 48).

For nearly two weeks, there was no further action although the wives and friends of Jones and Jensen repeatedly importuned the officials to act.

In the meantime, Robert returned to the valley and was drawn into the discussion of what action would be taken against the Morrisites. He was informed that "The leaders of this people defied the authority of the law. . . . Among other depredations they arrested and imprisoned several citizens and sentenced them to death without trial, refusing to surrender them on the order of the court" (n.d.ª, 39).

The next official action came on June 10, when Kinney issued a writ to either U.S. Marshal Henry W. Lawrence or Robert T. Burton, ordering the arrest of Joseph Morris and four other high Morrisite officials. Lawrence, who was opposed to an armed confrontation with the Morrisites, had already left the territory for the East, leaving Robert as acting U.S. marshal, with the other deputy Theodore McKean as next in command (Howard 1976, 124–25).

In later years, blame for the subsequent events at Kingston Fort was variously assigned to Judge Kinney, Frank Fuller, territorial secretary and acting-governor, Brigham Young, and Robert T. Burton. Reportedly Kinney was incensed when he learned that the legal writ had not only been disregarded, but burned as well, and he appealed to Fuller to call out the militia to act as a *posse comitatus* to enforce the process of the court. Kinney later insisted that he did not take any steps without counseling with Brigham Young. Conflicting accounts exist of almost every step taken from June 10 to 15, and it is probably impossible to know or understand today exactly what did happen.[3]

Brigham Young, according to Whitney, "was very much averse to the execution of the process, fearing it might result in bloodshed" (2:53–54). Robert described similar fears in his biography:

> After repeated petitions and affidavits had been made, Judge Kinney, chief justice of the Territory, came to me as acting Territorial marshall saying, "Mr. Burton, you must go and serve some

writs on these lawless men (naming them) as the law must be honored and that he could not withstand longer the petitions of those whose husbands and friends were doomed to death by the lawless band."

I at first refused to go but after repeated urgeing by the judge and Governor I consented on the condition that I should have a strong overwhelming posse knowing the kind of people to be dealt with, but thinking this would awe them into submission to the law and there would be no bloodshed.

On the 10th day of June affidavits were issued by Dept. Territorial Marshall J. L. Stoddard and writs issued by the district court and an attempt made by the marshall to serve them. (See district court record.)

The next day other writs were issued directed to me as Territorial Marshall to take posse and arrest and bring offenders before the court in Salt Lake City (n.d.[a], 39–40).

This second writ, issued on June 11, was a writ of attachment specifying the offenses of the accused. Kinney also urged Fuller to order out the militia. Fuller did so, requesting Daniel H. Wells to furnish "sufficient military force to act as a *posse comitatus*, 'for the arrest of the offenders, the vindication of justice and the enforcement of the law' " (Whitney 2:53).

On the morning of June 12, "the proper arrangements having been made," Robert T. Burton left Salt Lake "with an ample force" and rode north toward Kingston Fort (n.d.[a], 41). That ample force included 100 men from Salt Lake, 100 men from Davis County, and 50 men from Weber County. Some reports cite up to 1,000 men being finally gathered into the posse, but no reliable resources substantiate that figure. Volunteers did join the posse as it moved through Davis County, and many citizens of Davis and Weber counties gathered on the bluffs and banks of the Weber River to watch this affair, but the posse itself had no more than 250 members (Stuart 1982). It consisted of a company of riflemen, one full company and a detachment of artillery with a six-pound gun and a brass howitzer (Anderson 1981, 119).

A large posse, however, was exactly what Joseph Morris wanted to fulfill his prophecies that the Lord would appear to fight the Morrisites' battles when the enemy came up against them (Anderson 1981, 120).

After the posse took position on the bluffs south of Kingston Fort, Robert sent a Morrisite herdsboy into the fort with a ultimatum directed to the Morrisites named in the writ, demanding them to surrender themselves and their prisoners within thirty minutes and warning them that if they intended to resist, "you are hereby required to remove your women and children; and all persons peaceably disposed are hereby notified to forthwith leave your encampment, and are informed that they can find protection with the posse" (in Anderson 1981, 120).

Mark Forscutt, one of Morris' twelve apostles, wrote that on the morning of June 13, Morris received a revelation that affirmed the army "to be that threatened so long. These men on the "bench" would demand the giving up of God's servants. They were to be denied. The enemy would then attempt the destruction of the saints; but God would deliver them out of their hands. None of the faithful should be destroyed" (in Anderson 1981, 121).

After the herdsboy delivered the message to Morris' counselor John Banks, the Morrisites gathered in the bowery. Another counselor, Richard Cook was just asking which command the people should obey, Burton's proclamation or the revelation, when the sound of the posse's cannon was heard and a ball crashed into the bowery killing two women and wounding a young girl. Hostilities were begun and the assemblage scattered (Whitney 2:54–55).

The accounts differ widely as to how much time had elapsed between the sending of the message and the firing of the first shot. Whitney wrote:

> It is certain that at least one hour, and very likely two, elapsed after Banks received the Marshal's proclamation before a shot was fired. The commanding officer was so averse to resorting to extremities that he repeatedly sent couriers from his position on the bluff down toward the fort to see if there were any signs of compliance or surrender. At length he ordered the officer in command of the artillery to fire two shots over the fort as a warning to the belligerents.

> The first shot passed high above the garrison and struck the oppo-
> site bluff. The second struck in a field between the posse and the
> fort, bounded in and did the deadly work in the bowery. Of this,
> however, nothing was known to the posse until after the surrender
> (Whitney 2:54–55).

One historian reports that several of Burton's soldiers testified the cannon was fired thirty minutes after the herdsboy was
given the note; Richard Young's 1890 history contended it was
two hours after the message reached the fort; Robert T. Burton
said he waited ninety minutes before ordering firing to com-
mence (Anderson 1981, 122).

Confusion reigned within the fort as the as yet unarmed
Morrisites scattered to shelter; then taking their arms, the battle
was underway. Robert testified at his trial in 1877 that firing
from small arms came from the fort, perhaps twenty minutes
after the first cannon was fired, and he positioned a "considerable force" on the east and west sides of the fort and returned
the fire (in Anderson 1981, 129). However, one of his men,
John C. Chambers, recalled that after the firing of the cannon a
rifle company was sent to take possession of a ravine and given
orders to fire catching the Morrisites before they could begin
their assault (JH, June 13, 1862, 2). During the first day's siege,
two Morrisite families ran from the fort and surrendered. Late
in the afternoon, posse member Jared Smith was killed. When
Robert Burton reported this to Fuller by messenger that evening,
Fuller replied: "The shedding of blood in resistance to civil authority renders execution of the law imperative. The service of the
writs submitted to you is expected at your hands and you have
been empowered to call to your aid a sufficient force for the
purpose. Let your acts be tempered with mercy; but see that
the laws are vindicated" (in JH, June 14, 1862, 2).

A heavy rain set in on Friday night and fell all day Saturday, June 14, preventing anything beyond aimless exchanges of
fire. However, Sunday, June 15, dawned bright and clear. John
C. Chambers writes:

> The rain having cased in the night, it was deemed wisdom by
> Col. Burton to renew operations and vigorously to storm the fort.

> The troops were accordingly called together, and after prayer by Bishop Cunningham were briefly addressed by the Colonel, who said, in substance that if the business they were called upon to do was right, it would be right to do it on Sunday, and if it were not right, it would be wrong to do it on any day. So he wished them to be prepared for a good day's work; he instructed the officers to be careful with their men and urged the men to be obedient to their officers, and he felt positive no lives would be lost (JH, June 15, 1862, 1–2).

Although it is disputed which side began firing first on Sunday, the attacks and resistance continued throughout the day. Anticipation was high among the Morrisites. Anderson summarized, "The advancing posse, the shortage of food, the fatigue, and the dwindling supply of ammunition seemed to conform perfectly to a revelation Joseph Morris had received that very morning. The revelation was profoundly optimistic, assuring the faithful Morrisites that all would be well and that Christ would deliver them that very day—for after all, it was Sunday, and Christ was the Lord of the Sabbath" (1981, 137).

Late in the afternoon, Robert ordered an assault on the west side of the fort where the Morrisites were firing through "portholes" in several cabins. Drawing upon his earliest military experience in Utah Valley in 1850, Robert had a rude but effective moving barricade built, consisting of a shield of brush and boards supported by wagon wheels. Manned by a dozen or more soldiers, the ominous-appearing battery so surprised and dismayed the defenders, who thought the machine was filled with explosives, that they ran from the westside cabins, allowing occupation by the posse. The Morrisites realized further resistance was hopeless and raised a flag of surrender (Anderson 1981, 139).

It was nearly sunset when Robert T. Burton saw the white flag; he moved forward to meet it accompanied by two men and a bugler. He insisted upon an unconditional surrender to the bearer of the flag and told the Morrisites to show acceptance of these terms by stacking their arms in the open space in the fort. As he entered the fort with a small force of men, he called for Joseph Morris and others named in the writ. Mormon and Morrisite descriptions of what happened next differ greatly. Wilford Woodruff's journal for June 18, 1862, reports Robert Burton's statement of that date to Judge Kinney:

> I placed some men to take Charge of the arms or guard them. Then Mr Morris made some remarks and asked me what I wanted. I said I wanted all the men who had taken up arms against me. Then Morris Said to the Croud, "all who will stand by me to the death lift up their hand and all as far as I could see lifted up their hands & made a rush as though they were going to the school House or some place to defend themselves. I ordered Morris to stop several times & followed him up. I had no arms but my revolver and as He would not stop I stoped him with my revolver. He was shot dead. Banks was also shot through the neck from which wound He died. Two women were shot at the same time which I vary much regret but it Could not be helped (WW 6:59–60).

Whitney's history adds these details:

> Nearly a hundred men confronted the deputy marshal and his slender escort. The moment was one of extreme peril. To dally was to court assassination for himself and the party. Twice he commanded the frenzied leaders to halt. They heeded not, and the struggle for the possession of the firearms had already begun. It was then that the commanding officer, seizing the pistol in his holster, fired twice at the leaders, while several of his associates did likewise. In all, perhaps a dozen shots were fired. When the smoke cleared away Morris was seen to be dead, Banks was mortally wounded, and two women, Mrs. Bowman and Mrs. Swanee, lay lifeless on the ground near their prophet. It is said that one of them hung upon his neck as he moved toward the arms, and several heroically sought to throw themselves between him and danger (Whitney 2:56–57).

The Morrisite War was over.

While Robert Burton maintained that "the loss of life [was] much to my regret" (n.d.ᵃ, 41), his Morrisite accusers, who eventually brought him to trial for the murders of the two women, and modern historians, who have tried to piece together the events in the fort after the surrender, have harshly judged him. He has been accused of "haste and overzealousness," "overreaction," and with "vengeance," with not trying to take Morris alive when he "could easily" have done so, and of murdering Bella Bowman because she called him a "blood-thirsty wretch" (see Anderson 1981, 141, 156; Howard 1976, 128–30; Anderson and Halford 1974, 52) In retrospect, Robert's original opinion that a military solution should not have been attempted seems to have been correct (Whitney 2:54). Once he was convinced to go, Robert gave to this assignment the same zeal and dedication that he had all previous campaigns. It is unfortunate that the second warning shot from the cannon went astray and also that the communications between the posse and the Morrisites were so inadequate. Robert Burton did not know that most within the fort truly believed this was the last great battle before the Second Coming and that when their ammunition was gone and all seemed lost, the Lord would appear to fight their battle and subdue the enemy. Undoubtedly both sides deeply regretted and were surprised at the outcome of the encounter.

Two days later the posse marched approximately ninety male prisoners into Salt Lake and turned them over to the authorities who admitted them to bail. Many of them found employment at Fort Douglas among the soldiers while awaiting trial, although some forfeited their bail and left the territory. Seventy-three Morrisites were convicted in district court in March 1863, seven for murder and sixty-six for resisting arrest, but they were almost immediately pardoned by a new governor, Stephen S. Harding. Harding sided with the anti-Mormon faction in Utah and the Mormons considered his pardon an effort to annoy them. Shortly thereafter, from the Morrisites who associated with the soldiers at Fort Douglas, affidavits began surfacing reporting "bloodthirstiness" and "cruelty" in the Marshal Burton's actions at Kingston Fort almost a year earlier. These men apparently had much encouragement from the federal authorities and Fort Douglas soldiers to decide what they would say happened (Whitney 2:100). It was not until 1863 that the Church was accused of persecuting the Morrisites or that Brigham Young's jealousy of Morris's following was suggested as a basis for the events at the Kingston Fort. In May of 1863, General Connor established a military post on the Bear River in Idaho, offering protection to Morrisite families who would go with him to build the community there. Eighty families, about 200 persons, went with the army and established Soda Springs, Idaho (CHC 5:52).

Robert Burton's actions were not questioned in 1862. After delivering his prisoners to court authorities, both Judge Kinney and acting-governor Fuller complimented him for the able manner in which he had discharged his duty and with so little loss of life (*Deseret News*, June 18 and 24, 1862). However, in 1870 he was indicted for murder in the deaths of Bella Bowman, Mrs. Swanee, and Joseph Morris. This was at a time, according to Lorenzo Snow, "when the judges of the Territory commenced their judicial oppression against the people of the Territory by ruling out the Territorial officers and ruling against the Territorial jury law (Snow 1873, 2) The "judicial oppression" was halted for a time by the celebrated Clinton v. Engelbrecht decision, in which the U.S. Supreme Court declared that the grand jury which brought this action and many others over a period of eighteen months was illegally drawn. All criminal proceedings arising in 1870 were declared void.

Seven years later another indictment was presented by a grand jury of the Third District Court. Robert was arrested at his home on July 27, 1877, and would have spent that night in the penitentiary except that Daniel H. Wells offered any amount of bail bond necessary to secure Robert's attendance when required by the court. Nineteen months later Robert was brought to trial on the charge of murdering Bella Bowman. The trial received much attention since Robert was now a counselor in the Presiding Bishopric of the Church and a prominent citizen of the city and state. The proceedings were covered in all Salt Lake newspapers and discussed on the streets of the city.

The prosecution, which was conducted by U.S. District Attorney P. T. Van Zile and his assistant, James H. Beatty, sought to prove that the killing of Joseph Morris and his followers was unwarranted, that Burton shot Morris because he said he would not give up and Mrs. Bowman because she called him a "bloodthirsty murderer" after he shot Morris. Robert felt that the testimony of the witnesses for the prosecution was full of bitterness and falsehood, but throughout the case he remained optimistic of acquittal. The jury was half gentile and half Mormon.

Robert's counsel included Judge Frank Tilford, a non-Mormon, Judge J. G. Sutherland, and three attorneys. Judge Sutherland's opening remarks referred to the one-sided manner in which the prosecution had presented the case. They had given no indication that Robert Burton had gone to the fort as an officer of the law and that he acted under judicial orders, orders of the very court in which he was being tried. Defense witnesses, who were called to refute much of the testimony of the prosecution witnesses, stated that Burton fired only twice and that the women were killed by accident. Robert took the witness stand, explaining in great detail the events of June 13 to 15, 1862, and his estimation of the situation within the fort after the surrender.

The courtroom was packed with many anxious friends when Judge Tilford arose on the morning of March 4, to deliver the closing argument for the defense. Robert Burton liked what he heard and noted in his journal that the court, jury, and spectators listened with marked attention to Judge Tilford's argument (1856–1907, March 4, 1879).

> He recounted the incidents leading up to the capture of Kington Fort and the death of Joseph Morris, and showed that the defendant, as an officer of the law, was justified in all that he did at that time; that he acted moderately, humanely and honorably, taking every possible precaution against the shedding of blood, and only at the last moment, when his own life and the lives of his men were in jeopardy, resorting of necessity to extreme measures. He also showed how witnesses for the prosecution—most of them Morrisites—had contradicted themselves and each other in their testimony, and expressed his convictions that one witness—Dan Camomile—had deliberately perjured himself in stating that the whole posse were inside the fort at the time Morris was killed and that Mrs. Bowman was shot by the defendant, on calling him "a d____d blood thirsty dog." It had not been proven that the defendant shot Mrs. Bowman, who fell in the midst of the melee, killed by accident. In conclusion Judge Tilford said: "We demand his acquittal as due to the welfare of the Territory, the security of life, and the enforcement of right;

we demand it as due to the court whose mandate placed him in the very peril that compelled the homicide; we demand it as due to the law whose process he was executing when resistance was offered; we demand it as due to humanity, whose noblest impulses are outraged by the prosecution of one whose only offense consisted of discharging his duty" (Whitney 3:43–44).

Prosecutor Van Zile had the last say, but Robert found that his words were "bitter, but not much argument" (1856–1907, March 4, 1879). He also thought that Chief Justice Schaeffer's charge to the jury was "honorable and fair and was virtually an acquital," yet he had some anxious hours the next two days while the jury was out. During that time he wrote in his journal, "I was left in suspense all day. Jury still hanging out not coming to an agreement, some one or two determined not to agree. Great excitement on the St. with all parties gentiles and Mormons" (1856–1907, March 6, 1879).

When the jury came back on the morning of the third day with a verdict of not guilty,[4] there was much celebrating. "News flew like lightning," Robert recorded on March 7. "I received the congratulations of friends in and out of the city. I called in my Counsel and other friends and members of the Bar to the Bank building where we had some wine. My family came together at 3 PM and dined with me. Had a very joyous time together, also many friends came to see me."

The *Deseret Evening News* and *Salt Lake Herald* newspapers published lengthy assessments of the trial, the *News* concluding that:

The trial of General Robert T. Burton, which has attracted so much attention for some time, was fitly closed this morning by a verdict of "not guilty," which we believe will be cordially endorsed by all classes of the people of this Territory, the only exception being a very few individuals, whose opinions have no real weight and who are swayed by unreasoning and groundless prejudice (March 7, 1879).

The March 9, 1879 issue of the *Herald* laid the entire episode to rest:

DISMISSED: District Attorney Van Zile, in court yesterday moved that the two cases against General Robert T. Burton for the murder of Morrisites, which were still untried [Mrs. Swanee and Morris], be dismissed, and good and sufficient cause for the motion appearing, the cases were accordingly dismissed. This action is only in accordance with general expectation and satisfactorily settles a matter that has long agitated the public. The friends of General Burton and those acquainted with the facts of the case were confident that the issue would result as it has and now that the affair has been thoroughly ventilated, it is to be expected that the various discussions and opinions in the matter will be at an end, and the whole case be allowed to die out, as in justice, it should have done years ago.

Notes

1. It is interesting to note that Robert T. Burton remained a Seventy and was not ordained a High Priest until September 2, 1875, after he served eight years as a counselor and eight years as a bishop. See R. T. Burton n.d.[b], Jensen 1:238, and R. T. Burton, High Priest's certificate, copy on p. 128.

2. The hotel still stands today north of Interstate 80 and east of Kimball's Junction. It has been owned by the Bitner family since 1908. See *Deseret News*, July 25, 1977, C1–2.

3. C. LeRoy Anderson has written an important scholarly study of the Morrisites, *For Christ Will Come Tomorrow: The Saga of the Morrisites*, Logan: Utah State University Press, 1981. Other sources are also used and cited in the bibliography. This chapter is based on Robert T. Burton's journals and personal history and his contribution to Orson F. Whitney's *History of Utah*, 2:48–57 and 3:35–44.

4. Anderson states the preponderance of evidence seems to support this verdict. Citing Burton's "honorable" character and the sudden and confused circumstances surrounding the deaths of Morris, Banks, and the two women, he concludes "The women were probably killed accidentally, and quite possibly by someone other than Burton. It must be remembered that Burton was on horseback and as such had to manage his horse as well as shoot at moving targets. . . . Actually, most accounts agree that there was renewed firing by several posse members when Burton fired at Morris, and at least eight or ten shots were fired by the posse. There is no doubt that Morris fell under Burton's bullets, but in all likelihood the others were shot by other posse members. . . . Even if Burton's bullets actually did strike one or both of the women, it was probably an unfortunate accident resulting from the attempt to stop Morris" (1981, 155–56).

Time for Family and a New Occupation, 1862–69

The 1860s after the Civil War were relatively calm years in Utah Territory, but Robert T. Burton found himself "constantly engaged." He was a husband and father, assessor and tax collector, sheriff, city councilman, military officer, and bishop's counselor; during these years he also became a businessman and a bishop. His sons were becoming young men and he spent much time instructing them in the fine points of horsemanship and working beside them at factory and farm. While he could not have foreseen that he would be gone from home frequently in future years, he trained his sons early to responsibly assume his duties.

When Robert Burton wrote his own brief biography, he wrote only nine sentences about the years between 1862 and 1869. He mentioned his service as federal collector of internal revenue, Salt Lake City council member, and Salt Lake County sheriff, announced his election as major general in the Utah Militia commanding the Salt Lake military district, and told of a new partnership to build and operate a woolen mill. In conclusion, he wrote: "Business accumulated on my hands very much with the various duties growing out of all these offices which added to the duties growing out of my Ecclesiastical position, Bishop of the 15th Ward etc., [and] kept me constantly engaged" (n.d.[a], 43).

However, his oldest son William S. Burton wrote much about these precious family years when Robert could take time from his church and community duties to be with his daughter, Theresa, and his older sons (1931 and n.d.[c]). He schooled the boys in horsemanship, including breaking horses for riding and for use as teams. Robert was very particular about the care, training, and use of his horses. He taught his sons to handle mules, to care for other stock, to build, and to farm. Robert was not their only teacher. Maria was skilled at butchering and taught William how to handle their beef and pork, including how to smoke the pork and dry the beef. Sarah had been reared to run a farm home and she taught the children to make butter and cheese, raise chickens, and other farm chores. The Burton children learned to work early and shared their chores equally, as well as their outings and amusements. Robert also taught his children self-respect, responsibility, perseverance, consideration for others, respect for their mother, their "aunts" and siblings, and devotion to the gospel and to modern Church leaders.

Robert trusted his sons and relied on them. William recalled when his father took him out of school to drive a team he would not trust to a hired man, although William was just thirteen years old.

> One of the horses in the team he wanted me to drive was father's favorite saddle horse, a sorrel called "Doc," a horse father kept just for his own riding and very seldom allowed a harness to be put on, nor do I remember anyone ever riding him other than father and me. As I got in the wagon and father handed me the reins he said, "Don't you let anyone else handle their reins and don't you let go of them until you are back home and the team is unhitched from the wagon." Then turning to the man he said, "You are to load and unload and let this boy handle the team and he will tell you what to do if anything more than I have already told you (1931, 5).

The Burton sons responded to their father's trust by working hard, remembering the details of animal care, and never knowingly letting him down.

Robert, who loved and valued a fine horse, was known throughout the valley for his animals. During the middle 1860s he acquired a fine brood mare known as "Doll." She was travelling west to California when a local boy, considered a "half wit," stole her as the party rested in Salt Lake City. The travelers reported their loss, but it was not until they reached California that Sheriff Burton found the horse and the thief. The boy's parents paid the California emigrants for the horse, which was in foal by a thoroughbred, then sold it to Theodore McKean. McKean really wanted Robert's fine saddle horse, so he offered to trade the mare and $150 for it. McKean thought the mare was windbroken, but Robert knew she was not and agreed to the deal. Doll lived for twenty-four years and bore some fourteen or fifteen colts, many of them prizewinners at territorial fairs. Robert gave his sons Doll's colts to raise and train (W. S. Burton n.d.^{c}, 41–44).

By 1862, Robert and his wives had twelve sons and one daughter, Theresa. William S., Robert T., Jr., Charles S., John H., LaFayette G., and Albert T. were Maria's sons. Albert died when he was nineteen months old on August 31, 1863, but no details survive of his death. Sarah's three sons were Henry F., Franklin G., and Alfred J.; Susan's were Willard C., Hosea M., and George W. Two daughters were born in the spring of 1864: Alice Maria born to Sarah on April 23, and Florence May to Maria two weeks later on May 9. On February 15, 1865, Susan delivered her fourth son, Walter James. In August 1866, two more children were added to the family—Mary Amelia (born to Maria on August 11) and Lyman Wells (born to Sarah on August 14). Susan's last child and only daughter, Sarah Elizabeth (Lizzie), was born February 29, 1868. Later that year, Sarah had another boy on December 29, 1868, named Elbert Turner. Thus, by 1869, the family included nineteen living children, fourteen boys and five girls.[1]

By 1864, Robert had begun the custom of taking one or more of his children with him when he was going to the farm, to the canyon for wood, on a journey with Brigham Young, and so forth. In the fall of 1864, Robert was asked to guard

Brigham Young on his annual trip to the southern settlements. As several of Brigham Young's teenage children were going on the tour, Robert invited sixteen-year-old Theresa and fourteen-year-old William to accompany him. The trip would seem long and uncomfortable to modern teenagers, but for Theresa and William it was a grand vacation, even though William had to be responsible for the principal baggage wagon and its team of mules.

Visits from President Young were community celebrations, times for feasting and rejoicing, and Theresa and William delighted in the receptions at each of the thirty-seven settlements. Schools were dismissed and children and teachers lined the streets to greet the arriving party. In the larger communities, companies of horsemen and bands formed welcoming parties; and more than once, "platoons of beautiful girls dressed in white" escorted the company into the city center. Fillmore residents favored the party with a banquet that included "armful after armful of the choicest fruits, meats, and vegetables of every variety" plus custard pies, frosted cakes, preserved fruits, and other delicacies. A dance was held in the elaborately decorated Capitol Building and actors furnished comical intermission entertainment (Arrington 1985, 309). Days later, Theresa and William enjoyed fresh fruits from the harvest in St. George, Utah's "Dixie," and were amazed to see cotton growing, harvested, and used by the Saints. Perhaps the best part of the trip was arriving back in the valley where a large party of Salt Lakers waited at Gardner's mill on Big Cottonwood Creek to welcome them home. Members of the city council, brass and martial bands, and hundreds of citizens lined the street and fell in with the company to escort them to Brigham's home (Arrington 1985, 309-10). It took days for the two Burton children to tell all the exciting details and stories of the tour which lasted twenty-nine days and covered 700-800 miles. The *Deseret News* reported "The reception given to the President and his company evidenced the universal confidence and good feeling of the people towards the constituted authorities of the Church" (in Nibley 1937, 392).

This feeling contrasted with the spirit in the Salt Lake valley where the California Volunteers, led by Patrick Edward Connor, and the judiciary appointed by President Lincoln were conspiring to keep the Saints in their place. Connor had filed the first mining claim in Bingham Canyon in September 1863, and visualized a great gold rush. On July 21, 1864, he wrote from his Camp Douglas headquarters to his friend Lieutenant Colonel R. C. Drum, Assistant Adjutant-General of the United States in San Francisco, outlining his strategy:

> As set forth in former communications, my policy in this Territory has been to invite hither a large Gentile and loyal population, sufficient by peaceful means and through the ballot-box to overwhelm the Mormons by mere force of numbers, and thus wrest from the Church—disloyal and traitorous to the core—the absolute and tyrannical control of temporal and civil affairs, or at least a population numerous enough to put a check on the Mormon authorities, and give countenance to those who are striving to loosen the bonds with which they have been so long oppressed. With this view, I have bent every energy and means of which I was possessed, both personal and official, towards the discovery and development of the mining resources of the Territory, using without stint the soldiers of my command, whenever and wherever it could be done without detriment to the public service (in Tullidge c.1886, 328–330).

Connor expected opposition from Brigham Young and other Church leaders and ostentatiously offered "protection" to the prospectors. Brigham Young had already made public his policy of benign neglect in October Conference, 1863, just weeks after the first claims were found in Bingham Canyon:

> If the Lord permits gold mines to be opened here he will overrule it for the good of his saints and the building up of his kingdom. We have a great many friends who are out of this church—who have not embraced the gospel. . . . We have a great many friends, and if the Lord suffers gold to be discovered here, I shall be satisfied that it is for the purpose of embellishing and adorning this temple which we contemplate building, and we may use some of it as a circulating medium (JD 10:253).

President Young also urged the members of the Church in numerous addresses to remember their common-sense duties—

building homes, making farms, planting orchards, establishing home manufacture, developing coal and iron mines and in other ways working to establish a great commonwealth to which Saints from around the world could gather. From the Tabernacle pulpit on October 25, 1863, he discounted the "glory of gold."

> Can you not see that gold and silver rank among the things that we are the least in want of? We want an abundance of wheat and fine flour, of wine and oil, and of every choice fruit that will grow in our climate; we want silk, wool, cotton, flax and other textile substances of which cloth can be made; we want vegetables of various kinds to suit our constitutions and tastes, and the products of flocks and herds; we want the coal and the iron that are concealed in these ancient mountains, the lumber from our sawmills, and the rock from our quarries; these are some of the great staples to which kingdoms owe their existence, continuance, wealth, magnificence, splendor, glory and power; in which gold and silver serve as mere tinsel to give the finishing touch to all this greatness. The colossal wealth of the world is founded upon and sustained by the common staples of life (in Nibley 1937, 384).

Robert attended the Sunday tabernacle meetings and it is likely his loud "amen" would have rung out after such a discourse. His commitment to Brigham's practical gospel led him to establish several business ventures beginning in 1864 and 1866.

Connor's great gold rush failed to materialize. Some of his California friends invested in the construction of several smelters, but the mining industry developed gradually because the gold supply was small compared to the abundance of low-grade silver and copper. It took the railroad and vastly improved refining methods to make mining profitable in Utah. Connor was greatly disappointed. However, as the months passed, he discovered the Church did not oppose his mining interests and its leaders were not "disloyal and traitorous," and he became less bitter.

President Lincoln's second inauguration in 1865 offered an opportunity to bridge some differences between the soldiers and the citizens. Robert and his associates on the city council discussed this in February 1865, and issued the following resolution/invitation on March 2:

> Whereas, Saturday, the 4th, instant, being the day of inauguration of the president of the United States; and whereas, also by reason of the many recent victories of the armies of our country; therefore, be it Resolved by the city council . . . that we cheerfully join in the public celebration and rejoicings of that day throughout the United States, and we cordially invite the citizens and organizations, military and civil of the territory, county and city, to unite on that occasion, etc.
>
> (signed) A. O. Smoot, Mayor (CHC 5:70)

March 4 was a day of "general and patriotic jubilee" that surprised the editors of the anti-Mormon *Union Vedette*, who gave an enthusiastic report of the day's proceedings as did the *Utah Telegraph* and the *Deseret News*. Undoubtedly Robert was at the head of his unit during the mile-long procession, which included military and civil officers mounted and in carriages, California Volunteer and Nauvoo Legion companies, and many citizens both walking and riding. Near a platform erected on First South, the citizens thronged around the military formations to hear orations from John Titus, chief justice of the territory, and William H. Hooper, Utah's delegate to Congress. Mayor Smoot, George A. Smith, Governor James Doty and General Connor occupied seats of honor on the platform. Such a show of unity was unique (CHC 5:70).

Little more than six weeks later, these same citizens and soldiers once again thronged the downtown streets to mourn and honor the assassinated Lincoln. Robert Burton, one of only two Mormons appointed to federal position by President Lincoln, was selected a member of the committee to arrange for the day of mourning set by Congress as April 19. On that day, 3,000 citizens and soldiers crowded into the Tabernacle to hear eulogies by Elder Amasa Lyman and Reverend Norman McLeod, chaplain of Camp Douglas. The Latter-day Saints greatly admired President Lincoln, whose policy toward them was expressed in three words, "Let them alone" (CHC 5:70). Though his death brought sorrow and anxiety, it also created a brief interlude of good feelings between the gentiles and Saints in the Great Salt Lake Valley.

Outside the valley, especially in central Utah, the settlers and the Indians were on the brink of war. Although Colonel O. H. Irish, superintendent of Indian affairs in the territory, with Brigham Young's assistance, negotiated an important treaty with many principal tribal chiefs on June 7–9, 1865, chief Black Hawk and his warriors or subchiefs were not parties to it. One of them, known as "Jake," son of the late Chief Arapeen, had been insulted in Manti in April sparking raids and revenge among those who followed Black Hawk (CHC 5:14–50). In April and May in San Pete and Sevier counties, Black Hawk's band first raided the cattle herds killing the herdsmen, then attacked the militia mustered into service against the Indians, and finally began killing settlers, including women and children. Three years of hostilities ensued in central and southern Utah, known as the Black Hawk War[2]. Though Robert did not lead troops in this war, he was involved in sending soldiers and supplies from Salt Lake and Davis Military Districts which were essential to the militia's success in these Indian campaigns, and twice was near the scene of attacks while on military business.

In October 1865, General Daniel H. Wells, who had been in Europe, revived and reorganized the Utah militia. Major General George D. Grant had resigned, and Robert was elected to fill his position, which included command of the Salt Lake Military District. Soon thereafter, he mustered the troops at Camp Utah, southwest of the city near the Jordan River, for three days of drilling on November 1–3. Apparently William attended the camp, because, on November 3, Robert wrote Maria that William was coming into the city to get her, Sarah, Theresa, and Merinda Young. He included some instructions for his men at the office and then added a fatherly postscript: "If you and the children would like to see the troops in line, watch when we come to the City and form on one of those Streets. Be in the Cariage and you can have a good view." In spite of his great responsibilities, he did not forget his children, who were delighted for a chance to see their father, the "General," and a parade.

Black Hawk's band in early 1865 was small—twenty to thirty warriors—but a few successful raids brought him prestige and his force grew to over a hundred men by winter, and to three hundred by spring 1866 (Whitney 2:191–92). Twenty-five whites were killed in the raids of 1865 (CHC 5:156). When the first three attacks in 1866 took seven more settlers, General Wells mustered all the men of Piute, Sevier, and Sanpete counties into the service as cavalry and infantry, and called on units from neighboring counties to help also. Many settlements had to be abandoned and Saints gathered to the larger communities where new forts were being built. Finally, companies from the northern counties were called out. On April 28, 1866, Robert T. Burton sent the first northern unit, a cavalry company from Salt Lake commanded by Heber P. Kimball (Nauvoo Legion, April 28, 1866). This company marched south, reporting to General Warren Snow, commander of Sanpete Military District, who sent them to assist settlers in Piute and Sevier counties who were moving back to Sanpete. In June, General Wells went into the field of action at Sanpete, establishing headquarters at Gunnison. He was accompanied by John R. Winder's cavalry company; an infantry company from Salt Lake followed. Through the summer, Indian attacks continued, but the battles between militia and Indians were indecisive (Whitney 2:196–99).

Robert sent fresh troops and animals from Salt Lake and other northern districts as needed during the summer. He was very particular about the soldiers chosen to go. His handwritten note to Franklin D. Richards on June 10, 1866, showed his personal interest in sending the best men for the campaign.

> Dear General
> You will excuse me for again refering to a matter refered to before in relation to so many inexperienced Boys going south on this detail. I have learned (how true I do not know) that from some of the districts Boys have been selected almost entirely. Fearing Monday might be to late [to] remedy this without giving feelings perhaps by a note

to the Cols something might be done and not interfere with the march of the Troops Monday if they were needed to move at that time.

Yours Truly R. T. Burton

P. S. From presant indications there may be need of good men at Sanpeet before they get there. RTB

A month later, July 7, Robert wrote General Wells in Gunnison that it was difficult to find animals for the cavalry which were not needed for farming, but he had sent sixty men "well armed and mounted. They are as fine looking lot of recruits as you would wish to see." The northern units returned to their homes in the fall of 1866, but were called out again in the summer of 1867.

Attacks were not limited just to central Utah, but ranged from Washington County in the south to Wasatch County in the north. On May 18, 1866, a band of marauders succeeded in driving off a herd of horses in Wasatch County. A few days later, Robert T. Burton, who was in the area to reorganize the local militia, took his military aid and a party of cavalry and thoroughly, but unsuccessfully, scoured the area for signs of the Indians (Whitney 2:200–01).

In late July 1867, General Burton rode to Sanpete County to inspect the troops, which were then under command of General William B. Pace of Provo. There had been no attacks in June and July, but during Robert's visit, Indians raided the herdgrounds at Springtown and attacked three men who were going to their hay fields. Generals Burton and Pace reported to Brigham Young on August 14, 1867, that one settler was killed and thirty horses stolen. A second settler died later from wounds suffered in this incident. The Indians were chased and defeated by the Mt. Pleasant and Ephraim cavalry and a number of the Indians killed (Whitney 2:208).

Although Colonel F. H. Head, new superintendent of Indian affairs, made peace with Black Hawk in August 1867, some of his followers continued the hostilities in the spring and summer of 1868. General peace with the Indians was achieved and a treaty signed at Strawberry Valley in August 1868 (CHC 5:152–53). The federal government refused to help the Utah militia during these Indian troubles and also refused to compensate the territory for the expenses of the campaign. The only recognition given the Black Hawk War veterans was from the Utah State legislature which awarded a medal of honor and $50,000 for the veterans in 1912–13 (CHC 5:157).

As the population of Utah Territory grew during the 1860s and new settlements were colonized, Brigham Young encouraged Church members to become self-sufficient, to develop home manufacturing and mills, and greatly reduce the necessity of importing goods from the east.

Responding to this challenge, Robert initiated several manufacturing enterprises. First, he formed a partnership with Charles Henry Wilcken to erect a grist mill and a saw mill in Daniels Canyon, southeast of Heber City. Wilcken came west with Johnston's Army, but deserted, was captured by Robert's men and brought to Salt Lake in October 1857. He was baptized into the Church in December 1857 and moved to Heber Valley (Seifrit 1987, 310–11). According to William S. Burton, the mills were built in 1864 (n.d.ᶜ, 24). Neither he or his father record the extent of Robert's participation in this venture, but perhaps he provided funds and labor to build the mills which Wilcken operated. In his memoirs, William describes many trips he and his brothers made to the mills to get loads of flour, lumber, and shingles (n.d.ᶜ, 24–25).

In 1866, Robert formed a partnership with Abraham O. Smoot and John Sharp to build a woolen mill on Parley's Creek (also called Big Kanyon Creek) in Salt Lake County. Their corporation was called A. O. Smoot and Company. Brigham Young had already built Deseret Woolen Mill there in 1863, and he sold the adjoining land to these three men for the Wasatch Woolen Mill. Eleven years later, they bought Brigham Young's mill and operated them both until March 1884. These two mills were only a quarter of a mile apart, located on either side of present-day Interstate 80 between 1700 and 1800 East, on land now occupied by the Salt Lake Country Club (see Chapter 17 for later history).

According to William, Robert paid his share of the property purchase price with a good four-mule team, harness, and wagon. Young William, who was at Brigham Young's office when the agreement was made, recalled that as they walked to the door, President Young said, "Now Robert, don't send to me a lot of wild mules that my men cannot handle." And Robert replied, pointing to his sixteen-year-old son, "This boy will bring them up" (1931, 7).

Contrary to their dignified reputations, Robert and Brigham and their peers loved a good joke. A few days later, Robert arranged for four mules to be brought to his barn, two tame and gentle and two wild as jack rabbits. With the help of his hired men, Robert hitched up the mules, putting a tame and a wild one together, one pair in the lead and the other "on the tongue." Then he and William got in the wagon seat and ordered the men to let them go. Off they flew, Robert skillfully keeping them under control and driving them for about half an hour until they had grown accustomed to the harness. Then he changed seats with his son and told him, "See if you can handle them." When he did, Robert told William to drive up to the president's office. William loved to tell this part of the story:

> Arriving there, father jumped out and soon came out of the office with President Young. As they came out onto the sidewalk, father said to me, "William, drive East about a block, then come back and pass us and go West a block and come back." I drove east as instructed, made a left hand turn, went past the office at a good trot, made a right hand turn at a good smart trot and again made a sudden stop near where father and President Young and quite a group that had collected were standing. President Young laughed and said, "Robert, I had forgotten when we made that bargain that William was considered one of the best horsemen in the country. I don't believe that one of my men could have done that with that team of partly wild mules, but the bargain stands." Then turning to me he said, "William, will you drive around to the barn and hold that team until my men get them unhitched" (1931, 7).

It was a proud boy who obeyed the president's order while all the brethren enjoyed a good laugh at their leader's expense.

Construction on the woolen mill began that summer. Abraham Smoot's sons joined the Burton boys in hauling rock to the building site. William and Owen Smoot worked at the site from Monday to Saturday almost the entire summer, returning to their homes in downtown Salt Lake on Saturday night. The main building was a three-story structure built of substantial rock, 33 feet by 90 feet in dimension. This building was finished by 1868, but it was several more years before the factory was in operation. Machinery to run the mill had to be shipped from the East; Robert ordered it when he served as a missionary in New York during the winter of 1869. He and Brigham Young, Jr., visited the mills of Massachusetts to learn new techniques and select equipment. Of course, all the machinery was run by water wheels, which had a combined force of eighty horse power. Over the years, A. O. Smoot and Company invested $60,000 in the factory (*Deseret Evening News*, September 8, 1881).

Robert had enlarged his home on the corner of First South and Second West many times during the 1850s and 1860s. He added a new dining room in 1864 or 1865 large enough to seat all nineteen family members at dinner and to house frequent quilting bees and other gatherings of extended family and friends. When Theresa and Lewis S. Hills[3] were married on October 17, 1866, the family celebration was probably held in this room. During these two decades, Robert had been purchasing land on the east half of the block where he lived and also south on State Street. When two babies (Lyman and Mary) joined the family in 1866, Robert decided it was time to build individual homes for each of his families.

Robert first built a two-story adobe for Susan on Second South on the third lot west of Second West (about 336 W. 2nd South), where she lived from about 1866 to 1878. Nathaniel and Rebecca Jones, Robert's sister and husband, were her close neighbors, living at the rear of the second lot north of Second South, around the corner on Second West (see illustration,

p. 134). Just west of Susan's home was a large fish pond which was used on occasion for baptisms, and behind the home a large garden area extended to the barns and outbuildings of Robert's first home (C. Burton 1969, 3, 11).

Deeds and other land records indicate that on May 9, 1855, Robert bought ten acres to farm located at present-day 2400 South between Main and West Temple Streets. (Main Street did not go through his property. It ended at 2100 South until the 1920s.) In 1856, he purchased ten acres directly across this plot through to State Street from his sister-in-law Elizabeth Burton; he added additional ten-acre parcels in 1863, April 1867, and February 1868 (Block 40, 10-acre Plat A, Big Field Survey, Salt Lake County Recorders Office, Salt Lake City, Utah). Robert eventually owned ninety acres in this location and had a small cabin and a hired hand living there in 1866–67 (see illustration, pp. 136–137).

Robert built Sarah's home on this farm enabling her to meet the needs of her large family through the years by raising chickens and selling eggs, butter, and cheese. Her lath and plaster home, begun in the summer of 1868, had four rooms in front, two downstairs and two upstairs with a hall running through the center where the stairway stood. In the rear was a large kitchen, another bedroom, and a pantry. William and Robert, Maria's oldest sons, hauled all the sand for the project from the banks of Big Cottonwood Creek where it crossed State Street three miles south of the farm. It took two days to haul each load and they made three trips a week until they had enough sand to build the home (W. S. Burton n.d.^{c}, 24–25).

Late in the summer, William and Robert got lumber and shingles for the farm house from the mill in Daniels Canyon. With a work team and wagon apiece, they expected to be gone four days, allowing two days each way, with a stop going and coming on the first and third nights at Kimball Hotel in what they called "Park Valley." After reaching the mill and loading their wagons, they were surprised by a big snow storm. Charles Wilcken insisted they stay with him, which they did for three or four days. The fourth day showed signs of clearing, and eighteen-year-old William, knowing their parents would be worried, decided to start for home even though Wilcken counseled them to stay. Robert, who was two years younger, followed his brother's lead.

The roads were bad and the going was slow and tedious because of the heavy loads on each wagon, but the boys made it safely to the Provo River crossing, some seven and a half miles beyond Heber City. There they discovered the bridge was out of repair and unsafe under the snowy conditions. Rather than turn back, William decided to ford the river. He carefully instructed Robert to keep the team going in the river, because if they stopped, the strong current would cut the gravel from under the wheels and the wagon would stick. William went first, driving his horses firmly and quickly to the opposite bank. When Robert's team was midway, they hesitated, and instead of "throwing the lash," Robert let them stop and could not get them started again.

Adding his own team to Robert's, William tried to pull the wagon free, but the reach[4] broke, the wheels pulled from the wagon, and the wagon bed dropped in the river. William had "an unenjoyable bath," but he did not give up. After unloading his own wagon, he went back into the river, transferred the load to his wagon, brought it to shore, then pulled out the empty wagon and proceeded to repair the reach with timber cut nearby. By dark, they had both wagons reloaded and drove about a mile and a half before taking shelter in an abandoned and dilapidated cabin nine miles from Heber City.

The boys had been gone five days, and Robert and Maria were terribly worried. On the morning of the sixth day, Robert hitched his best team to their light-spring wagon which had a new black oilcloth top, and he and Maria went in search of their missing boys. On the seventh day, they met their sons on the road to Silver Creek Junction. The boys had sensibly left half their load at the abandoned cabin and were making good time on terrible roads with half-filled wagons. Before long they were all back at Aunt Melissa's hotel, enjoying a good meal and exchanging stories of their adventures. William and

Robert, Jr., described their river crossing and the night spent in the leaky cabin with coyotes giving concert outside the door, while Robert and Maria told of a merciless hailstorm they had encountered which had punctured the new oilcloth top so it would have to be replaced again (W. S. Burton n.d.^{c}, 25–28). Robert was very proud of the way his sons handled this emergency even though better judgment might have avoided some of the problems. He continued to depend on them, preferring their service to that of older men; and they worked hard to be worthy of that trust.

Sarah moved into the farm home in the spring of 1869 after the birth of her sixth child, Elbert Turner, on the previous December 29. She had five sons, with ten-year-old Henry, the oldest, and one daughter, Alice Marie. The area in the 1860s was sparsely settled and Sarah's nearest neighbor lived four blocks away. Family members recalled that she was often lonely and sometimes frightened living there during the early years (A. Cutler 1976, 173).

On January 25, 1867, Robert was initiated into the Council of Fifty. Many of the council members at that time were growing older, having been originally appointed by Joseph Smith in 1844. Brigham Young planned to invigorate the organization by adding Robert and ten other men at this time (Hansen 1967, 143). Robert's journal entries over the next nineteen years mention his meetings with the council from time to time, with a great increase in activity during the presidency of John Taylor.

Later that year, Robert T. Burton was called and sustained as bishop of the Fifteenth Ward, after serving for almost nine years as counselor to Bishop Andrew Cunningham.[5] He was bishop for the next ten years, even while absent serving two missions and two years as a counselor in the Presiding Bishopric. He was a beloved bishop because he took seriously the needs of the people in his ward and truly cared for the poor. Of all the titles by which he was known, "Bishop Burton" seems to fit him best.

As a bishop he closely associated with two early Church members who had great influence on the development of Church policy and programs—Presiding Bishop Edward Hunter and Sarah M. Kimball.

Edward Hunter was called as presiding bishop in 1851, when his position was not well defined, although his predecessor, Newell K. Whitney, had had specific responsibility for managing tithing, establishing home industry, and caring for the poor. His background was prestigious compared to many Saints.[6] Socially and financially prominent in Pennsylvania before his conversion, Hunter was a farmer, leather curer, expert cattle breeder, handler, and judge, and a businessman. In short, "a person with great knowledge in temporal things" (Hartley 1985, 277)

Robert began attending the meetings of the Salt Lake valley bishops which Bishop Hunter held regularly. This was a form of "town meeting" which allowed the Presiding Bishopric to give instruction and receive feedback from the bishops, and over a period of years, many policies, programs, and projects grew out of these meetings. Although the presiding bishop was "President of the Aaronic Priesthood in all the World," Bishop Hunter's number one responsibility was tithing, which included the care of the poor. In both areas, he directed the bishops. Robert's own contributions to the Presiding Bishop's office were founded upon the principles he learned from Bishop Hunter from 1867 to 1873.

Sarah M. Kimball is best known for her role as a founder of the "Female Relief Society of Nauvoo" and for service in the Relief Society as General Secretary from 1880 to 1892 and as third counselor to Zina D. H. Young from 1892 to 1898. She also served forty years as president of the Fifteenth Ward Relief Society, working closely with Bishop Burton from 1867 to 1877. Brigham Young revived ward relief societies in 1867, and Sarah used her administrative talents and sincere concern for the poor and needy to develop her ward organization into an example for all other wards to follow. In all her efforts, she enjoyed the support of Robert Burton, also her neighbor (see diagram, p. 134). Their compassionate natures were very much alike, and together they tended to the temporal and spiritual needs of the poor, the sick, those in mourning, and the general membership of their ward (Mulvay 1976, 219–21).

After a year as president of the Fifteenth Ward Relief Society, Sarah Kimball reported to President Young and Eliza R. Snow that the poor, the sick and the sorrowful had been looked after "so far as we had the means and power to relieve and comfort them," and that, "We soon found an increasing treasury fund which it became our duty to put to usury" (in Mulvay 1976, 213). The women of the Fifteenth Ward had determined that if their society was going to manufacture and sell goods to fund their projects as Brigham Young had suggested, they would need a hall of their own. They purchased a lot with their small fund and received Bishop Burton's support in constructing a Relief Society Hall, the first in the Church. He not only pledged his cooperation but gave some of the first donations of time, materials, and money.

On November 12, 1868, Bishop Burton and a few other Fifteenth Ward priesthood members gathered with the Relief Society sisters to lay the cornerstone of the new building. Sarah Kimball led the ceremony with a silver trowel and mallet.

> The laying of the corner-stone of a "Temple of Commerce" by the Female Society of the Fifteenth Ward, Salt Lake City, took place yesterday. The novelty consists in its being a female enterprise developed under the fostering care of Bishop R. T. Burton. A large audience, composed in part of the members of the Society, was on the ground. At 2 p.m., after the usual form on such occasions, the following address was read by the president, followed by an extempore speech by E. R. Snow on Women's Relations to the Sterner Sex; a speech by Bishop Burton, commendatory and encouraging, and one by Mrs. Bathsheba Smith appropriate to the occasion (in *History of the Relief Society* 1966, 104)

In her address, Sarah Kimball expressed "thanks to Almighty God that the wheels of progress have been permitted to run until they have brought us to a more extended field of useful labor for female minds and hands," and she described the "unpretending edifice" which they planned to build, "the upper story of which will be dedicated to art and science; the lower story to commerce or trade." She recognized they were the first society to construct their own hall, but saw their actions as a "stepping stone to similar enterprises on a grander scale" (in *History of the Relief Society* 1966, 104).

Throughout the winter and spring of 1868–69, the men and women of the 15th Ward cooperated to build a fine structure. Twice Robert cosigned notes when Sarah Kimball borrowed funds for construction. On March 10, 1869, she borrowed $250; on April 20, $300. Relief Society minutes of the Fifteenth Ward note that each loan was paid in full in 1873. The building was dedicated in August 1869; Eliza R. Snow, general president of the Relief Society, composed a hymn and Brigham Young spoke, exhorting the sisters to train their minds and exercise the rights and privileges that were legitimately theirs.

The ward Relief Society minutes frequently refer to his attendance at meetings where he gave "much good counsel and encouragement to the sisters." At one meeting, Sister Kimball said, "Bro. Burton has always spoken in the most Fatherly manner" (January 4, 1870; April 21, 1870; January 6, 1876). Some years later, Robert presided at a joint meeting of the Relief Society and ward teachers to consider President Young's call for relief societies to build granaries and collect wheat. He donated $20 toward construction of the granary and served as chairman of an advisory committee to help the women decide the location and best type of structure ("Minutes," 1876). The Burton wives were also active in providing donations and services. For example, Maria was in charge of straw braiding for the Fifteenth Ward during the 1870s.

As the 1860s drew to a close, the completion of the transcontinental railroad ended the isolation of Utah Territory. Surveys in the 1850s determined the best route across the country and during the Civil War, Congress passed legislation offering financial aid to the construction companies. Originally targeted for completion in 1873, it was finished much sooner. Both Brigham Young and the gentile leaders in Utah supported the building of the railway, with Young confident it would benefit emigration and missionary work, and the gentiles positive it would aid in their mission of "regeneration." Both favored a route through Salt Lake City, but the northern route around Great Salt Lake was chosen because it was much less expensive to build.

Brigham Young knew the railroad would threaten the economy of the Mormon community. Trainloads of cheap imported goods and food would flood the territory, making profits for non-Mormon merchants and traders, destroying the local industries, and leaving Church members unemployed. He also knew that the unemployed would be forced to seek jobs in the mines which he preferred Church members to avoid. "Mines become exhausted," economic historian Leonard J. Arrington summarized. "Ghost towns develop; people move away; societies decay. Cultivating land, tending flocks, developing local industries using local resources—these were the activities which church leaders thought produced stable, contented societies" (Arrington 1958, 241)

Brigham Young's revival of the Relief Society with its mission of self-sufficiency was designed to mitigate the undesirable effects of the railroad. So was his revival of the School of the Prophets, an all-male, invitational forum, somewhat like the bishops meetings, but on a larger scale. Robert T. Burton was one of 900 men in the Salt Lake school which focused particularly on the development of economic policies in 1867 and 1868. To minimize the influx of undesirable newcomers, the school decided to take the contract (done in Brigham's name) to build part of the Union Pacific railroad, to establish locally owned cooperative enterprises, to reduce wages so local industries could begin to export goods, to build interior branch railroads, and to encourage LDS buyers to purchase imported goods through Zion's Cooperative Mercantile Institution, in effect boycotting gentile merchants (Arrington 1958, 245–49).

Robert both supported and benefitted from these policies. The future success of his woolen mill, still under construction, depended upon the implementation of these economic policies.

Although many prominent Salt Lake and Ogden men—including apostles, bishops, and community leaders—filled the railroad contracts, Robert Burton did not. This is somewhat surprising, since in November and December 1880, he supervised the building of the Utah Eastern Railroad from Coalville to Park City. He did not even go to Promontory Point with other community leaders on May 10, 1869, to observe the driving of the golden spike, but he did help plan a celebration in Salt Lake, to begin after news of the driving of the last spike came flashing over the telegraph wires to Utah's capital and simultaneously to other states in the Union.

This committee planned a meeting in the "new" tabernacle (the famous turtle-shell structure on Temple Square which was completed in 1867) with speeches from Governor Charles Durkee, Brigham Young, and other civic and church leaders and music from two bands. Six thousand citizens heard resolutions expressing gratitude to God for the accomplishment of "the iron road which bridges from ocean to ocean this vast land of liberty and progress." The business district was beautifully illuminated that night, a huge bonfire burned on Arsenal Hill, and fireworks were lit throughout the city (Whitney 2:258–59; CHC 5:239–45).

A week after the driving of the golden spike, ground was broken for the building of the Utah Central Railroad as planned in the School of the Prophets. Both Union Pacific and Central Pacific were bankrupt and defaulted on payment of their contracts to the subcontractors, merchants, and laborers, but the Union Pacific did come through with $500,000 worth of iron, construction equipment, and rolling stock. With this, the people of Utah built thirty-seven miles of railroad from Ogden to Salt Lake City without government subsidies. Fifteen thousand Saints gathered at a "grand dedicatory celebration" on January 10, 1870, when Brigham Young drove the last spike, of native Utah iron, with a steel mallet, both made at the public works factory. He boasted at the dedication that just as the Saints had subdued the barren country without assistance from their neighbors, "now we have built thirty-seven miles of railroad. . . . I thank the brethren who have aided to build this, our first railroad. . . . They have worked on the road, they have graded the track, they have laid the rails, they have finished the line, and have done it cheerfully 'without purse or scrip' " (in Arrington 1958, 272–73). The Saints were not finished either. The Utah Southern and Utah Northern railroads were built in the same way, eventually connecting settlements from southern Idaho to Beaver. Many Burton family members probably attended the Utah Central dedicatory celebration, but not Robert who was in New York preaching the gospel.

Between Joseph Smith's martyrdom in 1844 and 1869, the Church concentrated its missionary efforts in Europe, especially in the British Isles, and scattered points in Asia and the South Pacific. In the United States, a few local members proselyted in the big, eastern cities and a few missionaries traveled to the East after the Civil War; but the Saints did not enthusiastically share the gospel with the people who had rejected and persecuted them. After the completion of the transcontinental railroad, however, Brigham Young reconsidered this policy. Many eastern travelers visited Salt Lake City, and most were surprised to find the Mormons quite different from the popular descriptions printed in eastern newspapers. In 1869, Illinois Congressman Shelby M. Cullom introduced a bill aimed at greatly limiting the liberties of polygamous Saints; the Church now had to explain and defend its principles before the nation.

In response, the First Presidency called some 200 missionaries in the fall of 1869 to go east for the winter to proselyte, especially among their relatives and friends. Known as "railroad missionaries," these men were the first who could easily go east on the railroad during the fall and winter months when farming and business activities were slow. The majority were men of experience, early converts who had been in Utah since its settlement. Seventeen of them were bishops; others were high councilmen, city officials, and "well-known elders in Israel" (Irving 1974[a], 1974[b]).

Robert Burton fit this profile in almost every way. He had a great many relatives in both Ohio and New York and wanted especially to visit those who were Church members but had not moved west with the Saints. He also wanted to spread the gospel to those who had not heard it and to give a better understanding to those who scorned polygamy. Because the appointment of U.S. Collector of Taxes had been given to someone else and his sons, counselors, deputies, and assistants were all trained to assume his duties as sheriff, county assessor, and bishop, Robert was free to go. He arranged his affairs in the early fall of 1869, and on the morning of November 14, William drove him and two companions, Theodore McKean and William H. Hooper, to Ogden where they joined a large group of missionaries going east on the Union Pacific train.

Notes

1. See Appendices B, C, and D for lists of the children.

2. The history of the Black Hawk War is covered in Whitney 2:187–213 and CHC 5:146–58.

3. Lewis Samuel Hills was born March 8, 1836, in Amhurst, Massachusetts. His parents died when he was young, and he was raised by his uncle and aunt, Samuel and Elizabeth Hills. He arrived in Salt Lake City in 1862 and became prominent in city and business affairs. He was first involved with mercantile business, then in 1869–70, formed a bank with William H. Hooper and H. S. Eldredge which became Deseret National Bank, of which he was cashier for many years.

4. The "reach" is the pole connecting the rear axle of a wagon to the transverse bar over the front axle supporting the wagon bed.

5. Andrew Cunningham was a pioneer of 1848 who settled in the Fifteenth Ward. He was a counselor to Bishop Nathaniel V. Jones in 1851 and acting bishop from 1852–55, while Jones was on his mission to India. After a mission to Illinois from September 1855 to August 1857, Cunningham was a deputy sheriff to Robert T. Burton and with him built the Salt Lake County courthouse. He became Fifteenth Ward bishop in January 1859. He served almost nine years and resigned due to failing health not many months before his death on March 2, 1868 (Jenson, 2:370–72).

6. Principal sources on Edward Hunter are William E. Hunter, *Edward Hunter, Faithful Steward*, Salt Lake City: Publishers Press by the Hunter Family, 1970; and William G. Hartley, "Edward Hunter, Pioneer Presiding Bishop," in Donald Q. Cannon and David J. Whittaker, eds., *Supporting Saints: Life Stories of Nineteenth Century Mormons*, Provo: Religious Studies Center, Brigham Young University, 1985.

Railroad Missionary, Winter 1869–70

From November 14, 1869, to April 2, 1870, Robert served a mission in the East and was the presiding Church authority in New York City. He was reunited with family members in Ohio and New York and experienced both the highs and lows of missionary work as he worshipped with members, taught and baptized investigators, and suffered humiliation and rejection from persecutors. Mormonism was a favorite topic in the eastern newspapers, and many people were curious to hear and see what the Mormons were really like. But prejudice was rampant, and Robert especially observed it while tracting and proselyting on Long Island.

Crossing the prairies of middle America faster than he had ever traveled in his life, Robert T. Burton could not have helped contrasting the marvels of this train trip with the weeks he had spent walking across Illinois and Indiana during his first mission in the spring of 1843. Although he was called to New York, his immediate destination was Toledo, Ohio, where he had spent many months in missionary service in 1843 and 1844. He intended once again to teach his family members and acquaintances about the restored gospel of Jesus Christ and the true state of affairs in Utah Territory. The missionaries reached

Chicago on the afternoon of November 18, after only four days travel, but the industrial and metropolitan sights that greeted them must have made them feel years removed from Salt Lake City. Robert and Theodore McKean separated from the main group in Chicago, boarded a train for Toledo, and arrived there at 1 A.M. on November 19.

By afternoon, Robert had found both his oldest sister, Jane Leybourn, and, to his surprise, his younger brother, Charles. In 1849, Charles had left Salt Lake Valley for the gold fields of California. He had written to the family in Utah from the Northwest, but later took passage in a ship around Cape Horn, and finally reached Ohio. Robert met Charles's wife, Harriet Miner, whom he had married in Toledo March 20, 1860, and their young son, William Austin Burton, born January 21, 1861 (W. S. Burton n.d.ª, 11).

Although Jane Leybourn was sixty-three years old and a widow for the second time, Robert found her in good health and living comfortably on the farm at Tremainsville (West Toledo) with several of her married children nearby. Almost twenty-six years had passed since they had bade each other goodbye at the end of Robert's first mission, and their joyous reunion was long overdue.

The families of the four Burton sisters who remained in the eastern and midwestern states had kept in close touch. Although Sarah and Betsy died before 1869, Robert knew that he could find family members in Ohio, where Jane and Anthony Leybourn and Betsy and Joseph Roop had homesteaded in 1829; in Sublette, Illinois, where Sarah and Elijah Austin settled about 1850; and near Pultneyville, New York, where Ann and Waters Shipley raised their family near Water's boyhood home. While in Toledo, Robert learned that his nieces and nephews mostly lived near their parents or near one of the aunt's families, as if they had gone there to visit or work, then married and located nearby. Robert intended to visit them all.

During the ten days he spent in the Toledo area, Robert had many opportunities to explain his feelings for the gospel of Jesus Christ, to teach gospel principles, and to answer questions about life in Utah. We do not know if any of his relatives other than Jane had been baptized during his earlier mission; but wherever he went, he received a warm welcome and found a receptive audience. In his journal, he mentions in particular visiting Jane's children, William and Samuel Leybourn, John and Melissa Leybourn Bladen, and Henry and Eliza Leybourn Glenn, plus Henry and Sylvania Roop Houghton, "and many other friends and acquaintances whom I had not met with since the early spring of 1844" (1843–69, 76). He also spent a day looking about the city of Toledo, "noting the remarkable changes that had taken place in this city since my boyhood days" (1843–69, 76–77).

In 1843 and 1844, Robert had often held LDS meetings in the Tremainsville schoolhouse and often baptized his listeners afterward. On November 24, 1869, he once again found himself at the podium of the schoolhouse at Tremainsville, known then as Purara School, preaching the gospel to a large audience. He called for two meetings to be held the next Sunday, one at 2 P.M. at the Houghton schoolhouse (where he had last taught on April 23, 1844) and one for 6:30 P.M. in the Purara School. He spoke freely on the first principles of the gospel to full houses at each location. Undoubtedly, former converts and investigators attended at each place. No one was baptized this time, but he left some seriously contemplating the gospel. John Roop, twenty-two-year-old son of Betsy and Joseph Roop paid particular attention. Before Robert's return in the spring, John traveled to Salt Lake City and requested baptism, but he died tragically a few weeks later (R. T. Burton n.d.[a], 45).

Robert's days in Toledo passed quickly as he went from one family to another. Elder McKean had already gone on to New York; and on November 29, Robert followed him. During the next few months, he and Elder McKean labored daily with other missionaries from Utah: Elijah F. Sheets, Samuel D. Serrine, H. W. Brizzee, Byron Groo, Brigham Young, Jr., Nelson A. Empey, Charles W. Nibley, Henry Peck, Angus M. Cannon, Francis A. Hammond, Benjamin R. Hulse, William Bringhurst, and Elder Riter [first name not available]. William H. Hooper, territorial delegate to Congress, stayed with the elders in New York until late December, at which time Robert accompanied him to Washington, D.C.

Robert's first goal in New York was to locate the "family of saints" and he found them after searching two days. He then felt comfortable enjoying two days of sightseeing in Central Park and the city, including a visit to the Metropolitan Theater. He assessed New York City in a journal entry on December 2: "Saw the extremes of high class life."

At noon on December 5, the missionaries attended the small, humble Williamsburg Branch in Brooklyn, where the Saints were overjoyed to hear President Young's son and the other Utah brethren preach the gospel. After two hours of testimony bearing, Brigham Young, Jr., and Robert T. Burton, who apparently shared the leadership of the "Eastern States Mission" at this time, spoke. After a break, they met again at 6:30 P.M., and several more Utah missionaries spoke.

With missionary work underway, Robert and Brigham, Jr., evidently felt free to leave for a few days. They took passage December 7 on a boat bound for Boston, the center of the weaving and loom industry, an important interest to both of them. In Massachusetts, Elder Nathaniel H. Felt, a prominent Salem businessman before his baptism in 1843, had arranged for them to visit the major factories during the day while they enjoyed historical, cultural, and intellectual offerings in the evening. The first evening, they visited Bunker Hill. The next morning, the went by rail twenty miles north to Salem, where Elder Felt took them to the "Nacenkidy Factory" during the afternoon and to a rehearsal of the Oratorio Society of Salem in the evening with ex-Secretary of State, General Oliver. The next morning, a letter of introduction from General Oliver allowed them to tour the armory; and they visited principal factories at Lowell, Massachusetts.

After returning to Boston, they visited the Academy of Music to examine the large organ, perhaps on assignment from Brigham Young and others interested in obtaining an organ for the Tabernacle, and heard 150 to 200 musicians in rehearsal. Next, they traveled to Worcester, forty miles west of Boston, where they met with Mr. Crompton, whose factory was "the greatest loom factory in U.S." (1843–69, 84). There they purchased equipment for the Deseret and Wasatch woolen mills and arranged to have it shipped to Utah. With these tasks completed, Brigham Young, Jr., traveled to Philadelphia and Robert to New York City to begin intensive missionary labors.

Back in the city, Robert settled into a room at 66 Wannock Street, near the Hudson Railroad Depot, where he intended to stay through the winter, although he later changed his mind and moved to Brooklyn. He found that William Hooper was ill in his hotel room and required the constant attention of one or more of the elders. Robert spent many nights with him over the next two weeks and by Christmas Hooper was well again.

In spite of his hours devoted to Hooper and to business affairs, Robert rejoiced in the opportunities which came to preach at services of the Williamsburgh Branch and at meetings in nearby communities. A few Church members lived near Freeport, Long Island, and this became a center for missionary activity. Robert first preached there on December 15 and 16, teaching the history of the Church and bearing strong testimony of the gospel's restoration. Robert's daily journal entries contain few comments about the success of his labors, but offer evidence that the missionaries were dedicated to furthering the image of the Church as well as strengthening the local members.

Robert spent a great amount of time writing to his wives and children, as well as to Church and business leaders in Utah and on the east coast. His letters home may have described the lectures, plays, monuments, historical sights, and big city wonders that he observed daily. Early in December, he purchased and mailed gifts for his family at A. T. Stewarts Retail House and then enjoyed the holidays with his companions and the members of the Williamsburg Branch.

On December 30, Robert and William Hooper went by train to Washington, D.C. where Hooper was to remain for the congressional session. Robert assisted him in finding suitable rooms and getting settled, then Hooper served as guide and companion through two weeks of sightseeing and business in the nation's capital. First they visited the Capitol Building, Treasury Department, and White House. After New Years' Day, they visited with the heads of some federal departments and some senators. Robert met on January 5 with officials at the Treasury Department to "ascertain the state of my account as Collector of Utah." He felt the settlement was accomplished "quite satisfactorily" (R. T. Burton 1856–1907, January 5, 1870; n.d.[a], 44–45). He recorded in his journal visits to the War Department, where he met Secretary of War Boulwell, to the Navy Yard, to the House of Representatives and the Senate, and finally back to the White House where he was introduced to President Ulysses S. Grant.

Robert's return trip to New York included a two-day visit in Philadelphia where he counseled with the missionaries and local Church members about problems in the Philadelphia Branch. He recorded in his journal that he appointed Amos Russell Wright to preside over the branch and ordered all members to be rebaptized (1856–1907, January 14, 1870).

Robert did not stay in New York City very long after his return on January 15. The elders serving on Long Island had planned a series of meetings for January 20–23, including public lectures at the Christian Work School House. Joseph M. Benedict,[1] a young Mormon physician living in Freeport, arranged the meetings and provided lodging for Robert and other missionaries. Except for the Friday evening session when the hall was "well filled," the missionaries were disappointed with the attendance. On Sunday, they split up and held three separate evening meetings in Freeport, Baldwin, and Rockville. Attendance was better, and these meetings led to the baptism of members of the Brown (or Bower) family on Tuesday and Friday, January 25 and 28.

Many who attended these meetings were not interested in learning about the gospel but came to confirm the gossip and vicious rumors they had heard about the Church. Missionary labors triggered opposition, and while Robert was addressing a well-filled house at Baldwin, he sensed a "mob spirit." Although he was permitted to speak for over an hour and Angus M. Cannon for half an hour, when they dismissed the meeting, a large crowd gathered outside the hall shouting insults and threats (1856–1907, January 28, 1870). Two days later, two members of the local clergy called at Dr. Benedict's home "to talk on religious matters." Robert thought the two ministers, Mr. Burns and Mr. Weeds were "very ignorant and very nervous and dishonest." His earlier missions had taught him that opposition from ministers often increased interest in the Church. True to his expectations, a full congregation gathered that night in Baldwin to hear Elder Cannon discuss the coming forth of the Book of Mormon and Robert's testimony of the missions of Joseph Smith and Brigham Young. As the meeting closed, an insulting mob gathered; but just as quickly, friends surrounded the missionaries eliminating any opportunity for an attack (R. T. Burton 1856–1907, January 30, 1870).

The next day, January 31, Elders Burton and Cannon went by train to Patchogue, a large town about midway on the ocean side of Long Island. Elders Hammond, Riter, and Bringhurst had rented a hall and set up a meeting to begin at 7 P.M. At that hour, Robert was surprised to find that although the hall was well filled, only men were in the audience. He recorded in his journal, "The People seemed to be so prejudiced that they were actually afraid to bring their families. In consequence of this great prejudice, we did not deem it necessary to attempt further meetings in this place."

Fifteen miles northeast at Riverhead, the reception was no better. The elders spent the better part of the afternoon of February 1, trying to get a hall to preach in. Finally, a clergyman of the Swedenborgian Church promised his house as a meeting place. But when the elders returned to the minister's home after putting out their announcements, he refused to let them in, saying his trustees forbade him to use his home for their meeting. They were finally able to secure the court house for the next evening, and a crowd of a hundred listened to their message. They took up a collection during the meeting to pay the rent for the court house, but the amount contributed was very small.

Robert concluded from this that if the people were not anxious enough to hear the gospel to help furnish the hall, they might go without the gospel. The missionaries spent two nights with the one LDS family in Riverhead, the Puggsleys. At their home on February 3, the elders decided to separate; Elders Hammond, Bringhurst, and Riter went west on the north side of the island, and Elders Burton, Cannon, and Hulse returned to the west end on the south coast.

At Waterville, Burton, Cannon, and Hulse arranged with the Methodist clergyman and his trustees to use their church on the night of February 4. They distributed notices and went to the church at the appointed hour, only to have the minister meet them at the door and deny ever having given them consent to use the building. Robert asked for permission to speak to the people already gathered inside the church but was denied. As they turned to leave, a crowd gathered outside, shouting insults and threats and becoming more unruly by the minute. Members of the congregation ran past the missionaries and hid by an old mill at the side of the road. From their hiding place, they pelted the elders with eggs, chips, and rocks as they walked past, then followed them to the home of William Hawkins where they were to spend the night. Hawkins loaded his shotgun, intending to defend his guests, but there was no further action that night. His hospitality and protection were the only kindnesses the missionaries received on that part of the island. Robert recorded in his journal that the assault was performed by "some of the more reckless knowing it would meet the approbation of the Priest" (February 4, 1870). Needless to say, the next morning they left Waterville. They spent February 5 in Hempstead at the home of a Brother DeMotte, and were found by the other three elders a day later at Lot Brown's home where they held a Sunday meeting with Church members. Robert's journal seems to indicate relief at being back among friends in a "good meeting" where the sacrament could be administered.

In spite of the prejudice and mob spirit encountered on Long Island, Robert knew many good people wanted to hear the gospel. He went back to New York City, promising Dr.

260

Benedict he would return to Freeport as soon as possible. Ten days later, he and Elder Bringhurst braved a winter storm and terrible roads to keep that promise. They arrived late at the hall a large congregation was gathered inside, but as soon as he walked in the door, Robert knew something was wrong.

> The congregation seemed to be a very singular one and it was evident something more than usual was intended. We succeeded in getting order enough to open the meeting and I commenced speaking probably occupied about 15 or 20 minutes. Some got up and went out of the room and finally *three* men entered the room very abruptly and broke in on the speaker informing us that they had been appointed to come and break up the meeting and give us some 20 minutes to get out of the Town. The Friends of Truth seemed to be so much in the minority that they dare not do anything to restore order. Finally we were compelled to leave the House, but succeeded in doing so without receiving any injury more than abusive language. Left the mob ranting among themselves. They numbered so far as we could tell about 25 or 30 men (1856–1907, February 17, 1870).

All the meetings on Long Island were not like that one, however. Robert made three more trips before his mission was over and was able each time to give Saints and investigators "some good advice." One of the meetings was arranged by a Mr. Tappin, a wealthy merchant and man of influence in the town of Jericho. He not only entertained Elders Burton and Hammond and Dr. Benedict very kindly, but also arranged for a hall filled with people who listened attentively to one of Robert's lengthy sermons on the rise of the Church and the first principles of the gospel (R. T. Burton 1856–1907, March 2, 1870).

So the Utah elders experienced the entire spectrum from acceptance to rejection while they labored on Long Island. Certainly Dr. Benedict, who used his position and family standing to attract honest investigators, probably endured persecution because of his affiliation with such an unpopular religion. Yet he did not waver. He listened to his friends, the Utah elders, preach about gathering to Zion and, one year later, immigrated by train to Salt Lake City where he continued his medical career. There, he took care of Brigham Young during his last illness, founded Holy Cross Hospital, served as an advisor for the building of the Territorial Insane Asylum (see Chapter 18), and worked for better medical care until his death on July 25, 1896.

When Robert T. Burton wrote in his biography about his mission in New York City and on Long Island, he did not comment on the persecution and prejudice but chose rather to remember that "we had good success and baptized many persons" (n.d.ᵃ, 44).

Robert spent his last days in New York City arranging railroad passage for the elders returning to Utah, purchasing items for his family, friends, or Church associates in large retail stores, and setting the Church affairs in order. There also seemed to be many visitors in the city—missionaries returning from Europe, travelers from Utah in the East on business, and other railroad missionaries in need of tickets for their journey home. As these visitors came and went, Robert enjoyed evenings at the theater or touring the marvels of the country's largest, richest, and most modern city with them. When Samuel W. Richards came early in March, he and Robert went to the Opera House to see "The Widow's Temptations." These men, who had kept drama alive in the remote western desert in the 1850s, were awed by the production, the theater's furnishings, and the finery of the audience. Robert and Samuel enjoyed the evening so much that they were not even put out to discover when they left the theatre that the street cars had stopped running and they had to walk all the way to the ferry at the East River and back to their lodgings in Brooklyn at 2 A.M. (R. T. Burton 1856–1907, March 8, 1870).

On his next to the last Sunday in New York, Robert went with three companions to Plymouth Congregational Church to hear the renowned Henry Ward Beecher speak. Of the most popular preacher in the country, Robert wrote in his journal, "The speaker was more literal than sectarians usually are" (March 6, 1870).

He had been away only four months, but by the middle of March, it was time to return home. Robert, who had already traveled about 4,500 miles by railroad and steamship, had plans for a less than direct route back to the valley. Most of the elders left on the Erie Railroad, but Robert and Angus M. Cannon boarded the New York Central Railroad on the evening of March 15, headed for the home of Waters and Ann Burton Shipley in the village of Pultneyville. The closest rail station was Palmyra, New York—birthplace of Mormonism.

They could not have left at a worse time. A late winter storm was burying upstate New York. "The snow over the face of this Country exceeded anything ever witnessed here by the inhabitants," Robert wrote in his journal on March 18, 1870. By 8 A.M. the morning of March 16, their train was at a full stop, snowbound about ten miles east of Palmyra. All day long they sat with the winds howling, "slow blowing fearfully and nothing for the Passengers to eat." By nightfall, four more engines helped pull the train into the station at Newark, where the passengers spent a cold night in the cars. The next morning, five engines pulled the train on toward Rochester; Elders Burton and Cannon got off in Palmyra and found lodgings at the Palmyra Hotel. All the roads were closed, leaving no way for them to get from Palmyra to Pultneyville, so they remained at the hotel and enjoyed an evening of music performed by a fellow traveler.

Robert had never been to Palmyra before. His parents had immigrated to nearby Pultneyville, but that was four years before his birth and three years before Joseph Smith's first vision. As he and Cannon introduced themselves to guests and townspeople at the hotel as residents of Salt Lake City, Robert noticed a reaction and recorded in his journal that he felt "there was a very bitter feeling among the People in regards to the [Mormon] people" (March 17, 1870).

The next morning Robert and Angus Cannon were able to engage a team to take them to the small town of Marion, seven miles north of Palmyra. Here they met Robert's nephew, Burton Austin, twenty-two-year-old son of Elijah and Sarah Burton Austin, and two other nieces, whom he did not name. Burton was prepared to continue the journey with his uncle toward Pultneyville. They secured the services of another team and driver; but after going only half a mile, the driver became alarmed about the depth of the snow and refused to go any further. The travelers climbed down from the wagon, took their luggage in hand, and proceeded north on foot. After hours of tramping in faint wagon ruts, with the snow banks at the road's edge over their heads, they finally reached Williamson, a very small community still three miles from Pultneyville. Once again, they convinced a farmer to hitch up his horse and wagon, and this time they finished their journey. They had spent the entire day traveling—walking over five miles and riding about twelve— and finally stood at the door of Ann Burton Shipley's home at 7:30 P.M. She answered the door, but did not recognize them until Robert identified himself. Her surprise and warm welcome made the toilsome day's march worth every step.

Ann Burton was Samuel and Hannah's seventh child and fourth daughter, the last born in England. She was eighteen months when they immigrated. She married her cousin Waters Shipley in 1834, and settled for some time near Toledo but eventually moved back to his home town of Pultneyville, New York. They had eight children, six of whom grew to adulthood and lived nearby. Ann was fifty-four years old. Ann and Waters did not want to discuss religion with Robert but were most anxious to hear all about the family members in Utah and Ohio. Other Shipley cousins, brothers and sisters of Waters and their children also lived near Pultneyville. Robert met most of these relatives for the first time during this brief visit and found some of them interested in the gospel. Robert described his visit in his journal:

> Saturday 19: This morning Bro. Cannon and I went and called on some of my couzens. Also went to the Shore of Lake Ontario to look at the same. I thought [it] strange that a country that had been settled as long as this had neither RR nor Telegraph within 16 miles of the Town.
>
> Sunday 20: This morning went to see John & Thomas Shipley. Was received kindly. Had a very good visit with John. He seemed very anxious to learn of the gospel.

Robert spent the afternoon visiting at Ann's home; but as it neared evening, he decided it was time to return to Palmyra. The temperature was rising and the snow beginning to thaw. He was afraid if they waited longer, they would not be able to get back. He was almost right; it took eight hours, until 2:30 A.M., to reach Palmyra.

At 8:30 A.M., he, his nephew, Burton Austin, and Angus Cannon boarded the train for Toledo. There they stayed with his brother Charles, probably discussing the gospel and opportunities in Utah. Before the year was out, Charles, Harriet, and nine-year-old William moved to Salt Lake City. Charles and Harriet were baptized on March 5 and 6, 1872; William was baptized May 10, 1873.

From Toledo, they traveled to Sublette, Illinois, to visit Burton's father, Elijah Austin, for a few days. From there, Robert and Angus Cannon traveled to Omaha where they finally boarded a train for Utah on April 1. The train ride ended in Salt Lake City rather than Ogden, as the Utah Central Railroad, completed in January, now connected Salt Lake City with the East and West.

Robert's happy homecoming on April 2 was marred by the sudden and unexpected death on April 1 of his nephew, John Roop. John had come to Utah early in 1870, after Robert had converted him in Toledo while he was en route to New York. Robert attended his funeral on April 3 and arranged for him to be buried in the family plot in Salt Lake City Cemetery (n.d.[a], 45).

Robert was grateful to be back in Utah again, but his family was soon to discover that having him home was going to be the exception rather than the rule during the next few years. He traveled with Brigham Young on tours to settlements in Utah, Idaho, and Arizona. Next, Judge James B. McKean's legal raids and charges from the district court related to the Morrisite War would interrupt their family life. Finally, he was called on a mission to England in 1873 for two years. From the start, the 1870s promised to be a new challenge for each member of the Robert Taylor Burton family.

Notes

1. Joseph M. Benedict was born in Connecticut but moved as a child to Freeport, Long Island, where his father ran the County Asylum. He received his medical degree from New York University in 1867 and lived at Freeport, practicing medicine until 1871 when he came to Utah. He was prominent in Utah medical circles until his death in 1896 (*Biographical Record* 1902, 418).

Legal Raid of Judge McKean, 1870–72

For about a year, Robert spent his time "very pleasantly with my family and attending to public and private business." In September 1870, he was indicted for the murders of three Morrisites in June 1869. He began dodging the court officers because he felt sure that he could not get a fair trial and spent the next twenty months living "on the lam," until his indictment was set aside by a U.S. Supreme Court ruling that the grand jury was illegally drawn.

Robert spent the weeks following his return from New York attending to his family and business responsibilities until called in June to accompany Brigham Young on a wagon and train tour of the northern settlements through Brigham City, Clarkston, Oxford, Soda Springs, Bear Lake, and Cache Valley. Robert invited Sarah to accompany him. Her brothers were all living in Cache Valley at this time and she probably visited them, although Robert's journal does not mention it. Like some of the other trips, this was more of a vacation and Robert and Sarah enjoyed "a very agreeable time" (n.d.ª, 45).

Later, the annual tour of the southern settlements took Robert away for almost the entire month of September, as the party went beyond St. George into Arizona and up to the new settlements near Kanab. John R. Winder was Robert's traveling companion.

In between trips, Robert and his sons often worked at the woolen mill where they were putting in the new machinery from Massachusetts. Work at the factory continued throughout the winter of 1870–71, when a crew of laborers built and lined the shaft, attached the machinery, laid the floor, etc. Robert, who continued to serve as sheriff, county assessor, county tax collector, and city councilman, often went to the factory by way of the courthouse or the police station.

On January 7, 1871, Maria gave birth to her tenth and last child, a son named Heber Kimball. Robert divided his time between "home," "Susan's," and "the farm." The farm was a convenient stop between the city and the factory which allowed him to assist with the chores, supervise the planting and harvesting, and see the family almost daily. Robert began keeping a daily journal in January 1871 and continued until his death in 1907, recording each day's activities in a pocket-size leather calendar book. While all these details cannot be included, the journals have been a major source for the remaining years in his life story.[1]

From about 1863 until 1870, the federal officers appointed to administer the civil affairs of Utah had been "satisfactory officers" (CHC 5:317). However, during this time a number of agitators and adventurers in the state—among them army officers and young lawyers—had found that they could profit by renewing the conflict between the Mormons and the United States government. Expecting to assume all the appointed offices which the Cullum Bill would have made "gifts of the governor," these opportunists were bitterly disappointed when the bill did not pass the U.S. Senate. Upon the election of Ulysses S. Grant as president, these men lobbied with members of the capital's "anti-Mormon" coalition (which included Vice-President Schuyler Colfax and Reverend J. P. Newman, Grant's Methodist minister and an outspoken opponent of polygamy) to make sure that Grant's federal appointees would share their interests in establishing the authority of the federal government over the people of Utah through political, military, and judicial means (CHC 5:287, 317–18, 327–29).

When J. Wilson Shaffer of Illinois was appointed governor early in 1870, he reportedly boasted, "Never after me, by _____ ! shall it be said that Brigham Young is Governor of Utah" (in Tullidge 1886, 480). What Governor Shaffer could not accomplish with political maneuverings, Grant-appointee James B. McKean, chief justice of the territorial supreme court, took care of in the courts, aided by Judges Cyrus M. Hawley and O. G. Strickland.[2] Though men such as Robert T. Burton and Orson F. Whitney saw evidence of a conspiracy in the actions of these federal officials, it was more likely an overzealous attempt to sustain federal authority (Alexander 1966, 99–100). Before McKean arrived in Utah in August 1870, Hawley and Strickland had decided that the probate courts had no jurisdiction in criminal cases and set aside the territorial law on the selection of grand juries which said jurors were to be drawn by the territorial marshal from county assessment rolls. After ruling that the territorial courts were U.S. district courts, McKean opened the Third District Court on September 19, 1870, with a grand jury chosen by U.S. Marshal M. T. Patrick by "open venire" or open selection of jurors. Ostensibly, the judges were trying to obtain impartial juries, since they believed those selected from the assessment rolls favored the Mormons. However, open venire allowed Patrick to draw an entire jury of men opposed to Mormonism, and the Mormons felt they could not get an impartial trial.

The grand jury in September 1870 indicted Robert T. Burton for the murders of Bella Bowman, Mrs. Swanee, and Joseph Morris (see Chapter 12). Other prominent citizens, including Salt Lake City Marshal J. D. T. McAllister, Andrew Burt, Alexander F. Macdonald, and Brigham Young were also indicted by grand juries similarly chosen. Of the next eighteen months, Robert wrote:

> In August the legal raid known as the raid of Judge James B. McKean commenced and Prest Young and many others had to leave their homes as many trumped up charges were brought against them.

> And amongst the rest they made me very much trouble because
> of my having several writs, from the District Court, on some of the
> people known as Morasites etc. as before refered to in my journal.
>   But I met with friends every where I went who gave me every
> comfort (n.d.ª, 46–47).

This last statement refers to the times from September 1870
to April 1872 when Robert dared not spend the night at one of
his homes for fear of a raid and arrest. He had concluded he
would not get a fair trial by a jury chosen by open venire. During the day, Robert went quietly about his civic, business, and
religious affairs carefully avoiding court officers serving writs
against him and trying to arrest him. Some times were more
dangerous than others; for example, in March 1871 he spent
some twenty nights at homes other than his own. He slept some
nights at Brigham Young's mill farm (which was near the woolen
mills), others at the homes of Heber C. Kimball, J. Q. Knowlton,
Abraham O. Smoot, and others. On occasion, he went to Provo
and participated in Sunday meetings where he stayed with
Alexander F. MacDonald or William Pace. Unfortunately his
diary entries do not tell more than his comings and goings each
day. Undoubtedly much discussion and plotting took place
among these powerful men who had been unjustly accused by
the district court on a variety of charges or mistreated by the
U.S. Army troops. MacDonald, William Miller, and E. F. Sheets,
all Provo city aldermen, had had their homes damaged and
ransacked by soldiers during a drunken raid in September 1870
(CHC 5:341–42).

In September 1871, U.S. Marshal Patrick began using regular army troops as a posse to serve arrest warrants on men
like Robert who had successfully avoided his regular servers.
Robert had not spent a night at home since August 28, but
decided that it would be prudent to take a trip to the southern
part of the state with Maria and their youngest children. On
Friday, September 8, he was warned by his brother-in-law,
Nathaniel Ashby, that he was being followed. Robert recorded
in his dairy on September 9 that he boarded the train at his
farm and traveled as far south as the tracks were then laid. His

son Robert brought a buggy to the terminus, picked up his father, and drove on to Provo, arriving at 3 A.M.

Late the next night, messengers came to Alexander F. MacDonald's home, where Robert and his son were sleeping, to report that army troops were en route to Provo with arrest warrants from the district courts. Robert and Alexander, called "Mack," arose and went to the meeting house where they hid until 4 A.M. They spent the rest of the day at the home of Henry Saunders, along with Abraham O. Smoot and William Pace. Later they all spent an anxious night at R. D. Kirkwood's home, but learned that the troops were not looking for them. They had raided the homes of H. L. Davis and J. J. Baum, and shot at Baum as he fled in the night, although they did not hit him or arrest anyone. Baum had already been acquitted of homicide, but the district court was trying to prosecute him further (Whitney 2:592).

Maria and her children reached Provo on September 12, and were sent on to Spring Lake (near Santaquin). Under cover of darkness, Robert left Provo and was reunited with Maria at Spring Lake in the morning. Charles E. Burton, Robert's brother, and George W. Bean joined them at Santaquin and together they headed south, although Maria and the children were in a separate wagon and sometimes traveled ahead of Robert, Charles, and Bean.[3] Once Utah Valley was behind them, they began a more leisurely journey, stopping frequently with friends and relatives for a meal or a night. This was probably Maria's first and last trip to southern Utah; she much preferred being at home in Salt Lake. In Beaver, they visited Robert's widowed sister, Mary Burton White, and her daughter and son-in-law, Lucy and William Flake. In Pinto, west of Cedar City near the iron mines and factory, they spent two days with Maria's sister and brother-in-law, Eliza Ann and Charles Westover. After eleven days on the road, the Burton family members reached St. George, where they were warmly welcomed by their hosts, the John Youngs.

A new experience for them while in St. George was being able to "talk" to family and friends in Salt Lake via the new telegraph lines. Robert talked to someone in Salt Lake almost every night to get news from the district court. He learned that Brigham Young had been indicted by the Grand Jury for "lewdly and lasciviously associating and cohabiting with women, not being married to them" (CHC 5:395). This was an attempt to indict Brigham and other polygamists under Utah's own territorial laws, rather than the federal Morrill Anti-Bigamy Law of 1862 which was more difficult to prove. The territorial law against adultery and lewd and lascivious association dated back to 1852 and never intended to punish polygamy (CHC 5:394-95).

Robert and Maria began the trip back to Salt Lake on September 27. Again they traveled separately, but followed the same route through the middle of the state and met whenever possible. From Parowan, they went east through Bear Valley over to Circle Valley and along the Sevier River to Richfield where they visited Susan's mother, Elizabeth McBride. (Her father was on a trip to Salt Lake.) As on the trip down, Robert, Charles, and George W. Bean took time to explore and often conferred with the leading men in the scattered settlements. Maria and the children seem to travel during the day from one settlement to the next, but Robert rode early in the morning and late in the day, especially as they neared Provo and the danger of arrest increased. Maria left Provo for Salt Lake on the morning of October 11, while Robert started late in the afternoon accompanied by Alexander MacDonald. They stopped at the farm at 1 A.M. to keep their presence in the city a secret (September 27–October 11, 1871).

Robert's journal entries of October 12–24 reveal that he dared go to his home, farm, courthouse office, or the factory only at night and he was now accompanied by both MacDonald and O. Porter Rockwell, who had volunteered as their bodyguard (see Dewey 1986, 324). During the day they were often at a relative's home, and after dark, they would change locations for the night. They spent a day or two with Lot Smith in Centerville and felt safe out hunting in the foothills very early in the morning and returned by boat on the Great Salt Lake, a pleasant diversion which included dinner at "Genl Smith's" mid-way between Lake Side and the Bath House.

The next day was Robert's fiftieth birthday, and he long remembered it because he couldn't be with his family to celebrate. Instead, he was ill and stayed at the Theodore McKean's home all day, where several friends but no family members visited him. In spite of his illness, he was preparing another escape from the valley. At 10:30 P.M., Robert, MacDonald, and Rockwell were taken by team and buggy to MacDonald's farm on the east side of Utah Lake where they boarded a boat at 7 A.M. for the mouth of the Spanish Fork River. A buggy met them there, and they drove quickly on to Nephi where they joined Brigham Young's party which had left Salt Lake a day ahead of them. President Young had appeared in court on the charges against him and had been released until his trial, which was supposed to be held in March.

By now a good-sized company of brethren was headed toward St. George. Some were "on the lam" like Robert and MacDonald; others were accompanying Brigham Young to St. George to dedicate the site and break ground for the temple. They traveled through a snowstorm at Fillmore and continued on to Cedar City where the roads were extremely dusty. The entire trip was rushed, and Robert, who was still recovering from his illness, felt the pressure more than others. On November 2, they rode by moonlight into St. George at 10 P.M. after traveling for seven days. Conference convened in the basement of the new tabernacle the next day. The weather was unusually wet, windy, and cold, and both Robert and Brigham Young missed conference sessions because of illness. However, on November 8, Robert assisted Young in surveying and staking the temple site; and at noon on the ninth, about 500 Saints gathered on the temple block for the ceremonies. George A. Smith offered the dedicatory prayer, and President Young marked the ground where the southeast cornerstone would be laid, turning the first earth with a shovel and pick. The Santa Clara Brass Band and the St. George Choir provided music for the service, a fitting beginning for this monument to the faith and sacrifices of these early settlers (November 1–9, 1871; Nibley 1937, 475–76).

Robert was pleased that evening when President Young asked him to serve as steward "of the house," apparently assigning him the responsibility of keeping the accounting records and making whatever business arrangements were necessary for the boarding house, owned by Erastus Snow, which served as office and home for the men who accompanied Brigham Young.

Robert's journal entries depict the next six weeks as somewhat idyllic. There were long visits with Brigham Young, frequent dinner invitations from St. George families, evenings spent in "musick and singing," and parties at the St. George Hall. His sixteen-year-old son Charles had joined him and he was surrounded with friends, so he did not write in his journal of homesickness. However, he wrote many letters to the families in Salt Lake and "talked" via telegraph with family members often enough to know they were being sustained in his absence.

In mid-November, the Salt Lake men toured all the settlements between Toquerville and Long Valley, traveling through Pipe Springs, Arizona, and holding church meetings at each community. In Kanab, Robert witnessed an interview between Brigham Young and four members of Major John Wesley Powell's exploration party, who asked many questions about the Mormon people and the colonization of the area. In December, Robert led a survey party to Hurricane Bluff to locate a road. He spent four days on the mountain determining the best route and clearing rocks, brush, and trees to make the road passable.

Although these weeks were a pleasant respite from the harassment in Salt Lake City, Robert and the others anxiously awaited news about other indictments which was telegraphed each night. Judge McKean had taken no time off while Brigham Young was gone from the valley and, in fact, was considering other ways to imprison and discredit the Church president. Though he had said that Young's trial "on lewd and lascivious cohabitation" would not come up until March, he changed his mind and called for it in November. An extension was granted until January 9, when the new U.S. District Attorney for Utah, George C. Bates, promised that he would call up "The People vs. Brigham Young" and press it for trial (CHC 5:401).

But it was not this charge that brought President Young back from St. George in a winter storm. During November, Judge McKean had filed a murder charge against Brigham Young, Daniel Wells, Hosea Stout, and William H. Kimball. Apparently, the grand jury indicted them before Young left for Southern Utah, but the judge conveniently held it until the president was gone so it could be said that he had fled the territory. The murder charge dated back to the 1857 Echo Canyon war when William A. "Bill" Hickman supposedly murdered Richard Yates; in 1871 he claimed he committed the murder on orders from Young, Wells, Stout, and Kimball. (For a history of this case, see Whitney 2:630-42.)

News of the arrests of Wells, Stout, and Kimball was telegraphed to St. George on December 14. Though Brigham was counseled not to return to Salt Lake where he surely would be arrested, he quickly decided to go. "It is common knowledge to those who were closely associated with President Young in his career, that he was greatly influenced, and often against his own judgment, by what he called "the Light"; doubtless the inspiration of God to his mind. . . . So now on this question of his returning to face his enemies, he had said "*The 'Light' says, Brigham, return*" (CHC 5:402).

George A. Smith, William Rossiter, Alexander F. MacDonald, John Henry Smith, Robert and his son Charles were asked to return with him. Also in the party were Amelia Folsom Young and Bathsheba Bigler Smith, wives of Brigham Young and George A. Smith. Robert immediately began preparing for the trip and worked to leave the affairs of the boarding house in proper order. On December 16, the Saints held a big party at the St. George Hall, and after Sunday services on the seventeenth, President Young's party started north. Robert, Charles and MacDonald, however, were busy finishing up their business until Monday morning. Robert recorded in his journal:

Monday, 18th, 1871. After settling our business matters pertaining
to the Boarding house and bidding farewell to many warm hearted
friends, at 11 AM we started for the North. We had occupied Elder
E Snows large house since Nov 13 & both him and his family treated
us with every kindness not only in giving us the use of his own
modern house and many articles of furniture, cooking utensils, etc.
but in every way possible to add to the happiness of the Company.
We left with Bro Snow many articles of our household effects, etc as
a small reward for the kindness received.

The Burtons and "Mack," as Robert called him, caught up
with the main party in Cedar City on December 20, where they
were all met by Porter Rockwell, Joseph A. Young, and Orson
Arnold, who had come from Salt Lake to escort and protect the
prophet during his journey. One day out of Cedar City, storm
clouds gathered, and by the time they left Beaver the next morning, December 22, the snow was eight inches deep and the wind
was blowing hard from the south. The blizzard continued
through the next day's journey to Fillmore; sometimes they could
not see the horses pulling their own buggies and wagons for the
snow. Traveling on Christmas day into Nephi, they found the
roads muddy and rutted though the storm had lessened. In Nephi,
Heber C. Kimball, John Sharp, and A. M. Musser, who had
come from Salt Lake, awaited them. Between Nephi and Payson,
the blizzard struck again, but they could not wait it out; they
changed horses and moved on. In Provo and again in American
Fork, they were given fresh horses and pressed on toward the
terminus of the railroad at Draper where they arrived at 10:30
P.M. They had telegraphed word of their location, and many
friends were waiting with the engine and cars to take them into
Salt Lake. Lewis Hills had been sent to assist Robert and Charles
(December 20–26, 1871).

The many family members who were gathered at Robert's
home were disappointed to learn that he could not even spend
the night. He visited them briefly about midnight, then went to
William Jennings home. Maria came to see him there the next
day, and late that night he went to Nancy Garr Badger's home

where he was reunited with Sarah and her children. He spent the next day and night with Theresa and Lewis Hills.

Once again Robert lived his underground life. He worked on his assessment books and record books for the factory, he visited friends, met with Church leaders, occasionally went to the farm or to the factory to supervise, and spent every night at a different place. He was still bishop of the Fifteenth Ward, but had not attended services since the summer before. On February 13, 1872, the ward members planned "an entertainment for my benefit" at the courthouse. "This was a time long to be remembered" he wrote in his journal early the next morning. He was grateful to be honored, but seemed more pleased to see the many friends and neighbors he had not seen for a year and a half. George A. Smith, John Taylor, Wilford Woodruff, Orson Pratt, Lot Smith, and Angus Cannon spoke, Robert gave a short response, and then they all sang until 1 A.M.

On January 2 Brigham Young was arrested and arraigned in court on the murder charge. He was refused bail and confined to his home until the March term of court. Robert recorded in his journal that day his disgust at the obstinance of Judge McKean because "bonds could have been given to any amount and the Pres. had come 350 miles to answer to the charge without having been arrested." A marshal moved into a room at the Young home to guard him until the trial.

However, the federal judicial crusade actually doomed its own success by ruling out of existence the territorial marshal, who was the only person authorized to pay court expenses for territorial cases. The federal government refused to pay expenses for offenses "against territorial laws, to be punished in territorial courts, by territorial officers thereof." Of course, the territorial legislature refused to answer the appeals of the district judges and U.S. district attorney for funds to run courts contrary to territorial laws. And so March passed, the cases were not called up, and the grand and petit juries were dismissed because there was no way to pay per diem expenses (CHC 5:408–12).

Meanwhile, the U.S. Supreme Court was considering the appeal of the Engebrecht case which challenged the method of determining juries. Word around Salt Lake was that the territorial law would be upheld and all indictments would be quashed, so Robert began staying at home more often. He also went to the farm to supervise the spring planting. He was at home on the evening of April 15, when Angus M. Cannon brought the welcome news of the Supreme Court decision: "Jury unlawfully drawn; summonses invalid; proceedings ordered dismissed. Decision unanimous. All indictments quashed" (CHC 5:412).

Although press releases reported in the East that the "Mormons were turbulent and threatening" (in CHC 5:413), the citizens of Utah and especially the accused accepted the announcement calmly. Robert's "celebration" was probably quite typical. The next evening he went to the Salt Lake Theatre; and on Saturday, he walked around the ward, then entertained the MacDonalds from Provo at his home since they were both free to go and come without fear of the marshals. On Sunday, Robert attended the 2 P.M. meeting in the Tabernacle for the first time since October 1871. In the evening, he presided at his Fifteenth Ward service. The next week, he returned the MacDonalds' visit spending two days in Provo, visiting many friends and conferring with Abraham O. Smoot on factory business.

Within a week, the residents of Salt Lake City seem to have forgotten the entire episode. April Conference had been postponed because Brigham Young was in custody. A writ of *habeas corpus* was issued on April 25, and conference convened on the twenty-eighth with President Young attending both sessions. This was a time for true celebration and Robert listened intently to the prophet's "few words" about the reign of Judge McKean: "I have no reflections to cast upon these Courts. How much power, ability, or opportunity would I have to possess, do you think, if all were combined, to disgrace them as they have disgraced themselves? I have neither the power nor ability, consequently I have nothing to say with regard to their conduct. It is before the world, it is before the heavens continually" (in CHC 5:416).

Judge McKean was chief justice until March 1875 when he was removed from office less than a year after his reappointment (Alexander 1966, 96–98).

All this while, Robert had continued to hold the offices of sheriff, county assessor and tax collector, city councilman, and to supervise Wasatch Woolen Mill (R. T. Burton n.d.[a], 48).

On March 6, his oldest son, William Shipley, married his sweetheart Julia, daughter of Joseph and Mary Isabelle Hale Horne. Maria and Mary Horne were friends from Nauvoo, and William learned after his marriage that the two women had "betrothed" him and Julia as infants, yet never told them of the arrangement. The families were close friends, and the relationship grew naturally, with their courtship beginning when they were seventeen and sixteen. Julia was also particularly close to Robert's wife Sarah. When six-year old Alice had fallen seriously ill in 1870, Julia had asked William to take her to the farm where she remained until after Alice's death and funeral, taking care of the five boys and the farmhouse work. Robert was also fond of Julia, and William wrote that Robert and Sarah loved her like one of their own daughters (W. S. Burton n.d.[c], 45).

William and Julia lived on the farm after their wedding, and soon Julia was expecting a child. It was a particularly busy summer on the farm; and because Robert was often out of town William was in charge. He also supervised the factory and later regretted that they had had no time for a honeymoon. Julia's daughter was born prematurely in the early morning hours of November 26. Robert had brought his sister Melissa to the farm to help and thought all was well. However, without warning Julia's condition changed, and she died at 3:30 A.M. in spite of all Maria, Sarah, and Melissa could do. William wrote: "I have never seen father more affected even at the sick bed of his own children than when he realized she could not live" (n.d.[c], 45–46).

The infant was named Julia after her mother and was probably nursed and cared for by Sarah who had seventeen-month old Edward and was seven months pregnant with Theodore at the time. Julia's funeral was held in the Fourteenth Ward on

November 29, and she was buried in the family plot at the Salt Lake City Cemetery. Baby Julia lived just eleven months and died October 24, 1873. These were sorrowful times for the Burtons, but they had seen their share of miracles and kept going, facing the tragedies with great faith.

Notes

1. These journals are noted in the bibliography as covering the years 1856–1907. Before 1871, the entries are not continuous; after January 1871, the entries are daily and continuous to 1907. These journals have been cited as Robert T. Burton 1856–1907, (date). From this point, all entries that are cited as a date are also from these journals.

2. Thomas G. Alexander examines the conflict between James B. McKean and the Mormons from a broader historical viewpoint in "Federal Authority Versus Polygamic Theocracy: James B. McKean and the Mormons 1870–1875," *Dialogue* 1 (Autumn 1966) 85–100.

3. George W. Bean described his role during this time: "It fired some of us to action when he [McKean] permitted falsehoods to bring fine men and even Brigham Young to trial. It kept some of us busy at times to keep the brethren out of the clutches of his merciless Myrmidons. Many of the brethren had to be guarded safely through and between the settlements and again O. P. Rockwell and George W. Bean [referring to himself] were on duty. Many other brethren offered and quietly guarded our innocent leaders" (Bean 1945, 158).

16

Mission to England, 1873–75

Robert's opportunity to serve a mission in Europe finally came in the summer of 1873. He was called to England and served first as president of the Birmingham Conference and then the London Conference. As a mature missionary and an important business leader, he led a group of elders on a tour through Europe to visit the World's Fair in Vienna and view the latest mechanical inventions. In spite of his many administrative responsibilities, he left the mission office whenever possible to visit the Saints in their homes and attend their branch meetings, socials, and conferences. He loved the English people and rejoiced as those he termed "strangers" to the gospel were baptized.

It was conference time again, April 1873. A year had passed since Brigham Young was released from his "prison" at home. Robert T. Burton was once again sitting with the bishops at the front of the Tabernacle. He listened with great interest as the prophet transferred many Church business duties to the younger men who surrounded him. It was said that he was finally encouraging others "to bear off the burden of the Kingdom" (Nibley 1937, 489).

During the final session of the three-day conference, on the afternoon of April 8, Robert heard his own name spoken from the podium, called as a foreign missionary to England. Almost immediately he recalled a conference in Nauvoo more than twenty-seven years earlier when he and his brother William had been called as missionaries to England. That mission had been postponed, first until the Saints were out of Nauvoo, then until they were resettled in the Great Basin. After 1848, whenever it was time to send missionaries, Robert's responsibilities kept him closer to home. Indeed, some family members thought he seemed indispensable to Brigham Young as a bodyguard, an advisor, a military leader, a civil servant, and a companion. He was most definitely one of the circle of "younger men" who were being given increased responsibilities by the prophet. Undoubtedly it was Robert's legal release from the indictment for the Morrisite murders that permitted him to be called at this time.

Robert's journal entries indicate no hint of hesitation, surprise, or advance knowledge about the call. After years of ordering his life to be ready for *any* call from the prophet, Robert simply went home from conference, told his family of the assignment, and "commenced to arrange my public and private business to be ready to start at the appointed time" (n.d.ᵃ, 49). Because his public and private business affairs were extensive, preparation time was lengthy. He was not released as Fifteenth Ward bishop and his counselors, Joseph Pollard and Elias Morris carried on the work of the bishopric until his return. He made arrangements for others to perform his public duties and when his terms of office expired during his absence other men were appointed or elected as sheriff, county assessor, and city councilman.

His oldest son William had been called as a member of the "Arizona Camp" to colonize along the Little Colorado River in northern Arizona. Robert recorded in his journal April 10, 1873, that he had asked Brigham Young to release William "on account of my appointment." The release was granted on condition that another of the Burton sons fill the call. After a council at home, his second son, Robert T., Jr., accepted the assignment. Robert was engaged to Rosalia Salisbury, and they were married at the Burton residence on April 21 just two days before the camp's departure, Robert officiating. The Arizona camp left April 23 and returned late in 1873, having explored the Little Colorado for many miles without locating a suitable site for settlement.

During the next few weeks, Robert spent a seemingly disproportionate amount of time working on the books of the woolen mills. His main business activity in 1872 and 1873 had been supervising the woolen mills for A. O. Smoot and Company. At this time, the company appears to have been operating both the Wasatch and Deseret Woolen mills, although Brigham Young still owned the Deseret Mill. As supervising partner, Robert, with his sons and a hired foreman, had made these mills one of the successful home manufacturers of the territory.

As previously shown, Robert entrusted his farms and livestock only to his sons, and most particularly to William. In addition to farming, William served as deputy sheriff and may have also assumed the duties of county assessor during his father's absence. William was also responsible for his mother, Maria, his infant daughter, Julia, and his six younger brothers and sisters living at home.

Susan and her family lived on Second South. Her oldest son, Willard, was sixteen years old and assumed most of the manly duties for his family of three younger brothers, Hosea, George, and Walter, and his five year-old sister, Lizzie.

Sarah and her seven boys were living on the farm. They ranged from fifteen-year-old Henry to four-month-old Theodore T. Although William supervised the farm and there were hired men also, Sarah was left with much responsibility as she kept chickens and dairy cows, and sold both eggs and freshly churned butter to help meet the expenses of her family.

As his time of departure drew near, Robert was invited on Sunday evening, May 4, to the Church Historians Office where he and seventeen other elders and one sister were set apart by members of the Quorum of the Twelve. Robert was set apart first by John Taylor, with Wilford Woodruff and George Q.

Cannon assisting. Once the blessings were concluded, the apostles each stood to counsel the missionaries, many of them young men on their first missions. They were exhorted to be pure, to abstain from the very appearance of evil, to keep journals, to live the Word of Wisdom, to be on guard against impostors and those who would pretend to be friends, to avoid keeping company with young women in the field, and to never give the devil an advantage over them by going on his ground (JH, May 4, 1873).

The next Sunday, Robert gathered his family together at the farm where he baptized two of his children, Florence and Alfred, and enjoyed the company of his loved ones. That night he was the principal speaker at the Fifteenth Ward Sacrament Meeting and offered kind words and counsel to his flock of faithful Saints. He left the affairs of the ward in the hands of his counselors, Joseph Pollard and Elias Morris. While he was absent, the ward was organized as a branch of the United Order, with Robert as president and his counselors as vice presidents (JH, May 23, 1874).

The entertainments and farewells finally over, on Thursday, May 15, Robert went to see Brigham Young whom he loved and respected. Saying farewell was the last thing he did before leaving the valley, and calling on President Young was one of his first duties upon his return twenty-six months later. Some family members and friends accompanied the missionaries to Ogden the next morning, traveling on the Utah Central Railroad at 5:30 A.M. At 8:00 A.M. the missionaries boarded the Union Pacific train for Omaha and were on their way at last.

Robert's journey to New York City took him through Sublette, Illinois; Toledo, Ohio; and Buffalo, New York. Once again, he visited the Austins and Leybourns. He spent some time getting his sister Jane to relate the family's genealogy and history in England, jotting down these notes in the back of his 1873 journal to help him find family members in England: "My sister Jane says my parents were married in the Town or Parrish of Garthrope, Lancashire [sic], and that many of our relatives are in this place, some in Gilberdike, some in Burton Stather

[in] Hornsey or Auncy, a Bathing place. See the families of Gibson and Greensides."

In Buffalo, New York, he delivered a package of books from Brigham Young to the famous Grossenor Library. His schedule permitted him a few hours of sightseeing at Niagara Falls, which he thought was beautiful beyond description. In his journal May 24, he wrote: "The grandure of the falls surpasses all description." Within a few months, he would be able to compare this sight with Europe's most magnificent scenery. He was beginning a grand adventure as well as a concentrated period of church service.

During three days in New York City, he revisited some favorite places from his 1869–70 mission and friends from the Williamsburg Branch. One of his nephews (he mentions no name) spent a day with him and took him to the steamer *Idaho*, which he boarded on the afternoon of May 28, with Elders John Clark,[1] John C. Graham, S. C. Thurman, and a Sister Douglas and her son who were returning to England for a visit.

All the sights and wonders of the ocean became journal entries during a very pleasant Atlantic crossing. One day Robert saw a school of whales, another they passed a fleet of fishing vessels and a large sailing ship. He enjoyed shuffleboard, concerts, reading, and talking with other passengers. While many on board were seasick, Robert was not, and comforted those who were suffering when the seas were roughest. On Saturday, June 7, land was sighted and the ship docked in Liverpool on June 8.

The missionary effort of The Church of Jesus Christ of Latter-day Saints in England and Europe began in the 1830s and was fully mature when Robert T. Burton and his companions reached the mission office at 42 Islington Street, Liverpool. The European Mission was headed by Apostle Albert Carrington, who immediately assigned Robert to serve as president of the Birmingham Conference. As conference president, Robert was responsible for much more than the elders assigned to Birmingham. He was expected to help Church members emigrate to

Zion (including collecting, bookkeeping, and dispersing funds for the Perpetual Emigration Fund), to counsel with local leaders concerning their branches and members, to teach gospel principles to members and investigators whenever possible, and to represent the Church before the civic officials in negotiations touching any of the Church's interests. From the Liverpool office came weekly issues of the *Millennial Star* which served for a century and a half as a vital communications link for the British Saints and as primary publisher of doctrinal statements and interpretations, official policies, and current history of the Church in America and Europe. Robert was to note in his journal many times in the next two years: "Spent most of the day getting off the Stars."

While Robert was a very organized administrator of first the Birmingham Conference and later the London Conference, his journal reveals that he also spent time building Zion temporally as well as spiritually. He combined missionary service with tours of factories, military displays, fairs, exhibits, and "modern day" wonders and enjoyed cultural and historical experiences as well. Two years in England greatly enhanced the education and foresight of this dedicated Utah entrepreneur. However, these activities did not take him away from teaching the gospel or improving the image of the Church among the British people. He quickly developed friendships among the British; as he traveled to hold services or teach members or investigators, he asked them to show him their historical sites, the factories where they worked, and the cultural events important in their lives.

Perhaps his first three weeks in Birmingham as recorded in his journal are typical of the pattern of his mission. Elder Joseph Birch met him at the train station on Thursday, June 12, 1873, and took him immediately to a meeting at the chapel. He spent the next morning in the Conference House "becoming acquainted with the business of my Conference & sending out Stars etc" (June 13, 1873). In the afternoon, he and a companion went out visiting some of the Saints and returned for an appointment with a man who was curious "in regards to our faith."

On Sunday, three converts were baptized and confirmed at a morning meeting where Robert was the principal speaker. After evening services, several of the members came to the conference house to converse into the night with Elders Burton, Birch and A. B. Taylor.

As he became acquainted with the area, the people, and the missionaries, Robert became more and more pleased with his assignment to Birmingham, a large industrial city dating back to the tenth century. A regional center of England's Midlands located on a major river, Birmingham was fast becoming a principal industrial complex for the British Isles. In the 1870s, brass foundries, gun, jewelry, hardware, button manufacturers, and Cadbury chocolate and cocoa works were already established there (*Encyclopedia International* 3:37).

At an agricultural fair held in the Aston Park and Botanical Gardens, Robert met "the best Ladies & Gentlemen of Birmingham." He spent Tuesday, June 17, at the fair with Elder Birch and returned a second time two days later with Elder E. W. Snow and Sister Ivins and her daughter, who were housekeepers at the conference house.

On his second Friday in England he traveled a short distance to the town of Dudley where he visited a few strong LDS families and a castle which overlooked the country all around. He recorded in his journal on June 20, "This Castle is a very ancient structure erected 17th Century and gives a fine idea of those old times."

Following Sunday's meetings at Hockley Branch, which Robert often described as "the little chapel," and a baptismal service for four converts, Robert began a six-day tour of the adjoining towns in the conference. Elder Snow accompanied him. Coventry was their first stop. After calling on several member families and friends, they visited a large silk factory which manufactured ribbons. That evening, they held a meeting in the home of a Brother Reynolds. The next morning, they traveled to Rugby, which was a railroad center. "Came to the house of Bro. John Hill a very good man. Remained here today. Found no saints but this one family and apparently no one wishes to hear the Gospel." A train took them south from Rugby to Leamington, where they visited some member families who took them to tour Warwick Castle.

Stratford-on-Avon was their next stop. They visited Shakespeare's birthplace and the old church where he was buried, viewing the sixteenth century Shakespearean relics just as tourists do today. Apparently there was just one Church member there, a Brother Ballard, who fed them lunch before they left on foot for the small town of Lowby, some four miles distant. Lowby had a branch of twenty-five members, "very much scattered, many of them luke warm and all very poor." A meeting that night brought out only a few because "being farmers, many of them [were] away at work." The next morning they walked back to Stratford-on-Avon and took the train to Birmingham. The week's travels were ended and Robert was more familiar with the British Saints and their challenges. Elder John Mendenhall, a newly assigned elder met Robert at the conference house.

Twice during July, groups of Saints emigrated from Birmingham. Robert accompanied the second group of seventeen to Liverpool where he helped them board the *Nevada* on July 10, which sailed with 283 Saints and six returning missionaries. In Liverpool, he visited the park and docks in Burkenhead with John C. Graham and George Crismon and discussed with President Carrington his own upcoming tour of Europe en route to the World's Fair at Vienna, Austria, with Elders Clark, Herrick, and Naegle.

He returned to Birmingham for only a few days. John Clark arrived there from Sheffield on July 12, and they traveled together to London on July 16 to meet Lester J. Herrick of the London Conference. They visited in the London branches and also saw the sights of London while completing arrangements for their trip. The Bank of England, Guild Hall, Crystal Palace, Billingsgate Station, the Tower of London, Westminster Abbey, Hyde Park, the King Albert Memorial, Regents Park and Zoological Gardens, and Madame Tusands were all stops on a whirlwind three-day London holiday (July 16–19, 1873).

Elders Burton, Clark, and Herrick left London together on the evening of July 21, and traveled by train to Harwich where they boarded the steamer *Zealous Mousdell*, crossed the English Channel, and landed in Antwerp, Belgium. Their first impressions of Europe were the "very fine" cathedrals of Antwerp and the "splendid arcade 650 feet long occupied by a number of shops on each side—a very beautiful sight" at Brussels where they spent their first night. They arranged for a carriage to pick them up early the next morning for a visit to the battlefield of Waterloo. Robert had read a biography of Napoleon Bonaparte during his months of hiding in 1871, and he planned to visit all the significant memorials from the Napoleonic period during the tour.

The carriage left Brussels on a beautiful promenade, and the men were soon passing through the forest "on the Norelle Road made by the Emperor Napoleon in 1814" en route to Waterloo. In Robert's recap of his European tour written at the end of his 1873 diary, he described the sights in detail indicating his intense interest in the battlefields and historical places.

> We came to the Castle . . . where the . . . English rested protected by the Brick walls then new now old and bearing the mark of French Balls. From here we came to the Mont or Mount St. Johns and the position of the two Armies for night. Arrived there by 225 stone steps and capt by a stone top and the Lion on the top. This is the Center of the British Forces and from here we have a good view of the battle field and the position held by the contending forces. This is one of the most pleasant days yet spent. . . . We next visited the Church where many Officers are interred and from this point returned through the forest De Soignes to Brussels (July 23, 1873).

Although long accustomed to writing of his travels and experiences without much emotion, Robert's evident enthusiasm for Waterloo makes it a highlight among his experiences all of which were extraordinary for a man born and reared on the frontier of America. His journal entry for July 23 also described the modern citizens of the city, observed in their leisure that evening: "Thousands of People are sitting in the streets in the most

Public places drinking beer as is the usual custom, men and women by thousands."

The next morning, the three elders took the Belgium State Railroad eastward through Liege ("as we come near Liege it gets to be quite hilly resembling many parts of our mountains") and arriving in the evening at Cologne, Germany, on the Rhine River. The next morning, they met Elder John C. Naegle. He had left London a day late, and they were very glad to have him join them as he spoke German fluently. After climbing 250 feet to the top of the Cologne Cathedral for a "splendid view of the Rhine and surrounding country," the group proceeded by train to Bonn, where they purchased tickets to Koblenz on a steamer—the preferred way of viewing the beauty of the Rhine Valley. "This is said to be the finest part of the Rhine; the scenery is certainly very beautiful," Robert wrote on July 26.

In the nineteenth century, as yet today, sightseers went to the Rhine Valley to see the huge castles built centuries before to exact toll from passing ships. The elders hired a cab at Koblenz to drive some six miles back upriver to see one castle and "the old Moselle Bridge erected over 500 years ago." The next morning, they visited the castle and fortress of Ehrenbreiten on the opposite side of the river, commanding a view of the entire country at the confluence of the Moselle and the Rhine rivers. Robert wrote on July 27: "This is a very strong fort being built upon a Rock and approached by a circuitous route winding up the hill, secured by high walls from the bottom and by 2 deep moats and heavy gates. . . . This is justly termed the Gibraltar of the Rhine and has never surrendered except by starvation and is a place of Great Importance."

Continuing down the Rhine, Robert was impressed by the scenery which "can't be surpassed." From the Castle Klopp at Bingen, they enjoyed a panoramic view of the Rhine and its junction with the Main. In Mainz on July 28, Robert took note of the ever-present army, "This City like all others we have yet seen in Germany is full of Troops and this one is the most strongly fortified. Population of 50,000 and over 8,000 Troops quartered."

They left the Rhine at Mainz and went by rail across Germany to Würzburg, leaving behind the forest of pine and birch and entering country much flatter and more suitable for farming, which prompted this description later on July 28: "We are now in the Western Part of Bavaria. In this like all the other Rhine Provinces the Women perform much of the field labor and Cows are used mostly for team work on farms, seldom Horses or Oxen are used and when they are used generally only one horse [or] one ox is used."

At Munich on July 29, their arrival coincided with the return to the city of some of the last troops which had been fighting for the Northern German Confederation in France. A "vast concourse" of people greeted the soldiers with shouting and cheers. Prime Minister Otto von Bismarck of Prussia was holding a loose empire together with great military might under King William, who had been crowned emperor of Germany following the defeat of Napoleon III of France in 1871. Still Bavaria had its own king, and on July 30, Robert and his companions toured the "Kings Palace, thru all the apartments all of which were very elegant. . . . The floors being most all inlaid and the walls of Marble; the finish about the windows and doors Bronze. Statues, etc. were all very elegant."

From Munich they traveled eastward to Mühldorf on the River Inn, a tributary of the Danube, and along the beautiful Danube through Austria to Vienna, which they reached at 7:30 P.M. on July 31. Although the city was thronging with residents and visitors, the four American missionaries obtained rooms in a private house near the Maria Theresa Bridge which suited them for their short stay.

They spent the next two days at the world's fair. The first day they inspected the exhibits in the mechanical department, which was "over a half mile in length and filled with machinery." As might be expected, Robert recorded on August 1, "This is a fine sight . . . [I am] well satisfied with the Exposition and consider it one of the Grandest ever yet exhibited to Man!"

On Sunday, August 3, Robert was awake early to begin a letter to his family which he customarily wrote on the Sabbath when he was traveling. He described the country through which he had traveled and the technological wonders he had examined at the fair. Perhaps most exciting was his description of a momentous event which he and the elders witnessed during their second day at the fair and recorded in his journal for August 2. The elders had been on the grounds not more than an hour when "the word became circulated that his Highness the Emperor Francis Joseph of Austria and the Shaw of Persia would visit the Exposition." This caused great commotion among the throngs of fair visitors who began leaving the exhibits to gather on the streets and paths near the entrance, hoping to glimpse the noted rulers. The missionaries positioned themselves well and, after waiting for nearly two hours, finally saw the monarchs entering the grounds in a beautiful carriage drawn by six gray horses. Throughout the day, as the emperor and shah moved from exhibit to exhibit, the crowds rushed to see them, finding the sight much more interesting for the moment than the fair.

When Robert walked out to see the city of Vienna, he thought it "the finest City I have yet visited." But all was not admirable as the broad streets, rows of trees and fine blocks of buildings made it appear. He found that "the people many of them seem very poor notwithstanding the fine appearance of the City. Women compelled to drudge while large Armies of men are maintained at enormous cost" (August 2, 1873).

Unfortunately, they were able to stay only three days, two at the fair and one sightseeing at the palace and parks of Vienna. By Monday morning, they were traveling again. They traveled from Vienna to the port of Trieste on the Adriatic Sea through mountains which made the travelers feel quite homesick. In his biography, Robert mentions a great epidemic of cholera. He wrote, "Our visit to this ancient city [Vienna] was somewhat marred by the prevalence of cholera in the vicinity." (n.d.[a], 51–52) There was also cholera at Trieste, which prevented them from traveling to Venice by steamer. "In consequence of the prevalence of Cholera we were compelled to proceed by rail passing through some very nice country into Italy" (n.d.[a], 52). Robert described this trip on August 6: "We are now in a better

County, fruits and vegetables looking better but very dry. Much of the vegetation is drying up for want of Rain, hundreds of acres of corn is dead and will not amount to anything. We now come to Conegleano and Treviso near the foot of one of the largest Mountains we have yet seen, called by the Italians the Mountain of Mountains."

Although they arrived in Venice at 7 P.M., they wasted little time going out to see the city. " After supper, [we] hired a gondola and visited some of the principle objects of curiosity and spent the evening in the Grand Plaza of Saint Mark. The people were here by the thousands, a fine Band playing at the stand in the Center" (August 6, 1873). From Venice, they went straight across northern Italy to Milan. "This has been the most dusty day I ever experienced in a RR car," Robert wrote on August 8. After visiting the Arco Della Peace founded by Napoleon I, they traveled north, crossing by boat the beautiful pristine lakes of Como and Lugano, at the base of the Italian Alps.

Before railroads covered Europe, travelers used large stagecoaches, known as diligences, which dated back to the eighteenth century. From Lugano at the northern end of the lakes, the elders traveled by diligence into the high Alps, traveling all night and the next day, crossing St. Gotthard Pass during the morning hours. Robert concluded in his journal on August 11, 1873, "This is the finest Mountain scenery I have ever seen."

They were in Switzerland when the diligence reached its terminus at Fluelen, a city on the eastern shore of Lake Lucerne, and the elders took a steamer to Lucerne at the west end of the lake. During these weeks of travel they had no contact with other missionaries or Church members. However, in Lucerne they met Elder Johannes Huber, president of the Swiss/German Mission, and his companion, Elder Keller, who came from Bern to see them. Robert recorded on August 12, "We had a pleasant visit; are looking at the City. It is finely situated and a beautiful Country, much like our home in the mts."

After viewing Switzerland from the summit of Mt. Rigi across Lake Lucerne, they left Switzerland, leaving Elder Naegle with Elders Huber and Keller. Elders Burton, Clark, and Herrick traveled northwestward through France, arriving in Paris at mid-morning on August 14, where sights from Napoleon's time were the main attraction. Robert wrote in his journal: "After breakfast hired a cab and drove through the City visiting at the Arch of Triumph Erected 1836 by Napoleon. . . . We next came to the large Park [Tuilleries Garden] and returning pass . . . the Tomb of Napoleon. Came to the Panorama of the Defense of Paris. This is one of the most wonderful works of Art." On Sunday, August 17, they went by train to Versailles, "visiting first the gallery of paintings in the Palace of the Emperor, then to the beautiful gardens & grounds laid out some nearly two centuries since. These are finely laid out."

Paris was the last city on the continental tour. Two days later Robert Burton and John Clark were back in Birmingham where Robert was relieved to find everything going well in the conference and a large stack of mail from home. His last journal notation on August 19 concluding the tour was simply: "2844 miles." These unassuming gentlemen from the heart of the barely settled American desert had traveled nearly 3,000 miles by train, steamer, and coach seeing sights of history, natural beauty, industry, geography, and culture that they would never forget.

Preparations for a conference in Birmingham were underway, and Robert quickly found himself caught up in the work, getting ready for the arrival of the visiting authorities. President Carrington and five other elders arrived on Saturday, August 23. Robert recorded that "We had a good visit together" and a "splendid conference." The elders stayed two days to tour the Gellets Steel factory, an electro plate factory, and Aston Park, and they enjoyed a concert put on by the Saints at Hockley Chapel.

As the weeks and months of missionary work continued, Robert recorded in his journal many details of his visits to members, investigators, branches, factories, and sights. Certain things always brought him greater satisfaction. He was happy when there were "strangers" at the branch meetings and when "the house was well filled." "Strangers" were most often potential investigators, persons inquiring about the Church for the first time. He wrote of baptismal services and confirmation meetings, which were potent spiritual times. For example, this entry was made on Sunday, August 30, 1874: "At 2 1/2 attended meeting at N.L. Many strangers present. After a short meeting repaired to Bath house and baptized 5 persons. Several strangers attended the performance of the ordinance. 6 1/2 Again attended meeting same place. Had a full flow of the spirit and all present were inspired. Some strangers came and were administered to."

He often wrote of healing the sick through priesthood administration. The first mentioned healing took place at Dudley, near Birmingham, just prior to his continental tour. A Brother Rubury, who had suffered a stroke, was near death when Elders Burton and Snow administered to him on Sunday, June 29, 1873. Two months passed, and Robert again visited the Dudley Branch. He was invited to tea at Brother Rubury's home, where he observed and recorded in his journal on August 27, that he was "miraculously healed." Robert administered to Sister Rubury during a visit at Christmastime, 1873. Although she had been "very sick," Robert wrote on December 27, after a blessing "she was better." Following the Sunday evening meeting of the North London Branch on January 25, 1874, Robert reported that, "many sick came forwards . . . and [were] administered to."

After serving four months in Birmingham, Robert was transferred to London on his fifty-second birthday, October 25, 1873. He was well acquainted with the elders serving in London, the conference house at 20 Bishops Grove, and the London branches, so he resumed work immediately. His second day in London, he attended priesthood meeting in the North London Branch, the 2 P.M. worship service at Lambeth Branch, and the 6:30 service at Whitechapel. It was a long but exhilarating Sabbath.

He had not been in London very long when a reporter from the *Daily Telegraph* wrote seeking an interview. Newspapers at the time were not known for being fair in their comments about the Church, but Robert granted this reporter the opportunity to discuss religion with him and, following the interview, wrote in his journal on November 13, 1873, that "He seemed well satisfied and promised to make a fair report."

From Robert's journals, it is evident that he spent a significant amount of time writing letters. He wrote frequently to other missionaries, especially to President Carrington and later to President Joseph F. Smith. He wrote to Church members in the London Conference, to other persons with interest in the Church, and to agents, prospective emigrants, and others. In addition, hardly a day passed that he did not write to someone in Utah—either Maria, Sarah, Susan, William, Willard or one of the other children, friends, city officials, one of the apostles, his counselors in the Fifteenth Ward, his business associates, and sometimes to his brother or sisters in Utah, Ohio, or Illinois. Considering the length of time it took to pass mail across the ocean and the continent, it seems amazing how many letters were exchanged. Unfortunately, only one of these many letters has been found among family records. It was written to Heber, Robert's four-year-old son, and is dated London, April 21, 1875:

> My Dear Boy Heber
>
> I received a very kind letter from your dear Mama Monday last (19th) and she therein suggested I had written to most all the others but not to you and Edward so I thought I would send you this and enclose with it a little [picture] so you could see if you remembered any one resembling it, as it will be about two years since you have seen Papa when this reaches you.
>
> You are now getting to be quite a large boy I presume. Do you go to school with Florence, Mary & Lizzy. If so you will soon learn to read and write, so that when I come you can read to me. I hope you are very kind and good to little sisters and to dear Mama also. You will please let Lizzy and Walter, and the others read this or have it read as [I] cannot write them all at one time.
>
> Also please give my love to them all. May the Lord bless and preserve you all is the constant prayer of your affectionate father,
> R. T. Burton.

Most of the time the news Robert received from Utah was good, and he was pleased that the Lord was caring for his family and his interests during his absence. However, when he received word of the death of William's tiny daughter, Robert wrote on November 15: "This is the most painful intelligence received since leaving home. She was a fine child and much beloved by the family." The next day was the Sabbath and he spent the morning writing his consolation and love to William.

Albert Carrington was released as European Mission president in October of 1873, and Lester J. Herrick, who had toured Europe with Robert, served temporarily until the new president, Joseph F. Smith, arrived in March of 1874. President Smith was only thirty-five years old, yet he had been an apostle and counselor in the First Presidency for seven years. This was the second of his three missions to Great Britain and Europe. His arrival on March 21, 1874, prompted a series of conferences which Robert attended, allowing him to visit almost every part of the British Isles.

The first conference was held in Sheffield, famous for its iron works; the next Sunday they were in Nottingham where the meetings were "well attended and good spirit was manifested." To travel to Wales, Robert rode what was said to be the "fastest train in the world," which traveled at the rate of one mile per minute. The conference in Glasgow permitted Robert his only opportunity to visit Scotland, where his brother William served and died in 1854. In this especially memorable week, he enjoyed speaking to the Scottish Saints so much that he took up the entire morning session of the conference on April 26, 1874. The next day, Elders Archibald McFarland, Robert McQuarrie, W. Fife, and others showed off the magnificent sights of nearby Dumbarton Castle and Loch Lomond, where they had a "fine row on the lake." Tuesday and Wednesday were spent in Edinburgh where Robert visited Chapel Royal, Royal Scots Academy, the House of Parliament, the Palace of Holyrood, and saw the troops drilling at Queen's Park (March 21–May 1, 1874).

London's conference was scheduled for May 17. Whether the date was planned or coincidental, it was the same weekend Alexander II, czar of Russia, was visiting the English royal family. The conference sessions were held on Sunday and "many strangers [were] present, some of whom gave their names for baptism." On Monday, the London Saints gave a concert in honor of the visiting Church authorities, including Joseph F. Smith who was leaving for Denmark on Tuesday. The elders tried to see the czar as he passed through the city, but the crowds were too great. On Tuesday, May 19, however, Elders Burton, Hardy, and Squires took the train to Aldershot where they witnessed a military grand review and mock battle of 17,000 troops, held before the czar and the Prince of Wales. Robert thought the battle included "many fine military manovers." He was not disappointed in the review or the "good look" he had of Alexander and his lieutenant as they returned to the rail station.

In May and June, emigrating Saints prepared to depart. Robert sent a flute to fourteen-year-old Frank with someone in the first group. In June, Robert sent a young girl (name unknown) from Birmingham to live with Sarah on the farm. Robert went to Liverpool on June 10, to help her get on the *Nevada*, and to introduce her to the Saints from London who were to watch out for her during the long trip.

From Liverpool, Robert went to Yorkshire searching for his family and ancestry. First he and his companion, M. H. Hardy, went to Leeds where they stayed three days with Joseph Burton, a member but not a relative. On June 15, he and Elder Hardy took a train to Goole on the Ouse tributary of the Humber River, which put Robert back in the area from which his parents emigrated in 1817. In his journal of June 16–20, he made notes of the genealogical search begun there:

> Tues 16 At 9 AM left Capt. Wright at Goole for Hull by boat down the Humber . . . Came by R. R. to Hornsea on the sea coast, a small village where I found a cousin by the name of Elizabeth

Potter who is quite old. Received us kindly and stayed with them tonight but got but little information of my father's family. She lives in big house occupied by her family for 300 years.

Wed 17 Wrote my wife Maria and at 11:15 AM came to R. R. station for Hull where we arrived at 12 N. . . . 5 PM Came by boat to Garthrope [Garthorpe] to the former Residence of my parents in hopes to find some relatives but did not succeed very well the most of them being dead. Found one cousin by the name of Gibson. Came to an Inn at Luddington and stayed tonight.

Thurs. 18. At 8 1/2 AM came to Luddington Church yard. Found the graves of my Grandfather and mother and two children, a brother and sister, an Uncle and many other relatives. From the tomb stones I was enabled to get the dates of birth, death, etc. 12 1/2 PM Called on the Rector of the Parrich who treated me very kindly but could give no further information of value to me. We then came to Eastoft to M. Wm Burtons in hopes to get some information but could trace nothing furthur. . . .

After visiting back in Hull with Church members, Elders Burton and Hardy boarded the steamer *Hamburgh*, "passing down the Humber into the German Ocean via Grimsby to Yarmouth & passing around the coast. Had a beautiful passage, no rough weather although rather cold for the season." The ship passed up the Thames and landed in London after a twenty-four-hour voyage (June 20–21, 1874).

This trip added another 750 miles to the 2,000 which Robert had traveled and recorded since March. On the day of his return, June 23, he had a most interesting meeting with a Jewish Rabbi, Mosel Malkman, who called at the conference house with a letter of introduction. The rabbi was soliciting aid to build an orphans' school in Jerusalem. Robert does not indicate if he was able to help, but it is significant that the rabbi knew of the interest of the Latter-day Saints in the Holy Land and sought their assistance in his project.

While traveling in September 1874, Robert and M. H. Hardy visited Oxford University and also called upon the family of future apostle James E. Talmage, then twelve, in Hungerford. The Talmages were early converts to Mormonism in England, and James E. was a third-generation member of the Church.

His father, James J. Talmage, walked with the missionaries five miles from Hungerford to Ramsbury, where they were guests of his widowed mother and held a meeting the night of September 18 (September 18–19, 1874). The Talmage family emigrated to Utah in 1876 (Talmage 1872, 1–10).

Between Christmas and New Year's, he traveled to Brighton, a resort city on the seaside south of London, where he performed the marriage of a widower, J. Simmons, and Dora Turner. Robert noted in his journal on December 28 that Brother Simmons expressly requested the ceremony was done "thinking that the circumstances of his children required a variation from the casual service made to many in this country."

Robert closed out 1874 with a journal entry summarizing his year:

> Thurs. 31 Very cold. Still spent this AM in attending to Conference business, reading & answering my letters, etc. Also wrote my wife Sarah & son Frank and at 6 1/2 came to Pentonville & attended a Social Party among the Saints of the N. L. Branch. Had a very good time. There were many present who were not in the church & took part with us, seemed to enjoy themselves much. Dismissed at 11 and came to Conference House. Thus ends the year 1874 during which I have traveld thousands of miles in England and some in Scotland & Wales, attending meetings, etc. in all of which the blessings of the Lord has been with me by sea and land.

In 1875, Robert investigated some of London's progressive facilities, hoping to bring home valuable new ideas to the ever-growing Salt Lake City. He visited the owner of White Brothers Limited, at the request of J. H. Rumell of Salt Lake, "in relation to establishing in Utah an agency for his celebrated cement." He arranged with a representative of the London Utilities for a tour of the subways beneath London to see how gas was distributed throughout the city and also toured the London Hospital. Journal notes on February 3 and 5 include the statistics and details of construction and operation for future reference. On May 25, he visited the arsenal at Wolrich to examine the most modern manufacture of large guns, some weighing eighty-one tons. On May 29, he attended a military review at Portsmouth, paying close attention to the infantry and artillery.

But his most significant experiences in 1875 definitely resulted from missionary activity. His days were filled with appointments to discuss the gospel with "strangers" inquiring about the Church. Along with his January monthly report, Robert included a letter to President Joseph F. Smith describing the tenor and spirit of the London Conference:

London, England, Feb. 8, 1875

Pres. Joseph F. Smith

Dear Brother: Knowing the very great interest you have always manifested in the onward march of the Latter-day Kingdom and the spread of the gospel of Christ among the people, I write you a few lines advising you of our progress in this part of the mission over which you preside.

I am very thankful that I can report to you that the cause of truth is moving steadily onward in this conference, and at no period since the commencement of my labors here have the prospects been so cheering as at present. The Saints exhibit more life and faith, meetings better attended and a more earnest spirit of inquiry is evinced by strangers who attend our meeting from some of whom we receive pressing invitations to visit them, and converse upon the faith and doctrines of the Savior as taught and practiced by Him and His apostles, and restored to the children of men by the Angel through the Prophet Joseph.

Quite a number have been added by baptism since you were here in November last. Yesterday four were baptized at Spring Baths (London) and notwithstanding the inclemency of the weather yesterday, some of our meeting houses were well filled and other names were handed in for baptism.

. . . In [Southhampton] we find great difficulty in obtaining a suitable meeting room, this however as you understand is one of the great difficulties we experience in almost every instance, in consequence of the great prejudice in the minds of the people, and their almost entire ignorance of the faith and belief of the Latter-day Saints. Those whose crafts are in danger are still earnestly seeking by misrepresentation to keep the prejudice alive. But we rejoice in the Lord God of Israel, that, however much His enemies plan and propose He still disposes and overrules all things for the good of His people and the ultimate redemption of Zion. . . .

All [the missionaries] are in the enjoyment of excellent health and spirits, laboring earnestly and hopefully for the promotion of the Kingdom of God upon the earth.

Your brother in the Gospel,

R. T. Burton

Almost two months later, a similar letter recounted increased missionary activity and stressed the need for more elders:

London, March 31, 1875

Prest. Smith

Dear Brother, — We are still quietly moving along in the good work in this Conference, and feel renewed spiritual strength and fresh encouragement at every step in the onward march of Truth. On Sunday last I baptized seven at Pentonville, and after the evening meeting (in the same place), which was well attended, other names were handed in for baptism, which will be attended to next week.

In some of the Branches in the country we are also having much encouragement, through additions to our numbers by baptism; and urgent requests for the American Elders to return at the earliest possible date, and attend to baptizing them; while others are anxious to learn something more of the Gospel of Christ, as believed in and taught by the Latter-day Saints.

The brethren who are laboring with me are in good health and are working with commendable zeal and earnestness. But as you are aware, our field of labor is very large, and the laborers by no means too many.

I am every day more and more confirmed in the opinion, expressed in the Council of Elders in Liverpool soon after your arrival in England, regarding the number of missionaries needed in the European Mission. It is very true the people are poor in many cases, but it is equally true that the only way to benefit them is by the earnest and devoted labors of good, faithful men, teaching them correct economy and true principles, and the blessings of the Lord will follow. Ignorance, vice and prejudice will gradually give way before the light of eternal truth, until the reign of universal peace is ushered in, and Christ will reign as King of King's and Lord of Lord's.

The brethren join me in love to yourself, and all the Elders in the Office.

Yours in the Gospel,

R. T. Burton

Robert's mission was nearing completion now, but he had several projects to finish before he left England. First, he spent several days collecting all previous volumes of the *Millennial Star*. As he visited long-time Church members, he would ask for old issues which were missing from the conference files so that he could have bound a complete set (March 23 and April 13, 1875). He visited the House of Commons and heard some of the principal members debate. He had his picture taken (see p. 129) and purchased books for his children. He also made a trip to the Isle of Jersey, which lies, with the Isle of Guernsey, just off the coast of France across the English Channel, seeking an affidavit to prove the death of Marvin Ducrecne for some one in Salt Lake. There, he enjoyed a visit with a small but faithful group of Saints. This visit prompted him to write a letter to Elder Edward Hanham at the European Mission office in Liverpool dated June 8, 1875, recommending that missionaries be sent more frequently. He wrote:

> I returned late Saturday evening from a visit to the Saints on the Isle of Jersy—there are some good people there, but they much need the labors of a good faithful Elder among them. They are so far away from "headquarters" that they seldom enjoy the privilege of a visit from an Elder that has come from Zion. A new generation has grown up since there was much if any preaching on the Island by the Latter-day Saints.

Robert T. Burton was scheduled to leave England on June 16, with a company of emigrating Saints which included several members of the London Conference led by President Peter Romeril[2] of the Whitechapel Branch. Their last Sunday in England was set aside as a district meeting, and the five or six London branches held joint services at Eastern Hall on East India Dock Road. President Smith came to London to attend and preside, but the departing missionaries and members were the center of attention.

This last Sunday was the spiritual climax of Robert's mission. He had anticipated a "glorious time" and was not disappointed. A number of American missionaries addressed the first session which Robert described in his journal on June 13 as "one of the best meetings we have ever had since I have been on my mission." At the 6 P.M. service, the hall was filled and the "Saints were full of the spirit of the Lord."

As Robert stood to make his farewell address, the faces of his beloved London Saints were streaming with tears. He could hardly speak. Never had he witnessed such an outpouring of emotion. He had been more than a missionary during his twenty-four months in England. He was a counselor and friend to the faithful members who were preparing for emigration and to the new converts who were often very poor. He performed their marriages, healed their sick, comforted them in bereavement, and stood by them when family and friends rejected them for their new religion. He had celebrated with them on holiday picnics, enjoyed their concerts and socials, visited their factories, fairs and festivals, as well as their baptisms and confirmations. He offered these words of farewell:

> I feel that I would not like you to go unless I said a word or two. What is the Gospel? It is the plan of salvation, a system which lays hold on a man that may be in the most despondent circumstances and lifts him up. Gives him wife and family—gives him a right to live in the great future. But, says one, it brings persecution. Well, if it does, it also brings consolation, peace and happiness. I ask you who have received it, what would you take in exchange for it? I answer, nothing. You have the promise of life eternal. What does the doctrines of men promise? I have heard that one of their popular preachers should say that a thousand souls could be compressed into a square inch of space. But what does the Gospel of Jesus Christ promise to you? That you shall be united to God—to wife—to children and friends, in the great hereafter.
>
> As this may be the last time I may speak to you in this land, I would ask you my brethren and sisters, what have we received? Do we know that when we lay these bodies down that we shall rise to eternal life? How shall we account for the great blessings received from God? Shall we barter them away for the evils of the world? I trust not. I hope the intelligence we have received will remain with us. If this be the case we shall be careful not to enter into those places that are contaminating to Saints of God. Now I have left a

family at home that are dearer to me than anything in the world except the kingdom of God, and yet, my brethren and sisters, I leave you with regret, for I have spent a happy year and a half with you; I can say I have tried to benefit you. It has been my study by day and by night and now that I am about to leave you, I would ask you to live your religion, so that you can claim the blessings of the Lord here on earth, and come to Zion to enjoy them. I am glad of the privilege of speaking to you tonight, for it was my desire to labor with you until the last minute. Now I bid you farewell, and I hope that you will all live in such manner that you will be accepted of the Lord. I take this opportunity to thank you for your many acts of kindness. I say unto you in the name of Israel's God, may God bless you—may His peace and blessings be in your habitations (JH, June 13, 1875, 4–5).

Two days later many of the London Saints gathered at the train station to send off fifteen members and Elders Burton and Hardy. Besides Peter Romeril, his wife Elizabeth, and their three-month-old grandchild, the company included Charlotte Young, age 35; John Badham, 11; Thomas Hull, 22; Sarah Warren and three children, Elizabeth, Catherine and Rosa; Peter and Jane Ellis, both age 50; and three members of the Frewin family, ages 21, 19 and 17.

At Liverpool, the company was joined by ninety Saints from throughout England, including the James Ferguson and Edward Warren families from Birmingham and the Joseph Burton family from Leeds, close friends of Robert's, and fifty-seven Swiss and German converts. Returning elders Elijah N. Freeman, Peter Sinclair, and Jacob Zundel completed the company of 167. On June 16, 1875, they boarded the 3,238-ton *Wisconsin*, one of the most important vessels in the Mormon migration from England. The *Wisconsin* was a Guion steamer with an iron hull, single screw, two masts, one funnel, three decks, and an average speed of eleven and a half knots (Sonne 1983, 128)

From on board the *Wisconsin*, Robert wrote a letter to President Smith which was mailed at Queenstown before they put out to sea:

June 17, 1875

Dear Brother—We left our mooring yesterday at 5:30 P.M., and at 8 we called the Saints together and organized with the following officers:

Thomas Hull, clerk and historian for the company, which is divided into two wards—English and Swiss—Peter Romeril, Prest. of the English Ward, with Edward Warren officer of the guard, and Joseph Eerstner, Prest. of the Swiss Ward, with Jacob Zwahlen officer of the guard.

We meet for morning prayer at 7 and evening at 8 o'clock.

We moved slowly until we had passed the bar, after which we steamed smoothly and pleasantly along to this place. All are feeling well, very little sea-sickness. Every one is as comfortable as could possibly be expected.

Elders M. H. Hardy, Peter Sinclair, E. N. Freeman, Jacob Zundel, join in love.

Your brother, R. T. Burton

Robert's letter was somewhat premature and optimistic, since the ship was not yet at sea. Two days later, the seas became very rough, and the reeling and rolling ship made many seasick. During the ten days at sea, Robert tended to the needs—both spiritual and physical—of his company. Because he was not bothered by seasickness, even on the roughest day, he spent his time encouraging the Saints to get up on the deck when they could and tending to those who could not leave their bunks. He wrote in his journal on June 21 that his good health allowed him "to be among the people all the time extending aid to them." He was pleased that the ship made exceptionally good time in spite of the rough seas and head winds. The only tragedy was the death of the tiny grandchild of Peter Romeril, who was quietly buried at sea on the evening of June 25, the day when the seas were roughest. Two days later, clear weather permitted a view of land ahead and all the people were up on deck "full of excitement." That afternoon they docked at New York City's Pier 46; and the next morning, those staying with the company went to Castle Gardens to prepare for the rail passage to Utah (June 16–27, 1875).

In New York City, Robert met with William C. Stains, emigration agent for the Church, and John W. Young as well as Edward W. Tullidge, who was researching the early history of Utah for his book, *Utah and Its Founders*. Robert and Tullidge spent several hours discussing history and biography on Tuesday, June 29.

That evening, the company left New York City in four rail cars and were soon traveling across Pennsylvania, Ohio, and Illinois en route to Utah. The trip was uneventful except for a collision with an empty freight car in Iowa which caused a three-hour delay. On the morning of July 3, they transferred to the Union Pacific line at Omaha. They held meetings on the cars on the Sabbath; and on Monday evening, they stopped in Laramie where the emigrants viewed their first Fourth of July celebration.

A telegraph message had alerted the Burton family members that the company was crossing Wyoming, and by Wednesday as many as could get away went to Ogden for Robert's arrival. Maria, Theresa and Lewis Hills, and eleven-year-old Florence took an express train up the canyon to Echo where they met the train and brought Robert back for a grand reunion in the Ogden station. The emigrants were settled in Ogden for the night, and then the welcoming party and returning missionaries rode to Salt Lake where an even larger group of friends and family were gathered at the station.

The "welcoming home" festivities continued for several nights as more and more friends called, choirs and bands serenaded, and finally Robert reported his mission to a crowded chapel at "my own ward" on Sunday evening, July 11. The local newspapers reported the return of such a popular citizen. On July 9, 1875, the *Salt Lake Herald* described Robert's homecoming:

An Ovation

The return to his home in this city of Elder R. T. Burton, who arrived on Wednesday evening in charge of the company of 170 Swiss, Scandinavian and English immigrants, was made the occasion of a quiet ovation to that gentleman. Members of his family met the immigrant train at Echo city, where Mr. Burton joined his relatives and came to Ogden in the afternoon express. There he was met by a party of relatives and friends who had chartered a coach from this city. After the arrival at Ogden of the immigrants, and their comfort for the night had been arranged for, Mr. B. and his friends came to Salt Lake, and found at the depot another party of friends. At his home the same evening the 15th ward choir, Professor Griggs leader, called upon him and enlivened the occasion with appropriate songs. Later the theatre orchestra band (Prof. Mark Croxall) serenaded the gentleman. Mr. B. will not soon forget his welcome home.

Notes

1. John Clark was an English convert who settled in the Fifteenth Ward upon his immigration to Utah in 1851. He served in Robert T. Burton's command during the Utah War, observing the movement of the army in October 1857 and remaining in the mountains most of the winter. He was clerk of the Fifteenth Ward for over twenty years. During this mission to England, he toured Europe with Robert, was president of the Sheffield Conference, and had charge of the business department of the mission office in Liverpool (Jenson, 1:775–76).

2. Peter Romeril (also spelled Romreal) and his wife Elizabeth lived in Salt Lake City and remained Robert's close friends. They died within a week of each other in late December 1879; Robert attended both funerals in the Nineteenth Ward.

17

Call to the Presiding Bishopric, 1875–77

Brigham Young's death on August 29, 1877, marked the end of an era. During the twenty-eight months before his death, Brigham had sought to recommit the Saints to a higher spiritual unity and "set the Priesthood in order." As a new member of the Presiding Bishopric in 1875, Robert T. Burton traveled with the apostles preaching the United Order. He later returned to many communities to encourage the payment of tithing and to help reorganize stakes and wards. Although he was both a ward bishop and counselor to Presiding Bishop Edward Hunter from June 1875 to June 1877, he also found time to make a significant contribution to the territorial legislature.

During the spring of 1875, word must have reached Robert in England that he had been called as second counselor to Presiding Bishop Edward Hunter, even though he made no mention of it in his journal. So, for the last months of his mission in England, he was president of the London Conference, bishop of the Fifteenth Ward, and counselor in the Presiding Bishopric, though he held the priesthood office of Seventy. Such simultaneous service, unheard of today, was possible before President Young set about putting the priesthood in order in the spring and early summer of 1877.

Three days after his return from England, Robert visited Brigham Young to report his missionary labors and to receive instructions concerning his call to the Presiding Bishopric. While Robert was in England, President Young had begun preaching the principles of stewardship and consecration, advising the Saints that the complete consecration of material possessions could help them achieve higher spiritual commitment and unity. This led to the establishment of the St. George United Order in February 1874 and communal settlements like Orderville and Kingston in Utah and Sunset in Arizona. But communal living was not mandatory. It was possible to live the law as a cooperative system in families and wards, and it was this phase of the movement that Brigham explained to Robert on July 9. At a general priesthood meeting on July 13, President Young announced that all Saints would have an opportunity to renew their baptismal covenants to indicate their commitment to living the principles of the United Order.

In St. George, a list of rules of conduct was drawn up in 1874 and those afterward who joined the "order" generally subscribed to these rules:

> We will not take the name of the Deity in vain, nor speak lightly of his character or of sacred things.
>
> We will pray with our families morning and evening and also attend to secret prayer.
>
> We will observe and keep the Word of Wisdom according to the spirit and the meaning thereof.
>
> We will treat our families with due kindness and affection, and set before them an example worthy of imitation. In our families and intercourse with all persons, we will refrain from being contentious or quarrelsome, and we will cease to speak evil of each other, and will cultivate a spirit of charity towards all. We consider it our duty to keep from acting selfishly or from covetous motives, and will seek the interest of each other and the salvation of all mankind.
>
> We will observe the Sabbath day to keep it holy, in accordance with the revelations.
>
> That which is committed to our care, we will not appropriate to our own use.

That which we borrow we will return according to promise, and that which we find we will not appropriate to our own use, but seek to return it to its proper owner.

We will, as soon as possible, cancel all individual indebtedness contracted prior to our uniting with the order, and, when once fully identified with said order, will contract no debts contrary to the wishes of the board of directors.

We will patronize our brethren who are in the "Order."

In our apparel and deportment we will not pattern after nor encourage foolish and extravagant fashions, and cease to import or buy from abroad any article which can reasonably dispensed with, or which can be produced by combination of home labor. We will foster and encourage the producing and manufacturing of all articles needful for our consumption as fast as our circumstances will permit.

We will be simple in our dress and manner of living, using proper economy and prudence in the management of all intrusted to our care.

We will combine our labor for mutual benefit, sustain with our faith, prayers, and words those whom we have elected to take the management of the different departments of the 'Order,'and be subject to them in their official capacity, refraining from a spirit of fault-finding.

We will honestly and diligently labor and devote ourselves and all we have to the 'Order' and to the building up of the Kingdom of God (CHC 5:485–86).

President Young assigned members of the Quorum of the Twelve and other General Authorities to take the message of the United Order to the Saints. From July 17 until October, Robert traveled with a "team" of apostles and other elders to stake conferences in Utah and southern Idaho where they called for a spiritual awakening of the people and rebaptized quorum, ward, and stake leaders as a symbol of renewing their covenants and entering the new order. After October General Conference, the principles were taught to the Saints in the Salt Lake Valley. Brigham Young described these efforts to Apostle Carrington, then back in England:

> Meetings of the Priesthood have been held in this city, previous to the members of the various quorum renewing their covenants at the waters of baptism. At these meetings the brethren of the Quorum

of the Twelve Apostles and others have spoken and counseled with the power of the spirit of the Most High, calling on the Elders to awaken to a newness of life, to shake off all lethargy, to settle all difficulties they had with their brethren, and if in the wrong to make restitution, and if not in fault to forgive. These teachings have been attended with the happiest results, many have arisen to a comprehension of the importance of the times and of the work in which they are engaged (in Nibley 1937, 519–20).

In no way did Brigham Young feel that his apostles and close associates were above the need to recommit themselves; and on August 31, Robert described in his journal a special meeting held in the Old Tabernacle "for the purpose of uniting together in order of the new covenant." Robert, Maria, and William, along with several members of the Quorum of Twelve and their family members, committed themselves to the covenants of the new order during the meeting and afterward were rebaptized at the Endowment House. The following baptism prayer was used: "Having been commissioned of Jesus Christ, I baptize you for the remission of your sins, for the renewal of your covenants with God and your brethren, and for the observance of the rules of the holy United Order which have been said in your hearing, in the name of the Father and of the Son and of the Holy Ghost" (in Arrington 1985, 380).

Two days later, September 2, 1875, Brigham Young ordained Robert Taylor Burton to the office of high priest and set him apart as second counselor to Bishop Edward Hunter. Thus, Robert reconfirmed his commitment to the kingdom of God and began to serve in a position that he would occupy for the remaining thirty-two years of his life. Because he had accepted every call and assignment from President Young for more than thirty years, neither the United Order nor his new position greatly changed the pattern of his life.

When Bishop Edward Hunter had been called in 1851, the Presiding Bishop's office was barely defined. As a businessman "with great knowledge in temporal things," Hunter was well chosen to direct the temporal affairs of the growing Church. A modern biographer has given this perspective on him:

> He was a pioneer Presiding Bishop in two ways. First, he presided during most of the Mormon pioneering years and longer, from 1851 to 1883. His firm hand on the Church's temporal reins helped steer it through dramatic transformations in size and procedures. During his thirty-three year term, the Rocky Mountain Saints' population grew from 11,000 to over 120,000, and the number of wards increased from forty to about three hundred. Because he had direct responsibility for people and resources, such explosive growth in the basically cashless desert oasis taxed his executive talents.
>
> He also pioneered in terms of the office and calling of Presiding Bishop. . . . Bishop Hunter firmly carved the Presiding Bishop's niche into the Church's General Authority hierarchy (Hartley 1985, 276).

At the time Robert became his counselor, Bishop Hunter was effectively administering the two most important responsibilities of the Presiding Bishopric: the tithing system, with the corollary task of caring for the poor, and the leadership of the Aaronic Priesthood. Robert's experience as businessman, farmer, cattleman, and bishop paralleled Bishop Hunter's, and he was immediately comfortable carrying his share of the responsibilities. This included "encouraging, receiving, storing, allocating, and accounting for animal and produce tithes, properties, labor tithes, and some cash" (Hartley 1985, 280). The Bishopric (Leonard W. Hardy was the first counselor) worked out of the General Tithing Office on the corner of Main Street and South Temple, where Hotel Utah now stands. (See photograph, p. 129)

Although the principle of paying tithing was not yet firmly rooted among the Saints in general, the tithing system was already extensive and complex (See Table 1). Robert's journal entries indicate that he was involved in almost every aspect of the system—from administrative decision making to paying Church employees. He was particularly involved with the Church's livestock herds and associated farming enterprises. He traveled to Illinois and New York to purchase breeding bulls to improve the quality of the Church herds. His well-trained sons were at times employed on the Church ranch and farm. Even though Bishop Hunter used traveling and regional bishops, and later bishop's agents, to supervise the tithing and storehouse

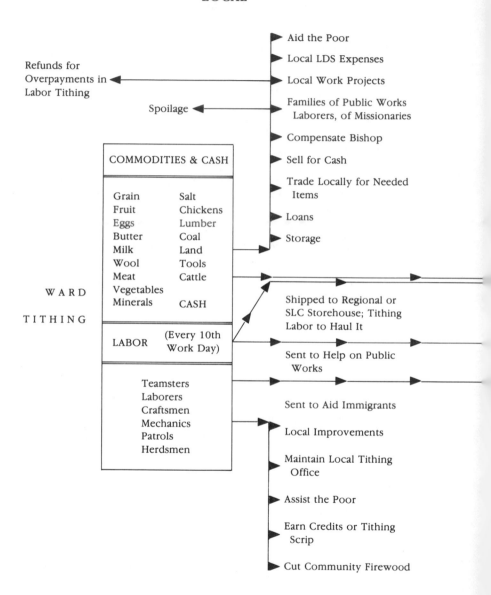

TABLE 1. Tithing System During the Era of
Presiding Bishop Edward Hunter, 1851–1883

REGIONAL OR GENERAL

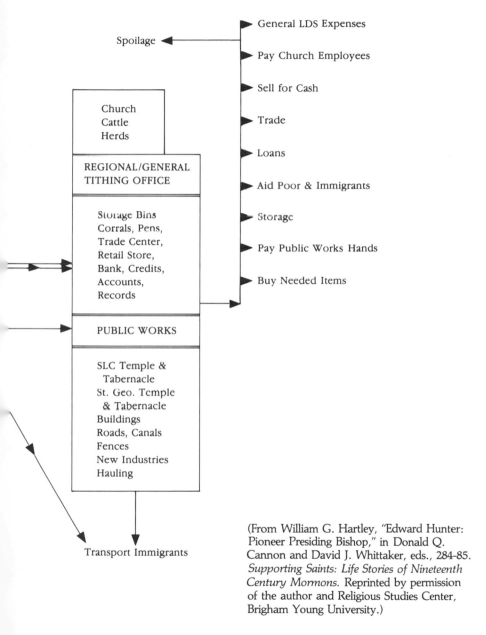

Spoilage

General LDS Expenses

Pay Church Employees

Sell for Cash

Trade

Loans

Aid Poor & Immigrants

Storage

Pay Public Works Hands

Buy Needed Items

Church
Cattle
Herds

REGIONAL/GENERAL
TITHING OFFICE

Storage Bins
Corrals, Pens,
Trade Center,
Retail Store,
Bank, Credits,
Accounts,
Records

PUBLIC WORKS

SLC Temple &
 Tabernacle
St. Geo. Temple
 & Tabernacle
Buildings
Roads, Canals
Fences
New Industries
Hauling

Transport Immigrants

(From William G. Hartley, "Edward Hunter:
Pioneer Presiding Bishop," in Donald Q.
Cannon and David J. Whittaker, eds., 284-85.
*Supporting Saints: Life Stories of Nineteenth
Century Mormons.* Reprinted by permission
of the author and Religious Studies Center,
Brigham Young University.)

315

system in the settlements, Robert also traveled extensively on behalf of the Presiding Bishopric.

From September 7 to October 6, 1875, Robert traveled with John Taylor, Daniel H. Wells, and Franklin D. Richards teaching the Saints of central and southern Utah about the United Order and encouraging them to greater spiritual unity. In Nephi on October 5, Robert rebaptized twelve of the principal brethren of the stake after which they were confirmed on the spot. William accompanied his father on this trip, which again permitted them to visit family members in Beaver, Cedar City, and Pinto. Robert was pleased to see much growth in the settlements, especially St. George and Kanab. He was particularly impressed with the construction of the St. George Temple, "which is a very creditable building," he wrote in his journal on September 22. "Many important improvements have been made here since [I] last visited this place."

While in St. George, Robert and William received their patriarchal blessings from William O. Perkins. Robert's blessing follows:

St. George, Sept. 24, 1875
A P. Blessing on the head of Robert Taylor Burton, Son of Samuel & Hannah Burton, Born in Essex Co. Canada West. Oct. 25, 1821.

Brother Robert: In the name of the Lord Jesus Christ I place my hands upon yr head & seal upon you a Fathers Blessing. Your line is of Joseph thro the loins of Ephraim. You are a lawful Heir to the fulness of the Priesthood. You agreed with your Father that you would come forth in the Dispensation of the fulness of times. He placed his hands upon your head & gave you yr name & blest you and sent you to this Earth to receive a body. He had yr name registered in the Lambs Book of Life and thro your firmness [?] in the gospel there it will remain forever. Your Father is well pleased with you for you was well proved & tried when you was with him. For you stood by Him in that great Battle that was faught with Lucifer. You saw them cast down to Hell & you have come after them to be further tried & proven. And the Heavenly host shouted for joy when you entered into this kingdom. And you have been faithful as a man of God, and the blessings of the Heavens above are upon you, and the Earth will yield forth her Rich blessings for you. In due time you will return unto this land and Enter into the Temple of the Lord

and go thro the ordinances of that House for yourselves & for yr
Dead. There you will see many of the Saints with their resurrected
Bodies & if you desire it, you will see Jesus your redeemer & the
Glory of His Presence will be upon you. You will be Chosen to go
to the Center Stake of Zion and you will go with power from on
High. There you will accomplish a great & mighty work. You will
have an Inheritance in Zion that will be beautiful. You will make
that as a paradise. You will have more wives given you of the Lord
& yr posterity will be very great & powerful in the Holy Priesthood.
That Communication will be kept up between you & yr redeemer.
Your body will be Strong and full of Light. You will have Holy
Messengers to visit you from time to time. The vail will be taken
from you & you will know them by name. They will hand you a roll
of yr dead that have Believed the Gospel. You will Enter into that
Temple & with your wives go thro all the ordinances of that House
for yourselves and your dead. You will have power to Call your
Dead forth. They will Stand upon their feet as a Great Army, for
you will be a pillar in the House of the Lord for you are one of the
Hundred & forty & four thousand that Shall Stand upon Mt Zion &
I bless you in your body limbs & joints, that they become strong &
active that you may do all this work to the Glory of God. I Seal you
up unto Eternal lives, and upon your head a Crown of Celestial
glory in the name of the Lord Jesus Christ. Amen (Member Services,
Historical Department Library).

Robert and William returned to Salt Lake just in time for
October Conference, during which the new tabernacle was dedicated. In the first afternoon session, October 7, Robert spoke
for an hour on his experiences as a missionary in England.
Robert considered it a "very important conference" because of
the valuable instruction given and the large number of missionaries called, including his son Charles, who was twenty years
old. Charles left November 2 for the Australian Mission where
he served honorably for sixteen months, returning home in February 1877. He was the first of Robert's posterity to serve a
proselyting mission. It pleased Robert immensely to send out
his sons (and later grandsons) as missionaries, and he wrote
many letters to them with news of the family and encouraging
counsel.

After October Conference, Robert began preparing his own
ward members to make their new covenants "on the principle

of union." One Sunday, November 21, he devoted both ward meetings to discussing spiritual unity, speaking at length from John, chapter 17. Later that week, he met separately with the brethren and sisters of the ward, taking time in each meeting to read and discuss the rules of the United Order. He found that the sisters were unanimous in desiring to renew their covenants and "most of the Brethren" agreed to do so (R. T. Burton 1856–1907, November 25–26, 1875). The next Sunday's meetings were also devoted to instructions concerning the United Order; and on the following Thursday, December 2, the Fifteenth Ward fast meeting adjourned early so that members could go to the Endowment House where some 300 of them were rebaptized. The ward members had previously formed the Fifteenth Ward Industrial Association as a cooperative venture, operating the Fifteenth Ward Store, but now were further committed to living the spiritual principles of the order. An additional hundred members were rebaptized on January 20 and another hundred following on May 11, 1876.

According to historians, the Council of Fifty, originally organized by Joseph Smith to provide political leadership for Nauvoo and which established the first civil government in the Great Basin under the leadership of Brigham Young in 1849, continued to influence political and civic matters up to the 1880s (Hansen 1967, 137). Members of the council were often nominated and elected without opposition for territorial positions, including the legislature. Robert Taylor Burton became a member of the Council of Fifty in 1867 (see Chapter 13), and probably not by coincidence was elected in August 1875 to the council of the legislative assembly, representing Salt Lake, Tooele and Summit Counties.[1] In January 1876 he began the first of two terms (he was reelected in 1877) in the legislature. He made three important contributions to the territory by (1) helping create a new penal code, (2) compiling and publishing the existent laws of Utah, and (3) chairing the committee which wrote an important revenue bill. His many years in law enforcement and as county assessor and collector of taxes gave him valuable experience for these legislative assignments.

According to Robert's journal, most of his time during the 1876 legislative session was spent in meetings of the Judiciary Committee developing the new penal code. The committee used the California statutes as a basis for the new Utah code. The new act, which received the approval of leading gentile and Mormon lawyers, contained twenty sections, describing the duties of courts and how punishments are determined, defining "crime," "public offense," "felony," and "misdemeanor," and defining and setting punishments for crimes against the person and against public decency, including sexual crimes. Because the California statutes did not mention punishing adultery, fornication, or lascivious cohabitation, the old law which Judge McKean had tried to use to punish polygamists was removed. The code was passed by the legislature and signed by Governor George W. Emery on February 18, 1876 (*Compiled Laws* 1876, 564–651; CHC 5:603).

That same day, the legislature passed an act appointing Abraham O. Smoot, Silas S. Smith, and Robert T. Burton as

> a committee to arrange for, and supervise the compilation and publication of all the Acts and Resolutions passed by the Governor and the Legislative Assembly of the Territory of Utah, now in force, including those passed during this twenty-second session, together with the Declaration of Independence, Constitution of the United States with amendments thereto, the Organic Act of this Territory, and such other laws of the United States as the committee may deem specially applicable to this Territory (*Compiled Laws* 1876, iii–iv).

This was not the first compilation, but evidently the committee determined to make it more complete than previous attempts. The committee spent many days during the next nine months researching the laws to be included in this publication. They spent days in the Salt Lake and Provo courthouses, working jointly and separately. According to the Preface in their publication, they paid particular attention to the legislative directive to publish the laws "now in force" and therefore reduced previous published acts by consolidating amendments and omitting acts private in nature which did not belong to the general statutes (*Compiled Laws* 1876, iv). In October they met for an extended session in their committee room, which they rented from Sarah M. Kimball who lived across First South from Robert's residence. In September, they took some drafts of their compilation to the Deseret News Press; and by November, they were working on an index to the laws and reading proof. They often conferred with Governor Emery and reported to George Q. Cannon in Washington, D.C., who evidently was to arrange for money from the federal treasury to cover publication costs. They sent two advance copies of the laws to Cannon in Washington on December 8, and subsequently, an appropriation was approved in the U.S. Congress "in aid of the compilation of the Laws of Utah" (R. T. Burton 1856–1907, December 8, 1876 and January 5, 1877). On January 6, they received a portion of the appropriation ($1,031). Committee members spent January 8–10, checking the printed books; and finally on January 15, they sent two bound volumes to Cannon in Washington.

During the 1878 session, Robert was chairman of the Revenue Committee. (He also served on the standing committees on judiciary; education; agriculture; trade and manufacture; militia; general incorporations; irrigation and canals; railroads; and on revisions.) The committee wrote a new Revenue Act (the first was written in 1865) which was considered one of the most significant and beneficial pieces of legislation approved during the session (*Salt Lake Herald*, February 24, 1878). The bill established an *ad valorem* tax on all taxable property of three mills on the dollar for the territory and three mills on the dollar for district schools. It also defined in detail the property tax exemptions (including houses, buildings, and land owned by religious denominations for public worship), indicated that the property of corporations should be assessed and taxed, and made other major changes (*Compiled Laws* 1888, 1:718–25). While preparing this bill, the Revenue Committee met in long sessions, sometimes until late in the evening.

According to the *Salt Lake Herald* of February 24, 1878, Governor Emery (appointed by President Ulysses S. Grant in 1875) was disposed to "work harmoniously with [the lawmakers] for the general good." Several times during the session,

Robert conferred with the governor, yet an "eleventh hour compromise" between the executive and the legislators was still needed on February 22 to get passage of a bill the governor would sign. The legislative council stayed at City Hall (where all sessions were held) through the night, awaiting the governor's action on their bills and finally adjourned about noon on February 23. The next day, the *Herald* applauded the work of the legislature and the governor:

> The session of the legislature has come to a close, and all things considered, we have nothing but words of commendation for the law-makers. . . . As the result of the legislative labors many good and necessary laws have been enacted. Among the most important are the revenue act, the act increasing the jurisdiction of justices of the peace in criminal cases, . . . the criminal procedure act, the act providing for official elections to fill vacancies, the act for the preservation of game and fish, . . . and the election law. . . . The governor had it in his power to nullify any part or all of the work of the assembly, and had he yielded to the desires and demands of a certain class he would have exercised his extraordinary power for the bad. We are pleased to think he acted for the best interests of the public, . . . [and] the action of his excellency is deserving of credit and commendation.

Unfortunately, Governor Emery worked so well with the Church that non-Mormons felt their position was not being adequately represented. When his term expired in 1880, newly-elected President Rutherford B. Hayes, who had taken a hostile position toward the Church, did not reappoint Governor Emery (CHC 5:607–8).

On January 18, 1877, immediately after completing the legislative laws project, Robert boarded the Utah Central Railroad for Provo to begin "a mission through some of the southern settlements." This "mission" was typical of many trips he undertook to examine tithing property and preach to the Saints the importance of paying tithing. He and his companion, Elias Morris, inspected the tithing stores, granaries, barns, and stables in Provo, Nephi, Fountain Green, Moroni, Spring City, Ephraim, and Manti. Bishops in each community would give him an inventory of their tithing commodities and cash on hand so that Robert could decide what should be kept for local use and what should be shipped to the General Tithing Office. In one community, he reported "not much spirit of paying tithing" but two days later described Ephraim as "one of the finest settlements in the County [with] a pretty good spirit of paying tithing." The Saints of Ephraim filled their meetinghouse with "an attentive audience who exhibited life and animation." After days of travel on snow-packed roads, the spirit of such a community lifted Robert's spirits. He and Elias continued as far south as Manti, then returned to Utah County where they held meetings in Santaquin, Payson, Spanish Fork, Provo, American Fork, and Alpine. Robert gave "instructions as the spirit suggested" to each congregation. In Provo, he and Elias toured the Brigham Young Academy, "one of the finest schools in the Territory, near the most perfect order" (January 18–February 2, 1877).

Two significant events occurred on May 28, 1877.

At 12:30 P.M., Robert and his business partner, Abraham O. Smoot, met with Brigham Young in his office. With John Sharp, these four men were proprietors of the two most successful woolen mills in the valley. Brigham Young had built the Deseret Woolen Mill in 1860, while the other three men had followed with Wasatch Woolen Mill in 1868. A. O. Smoot and Company had been operating both mills and now negotiated purchase of Young's Deseret Mill, including the land surveyed that very morning as 46 and 55/100 acres. (See photograph, p. 124). Newspaper articles from the *Deseret Evening News* on July 10, 1874, and October 6, 1876, report that wool cloth woven at the Deseret Mills "has not been surpassed in that class of textures in this Territory. It is really excellent, both in appearance and quality . . . " and that "in point of quality they are as good as need be desired by the most fastidious wearer . . . equal to the best Scotch tweeds."

In April 1878, Robert rented the mills from his partners and operated them under the corporation of Burton, Sons and Young. Three years later on September 8, 1881, the *Deseret*

Evening News again extolled the quality of products of the two mills:

> **The Wasatch Woolen Mills**—A delightful ride of six miles through the green meadows and ripened fields south and east of the city, brings us to the Wasatch and Deseret Woolen mills, situated near the mouth of Parley's Canyon. These mills are now entering upon their third year under the proprietorship of Messrs. Burton, Sons, & Young, under whose efficient management they are flourishing, and give every promise of another successful season. The two buildings are about a quarter of a mile apart, the upper or Deseret Mill having been established about 17 years ago, by the late President Brigham Young, while the Wasatch Mills, a substantial rock, three story structure of 33 feet by 90 in dimensions, was built in 1867–8 by A. O. Smoot and Company, at a cost of $60,000, including machinery. Adjacent to the main building, is a large frame house used for finishing and dying [sic] purposes. The machinery used in these mills consists of the following: two renovators, two pickers, four sets of Bridesburg cards, three spinning mules, and one jack, running in a joint capacity 1,260 spindles; thirty-one power looms, two hydraulic presses, one screw press, two shearers, besides gigs, nappers, spoolers and twisters, bleach house, dye vats, scouring boxes, fulling mills, etc., etc. The machinery is all run by two Leffel water wheels, 20 inches and 28 inches in diameter respectively. The former has an 18 foot head, the latter a 22 foot head, representing a combined force of 80 horse power.

The article continues with a lengthy description of the process by which the raw materials are converted into cloth and concludes:

> Last year their product was 80,000 yards of cloth, 13,000 lbs of yarn, besides about 800 pairs of blankets. They employ about 50 hands, of both sexes, the pay roll amounting to between $400 and $500 per week. The mills are superintended by W. S. Burton, one of the firm, and the warerooms in the Emporium Buildings, are under the management of Messrs. M. M. Young and C. S. Burton. We are pleased to find the mills in such a prosperous condition and trust it may continue. These and all similar enterprises deserve the hearty and substantial support of the people of Utah.

From Robert's journals, we also know that he did much of the bookkeeping for the mills over many years, while he employed James McGhie to manage the factory throughout the 1870s.

The second event on May 28, 1877, was a family party in honor of Robert's son John's twentieth birthday. Two months earlier, John was stricken with a serious illness, described by Robert as "lung fever." For three weeks he lay between life and death. Robert personally attended to John's care, the graveness of this illness overshadowing all other activities and responsibilities. Though it was time for spring planting and Robert was also busy establishing a cooperative tannery, he hurried through his meetings and dashed to the farm and back so that he would be gone from John's bedside only for short periods. John received many priesthood administrations, and each one brought some relief. After four consecutive days of calling in the elders, Robert recorded in his journal on April 4, "John is a little better this morning although very sick [and] yet requires all my attention. I am with him all the time." John did not die, but he was weak and low for many weeks. As he had done with William years earlier, Robert took John out in the carriage in the spring air, and the treatment did him more good than anything else. He gradually regained his health, and it was a very grateful family that gathered at the Burton residence to celebrate his birthday.

Brigham Young's periods of poor health were also the subject of much discussion. He spent the winters in St. George because he felt better there, and in 1877 he held April General Conference in the St. George Tabernacle. He concluded the conference: "As to my health, I feel many times that I could not live an hour longer, but I mean to live just as long as I can. I know not how soon the messenger will call for me, but I calculate to die in the harness (in Nibley 1937, 528).

After this conference, Brigham Young began what proved to be his final contribution to building the kingdom, setting in order the priesthood quorums and stakes, beginning with the Quorum of the Twelve. He released from their stake callings all the apostles who were presiding over stakes, telling them that their mission was larger than a single stake. He then sent them out to reorganize the stakes, wards, and quorums. He personally called a new presidency for the St. George Stake in April, and his last public appearance was at the reorganization of the Brigham City Stake on August 19. In all, he added seven new stakes to the thirteen existing ones and created 140 wards to make a total of 241. Hundreds of men were called to stake presidencies, bishoprics, high councils, and quorum presidencies. His counselor, George Q. Cannon, described this endeavor:

> He set the Priesthood in order as it has never before been since the first organization of the Church upon earth. He defined the duties of the apostles. .. Seventies . . . High priests, the duties of the elders and those of the lesser priesthood, with plainness and distinctness and power—the power of God—in a way that it is left on record in such unmistakable language that no one need err who has the Spirit of God resting down upon him (*Deseret News Weekly*, September 3, 1877).

Brigham Young wrote to his son Willard on May 23, 1877, that he had undertaken this program "to give greater compactness to the labors of the priesthood, to unite the Saints, to care for the scattering sheep of Israel in these mountains who acknowledge no particular fold, to be in a position to understand the standing of every one calling himself a Latter-day Saint, and to consolidate the interests, feelings and lives of the members of the Church" (in Arrington 1985, 394).

The reorganization very much affected Robert and his family. At a special conference on Sunday, July 22, Church leaders divided the Sugar House Ward, creating Farmers Ward with boundaries that included Robert's farm. The new ward held its first services in the home of "P. Young." By December, the ward members had built a brick school house south of the Peart property, near the end of the lane which led to the paper mill, in which Church meetings were held (JH, July 22, December 19, 1877). In 1891, they built a large chapel on State Street just below present-day Seventeenth South. For decades, the Burtons were active members of Farmers Ward, and later divisions of it such as Burton Ward and McKinley Ward. Robert frequently attended Sunday morning services with Sarah and whatever children were staying at the farm. In the evening, he would attend Sacrament Meeting at the Fifteenth Ward in the city.

Robert also attended the bishops' meetings held twice a month, which traditionally had been a forum for discussion but which now became the vehicle for orientation and instruction during this time of change.

As a member of the Presiding Bishopric, not only were Robert's own responsibilities clarified during this time, but the lines of authority between the Presiding Bishopric and the stake and ward leaders were tightened and strengthened, making his work in the Presiding Bishopric more effective and efficient.

Last of all, after sixteen years in the bishopric of the Fifteenth Ward, Robert was released at a special conference held Wednesday, June 27, under the direction of President Daniel H. Wells. Robert's counselor, Joseph Pollard, was chosen as the new bishop (R. T. Burton 1856–1907, June 27, 1877).

Brigham Young kept up his busy schedule through the long, hot summer of 1877. During the afternoon of Thursday, August 23, he felt nauseated but insisted on attending the bishops' meeting in the Council House at 7 P.M. where Robert heard his instructions on the duties of the Presiding Bishopric and its relationship to the Bishops' Council. He told the bishops that it was their responsibility "to look after every member in their wards, and not retain to fellowship those who utterly refuse to attend to their prayers, tithing and other duties." He also made it clear that representatives of the bishop such as the priests and teachers should visit the homes of the ward members weekly when possible, and at the very least "every member of each ward should be well and thoroughly visited at least once a month" (in Arrington 1985, 395).

Upon returning to his home that evening about 11 P.M., President Young was struck with violent cramps, vomiting, and purging. The family called in Doctors Seymore B. Young, Joseph M. Benedict, Denton F. Benedict, and W. F. Anderson. They began an immediate treatment of a mild opiate for pain and gave him constant attention over the next several days. They called his illness "cholera morbus," (cholera being an infectious disease characterized by diarrhea). It is more likely that he had either a ruptured appendix, mesenteric thrombosis, or diverticulitis, but these conditions were unknown at the time (Bush 1978, 92–103; Schoenfeld 1977).

In spite of medical attention, continual nursing from family members, and repeated priesthood administrations, Brigham Young continued to experience excruciating stomach pains and each day was weaker than the day before. Toward the end, doctors increased the opiates, and he fell into a restless sleep.

On Wednesday, August 29, Robert was at his farm plowing when a messenger arrived with news that President Young was not expected to live. Robert rushed to the city, arriving at Brigham Young's office shortly after 2 P.M., where he found members of the family and Church leaders gathered at his bedside. Robert joined a circle of brethren in a last administration, in which they dedicated him to the Lord. Robert then ran to the Presiding Bishop's office and brought Bishop Hunter back to the office. "His family were taking a last look," Robert recorded in his journal that night. "He was then Dieing, expired at 4 PM without a struggle in the midst of his family and friends."

Brigham Young left detailed instructions in his will regarding not only his funeral service and disposition of his body, but also the manner of mourning by family and friends. "At my interment I wish all of my family present that can be conveniently, and the male members to wear no crepe on their hats or their coats; the females to buy no black bonnets, nor black dresses, nor black veils; . . . . The services may be permitted, as singing and a prayer offered, and if any of my friends wish to say a few words, and really desire, do so" (in Arrington 1985, 400).

Robert was occupied for two days taking care of funeral arrangements, including the decoration of the Tabernacle and organization of the procession. At 6 A.M. Saturday morning, September 1, he was at the Lion House to assist in laying the president's body in his specially prepared coffin. It was made according to Brigham's request:

I want my coffin made of plump 1 1/4 inch redwood boards, not scrimped in length, but two inches longer than I would measure, and from two to three inches wider than is commonly made for a person of my breadth and size, . . . and the coffin to have the appearance that if I wanted to turn a little to the right or left I should have plenty of room to do so." (in Arrington 1985, 399–400).

The coffin was encased in a metallic covering, which included a plate glass big enough to allow a view of the body. With male members of the Young family, several of the apostles, the Presiding Bishopric, and Church employees in attendance, Brigham Young's faithful clerks and workmen bore the coffin to the Tabernacle. At the Tabernacle, the coffin was draped in white and wreathed in flowers, and when all was ready the doors were opened to admit the thousands come to honor the departed leader. Robert remained there all day and into the evening, leaving only for a quick meal. At 10:30 P.M., he went home to sleep, but the building remained open all night as more than 18,000 filed silently through.[2]

Early Sunday morning, Robert returned to Temple Square to make sure that all was in order and no detail overlooked that would mar the funeral services. At 10 A.M. he had the doors opened, and by noon, the huge hall was filled, including the aisles, doorways, and every standing place. Twelve thousand were inside, and many more gathered on the grounds. The great organ and an orchestra played solemn funeral marches as prelude, and the Tabernacle Choir provided hymns during the service.

The funeral was not long, but included the elements suggested by Brigham himself: singing, prayers, and "a few words" from his friends Daniel H. Wells, Wilford Woodruff, Erastus Snow, John Taylor, and George Q. Cannon. After the benediction, the choir sang "Unveil Thy Bosom, Faithful Tomb" while a procession of some 4,000 Saints formed.

Robert T. Burton was pleased that the formation and movement of the large cortege was "very orderly." He had arranged for ropes to hold back the dense crowds so that those accompanying the coffin to the cemetery could walk eight abreast along South Temple and up the hill to the Youngs' private cemetery, which at that time commanded a view of the valley south and west. Participants walked in the following order: Tenth Ward Band; Glee Club; Tabernacle Choir; press reporters; Salt Lake City Council; President Young's employees; President Young's brothers (Joseph, Phineas, and Lorenzo D. Young); the coffin, borne by Young's clerks and workmen with nine of the twelve apostles and the Presiding Bishopric as pall bearers; counselors in the First Presidency; the family and relatives; Church Patriarch; First Seven Presidents of Seventies; stake presidencies and high councils; bishops and their counselors, high priests, elders, seventies, and lesser priesthood; and the general public. Under beautiful blue skies, the Glee Club filled the air with Eliza R. Snow's hymn, "O My Father," Wilford Woodruff dedicated the grave, and the casket was slowly lowered into the stone vault, built as directed in the southeast corner of the cemetery.

For thirty-three years Brigham Young was a prophet and for thirty-three years a friend, advisor, teacher, and exemplar for Robert T. Burton, and through Robert, to his oldest sons. In 1905, Robert wrote of the first time he saw Brigham Young addressing the saints in Nauvoo, looking "strikingly" like the martyred Joseph Smith Jr.: "It was a positive indication to me where the succession had fallen, and from that time until the death of President Brigham Young, I never had one doubt, never thought that I was deceived. I believed, still believe and I know that he was the legitimate successor to the Prophet Joseph Smith" (R. T. Burton 1905).

As requested by his prophet friend, Robert showed no public grief. Rather he turned to the tasks at hand and prayed that his life would reflect this tribute to Brigham Young, written by Orson F. Whitney (2:849):

> He loved his people; their high destiny
> Will be a monument to Brigham Young.

Notes

Leonard J. Arrington's *Brigham Young: American Moses* (New York: Alfred A. Knopf, 1985) is a scholarly and fascinating biography of Brigham Young's life. His bibliographical essay (500–509) lists many other sources and studies pertaining to Young's life and contribution to Church and community. His life was entwined with Robert's from 1844 to 1877, and William S. Burton wrote that his father was considered "one of President Brigham Young's councilors, although he never had that title" (n.d.^{c}, 33).

1. The territorial legislature was divided into two bodies, the council and the house. Robert was one of twelve members of the council.

2. Robert indicates in journal entries on September 1 and 2, 1877, that there were 18,000 mourners, while Whitney's *History of Utah*, 2:846, indicates there were 25,000.

The Calm
Before
the Storm,
1877–84

The seven-year interval between Brigham Young's death and the raid against polygamy might be seen in the life of Robert T. Burton as the relative calm before the storm. Though these years were not easy, Robert made significant contributions to improving conditions for the poor and the mentally ill. The family memoirs of this time reveal many satisfying times for the Burtons.

Each night from 1877 to 1884, as Robert sat down to pen a sentence or two describing his activities, he could view the day with satisfaction. Though before 1877 he was constantly busy, often with more projects and travels than would seem possible even in the twentieth century with modern aids like cars and telephones, during these years, he accomplished more for Church, family, and community than ever before.

At this time, Robert was in his late fifties and in good health. A comparison of his journal entries, historical material, and newspapers of the time indicates that very little occurred in general Church administration and the Salt Lake civic and business community to which he was not a party. Most considered him a prominent citizen, evidenced by the attention given to his trial on murder charges stemming from the Morrisite War which took place in early 1879 (see details in Chapter 12). He was rearrested on July 26, 1877, and appeared in court on September 27, where he pled "not guilty." Even though he requested a speedy trial, it was first set for December 1877, then postponed again and again until February 1879. During the latter months of 1877 and all of 1878, he spent much time preparing for his defense. Fortunately the case was concluded during the years when the judiciary acted with fairness in cases involving Mormon leaders. A jury composed equally of Mormons and non-Mormons acquitted him. After passage of the amended Edmunds Act in 1882, those who practiced or even believed in polygamy were excluded from jury service, making it impossible for Church members to receive trials by impartial juries. If Robert's trial had been delayed into the 1880s, it might have had a very different outcome.

After the death of Brigham Young, John Taylor assumed leadership of the Church by virtue of his calling as president of the Quorum of the Twelve until October 1880 when he was sustained as president of the Church. He relied heavily on the Presiding Bishopric to run the temporal affairs of the Church, encouraging improvement and greater accountability in the tithing system especially in the stakes and wards scattered throughout the territory. Members of the Presiding Bishopric attended every event of importance—temple dedications, laying of cornerstones, groundbreakings, quarterly stake conferences, jubilee celebrations, and councils. President Taylor reorganized the Council of Fifty in 1880 and Robert faithfully attended the meetings which were held at April and October Conference times.

Despite the great emphasis on developing united orders, by 1878 most of them were failing, and President Taylor recognized a need for some new type of economic planning. The goal remained the same—establishment of an independent kingdom of God—but Church leaders thought the Lord "would not be displeased" if they tried cooperation on a less intensive scale (Arrington 1958, 341–42). So, using as a pattern a board of trade which had been functioning in Cache Valley since 1872, they established Zion's Board of Trade in 1878 with John Taylor as president, William Jennings and Edward Hunter as vice presidents, and a board of directors of fifty men, including the "leading men" of each valley or stake. Robert T. Burton was an active member of this board.

The plan called for each valley, county, or stake to have a board of trade to encourage and strengthen cooperative marketing and buying, to develop new industries, and to regulate trade in the interests of the group as a whole. The representatives of these individual boards would meet as the Central Board of Trade in Salt Lake City at conference time each April and October. Leonard Arrington has described the movement as an attempt by Church leaders to get together the best business and professional people to work out solutions to economic problems (Arrington 1958, 344).

President Taylor introduced the concept to the Church in General Conference, October 8, 1878, the day before the official organization of the Central Board of Trade:

> Our true policy is to make, as far as possible, at least what we need for home consumption, with an eye to future exports of those articles which we can sell abroad at a profit. To determine what can be produced and manufactured to the best advantage, on sound business principles, in this Territory, and to devise measures by which those articles can be produced for the benefit of the community and the advantage of all engaged in these enterprises, . . . are the purposes which will be served by the organization of Zion's Board of Trade.
>
> And when we get things into a proper fix we will pull with a long pull and a strong pull and a pull all together. We will strive to be one; . . . we will begin with this, and then cooperate in all the different Stakes, . . . And we will keep working and operating until we succeed in introducing and establishing these things that God has desired, and until Zion shall be a united people and the glory of all the earth (JH, October 8, 1878).

At the Council House the next day, Robert witnessed the formal organization of Zion's Central Board of Trade by "the 12 and some of the prominent Brethren." He was selected as a member of the Board and the Executive Committee (Taylor 1878; R. T. Burton 1856–1907, October 9, 1878).

One project already functioning which fit nicely into the Board of Trade policy was the cooperative tannery, called Deseret Tanning and Manufacturing Company. From the tannery committee's first meeting in June 1877, Robert invested his time and business expertise in this project. He sat on the board of directors and went to Chicago in November 1877 with John R. Winder, to tour the most modern tanneries in America and order equipment to be installed in the building under construction in the Nineteenth Ward. President Taylor dedicated the tannery on March 23, 1878.

One of the least known activities of the Board of Trade began with discussions about the high price of coal in Salt Lake Valley and led to construction of the Utah Eastern Railroad. Fuel to heat homes in the valley had been a constant problem over the years. Settlers exhausted nearby timber supplies within the first decade. By 1860, vast deposits of low-grade bituminous coal had been discovered in Summit, Sanpete, and Iron counties, but transporting it to Salt Lake was difficult and expensive. The mines near Coalville, Summit County, produced coal that burned clean, but it "slacked" or disintegrated quickly and could not be stored from summer to winter. It needed to be shipped during the winter for immediate use, but wagon transportation was undependable and risky. The completion in 1870 of the Union Pacific railroad through Echo Canyon to Ogden and the Utah Central Railroad from Ogden to Salt Lake should have solved the transportation problem. Unfortunately, the Union Pacific was lead by unscrupulous men who controlled the price and availability of coal by setting the rates and allocating the cars between Echo and Salt Lake. Called a "soulless monopoly" by Salt Lake newspapers, the Union Pacific charged $10 per ton during the winter of 1877–78, and many poor Salt Lakers went without heat that winter because they were unable to pay the exorbitant price.

The injustice and suffering caused by these prices became a regular topic at the meetings of the Presiding Bishopric with the Salt Lake bishops, where the bishops complained that the Union Pacific had "negotiated" with the Summit County mine owners to take all their output "with the proviso that none be sold to any other purchasers." Mine owners could no longer sell to men with teams who had been carrying Salt Lake merchandise to Coalville to barter for coal. Tithing produce had been bartered this way with the coal going for welfare purposes and to heat Church office buildings, chapels, and businesses. When Union Pacific allocated fewer and fewer cars to carry Summit coal and filled the needs of the Salt Lake market with coal from their own mines near Rock Springs, Wyoming, in 1877, it was the last straw. Unable to ship on Union Pacific and unable to sell to anybody else, the Coalville mines were "starved out" of the coal business and had to lay off their miners (Arrington 1955, 44–45).

The Church purchased a mine in Summit County in August 1877 and worked it with unemployed Mormon miners. They transported the coal into the valley by wagon teams whenever weather permitted.

By the fall of 1879, Board of Trade officials and the Presiding Bishopric had decided to resurrect a plan to build a railroad south from Coalville to Kimball's Junction and down Parley's Canyon to the valley. To finance construction of the railroad, an alliance was made between several Mormon capitalists and a group of non-Mormon silver mine owners from Park City who wanted both a railroad connection and a supply of cheap coal.

The Utah Eastern Railroad Company was incorporated December 27, 1879, with Robert Taylor Burton on the board of directors to represent the Board of Trade and the interests of the Church. Directors and principal stockholders besides Robert included Robert C. Chambers, George M. Scott, Henry Dinwoodey, Francis Armstrong, Edmund Wilkes, John A. Groesbeck, Joseph M. Cohen, and Robert Harkness. Each subscribed for fifty shares of stock, except Robert who subscribed for only five shares (Arrington 1955, 46).

Robert took this assignment seriously because of his strong conviction that it would relieve the suffering of the poor and benefit every resident of the valley. From the day of incorporation, Robert's journal records his dedication to getting the railroad built as soon as possible. Four days after incorporation, he sent his team and sons Alfred and Robert to begin surveying near Park City, which Robert called "Parley's Park," or simply, "the Park." He began soliciting subscriptions among the bishops and Church members, and spent days in the UERR office working out the legal and land arrangements. In Salt Lake Bishops' meeting, he urgently sought the aid and influence of ward leaders, claiming that "This was no private speculation; it had been commenced for the express purpose of benefiting and blessing the poor" (*Deseret News*, June 11, 1880).

During the fund-raising campaign, articles in both the *Deseret News* and *Salt Lake Herald* emphasized the public nature of the road. A May 19, 1880, *Deseret News* editorial said: "If the people build and own the road, no matter whether a ton of coal is freighted upon it or not, so long as coal is sold in Salt Lake City for $4 a ton or less, the people will gain largely by the investment." The *Herald* editor explained on June 20, 1880: "The Utah Eastern was not devised as a moneymaking scheme for a few individuals. . . . The Company was organized and the road is to be built for the purpose of breaking a monopoly that is sorely suppressing the people."

During 1880, the organizers of the Utah Eastern also formed a corporation known as the Home Coal Company, which acquired a number of important coal mines in Summit County, and contracted with the Park City mine owners to deliver this coal to their mines, assuring the railroad of business even if crowded out of the Salt Lake City market (Arrington 1955, 51).

Capital stock in the railroad enterprise paid for early stages of construction. Robert convinced the property owners to grant right of way permission in exchange for company stock. Contracts for grading and for 60,000 railroad ties to timber the first twenty-one miles of track were awarded in May 1880 and by the middle of June 400 men and 150 teams were at work on the grading. The overwhelming majority of the men were paid in stock (Arrington 1955, 50).

Utah Eastern officials were concerned from the beginning that the Union Pacific would try to take over the railroad by buying the controlling interest, so stockholders devised a plan to keep power in their hands, regardless if the stock was sold. Under the plan, three trustees were elected in whose hands was placed a majority, or $400,000, of the stock. This stock was to be inalienable for fifteen years, which meant the stock could be sold but would still be subject to the control of the trustees for voting purposes. John R. Winder and Leonard W. Hardy from the Presiding Bishop's office and Fred H. Auerbach, a non-Mormon Salt Lake businessman, were chosen trustees (Arrington 1958, 347, 501).

Although large numbers of Latter-day Saints subscribed labor and cash to buy stock, the company collected only half the amount needed to buy the iron rails and rolling stock (engines, cars, etc.). The Ontario Mining Company of Park City agreed to advance cash ($186,000) in exchange for mortgage bonds and a bonus of treasury stock. This sum purchased twenty-five miles of track, enough to link Coalville with Kimball's Junction and Park City.

Grading was finished in August, and the iron and rolling stock were delivered in Coalville late in October. Robert had been busy with railroad business almost daily in Salt Lake with an occasional trip to Coalville; but on November 3, he traveled to Coalville where he and Francis Armstrong took charge of the construction crew. It was very late in the year to begin such a project in the Wasatch Mountains, but the Union Pacific's efforts to build a parallel broad-gauged line from Coalville to Park City and drive the UERR out of the Park City market pushed the UERR forward.

They laid the first track November 4. The next day, they fired up the engine and moved it onto the track. Using it, the crews expected to lay a mile of track a day, but on November 9, the first snowstorm of the year hit the mountains, and crews lost time as they cleared the grading with shovels before laying track. Through long cold days, Robert's determination kept the crew working even though he often wrote in his journal that it was *"very cold,"* and he was having a hard time getting the men out to work in the snow each morning. He led the crew every day—seven days a week for eight weeks—except when he made one trip back to Salt Lake, November 14–18 (see R. T. Burton 1856–1907, November 4–December 23, 1880).

In seven days, they laid the track to Wanship. Nine days later, the crew was laying track along Silver Creek, and two days later they were going over the divide. Five days later, the railroad reached the ranch of William and Melissa Kimball. The ranch marked the junction of the road into Park City and now became the railroad junction as well. Near Kimball's Hotel, a station house was eventually built. The title, "Kimball's Junction," still marks this site.

Construction was slower after they passed the junction because winter storms intensified, grading wasn't finished, and ties were not laid. But the work did not stop, and Robert continued to lead the men out each morning and work with them until dark. Each night, Robert wrote a sentence in his small, black journal, describing the conditions that day: "Snowing and blowing hard but still continue work," "Hard work to get material forward on account drifting snow," "No train through, blocked in snow," and "Drifting too bad" (November 28–December 5, 1880).

The crew inched forward, laying a half mile or less each day until the rails reached Park City, on Saturday, December 11. Coal had already been delivered at Kimball's Junction from which point it was being freighted down to the city, and on December 13, the first coal reached the mining community at Park City. All the available iron for rails was used up at this point, but the UERR won the construction race by almost a month. The Union Pacific track reached Park City in January 1881. In recognition of Robert's leadership, the UERR named one of its engines the "General Burton" (*Park Mining Record*, May 27, 1882).

Robert stayed ten days attending to railroad business, paying the hands, and overseeing delivery of coal at both the Park and the Junction, until the day before Christmas when he left

Kimball's ranch by sleigh for home. Unfortunately, the snow in the valley gave out, and it was a tired father who walked the last two miles to the farm, arriving just in time for Christmas Eve with his children.

Confident in the success of this venture, two days later Robert was back at his desk in the Tithing Office. He also enjoyed family Christmas and New Year's activities, including the blessing of his son Robert's fourth son, Don Carlos, and the wedding of Willard and Mary Jane Gardner which took place on January 6. Willard left January 24 for a mission to the Southern States, where he labored principally in North Carolina.

Railroad business continued to take up Robert's time for the rest of the winter and also periodically over the next four years. After a year of operation, the UERR was reported to be working at near capacity and paying its own way, although there were never enough profits to pay dividends. Twice, the board of directors began plans to extend the track from Park City to Salt Lake City, but interference from the Union Pacific stopped the project.

As previously noted, when the Utah Eastern was incorporated, the stockholders placed the majority of the stock in the hands of three trustees and made it "inalienable" for a period of fifteen years. However, only 1,638 shares of the original 7,000 were sold in the public subscription, netting only $82,400. To secure the cash needed for tracks and engines, Robert C. Chambers, president of Utah Eastern and superintendent of Ontario Mining, bonded the railroad to J. B. Haggin, vice-president of Wells-Fargo and the Nevada Central Railroad Company, and president of Ontario Mining. Later, Haggin put up $186,000 to buy second mortgage bonds on the condition that he receive a stock "bonus" which gave him control of the Utah Eastern. Then in the fall of 1881, without the knowledge or consent of the trustees, Chambers transferred 2,232 shares of treasury stock (twelve shares for each of 186 bonds) to Haggin, giving him more stock than all the other stockholders put together. In the fall of 1883, the Union Pacific purchased the Utah Eastern bonds from the San Francisco partnership of Haggin and Lloyd Telvis.

They also secured from the firm a proxy to vote the bonus stock and later the stock itself (Arrington 1955, 56).

This complicated and somewhat devious arrangement between Chambers, Haggin, and the Union Pacific came as a surprise to the trustees, board of directors, and stockholders of the Utah Eastern at the annual stockholders meeting, November 19, 1883. The representatives of the Union Pacific came to the meeting, voted the bonus stock, and elected their own slate as board of directors, replaced the management, and removed the books of the UERR to Union Pacific headquarters in Omaha. Almost immediately, they transferred the rolling stock to a Union Pacific subsidiary, the Utah and Northern Railroad, in effect closing down the Utah Eastern and allowing the Echo and Park City road to absorb the coal contract between Utah Eastern and the Ontario Mining Company (Arrington 1955, 57).

Robert's journal entries only hint at the anger and frustration of the now-minority stockholders and the residents of Salt Lake City. They instituted a number of investigations and legal steps over the next two years, but the results were inevitable; the mighty Union Pacific had won again. If managed properly, the railroad could pay its debts, but the superintendent, a Mr. E. Dickinson, chose not to run it at all. A year after the takeover, Charles W. Penrose described "The Injustice of a Great Corporation" in a November 18, 1884, *Deseret News* editorial:

> The U. P. [Echo & Park City Railroad] is in fine condition, conveying both passengers and freight, . . . chiefly coal for the Ontario. The U. E. is dilapidated and empty; its rails are twisted, its roadbed sunken, its bridges falling into decay, and the whole concern going rapidly to destruction. It is a standing but crumbling shame to the Company which has wrought this ruin.

By February 1885, when Judge Charles S. Zane appointed a receiver and it appeared that sufficient prodding by the minority stockholders could force him to get the railroad back on its feet, the antipolygamy campaign was in full swing and the important minority stockholders, including Robert Burton, were forced to go "underground" to avoid jail. They could no longer fight for the railroad. On February 21, 1887, the Union Pacific bought the Utah Eastern at a bankruptcy auction, bidding $25,000 for the roadbed, locomotives, cars, and other properties (Arrington 1955, 56–63).

However, all along Robert had been most interested in helping the community and the poor, and this had been somewhat accomplished. Through the Board of Trade, he and other leaders worked to increase employment and production in all the communities. In the early 1880s, the Board of Trade actively supported the construction of a Denver and Rio Grande railroad from its rich new coal mines in Carbon and Emery counties, signaling the end of the Union Pacific monopoly. Countering the monopoly and discriminatory tactics of the Union Pacific Railroad during its heyday in Utah became the board's most outstanding accomplishment (Arrington 1958, 348–49).

Robert's involvement in the Utah Eastern was a direct result of his positions in the Central Board of Trade and the Presiding Bishopric, but his appointments to the board of regents of the University of Deseret and the board of directors of the Territorial Insane Asylum were most likely the result of service in the territorial legislature. As with the tannery board, the canal board, the railroad board, etc., Robert did not give token service to these responsibilities. Under his direction, the university and the asylum constructed the first buildings specifically for their use.

Although the University of Deseret, which became the University of Utah in 1892, was founded by the legislature in February 1850, it was well into the 1870s before President John R. Park received financial commitment from the territorial treasury and support from the chancellor and board of regents to give the university stability as an institution of higher learning.[1] When Robert T. Burton was appointed to the board of regents in February 1878, the University of Deseret had been offering classes for five consecutive years, and the student body had grown from eighteen students in 1872 to nearly 200 (Chamberlain 1960, 102–12). The faculty included Dr. Park, Joseph B. Toronto, and Joseph T. Kingsbury. The campus had moved from the Council House on the corner of Main and South Temple (where William S. Burton attended classes in 1869) to the Union Academy Building, formerly named the Union Hotel because it stood adjacent to Union Square, a block-sized park where West High School now stands on the corner of Second West and First North. Union Academy was a long, two-story adobe building, divided into three classrooms with a library, office, labs, and museum.

Classes at the "university" did not lead to a four-year degree, but to a one-year normal degree or a one-year certificate course under the Academic Department. Since the territorial schools were not graded nor well developed enough to provide preparatory classes for college-level work, the university was more like a high school which accomplished that preparation. The goal of the regents during the eight years of Robert Burton's service was to develop a true university for the territory. Chancellor at this time was George Q. Cannon, and other regents appointed by the Twenty-Second Territorial Legislature on February 22, 1878, included Karl G. Maeser, David McKenzie, W. W. Cluff, John T. Caine, George J. Taylor, George Reynolds, William Jennings, James Sharp, H. S. Eldredge, D. O. Calder, and Moses Thatcher (*Salt Lake Herald*, February 23, 1878).

Robert served on the Executive Committee, and also the Building Committee, which placed the institution's major problem on his shoulders. The old academy building was "totally unsuitable and inadequate" for the university (Chamberlain 1960, 121). In 1879, unsuitable school facilities forced the university to terminate a one-year experiment in having a primary and intermediate school "graded to" the university. But the greater struggle was for an adequate building for the university itself. Robert worked diligently with Dr. Park and the regents to obtain funding from the legislature and to choose a site for the campus. His journal records that on March 21, 1880, Robert drove Dr. Park in his buggy up into the foothills north of Salt Lake City to the area known as "Arsenal Hill" looking for a site for the university.

The Board of Regents asked the 1880 legislature for $50,000 to purchase land and initiate the construction of a suitable building. The members of the Appropriation Committee, who claimed to be supporters of the university, recommended only $20,000—$10,000 in 1880 and $10,000 in 1881. "Subsequent legislators, they expected, would see the advisability of continuing to make such appropriations as would be necessary for the University of Deseret to become 'a first class college, a credit and blessing to the Territory' " (Chamberlain 1960, 122).

Since according to its charter, the university had to be located in Salt Lake City thereby making the city the chief beneficiary of the institution, the Building Committee petitioned the city council to donate one of its several available parks or other vacant land as a site. After considering several city parks and city-owned land on Arsenal Hill, the council finally agreed

> that a donation be made to said University of the grounds known as Union Square, . . . (such grounds being, in our opinion the most suitable for the purposes mentioned, and of any owned by the corporation), upon condition that the chief building of said University be erected and maintained on said grounds, and that the said building be used exclusively for educational purposes (in Chamberlain 1960, 122).

Work on the foundation of a large and spacious building began in July 1881, and continued until January 1882, when the legislature approved a second appropriation of $40,000 to continue the construction.

However, the University of Deseret became the unfortunate victim of a battle between the legislature and Governor Eli H. Murray, and for a time it appeared the building would not be finished. Murray maintained that Section 7 of the Organic Act of the territory gave him the authority to appoint certain territorial officers, including the chancellor and the board of regents for the University of Deseret. But legislatures between 1850 and 1878 had passed laws making the disputed positions elective either by the legislative assembly or by the people. For example, Section 574 of the *Compiled Laws of Utah* (1876) provided that the chancellor and board of regents be chosen by a joint vote of both houses of the General Assembly (see Whitney 3:198–200). When the legislature refused Murray's nominations in 1882 and again in 1884, he retaliated by vetoing the $40,000 appropriation for the university building fund and $15,000 marked for tuition for eighty normal students.

Without the 1882 appropriation to continue construction, the Building Committee arranged to cover the basement walls to protect them from storms and further minimize deterioration of materials on the grounds. A year later, however, Robert T. Burton and the other members of the board took matters into their own hands and voted to finish the building with money from public subscriptions, either in the form of loans or voluntary contributions. They raised twelve thousand dollars almost immediately, which included Robert's contribution of $500. Eventually, they raised $28,000 and the regents borrowed $7,000 from a bank, which completed the walls and roof.

The regents expected the 1884 legislature to reimburse the citizens and to continue construction, but again Murray vetoed the 1884 appropriation of $50,000 and the 1886 appropriation of $60,000. On March 16, 1886, President Cleveland removed Governor Murray from office "for cause" (CHC 6:173–75). In the interim years, the regents made small amounts of money available to the Building Committee. The first floor was completed "in the rough" so that classes could be held there in the fall of 1884; the second floor was likewise completed in 1885 (Chamberlain 1960, 124–26).

Robert watched over the construction and worked alongside the laborers when it was necessary to protect the unfinished structure, but his term as a regent ended before construction was complete. The 1888 legislature appropriated funds to complete the building which became known as University Hall and to pay off the indebtedness. By the time it was finished in 1891, it was already grossly inadequate due to growth in student body size and course offerings (see photograph, p. 130).

During Robert's term of service, enrollment increased to 330 and the university added a two-year normal course for training teachers and an academic department with a two-year classical preparatory course "to prepare students for entering the freshman year of any of our best classical institutions." In 1884–85 they added a four-year course leading to a bachelor of science degree (Chamberlain 1960, 129–30).

Many of Robert's children studied at the university, including William, who attended in the 1860s, Charles, John, and Willard, who attended in the early 1870s, and Virginia in the 1890s. Charles also was appointed as a regent in 1884 but did not serve because of the conflict with Governor Murray. Robert's son-in-law, Lewis S. Hills, was a member of the board of regents from 1890–96. Hundreds of Robert's descendants are alumni of the University of Deseret or the University of Utah.

In February 1880, the legislature appointed Robert to the board of directors of the Territorial Insane Asylum, which had just been created by legislative act. Before this time, the Salt Lake City Insane Asylum and Hospital was the only institution which specifically cared for the mentally ill. The Board of Directors met for the first time on March 17, 1880, and elected Robert president, with Warren H. Dusenberry as vice-president, John R. Winder as secretary, and Lewis S. Hills as treasurer. The legislature appropriated $25,000 and instructed the board to choose a site in Salt Lake, Utah, Davis, or Weber counties for the location of the institution, "upon the grounds of healthfulness, adaptability to the purposes of the institution, cost of material for construction and convenience of access from the different portions of the Territory." The building was to accommodate not more than 250 patients (McKell 1955, 305).

In April, Robert and the seven members of the board examined a number of sites along the Wasatch Front. Governor Murray was very much interested in this project and accompanied the board to Farmington and Ogden on April 20–21. On April 27, the board looked at sites in Salt Lake County, then traveled to Provo the next day to look at a number of sites there (April 20–21, 27–28, 1880). However, the territorial warrants were not immediately redeemable "without extensive discounting," and it was more than a year before the board announced that forty acres of land had been purchased one and a quarter miles due east of the Provo court house. Just as Salt Lake City had helped select the university site, so Provo city council and Utah county court donated funds to help purchase this land (McKell 1955, 306). The board of directors reported on August 4, 1881:

> The site chosen for the Asylum is upon an elevated position at the east of Provo City, being immediately at the head of its principal street, affording good facilities for drainage and ventilation and is remote from noisy trades and manufactories without being intersected with public roads or thoroughfares, has excellent water facilities, having a spring of ample supply, with an elevation of 530 feet, furnishing about 1000 gallons per hour. . . .
>
> Forty acres of land have been purchased for the sum of $1801.10, most of which is of excellent quality for agriculture and horticulture, the remainder pleasantly situated for ornamental grounds (in McKell 1955, 306).

Joseph M. Benedict, whose father was superintendent of a county insane asylum in Freeport, New York, advised the board in the planning of the institution. Dr. Benedict visited similar institutions in the East and tried to select the best features of each for the new asylum.

The Territorial Insane Asylum was the first building of what later became the Utah State Hospital, still located at the head of Center Street in Provo (see photograph, p. 130). From a history of the hospital, it appears that this first board of directors showed considerable insight in planning not just an adequate building, but an admirable institution, embracing all the improvements and conveniences of a modern asylum, "worthy of a great and good people, and commensurate with the wealth and population of the Territory" (McKell 1955, 309).

While Governor Murray was harassing the University of Deseret Board of Regents and vetoing its appropriations for construction of University Hall, he was cooperating with the directors of the asylum and approving its appropriations of nearly $100,000 in 1880, 1882, and 1884. Ironically, in both situations he was dealing with Robert T. Burton. On July 15, 1885, Robert led a delegation of church and civic officials to Provo on the D&RG railroad, to participate in the dedication of the Utah Territorial Insane Asylum (*Salt Lake Tribune,* July 15, 1885).

In August of 1880, Robert had again been elected as Salt Lake County assessor, which included the responsibility of voter registration. He frequently mentions going to his office in the county courthouse where he worked on the tax rolls and met with his deputies.

As registrar, he became a central figure in an interesting court case during the 1880 election for Utah's delegate to Congress. Encouraged by Governor Murray's political opposition to the Latter-day Saints who were represented by the People's Party, the Liberal Party revived after some years of inaction. Anti-Mormon, anti-polygamy rhetoric from Murray and other speakers dominated it's nominating convention. The party nominated Allen G. Campbell, a non-Mormon mine owner from Beaver, to represent Utah Territory in Congress. Although the party managers had no hope of winning a majority of the votes, they made every effort to influence the election, including an attempt to disfranchise the women of Utah who had been given the right to vote by the 1870 Territorial Legislature and Acting Governor S. A. Mann. The Liberal Party brought a writ of mandamus before the Supreme Court of Utah Territory to compel Robert T. Burton, registrar of Salt Lake County, "to erase and strike off from the list of voters of Salt Lake county made by him . . . and of all women whose names appear on the aforesaid list" (in CHC 6:5). The Liberal Party based its attack on two grounds: (1) the territorial law of 1859 only provided for males and *taxpayers* to be voters, while the law of 1870 extended the privilege of suffrage to women without requiring them to be taxpayers; and (2) women were not required to be "citizens" within the ordinary meaning of that word, since women could vote if they were wife, widow, or daughter of a native-born or naturalized citizen (CHC 6:5).

Robert refused to remove the names of women voters and appeared before the Supreme Court to argue that the court did not have proper jurisdiction in this action, nor did the petition contain facts sufficient to constitute cause of action. The Supreme

Court held that it did have jurisdiction in this matter but that the validity of the law could not be brought into question in that type of proceeding. The court found "that there is a law on our statute books in reference to registration, compelling the respondent to do what we are asked to compel him to undo. We cannot, for the purpose of this proceeding inquire into its validity. Having satisfied ourselves that the duty required by the statue to be performed has been performed, nothing is left for us to do" (in CHC 5:6).

Thus, the court refused to compel Robert to remove the names of women from the registration lists, and the women voted. The People's Party candidate, George Q. Cannon, was overwhelmingly elected by a vote of 18,568 to 1,357. Many months later, Cannon was denied the seat to which he had been elected because the newly passed Edmunds Act made it unlawful for a polygamist or any person cohabitating with more than one woman to hold any office or place of public trust in any territory of the United States.

It might not be surprising if Robert's substantial and time-consuming duties during this time caused him to neglect his family, but his diaries during these years show quite the opposite. There is evidence of rich and satisfying family experiences, ranging from births and weddings to remarkable healings and heartrending deaths, family holiday celebrations and summer outings, and the construction of modern, spacious homes.

While Robert did not take time for introspection in his daily diary notes, his entries say much about the importance of his family to him. Unlike some polygamist families, the Burtons all lived in Salt Lake City where there was opportunity for daily interaction between the busy patriarch and his wives and children. No written memoir or family story mentions jealousies or unhappiness. In 1885, Robert said that he did not know of any feelings that were not harmonious in the family (Burton Family Association, October 25, 1885). The close family experiences of these years were a great comfort to Robert during the difficult years after 1885.

Robert rarely traveled by buggy from downtown Salt Lake to the farm on South State Street or anywhere else without a family member at his side. He had begun this practice many years earlier when he would choose William, Robert, or Charles to be his teamster when he traveled outside the valley. In the late 1870s and early 1880s, he had nine teenage sons from which to choose a driver and eight younger children who loved to go with their father back and forth between his homes. He usually noted in his diary who accompanied him, for instance, Sarah and the little children, Mollie (Willard's wife), Annie (Henry's wife), Lizzie (Susan's daughter), or often "Mrs. Burton," as he described Maria.

He also continued to select family members to accompany him whenever possible on Presiding Bishopric business. In August 1879, Robert combined business in Bear Lake with a camping trip with his sons LaFayette (called Lafe or L.G.) and Henry and his nephew, Ranch Kimball. The first day they traveled up Parley's Canyon to Kimball's Ranch. He and the three boys left there in a wagon early the next morning, riding along the Weber River to Coalville, then northward to Echo Canyon. The next day's ride went "via Wasatch" to Woodruff through beautiful mountain terrain. While Robert had appointments to fill in Randolph and Bear Lake, he spent most of the week's time with the boys camping and fishing and also visiting isolated ranch families. He mentions Brashers, Collets, Groos, and Beckworths. He fished with the boys on Smiths Fork and Thomas Fork on the Bear River, then traveled to Logan via Lake Town and Meadowville. From Logan, Robert took a train to Salt Lake while the boys returned more leisurely with the wagon.

With some forty members in the immediate family, birthdays occurred almost weekly and each required a family gathering of large or small proportions. For Willard's twenty-first birthday, Susan had a family dinner on Sunday afternoon. When Mary and Lyman, born three days apart, turned twelve in August 1878, they had a joint birthday party at the farm, most likely in the grove of trees north of the house. Robert wrote in his diary that most of his children and grandchildren were at the farm for the occasion. This grove was the setting for many family gatherings, including birthday parties, holiday picnics, and Sunday afternoon visits. Other times, the grove was a wonderful playground for children and there were always children around the farm.

Robert's last three children were born to Sarah between 1877 and 1884. Virginia Louise, whom the family called "Genie," was born December 2, 1878; Austin Garr was born November 26, 1881; and Hardy Garr was born July 11, 1884. The generations were overlapping now, as Theresa, William, Robert, Henry, and Willard all had young children by 1883. Theresa's six children were the same ages as a number of her brothers and sisters, so family parties at Lewis and Theresa's were popular with the Burton family.

Almost every holiday called for a family gathering. Thanksgiving dinner was held in 1877, 1878, and 1881 at the Hills. During 1877, Lewis and Theresa built a spacious and elegant new home on their property through the block east from Robert and Maria's home at 126 South First West (now Second West). Lewis founded the Deseret National Bank, with William H. Hooper and Horace S. Eldredge, and was cashier there for many years, as well as a prominent civic servant. His home has recently been described as a "mansion" in "Victorian Italianate" style (Goodman 1987, E5). It is one of few from its time period still occupied in downtown Salt Lake. Walking through the large parlor and dining room downstairs, it is possible to imagine tables set end to end, covered with fine linens and loaded with food prepared by Theresa and Robert's three wives. There is a splendid staircase in the front hall, where children might have played while waiting the dinner bell. The ornate moldings and wood paneling reflect warmth and fine craftsmanship. The home has two full stories, with an attic tucked under the roof, and was built of fine red brick with white stone quoins at the corners and two-story bay windows fronting the street.[2]

Christmas was on Sunday in 1881, and Robert and Maria invited the older children and their wives or husbands to Haven Villa for dinner in the afternoon. The next morning, all the younger children and the grandchildren came for a party. They decorated a Christmas tree and had presents for everyone. Robert recorded in his diary that it was "a very good time, general joy and gladness."

Often the family included Robert's widowed sisters, Rebecca Jones and Melissa Kimball, and their children in the celebrations. Visits from the Westover, White, Garr, Ashby, McBride, or Badger families, or other relatives from Cache Valley, Beaver, or southern Utah also called for family get-togethers. When Samuel Leybourn, son of Jane Burton Leybourn, came from Denver to visit in September 1877, the family feted him every night at a family dinner as he became acquainted with his many cousins.

The first family wedding of this period (1877-84) was Charles's marriage to Julia Young, daughter of Brigham Young[3] and Susan Snively Young. They were married in the Endowment House the morning of May 7, 1878, at 11 A.M. Their wedding party for members of the two large families was held that afternoon at President Young's residence. William served a mission in England from May 1877 to May 1879 and shortly after his return married Eloise Crisman, daughter of Robert and Maria's close friends, George and Mary Louisa Crismon. They were married on June 11, 1879. On January 6, 1881, Willard married Mary Jane (Mollie) Gardner, daughter of Henry and Margaret Gardner. In January 1883, the family had two weddings in two days. Robert performed the marriage of John and Kathleen or Katherine (Kate) Ferguson, daughter of James and Phyllis Ferguson, on January 10, and the next day he witnessed the wedding of Henry and Anna Eliza Gibby, daughter of William and Catherine Gibby. The brides' parents hosted wedding parties for each couple.

Many years before, when he was a new father, Robert began a tradition of blessing his children that has carried into recent generations. As each child was born, he gave them their name and a father's blessing at home when they were about eight days old. Later, he took them to the appropriate fast day meeting and again named and blessed them to place the name on

Church records. He also blessed his grandchildren at home as close to their eighth day as possible. Often, he performed these blessings and the baptisms for the eight-year-old children and grandchildren at family gatherings.

Robert refers so often to music whenever the family got together that it is not surprising to discover that, beginning October 18, 1882, Evan Stephens taught a singing class at the farm for the Burton children and their friends. On the next Thanksgiving Day, they held an examination or recital. The children also sang in the Tabernacle for special jubilee programs and held other concerts in Social Hall under Stephens's direction. Robert mentions bringing him to the farm from the city for the classes which were called the "Farmers Ward Singing School," but later Evan Stephens built a home on Main Street just north of Twenty-first South and became a member of Farmers Ward.

Although family gatherings were most often parties with music and occasionally dancing, the Burton children also loved to go sleighing when the weather cooperated. Sleighs were necessary to get around the valley when the roads were snow covered and the temperatures below freezing, but many times Robert took the children out riding just for fun. Ice-skating was another favorite activity, according to William's stories about his youth. In the summer, the Great Salt Lake attracted families, Sunday Schools, the "Old Folks," or other groups. On August 6, 1884, Robert took several family members to Black Rock beach for an outing with members of the Fifteenth Ward. It was very hot, and Robert took his little children into the lake on a boat, providing a "pleasant afternoon" for them. The next week, he returned to the same beach for a reunion of members of the London Conference.

All family experiences are not joyous, and a family as large as Robert's could not avoid sickness, accident, or death. Two of Robert's children died in childhood—Maria's sixth son, Albert Temple (born January 29, 1862; died August 31, 1863) and Sarah's first daughter, Alice Maria (born April 23, 1864; died

21 August 1871). There are no journal notes describing the anguish of those times, but undoubtedly the entire family mourned.

Late in April 1878, eighteen-year-old Frank, Sarah's second son, suffered what Robert called "a violent attack of brain fever." The attack was so sudden and so severe that priesthood administrations, constant nursing, and a physician's attention brought no relief to the sick boy. He fell ill on Friday evening, and on Tuesday morning, he died. Robert had been at his bedside for nearly forty-eight straight hours, in anguish because "we could do nothing that appeared to give relief." He recorded in his journal on April 30. "My son Frank departed this life at 7 A.M. after four days of terrible suffering, but full of patience and love amidst all his pain. He departed full of faith and hope."

As his body lay in the farmhouse for viewing, Robert recorded on May 1, that "a delegation of young men from the YMMIA came and stayed with us on account of Franks death. All the neighbors & friends are very kind." The funeral took place May 2, 1878, in the Fifteenth Ward where "the house was very full and many departed [as they] could not get in." Frank was known as a talented and righteous young man, who at age sixteen was ordained an elder and received his temple endowments.

Robert recorded many other instances of illness among the children. Chapter 17 describes John's bout with "lung fever" during the spring of 1877, but family members also endured epidemics of diphtheria, measles, mumps, and other illnesses. The Burton children avoided diphtheria during the winter of 1879–80, but many of their friends died or were very ill. Robert writes about the children at the farm having mumps in January 1882 and measles in January 1883. During these years, Robert almost always helped care for the sick children, especially through the long nights. The wives also assisted each other at these times, as well as when Sarah, Theresa, or one of the daughters-in-law gave birth.

On September 14, 1880, Robert's son Charles was accidentally shot in Moroni, Sanpete County. When a telegraph message reached Robert that evening at the farm, he secured a special train to take Dr. Joseph Benedict, Maria, and Charles's wife, Julia, to help him. The trip took most of the night. They left the train at Nephi and traveled by wagon to Moroni, arriving at 5:30 A.M. To their relief, Charles was not hurt as badly as they had feared. They carefully moved him back to Nephi, caught a train for Salt Lake City that afternoon, and took Charles to Haven Villa to recuperate (September 14–15, 1880).

Haven Villa was constructed in 1878. First, Robert had a new home built for Susan and her children on Second West, four lots south of his primary residence on the corner of First South and Second West. Construction began in the fall of 1877 with Robert's brother Charles apparently as the builder. Family members often referred to the home as the "redwood house." It was a double-house or duplex, although it is not known if it was built that way originally (Raybould 1978). Susan moved in on January 2, 1878, with the help of family members.

Just two weeks before Susan's home was finished, a large fire threatened Robert and Maria's home. The alarm came while Robert was attending sacrament meeting at the Fifteenth Ward on December 23, 1877. Maria ran to the church to get Robert, and he and others returned to find a building immediately west of his home being consumed by flames and other structures threatened. Robert owned the burning building, but J. H. Clemetshaw, a trunk maker, occupied it. The building and Clemetshaw's entire inventory of trunks, tools, and materials were destroyed ("Trunk Factory," 1877). Members of the Burton family and the ward quickly tore down the fence between the outbuildings and the Burton house, then stripped blankets off beds, soaked them, and used them to stop the fire as it moved toward the house.

Robert's loss was estimated at $600, but the scare moved him to replace his old adobe and frame home with a modern brick one. Four days later, Robert and Maria met with a Brother Terns to discuss plans for a new house. On March 21, Maria and her children moved to the "redwood house" where they lived on one side of Susan's home while the new home was under construction. The next day, March 22, all the younger children held a party at the old house before it was torn down. The home had been added onto many times in its nineteen-year history and there were many family memories of the times when all three families had lived there together (see drawing by LaFayette G. Burton, p. 117). Construction of the new two-story brick house, with a basement, took about a year. Robert referred frequently in his journal to his part in the process. For instance, on July 16, 1878, he went to the brickyard in Kaysville to select brick. Hired men appear to have done the labor although Robert's sons, especially John, may have been involved. Some family members remember that John designed and built this home, but Robert does not mention this particularly. John was very much interested in construction and architecture. He later studied architecture under a Mr. Furber in Chicago and N. B. Bacon in Toledo (see photograph of Haven Villa on p. 135). Robert was particularly busy during this year with the trial for the Morrisite murders. The trial ended March 7, and the family began moving into the new house on Wednesday, March 12. Robert wrote that he spent Friday "arranging things in new house."

The new house definitely allowed more room for family dinners and socials. On Robert's next birthday, October 25, 1879, the entire family came to Haven Villa in his honor, "the children enjoying themselves, dancing and with music, etc." The largest room happened to be in the basement, and often the family cleared it out to make room for games and round dancing (Raybould 1878). Maria's children also built new homes on the block adjacent to Haven Villa. The block is illustrated on pp. 132–33 as it might have looked during the 1890s.

Ten years later, Robert had a new house built on the farm for Sarah and her family. Virginia Burton remembered that in the spring of 1889 Robert had workmen divide the old home before moving it in order to save the garden in front of the home, which had been landscaped by Maxwell, a Salt Lake florist (A. Cutler 1976, 185–85). Part of the old plaster house was moved to the north side of the lot and the family lived in it until the new two-story brick home was finished that summer. The house, according to Virginia had eight rooms, plus a pantry and bath. "We had our first bath tub and running water," she said, "We had a jack pump. It pumped water to a tank on the roof. It had only a small force but if it pumped all day and night, it was sufficient for our needs" (A. Cutler 1976, 185) (see photograph, p. 135). The new farm house was built at the end of Robert's four years living on the so-called "underground," and he recorded many visits to the farm during the summer "to see how my men are getting along on the house."

As early as 1879, the citizens of Utah Territory were becoming increasingly concerned about the anti-polygamy campaign (usually called the "Mormon question") developing in the East. But when the Edmunds Bill became law on March 22, 1882, and George Q. Cannon was denied his seat in Congress five weeks later because he was a polygamist, apprehension swept through the Latter-day Saint people. The Edmunds Bill was an amendment to the Morrill Anti-Bigamy Act of 1862 and defined polygamy as a felony. According to the act, every person with a husband or wife living, who married again after the Edmunds Act became law, or who simultaneously, or on the same day, married more than one woman, was guilty of polygamy. The fine for breaking this law was $500 and/or imprisonment for five years. Polygamous living or "unlawful cohabitation" was made a misdemeanor punishable by a fine not to exceed $300 and imprisonment not to exceed six months, or both. The bill also disfranchised polygamists, declaring them ineligible for public office, and excluded from jury service those who lived in or believed in polygamy. All registration and election offices were declared vacant and a board of five commissioners was to be appointed by the president of the United States—the notorious Utah Commission—to perform the duties of registration and election officers (Larson 1971, 95).

From this time on, Robert's journal includes sporadic comments about preparations by Church authorities to counter government action against the Church and its members. Initially the Council of Fifty became very active, often meeting for several days in a row, especially in June and August 1882, June 1883, and other times in 1884 (June 21–27 and August 21–September 1, 1882). Robert does not name the council specifically in his notes, but says, "This Council was organized in Nauvoo by Joseph the Prophet." It traditionally met at April and October conference time. During this time Robert wrote a new will reflecting changes in his business affairs, traveled to Logan where he "participated in an organization securing the Logan Temple for Educational & Scientific Purposes" on July 10, 1884, and visited various rural communities where Church cattle herds were transferred to semi-public livestock associations; each of these activities related to Church efforts to protect their property from government seizure. On the Fourth of July 1884, Robert commented in his journal that there was no public celebration except "some of the rabid Gentiles undertook to celebrate, but it was very faint indeed." Whereas, Robert had been marshal of a Twenty-fourth of July parade in 1880, "one of the grandest displays ever seen in the West," in 1884, he mentions no parade or entertainment in the Tabernacle to commemorate the arrival of the pioneers. It was subtle, but life in the valley was changing and the Latter-day Saints seemed powerless to do anything about it. On the Fourth of July 1885, Robert wrote: "Independence Day, but not much liberty for L. D. Saints as the spirit of persecution among a class of people and especially Government Officials makes the Saints feel *sore indeed*" (emphasis in original).

One example which illustrates the feelings of the Saints toward the government and judicial oppression occurred in 1879 during one of the first trials for violation of polygamy laws. It was not the trial nor conviction of John H. Miles that created a sensation in Utah, but the imprisonment of Daniel H. Wells for alleged contempt of court during the trial when he would not answer questions about the endowment ceremony and clothing. He was fined $100 and sentenced to two days in the penitentiary, but to the Saints he was a hero. During his brief imprisonment, they planned a public demonstration as "an expression of admiration" upon his release, placed announcements in the Salt Lake papers, and sent special messengers to the surrounding settlements.

At the end of Wells's second day of imprisonment, Robert T. Burton escorted President Wells from the penitentiary to the Burton farm home where he was Robert's guest for the night. In the morning, President John Taylor, members of the Quorum of the Twelve, and hundreds of prominent priesthood and civic leaders from northern Utah arrived at Robert's farm to escort President Wells to the city. There were presidents of stakes, high councilors, bishops, mayors, and city councilors with several bands from Bear Lake, Cache, Box Elder, Weber, and Davis counties on the north and Utah and Juab counties on the south. President Wells rode with President Taylor in a barouche carriage drawn by four white horses, followed by the procession of carriages and horsemen, past "a vast concourse" of Saints, including formations of the Sunday Schools, Relief Societies, Mutual Improvement Associations, priesthood quorums, and so forth. Everywhere the American flag was in evidence, carried by the marchers and festooned throughout the Tabernacle, where a spirited meeting was held with speeches and band music. While the Church's enemies accused them of dishonoring the flag, to the thousands of Latter-day Saints caught up in the event, it was a time to honor the flag and the principles of religious liberty which they valued (CHC 5:544–50; R. T. Burton 1856–1907, May 5–6, 1879.)

Surely the Saints must have realized after 1882 that if one man could be imprisoned—even so briefly—for honoring his temple obligations, greater trials were in store for them when prosecutions began under the Edmunds Act. There were no convictions until November 1884, although several women were sent to prison for contempt of court prior to that date.

There were three significant changes in Robert T. Burton's responsibilities prior to 1885: he resigned as county assessor, he became first counselor to a new Presiding Bishop, and he sold his interest in the woolen mill.

When the Edmunds Bill was passed in 1882, Robert was serving a second time as Salt Lake County assessor. Because polygamists were ineligible for pubic office under the bill's provisions, Robert had to resign, and his son William replaced him in 1883. Of course, Robert was no longer registrar either as the Utah Commission supervised voter registration.

On October 16, 1883, Bishop Edward Hunter died. Until the next April Conference, the work of the Presiding Bishopric fell upon his counselors, Leonard W. Hardy and Robert T. Burton. When William B. Preston, president of the Cache Stake, was called April 6, 1884, to replace Bishop Hunter, he kept both as his counselors. Bishop Hardy died July 31, 1884, and Robert was subsequently sustained as first counselor to Bishop Preston, with John R. Winder as second counselor (R. T. Burton 1900).

The Wasatch Woolen Mill, operated by Burton, Sons and Young during the early 1880s, provided employment for several of Robert's sons and income for the large Burton family. However, on March 20, 1884, Abraham O. Smoot, John Sharp, and Robert T. Burton sold the mill to James Dunn of Provo and John C. Cutler of Salt Lake City for $13,000 (*Deseret News*, March 21, 1884). Deseret Mill, built by Brigham Young, was not sold, but it had not been operating.[4] Building and operating the mills had been significant ventures for the Burton family for nearly twenty years, giving the older sons experience in manufacturing, supervision, and retail sales from which they went on to successful careers in other growing Utah institutions.

In summary, 1877–84 were eventful years for Robert and his family. While he personally experienced the just conclusion of his trial for murder dating back to the Morrisite War, the Saints experienced many instances of injustice. Though remarkably they did not strike back, neither did they capitulate to their persecutors. Rather, they prepared to peacefully resist with all their might enforcement of the Edmunds Act and later the Edmunds-Tucker Act, legislation whose ultimate goal was the temporal and political destruction of The Church of Jesus Christ of Latter-day Saints and its people.

Notes

1. For a complete history of the university, see Ralph V. Chamberlain, *The University of Utah, A History of Its First Hundred Years*, Salt Lake City: University of Utah, 1960.

2. The Hills' home has been restored since 1977 by Jonathan Sweet, who lives and operates the Hills' House Antique Gallery therein. It can be visited daily during business hours or by appointment.

3. Julia was adopted by Brigham Young following his marriage to Susan Snively, her mother.

4. Much later, some of the mill buildings were used as an isolation ward to quarantine individuals with small pox and were referred to as the "pest house" (C. Burton to T. M. Burton 1953).

19

On the Underground, 1885–90

Intermingled with Robert's official role during the polygamy raids as a trustee for The Church of Jesus Christ of Latter-day Saints is the story of his personal life on the "underground." For four years, he was constantly on guard to avoid arrest by the U.S. marshals for "unlawful cohabitation." Initially, he chose to travel outside of the territory, taking care of cattle and tithing business for the Church. After months of poor health, undoubtedly aggravated by the absence of familiar home and family routines, he returned to Salt Lake City and worked with the First Presidency and Presiding Bishopric to save the Church's property during months of litigation and receivership.

There was nothing suspicious about the buggy which pulled up to the home of William Gibby at 8:30 on the evening of January 31, 1885. The drawn curtains shielded the passenger from view, but they could just as well have been protecting him from the cold night air. The Gibbys were long-time friends of the coachman, William S. Burton. William went inside, leaving his passenger in the buggy, and returned a few moments later with a man bundled and hidden in an overcoat, scarf, and hat. The second man climbed in the buggy, and William guided the horses on a unhurried ride through the streets of Salt Lake City.

The two gentlemen out for a "pleasant ride" were none other than President John Taylor and Robert T. Burton, at that very hour avoiding the federal marshals with warrants to arrest them for polygamy and/or unlawful cohabitation. Of course, the conversation that night between Robert and his prophet/friend is nowhere recorded, and yet it is not difficult to surmise. Undoubtedly Robert wanted to know what course of action he should take, and John Taylor counseled him that he should take care of himself the best he could and avoid being caught in any of the snares of the federal officials. President Taylor preached this same counsel publicly the next afternoon in the Tabernacle in his final public discourse:

> Would you resent these outrages and break the heads of the men engaged in them, and spill their blood? No, avoid them as much as you can. . . . What! won't you submit to the dignity of the law? Well I would if the law would only be a little dignified. But when we see the ermine bedraggled in the mud and mire, and every principle of justice violated, it behooves men to take care of themselves as best they may. That is what I have told people while I have been in the south—to take care of their liberties, to put their trust in the living God, to obey every constitutional law, and to adhere to all correct principles. But when men tamper with your rights and with your liberties, when the cities are full of spies and the lowest, meanest of men are set to watch and dog your footsteps; when little children are set in array against their fathers and mothers and women and children are badgered before courts and made to submit, unprotected, to the gibes of libertines and corrupt men, when wives and husbands are pitted against each other and threatened with pains, penalties, and imprisonment . . . when such a condition of affairs exist, it is no longer a land of liberty, and it is certainly no longer a land of equal rights, and we must take care of ourselves as best we may, and avoid being caught in any of their snares. . . . Would you fight them? No. I would take care of myself as best I can, and I would advise my brethren to do the same (in CHC 6:122–23).

Encouraged by recent court rulings supporting rigorous enforcement and interpretation of anti-polygamy laws, the marshals had, eleven days earlier, begun arresting prominent Church leaders, all of whom they presumed to be polygamists. Angus M. Cannon, president of the Salt Lake Stake, was captured on January 20, while the First Presidency was in southern Arizona. News of Cannon's capture reached Robert in American Fork, his first stop on a trip to inspect tithing properties in Utah, Juab, and Sanpete Counties. Warned that marshals were also after him, he hid a few days in Utah valley. When he returned to Salt Lake City, he stayed the first night at his son Charles's home and the next night and day in a room built into the new tithing barn behind the General Tithing Office for such a purpose.[1] He finally dared to go home and to the farm for a couple of nights, but "at the suggestion of a friend" he changed quarters to William Gibby's on Friday, January 30.

In his journal, Robert described the evening with President Taylor as "a pleasant ride" (January 31, 1885). One must wonder if he would have recorded it differently if he had known he would never see President Taylor again. John Taylor left his public ministry the next night and died on July 25, 1887, after two and a half years of hiding from federal marshals. He lived with families in Bountiful and Kaysville and directed the affairs of the Church through messages and messengers to Salt Lake. His counselors also went into hiding. Joseph F. Smith went to Hawaii until 1889, and George Q. Cannon was pursued all over the West, captured, escaped, then recaptured, released on $45,000 bond, and forfeited it to go into hiding in Arizona. The Council of Fifty never met again after President Taylor dropped from public life and was unable to influence decisions made after 1884.

Robert spent Saturday night and Sunday, February 1, at Lewis and Theresa Hills' home. Bishop Preston and other friends called on him Sunday afternoon. A few family members also came, and the spontaneous social which followed prompted Robert to record, "With singing and music the day passed very pleasantly."

With such seeming calm, Robert began four years of living on the underground, successfully avoiding arrest, trial, and imprisonment.

Until the arrest and trial of Angus M. Cannon, Church leaders, including Robert T. Burton, assumed they could conform to the provisions of the Edmunds Act by furnishing separate housing for their plural wives and ceasing to live with them, although still giving them financial support. However, the federal officials and the anti-Mormons were intent on destroying the political power of the Church hierarchy as well as ridding the country of polygamy, the "twin relic of barbarism" to slavery.

The key men in the drive were the federal judges and district attorneys whose prosecution and decisions made the anti-polygamy laws either effective or empty. Led by newly appointed Chief Justice Charles S. Zane of the Supreme Court of Utah Territory, the federal judges launched the judicial crusade late in 1884, using such tactics as selecting grand jury members according to their stated biases against Mormonism, seating all-gentile trial juries, imprisoning witnesses who refused to testify, denying bonds, and levying lengthy prison sentences on those convicted (Lyman 1986, 25). The *Deseret News* reported June 1, 1889, that Zane was "a good and able judge when not excited on the one [Mormon] question"; but on that question, he represented the biases of the Republican Party whose leaders had sent him to Utah to execute the Edmunds Act. He made his mission clear in one of his first polygamy trials. When John Nicholson chose allegiance to his family and religion over the law in question, Zane replied, "If you do not submit, of course, you must take the consequences, but the will of the American people is expressed [severely] and the law will go on and grind your institution to powder" (in CHC 6:112).

Although Church officials first decided they would fight each and every charge under the Edmunds Act, after only a few cases they were convinced that the Republican-appointed judges would not give them fair trials or sentences until they had abolished polygamy and destroyed the secular power of the Church. Latter-day Saints could not foresee either happening in 1885.

Three paths were open to polygamists like Robert Taylor Burton. They could submit to arrest, plead not guilty, and be convicted and sentenced to a fine and prison term. Men who chose this course were seen as heros by their families, wives, and loyal Church members. Polygamists could also be arrested, but could plead guilty and promise in court to obey the law on condition they could avoid a prison sentence. This course, exercised at first by only a few men, shocked many Church members who saw it as an abandonment of wives and sacred covenants and was deplored by Church officials. The third choice was to avoid arrest by leaving homes and families and living on the underground. John Taylor set the precedent by disappearing on February 1, and almost all the apostles and prominent Church leaders followed.

The underground was a network of hiding places, escape routes, warning systems, and assistance from Mormon communities which helped the so-called "cohabs" avoid capture during intensive "polyg hunts" conducted by a large force of deputy U.S. marshals. Saints built ingenious hideouts into homes and barns (such as the room in the tithing barn), and hunted men retreated into the canyons and even into Mexico or Canada (Larson 1971, 119–20). The marshals considered some men more wanted than others, and offered large rewards for their capture, and watched their homes and families intensely. Deputies particularly wanted to capture those who could lead them to the "safe retreat" of President Taylor.

Robert Burton seems to have stayed out of sight during the first few weeks of the hunts (January 20–February 6), but in mid-February he resumed normal activities, though always guarded by one of his sons or colleagues. It was quite well known that the city police were the eyes and ears of the underground although they pretended to be aloof from the entire game. Robert had many friends in the police department, and he changed his quarters more than once "at the suggestion of a friend." Significantly, he wrote in his journal of the formation of "a large force of special Police for the Protection of the City" during a January 13 meeting called by the mayor at the Social Hall. However, as long as Robert remained in Salt Lake City, he was in danger. Prudently, over the next eighteen months, he was away two-thirds of the time.

Robert's first trip, March 22 to May 27, was with Lewis S. Hills, Elijah F. Sheets, and Thomas Cutler; they went to the Midwest and East to purchase cattle for the Church and attend the New Orleans Exposition. At this time, Sheets was livestock agent for the Church, and he and Robert were committed to an extensive program to upgrade the Church's cattle and dairy herds. Both men were polygamists and on the underground. After visiting stockyards and packing plants in Kansas City and St. Louis, they went south by train to New Orleans where they spent six days examining the agricultural and manufacturing exhibits at the exposition and sightseeing in the city. From here Lewis went on to California while Robert, Sheets, and Cutler went north to the home of Robert's brother-in-law, Elijah Austin, at Sublette, Illinois. Robert and Elijah Sheets made this their home base while they visited prominent stockmen in northern Illinois, then traveled to Syracuse, New York where they inspected cattle bred on the farms of Smith and Powell. They were most interested in pedigreed Holsteins. After purchasing cattle, they had to make arrangements to get them all to one place for shipment to Utah, a complicated and frustrating task. However, they were not in a hurry and eventually made the necessary arrangements (March 22–May 1, 1885).

While traveling to and from New York, Robert again visited his relatives in Ohio and New York. In Pultneyville, New York, the husband of his sister Ann, Waters Shipley, was on his deathbed. Robert stayed until he died on May 3, 1885. Robert was not traveling with Elijah Sheets at this time and found it difficult to leave the Shipleys even though Sheets was waiting for him in Chicago. Robert extended all the comfort he could to his sister and her children and left sorrowfully, feeling "in all probability this is the last time I will meet my sister" (May 4, 1885).

Back in Illinois, Burton and Sheets completed their purchases, and on May 19, they loaded some of the stock in Sublette and traveled to Mendota. However, at Mendota they had a two-day delay getting a boxcar, and the trip to Salt Lake eventually took nine days, including time to unload and load the cattle three times as they changed trains. Transporting the cattle proved to be more exhausting than bringing hundreds of emigrants even greater distances.

Once in Utah, Robert took these cattle to what he called the "improved stock farm," apparently located near the Church farm on the Jordan River south of Salt Lake City. While avoiding the marshals, Robert supervised construction of a barn, recorded the pedigrees of the cattle, and conducted what Church business he could without appearing in public.

Robert was in Salt Lake City from May 28 until August 6, when he went north to Logan and southern Idaho with Moses Thatcher and Bishop Preston, to attend conferences, instruct the bishops, and inspect tithing property. In September, similar responsibilities allowed him to spend four weeks traveling through central and southern Utah as far south as Pipe Springs, Arizona.

For more than twenty years, Robert had been associated with Bishop John Sharp. During the summer of 1885, they had discussed the anti-polygamy crusade, so it may not have surprised Robert when the news reached him in southern Utah that Sharp had chosen the unpopular path and had pled guilty to a charge of unlawful cohabitation before Judge Zane. In making a formal statement before the court, Sharp explained that he had become the husband of more than one wife when such had not been contrary to the law. He said he understood the Edmunds Act did not require him to disown the mothers of his children as his wives; he intended to support his wives but promised to live within the provisions of the law "as construed by this Court and the Supreme Court of the Territory," until "an overruling Providence shall decree greater religious toleration in the land" (Whitney 3:421).

Judge Zane commended Bishop Sharp's decision, hoping that his example would help others to submit to the law. He then imposed the customary fine of $300 but no prison sentence. Others who chose this plea also avoided imprisonment but were very unpopular with the Saints. Robert does not give any clues about his feelings toward Bishop Sharp's action, although he probably knew more about the mitigating circumstances and struggle that had gone into the decision than did all those who severely criticized him.

Robert continued on the course he had chosen. He said later in court that from this time, he lived only with Maria. However, he saw Sarah when he worked at the farm and visited Susan in her home on special occasions. While he was in Salt Lake City, he moved cautiously, changing locations frequently from home to office to his farm to the stock farm and to the homes of his sons or friends.

On October 25, the Burtons held their first official "family meeting" at Haven Villa, on Robert's sixty-fourth birthday. For some time, Robert had contemplated organizing his family, and he had called his children and grandchildren together for this purpose. All his twenty-four living children were in attendance except Hosea and George, as well as his sisters, nephews, sons-and daughters-in-law, grandchildren, and friends—fifty-eight persons in all. By vote of those present they organized the Burton Family Association and named Robert their first president, with William S. Burton as vice president, Lewis S. Hills, secretary, Mary A. Burton, assistant secretary, and Julia Y. Burton, reporter. Now 102 years old, this association continues to meet on a date as near to October 25 as possible.

It is important to view the circumstances of the first family meeting and the speech delivered by Robert as president, patriarch, and concerned father in the context of the contemporary political situation. Because of the anti-polygamy raid, Robert was fortunate to be with them on such an occasion; and realizing this could be his last opportunity, he counseled them regarding their behavior as family members in the environment of

federal oppression and his decision to obey the Church leaders
and disobey the law.

> I may meet you many times in gatherings the same as the present
> but we can not tell what a day may bring forth; still, I trust I may
> have the opportunity of being present in my family circle many,
> many times on occasions like the present. . . . There are but two of
> my children absent today. I hope that whatever the circumstances
> are, this family reunion may be observed annually on the anniver-
> sary of this day whether I may be absent or present, whether I may
> have passed to the other world or been permitted to remain. I hope,
> I expect to live many years yet. . . . Of this however we have no
> assurance and must be satisfied with the decrees of Providence.
>
> I have throughout my life, endeavored to set an example wor-
> thy, my children, to be imitated by you; but to err is human, and I
> doubtless have made many mistakes. I do not ask you to pattern
> after those, but that which is good (which I trust predominates) you
> are at liberty to live by if you desire and I hope you do. I have never
> sought to enforce my religious sentiments upon any of you, my
> sons and daughters, only by practice and example, hoping that as
> you grew to years of accountability you could understand, and would
> appreciate them, for yourselves. But I desire to say this to you, my
> children, it is the religion of the Lord Jesus Christ that has been
> taught you from your infancy, and through it I have received noth-
> ing but benefit, joy and blessings.
>
> There is at least one request I would make of you—my children,
> if there be any feelings among you, any disagreements of any nature—
> you will not talk about them outside of our immediate family circle
> but kindly adjust them among yourselves. In our early days, when
> you were all small, and we had not the comforts and conveniences
> of life that we have at the present time, we all lived as one family,
> and if there were any feelings that were not harmonious they were
> never known. Now that most of you are grown if again there be any
> misunderstandings, any differences of opinion, do not talk about
> them, do not parade them before the public. Be forgiving and char-
> itable as brother and sister should be in the full sense of the word. . . .
> And now my sons, I desire to ask you—I beseech of you this; what-
> ever is your belief, whatever your religious opinions may be, I request
> that you will not, by a single word or act of any kind, try to destroy,
> in any way, the principles of our religion that I have all my life tried
> to establish by practice, by example, and by kind teachings. . . . I
> would ask this for the future; whatever your religious or social views
> may be do not by indiscreet acts or unguarded words drag down to

the dust, disgrace, destroy or attempt to do so, that which your
mother and myself have prayed for and labored unceasingly to
establish from our youth to the present time (Burton Family Association 1885–1953, October 25, 1885)

These words urged his children to be united at a time when
public disagreement with the outlawed doctrine of plural marriage divided many families. His safety in months ahead
depended upon the discretion of his children and their support
of his decision to go on the underground.

Robert spoke many more times to his family as he presided
at family meetings until his death. In addition to fatherly counsel, he gave reports of his personal and family history and genealogy. The minutes of the association have been a valuable
resource for this biography. Robert's birthday became a family
holiday, and his grandchildren were excused from school in the
afternoon to attend. Carl C. Burton, who was five months old
at the first reunion, recalled later reunions and "the wonderful
times we used to have when they were held in grandfather's
home on 1st South and 2nd West. . . . The refreshments
impressed me most as we all sat down to a well ladened [sic]
table covered with all kinds of good food to eat. . . . I recall
that grandfather and his fiddle played quite a part on the
program" (C. Burton 1969, 15). Beginning with the blessing
given Eloise Burton, the youngest grandchild, at the first reunion,
it became a tradition to bless the infants if not previously done
and to formally admit each of them to membership in the association.

On November 19, 1885, Robert began his longest period of
exile from home and family. He left Salt Lake with a contingent of stockmen representing Utah at the National Stock Convention in St. Louis, Missouri. Apparently they had been concerned about the reception their delegation might receive, but
Robert recorded in his journal on November 23, "Utah Delegation meets with marked courtesy and attention from Citizens
Comm[ittee]." Later, with that committee, they marched to their
place on the convention floor. As the convention drew to a
close, Robert T. Burton was elected vice president for the terri-

tory of Utah. After the convention, he led the Utah delegates on a tour down the Mississippi River by steamboat to the New Orleans Exposition. However, Robert was disappointed to discover that the display was "comparatively nothing to what it was last spring when I visited it" (December 5, 1885).

John Burton accompanied his father, and from New Orleans, they went by train to Toledo, Ohio, where John met many cousins living in the vicinity. They also visited the federal penitentiary in nearby Detroit where four prominent Arizona polygamists had been imprisoned as an additional harassment by the Arizona judiciary. Robert found that David Udall, C. I. Kempe, Ammon M. Tenney, and Peter C. Christofferson were "looking well considering their confinement and were very glad indeed to see me" (December 10, 1885). It is a wonder that Robert could venture into such an institution and be "treated very kindly" by the warden in spite of the warrants outstanding on him for the exact "crimes" of the men he was visiting.

Robert and John next traveled to Sublette, Illinois. There John left his father with Elijah Austin, went to Chicago on business, and returned to Utah. Thus, the brother-in-law who would not follow the Saints to the West now provided a haven away from Utah where Robert spent the greater part of the winter. Robert spent his days reading, writing letters, visiting with relatives and friends, and preparing a manuscript of his address to his family so that the complete, accurate text could be entered in the Burton Family Association minutes.

Elijah Austin had married Catherine (Kate) Carnes after Robert's sister, Sarah, had died delivering twins in 1859. He had eight living children from the two marriages. After the Christmas holidays, Robert and Elijah visited Abilene, Kansas, where Elijah had a second farm run by his son, Burton Austin. Elijah's daughter, Melissa, lived nearby with her husband, Robert McKennett, and family. Robert and Elijah returned to Illinois in a heavy snowstorm on January 22 and 23.

During the winter, Robert anxiously waited for the mail from Utah hoping for news that he could safely return home. He knew within four days about the arrest of George Q.

Cannon on February 12, 1886, near Winnemucca, Nevada, and followed subsequent events, culminating in Cannon's forfeiting bail and fleeing the state on the advice of President Taylor. About the time of Cannon's arrest, Robert began making arrangements to travel to Arizona to meet Bishop William B. Preston, who was continuing to conduct Church business during these unusual times.

In spite of cold and stormy weather, Robert left Illinois on February 23, and traveled back to Abilene, where he had arranged to meet his son William. After visiting five days with relatives in Abilene and conducting some cattle business in Kansas City, Robert departed for Arizona and William returned to Salt Lake City. Had they known Robert would be seriously ill within two days, perhaps William would not have not have left him to travel alone to Arizona or they would have remained in Kansas. But the illness came without warning during the train trip across New Mexico. Robert spent the entire day sick on his bunk in a sleeper compartment as the train ran from Albuquerque to Navajo Springs, Arizona, where he got off the train. He wrote in his journal on Sunday, March 7:

> Remained at Navajo Springs discussing in my mind if I should attempt in my present ill health to meet Bro Preston at St. John or go on the R.R. to St. Joseph and finely concluded upon the latter and at 2:10 P.M. Boarded cars again for West. Arrived at St. Joseph. Found no station as the settlement is one mile and a half off the road. Met here a Bro Peterson who assisted me by carrying my satchel. I made out to walk to settlement by resting on the way. Here I put up with John McLaws also met many other accquaintences but I am very feeble.

Miles away in Salt Lake City, William returned from Kansas City on March 7 and assured his mother that Robert was fine, but Maria felt differently. A poignant entry in her journal the same date says, "I have felt very lonly all day, could neither read nor write." A week later, news of Robert's untimely illness reached her in a letter from St. Joseph. "It has made me feel very bad. . . . When I read my husband['s] lettr, I can account for my uneasy feeling last Sunday" (M. Burton 1875–1919, March 7 and 14, 1886). Maria's brief journal entries during these years show that she bore her burden alone, without complaints. She kept boarders to help cover the expenses of her home; she cared for the elderly and the ill; she endured fear of subpoena and searches through her home; and she didn't dare write out her husband's name if she noted his whereabouts or letters in her journal.

Friends in the Mormon settlements along the Little Colorado River treated Robert kindly, but he continued to be ill. He first suffered from an infection or obstruction in the kidneys or bowels. Then after a storm, he caught cold and soon was coughing incessantly and unable to sleep at night. He sent a urine sample to Dr. W. F. Anderson in Salt Lake City for analysis but also received medicine from Holbrook, including Warners Safe Kidney & Liver Cure. "Commenced to take this in earnest," he recorded in his journal March 12, 1885. A conference at St. Joseph went on without him on March 13 and 14, although he felt better on the fifteenth, "as if the fever had broken." Robert also applied the cure he had used during his sons' illnesses—he got out of the house for a walk or a ride. On March 15, he walked out to the east of the fort at St. Joseph and the next day took a long wagon ride, and gave both credit when he felt better.

This episode reveals one of the most disheartening sides of the "underground." Many of the men were getting older and needed the comfort of their homes and families. Robert, who had formerly enjoyed excellent health, suffered frequent spells of poor health from this time on.

Bishop Preston arrived in St. Joseph on March 15. Robert's health had improved somewhat, and from March 18 to 23, they visited nearby settlements, such as Snowflake where Robert spent an afternoon with his niece, Lucy White Flake. On March 23, they traveled to Southern California, where they were met in San Bernardino by Lester J. Herrick. During three weeks of visiting friends, relatives, and cattlemen in San Bernardino,

Riverside, Los Angeles, Pasadena, Downey, Colton, and San Diego, Robert's only mention in his journal of his health was on March 28, "My health still on the improve."

On April 12, Robert and William Preston returned to Arizona, this time to the settlements at Maricopa (now Phoenix). Robert's brother Charles was living in Mesa and they stayed with him for a week while visiting the Saints and attending to tithing business.

While at Charles's home, Robert could get mail from Salt Lake City, and, on Saturday, April 17, was particularly delighted to receive letters from his children Theodore and Ada and also from Lewis S. Hills and his son, Herbert Hills. On the nineteenth, Robert penned letters in return to Ada, Virginia and Austin, and Herbert. Two of these notes have survived, revealing much about a lonesome father's feelings for his family.

Mesa City, Arizona
April 19, 1886

Dear Ada,

I received your very welcome letter written on the 9th on the 17th and was much pleased to have you tell me so much news about the family and the affairs at the farm, and if I could only step in to night about 6 o'clock and find two little boys and one little girl by the name of Virginia Louise and you, could we not have a merry romp about the Barn and find a lot of eggs for mama.

You told me a good many things that I was pleased to hear but you did not tell me how you intended to do about your music or rather what your mother intended for you to do about going to the city or if Maria was willing to teach you any more. You did not tell me how many little songs the boys and yourself had learned to sing together. I am much interested in those matters all most as in your day school. Of course, we'll give the day school the preference.

Now Aday, I hope you are doing the best you can to help your mama about the house and to take care of my little Hardy.

Lord bless you all.
Affectionately your father,
R T. Burton

Mesa City,
April 19th

Dear Geny and Austin:

I received such a lot of little letters the other day and have been trying to find time today to answer some of them as I expect to leave this place tomorrow.

I learned from some of those letters that you had some young colt and calves. One or two was Austins and one was Henry's and etc. but where is mine and little Hardies? Have we got none? If not I had better get one here and send it on the cars for him and me. What have you done with Dazy? I hope the boys have not sold him yet.

How about Sunday School, Geny? I hope you go. Is Austin big enough yet to go? Does Mama go with you to the meetings? If so it will please me very much to know that when Papa cannot be at home his dear little children are being learned while they are young to attend Sunday School and meetings and learned to pray to our Heavenly Father so that if Papa or Mama or any of the little Brothers and Sisters are sick, you could ask the Lord to make them well. I hope you are very kind to Annie so she has not gone to Cottonwood yet.

The Lord bless you my little ones.

Robert T. Burton

Ada was almost twelve years old, Virginia was seven, Austin was four, and Hardy just twenty months old. Annie was their hired girl, a Danish immigrant who lived with them many years.

On Sunday, April 18, Robert attended a sacrament service at Lehi, Arizona, where the congregation was mostly Indians, or Lamanites, as he referred to them. He wrote that they took an active part in the meeting and the Indian choir "sang very beautifully." He and Bishop Preston addressed this congregation, a later service in Mesa, and a priesthood meeting at 6:30 P.M. where they gave "good instruction to the Bishops, etc."

After President Taylor's visit to Arizona in January 1885, a number of Latter-day Saint families left there to found settlements in the northern Mexican states of Chihuahua and Sonora where polygamist families hoped to live without persecution or danger of prosecution. After Brigham Young, Jr., and Moses

Thatcher obtained permission to establish settlements from President Porfirio Diaz acting for the government of Mexico, the Saints began purchasing town sites. They named them Colonia Juarez, Colonia Diaz, and Colonia Pacheco, in honor of Mexican leaders, and promised allegiance to the Mexican government. The Saints faced and overcame many problems in establishing these communities along the Piedras Verdes and Casas Grandes rivers and in the state of Sonora (CHC 6:260–262; Hatch 1954, 1–38).

There were also a number of small Mormon settlements in the southeastern corner of Arizona near the Mexican border which Bishops Preston and Burton desired to visit along with the Mexican colonies. While in Mesa, they purchased a span of mules and a sturdy wagon, a number of barrels and kegs for water, and a supply of food for the long wagon trip. They left on April 21 with delightfully good weather and road conditions. Robert was fascinated with the road they traveled which was built by the Mormon Battalion in 1846 and with the Mexican ranches and architecture as they passed through Tucson. They traveled as fast as possible and arrived in St. David in time to speak at a 2 P.M. sacrament meeting on Sunday, April 25.

On Tuesday, April 27, Robert drove some ten to fifteen miles from the Mormon settlements to the booming silver-mining town of Tombstone. Most often remembered for its gunslingers, saloons, dancing girls, and the 1881 gunfight at the O. K. Corral, between 1880 and 1890 Tombstone had some 15,000 residents working in underground mine shafts that seemed to have inexhaustible supplies of silver. Robert's twenty-eight-year-old son, Hosea, was one of those miners. Robert found Hosea there in a "sorrowful" condition. "He has been absent from the family a long time," Robert wrote in his journal that night, "and had not followed my counsel, but had given way to drink and folly which makes me feel very sorrowful indeed and I will make another effort to save him." Robert brought him back to St. David to assist him on the trip to Juarez. That night, once again Robert wrote, "Feeling quite unwell today."

Robert continued to prepare the next day for the long trip even though his condition worsened, and Bishop Preston was in grave doubt about leaving. However, on the morning of April 29, Robert pressed him to leave because all the arrangements were made. Though he was sick throughout the trip, he called upon his personal courage and faith to sustain him as it had through other difficult campaigns.

For six days, their solitary wagon rode through barren valleys and mountains, stopping at springs, an army fort, or ranch at night. Hosea may have done most of the driving and cared for the mules while the other men were on constant lookout for unfriendly Indians. They were fortunate to be near Fort Bowie when their wagon broke the second day and were able to make repairs at the fort. Their route continued northeastward around the Chiricahua Mountains and through the San Simon valley, then southeastward across the corner of New Mexico, over Hatchet Gap Pass, and south into the Casas Grandes valley of Mexico. A great many Latter-day Saint families had traveled the route, and they had directions to friendly ranches. They were delayed once or twice when they lost the road and once when their animals strayed in the night. Water was scarce. They filled their barrels and kegs to the brim at every well and spring. Though it was springtime, it was extremely dry and feed for the animals was often scarce.

Even though Robert did not feel well, the evenings around the campfire provided quality hours for him to discuss with Hosea the principles which he hoped would convince this son to change his lifestyle and return to the family circle.

The sixth day from St. David, the group arrived at a Mormon settlement a few miles from La Ascension and found Apostle George Teasdale. The settlement, called "Camp Johnson," was temporary and Robert sensed discontent among the settlers, but after good land for a townsite was purchased they later built Colonia Diaz. Teasdale traveled with them down the Casas Grandes River where they visited Church members working land on the Colalitos Ranch belonging to a large development company. On May 7, they drove to Casas Grandes, "a

Mexican Town of some little pretentions" where they met with
two prominent citizens: the "Jefa Politico" and Senor Ignacio
Gomez del Campo, from whom the Saints purchased the land
for Colonia Juarez. Leaving there late in the afternoon, it was
only a short trip over a small range of mountains to the valley
of the Piedras Verdes (Green Rock) River where a large group
of Saints was establishing Colonia Juarez. Robert's old friend,
Alexander F. MacDonald, was president of the colonization company. The two Salt Lake visitors discussed at length the prospects for the new settlement with MacDonald and Teasdale.
Settlers had laid out the first town site January 10, 1886, and
were working to move from quickly built dugouts along the
river bank into adobe homes. They had constructed a dam,
completed a mile-long canal, and begun their spring planting
(Hatch 1954, 22–23). Their greatest difficulty was finding sufficient water, and this was an especially dry spring. The winds
blew constantly, day and night, in great dust storms. Bishops
Preston and Burton, with years of experience in farming and
cattle ranching, toured the area and conferred with the men of
the colony about possible agricultural areas, dams, and herd
grounds. Robert's health continued to be poor, but on days
when he felt better, he rode up and down the river looking at
improvements begun by the settlers.[2]

The visitors began their trip back to Arizona on Saturday,
May 15. Alexander F. MacDonald accompanied them as far as
the town of Casas Grandes where another council was held
with Senor del Campo. Two days later, Robert met Lot Smith
at Camp Johnson. He had letters from home for Robert and
Bishop Preston and some Salt Lake newspapers which were too
old to give any news of value about conditions in the city. As
Robert bade farewell to Alexander MacDonald and Lot Smith,
his friends for almost four decades, he must have wondered at
the circumstances that had brought them together in remote
Mexico. These men were stake presidents and community leaders in Arizona. Instead of enjoying the comforts due them after
years of service to the Church and loyalty to their country,

378

they were on foreign soil struggling to build new settlements just to live in peace with their wives and families. Perhaps Robert and his families would have considered this alternative had he not been in the Presiding Bishopric.

Each day after leaving Mexico, the wagon covered about thirty-three miles over dusty roads until on May 22, they reached Safford, a Mormon settlement along the Gila River in eastern Arizona. Robert had spent almost a month and traveled over 500 miles with Hosea, who left him in Safford and went to Globe, another Arizona mining town. Robert does not comment on the success or failure of his mission with Hosea, but it was probably significant that Hosea did not go back to Tombstone and in the fall was back in Salt Lake City to attend the second family meeting in October. At nearby Pima, Robert visited Susan's parents (and incidentally, Hosea's grandparents), William and Elizabeth McBride, now old and feeble, who had moved from Richfield in 1880 with their son, James Andrew McBride. William served as a patriarch to the Arizona Saints until 1890 when they moved back to Salt Lake City. The Saints in Pima were upset by Indian problems; and on the first day of Robert's visit, F. Thurston was killed by Indians at a lime kiln eight miles away. Erastus Snow was also in Pima and Bishops Preston and Burton counseled with him for several days about the Indian problems, the settlements in Mexico, and other items of Church business.

Now Robert and Bishop Preston became anxious to return home. They traveled to San Simon by wagon and took a train to Deming, New Mexico, where a break or washout in the train tracks left them stranded. Robert was suffering again from another attack of "bowel complaint" and tried to rest at the depot hotel while they considered their options which were to wait there an indefinite time or return through Arizona to California and go to Utah via San Francisco. Robert's thoughts were definitely on home and family as he sat in the hotel and penned another note to his children:

Deming, New Mexico
May 30th, 1886

Dear children, Ada, Geny and Austin,

I think I have not answered the last letter I received from Ada which came to me at Pima, Arizona and was read with pleasure—allthough I was very sorry to learn of the death of Aunt Mary Ashby. How lonely must the little children be without either father or mother. I allmost wish we had some of them for you to take care of if you would not plague them.

Ada said that Herbert and her was learning a song to sing for me when I return. I hope they are learning fast for I shall be much pleased to hear them sing when I come.

I have sent to your mother a little box in which is a few sheets of paper and envelopes when you wish to write. Also some little shells picked up by me on the Pacific Coast at Long Beach April 4th, 1886; you can keep them to remind you of where pa was on that date. With love to all the folks, Lord bless you all.

Affectionately your father,
R.T. Burton

The sentence about learning the song fast may have been the only clue to the family that Robert would be home soon. Federal marshals were known to question even small children concerning the whereabouts of their daddy, so Robert confided the time of his return only to William.

When they learned on May 31 the railroad north of Deming would be out indefinitely, the weary travelers boarded a westbound train which took them via Tucson and Phoenix to Los Angeles, then north to San Francisco, where they arrived about noon June 2, having covered 1,100 miles in about fifty hours. Two days later they left San Francisco on an eastbound Union Pacific train which arrived in Ogden at 8 A.M. on June 6. They remained at Lorin Farr's residence until William arrived to escort Robert home. He wrote: "Arrived at my home in Salt Lake City at 9:30 and happily surprised my family who knew nothing of my returning (accept Wm). Found all reasonably well" (June 6, 1886).

The next day, he wrote in his journal the total number of miles traveled: "I have traveled since Nov. 19th/85 as near as I can tell up to the date of my return to S.L. 1000 miles by horse and mule teams and 11,567 miles by RR making a total of 12,567 miles and much of the time in very poor health especially while traveling in private conveyance in an unsettled country."

For the next twenty-one months, Robert stayed close to home, even spending occasional nights at his own residence and at the farm. He also records spending many days and nights at the stock farm where his son Henry lived until mid-1887. His health gradually improved, despite periodic setbacks.

Though Robert kept busy working on his farm or the stock farm and conducting Church business with Bishop Preston and the new second counselor, John R. Winder, the difference in his life on the underground is seen in the things he could not do during this time. He never attended sunday school, sacrament meeting, or fast meeting, but spent his Sundays reading, writing, and visiting. He did not go to other public meetings or entertainments. He did not attend public political meetings, although he often wrote that the Church leaders met to discuss the "political" situation. He did not travel alone around the city; often one of his sons drove him early in the morning or late at night. He could not attend funerals, especially not those involving his own family members, and this was a painful sacrifice.

During the early morning hours of Sunday, May 29, 1887, John Haven Burton, Robert and Maria's fourth son, was murdered on a downtown Salt Lake City street. John was a promising young architect with a wife, a two-year-old son named Charles Haven Burton, and a second child on the way.

Robert recorded in his journal:

> Sun [May] 29. At the farm this morning about 9 oclock Wm and Heber came to see me with the terable intelligence that my Son John was murdered last night shot down in the Street. I was some minutes before I could realize everything about it. When I recovered from the shock I came with Wm and Henry to the City to my Daughters Mrs. Hills and remained here quite prostrated.

As testimony of eyewitnesses brought out the details of a senseless tragedy, family grief deepened and lingered, as indicated in Robert's journal entry three days later: "Family and myself are much oppressed by the murder of my Boy but are endeavoring to be reconciled to the will of providence."

The first newspaper reports, published just hours after the incident by the admittedly anti-Mormon *Salt Lake Tribune*, contained rumors and half truths that John was in "disguised attire" and "peeping in a window" at 1:30 A.M. The inquest later that day established that he was returning from City Creek Canyon where he frequently walked late at night pondering problems of his architectural projects. He was wearing work clothes instead of his customary suit. As he passed the saloon where A. H. Martin was working, John looked in the window. Martin, reportedly a very excitable person, may have supposed John to be a detective or spotter, trying to catch the whiskey men. Martin came out of the bar, pulled a revolver, and several times told John to put his hands over his head. John did and agreed to go to the police station; but after standing for some time, he grew tired of holding up his hands and let them drop. Witnesses testified that when Martin again told him to throw up his hands and submit to a search, he answered, "I'll be damned if I will!" and "Shoot if you want to." Martin then fired, and John Burton cried out, "What's the matter with you, are you crazy?", groaned, and fell to the ground (*Salt Lake Tribune*, May 29, 1887; *Deseret Evening News*, May 31, 1887, 2).

The two accounts of the incident and the inquest published in Salt Lake newspapers differed considerably, but an editorial comment in the June 2 *Salt Lake Tribune* seemed to summarize the community's feelings: "The acts of Martin, the slayer of Burton, and his own statement of the affair, give one at a distance the impression that he is an uncontrollable fool, liable to become excited at nothing and when excited an ungovernable and cowardly wild beast; a man no more fit to be trusted with a deadly weapon than is an unthinking and irresponsible child."[3]

Robert remained secluded at the Hills's home, but wrote in his diary on May 31, "This is a sad day to my family. We are preparing to deposit the remains in the cemetery. The funeral is at his late residence in the 18th [Ward] at 4 P.M. today. Every attention and respect was shown the family on the occasion." After the funeral, family and friends called on Robert who was in a second floor bedroom, physically and emotionally distressed.

It was more than a week after the funeral before Robert dared to call on Kate, John's widow, and Haven, as marshals could have been watching her home for him to visit. Kate delivered a daughter on July 25. Robert and John's brothers, William and Charles, blessed her and named her Phyllis Hardy Burton on August 23, 1887. Maria was devoted to Kate, Haven, and Phyllis, visiting them almost daily for many months. She brought Haven to her home and took him on outings. She planted flowers on John's grave and took water several times a week to keep them alive. She recorded one touching trip in her diary, "Saturday [June] 25. Florence, myself rode up to Kate[s], 11 A.M. We took Haven and visited John['] grave. The plants are growing nice. Haven carried water on to the plants. 'Poor boy,' he little realizes whose grave he was keep[ing] green." While she tried to lift Kate's spirits, she filled her diary with expressions of her own grief.

On November 19, 1888, Robert's sister, Rebecca Jones, died at her home after a lengthy illness. Robert wrote of her: "She has truly had an afflicted life with loss of husband and children but amidst all she has lived an exemplery life and has been prominent among L.D.S. in doing good" (November 19, 1888) He continued, "I am not able to attend [her funeral] by reason [of] the Continued Persecution against the people. However all was done that loving hearts & willing hands could do" (November 21, 1888).[4]

Although 1,004 polygamists were convicted of unlawful cohabitation between 1884 and 1893 (Grow 1954, 268), the only General Authorities captured were George Q. Cannon, Lorenzo Snow, who went to prison to test the constitutionality of the "segregation" principle (Larson 1971, 128–29 and 145–51), and

John Henry Smith, who was acquitted in 1885 (Whitney 3:398–99).

Robert narrowly missed being found by the deputies several times. On February 10, 1887, he and Bishop Preston worked at the Tithing Office with men on their staff from 6 A.M. to 7 P.M. The next day, Marshal Dyer and fifteen deputies appeared and searched the office and yard without success. Maria recorded in her diary on February 11, that they also surrounded and searched the Gardo House, Lion House, Assembly Hall, and Endowment House but found no polygamists to arrest.

On August 31, 1887, Robert recorded that four or five deputies had searched the Burton farm. Virginia later remembered what was probably this incident: "I remember one night when a horseman rode up to the south side of the house. . . . Somebody opened the door before we had time to even speak and he said, 'If Brother Burton is there, tell him to go. The marshall is after him' " (A. Cutler 1976, 178–79). She said her father escaped out the back and crossed the fields to the William Gibby home about a quarter of a mile north near the corner of Twenty-first South and State Streets.

She also remembered another time when the marshals came and her father was not at the farm.

> But Edward and Theodore were there, and they were teenagers, and did they have a good time. They took those two marshalls all over the farm, through the big red barn where the cows were, through the old carriage shed and the harness room, and the big hay barn and through the chaff hole and through the big hay barn at the back. It was a big place and full of hay, and I think they had to look under the hay even, to see where my father was. But they didn't find him, and the boys had a very fine time at that time leading these two men around. And if you had known Theodore and Ed you would know what a grand time they had about it. (V. Cutler 1955; also in A. Cutler 1976, 179).

The underground communication system was highly effective both in the Salt Lake Valley and throughout all the Mormon communities where the federal marshals pursued the cohabs. Robert must have benefitted greatly from the signal systems and codes, for he traveled a lot and met with Church leaders who were sought as much as he was. Family oral tradition says that he used the alias "Taylor." His light grey hair was dyed black and he tucked his long beard into his coat when he went out. Virginia said her mother (Sarah) took her young children to the Church farm to see their father one day, but they didn't recognize him. "We children didn't know him and he felt very bad about it. The disquise [sic] worked so well, what could he expect?" (A. Cutler 1976, 179).

Although Virginia was not yet ten during the underground days, she remembered this as "a very anxious period for my mother. She never really had a minute that she wasn't anxious about my father because he couldn't come home only as he came on the sly, because somebody was always watching for him. . . . [I] remember how careful mother must be of us younger children not giving information about father" (A. Cutler 1976, 178).

The daily entries in Robert's journal only hint at the strain under which he and all the family members lived. They also inadequately describe the complicated business transactions which occupied his time as a member of the Presiding Bishopric.

When the Edmunds Law of 1882 did not bring polygamy to an end, anti-polygamist crusaders amended the law to increase the pressure. In February 1887, the Edmunds-Tucker Act became law without the signature of President Grover Cleveland, who as a Democrat hoped to keep the favor of the Church leadership, thinking that Utah might eventually enter the Union as a Democratic state.[5] This new act contained provisions to destroy the Church politically and economically. The Church was disincorporated, its property over $50,000, held in violation of the 1862 law, escheated or reverted to the federal government, to be disposed of by the Secretary of the Interior, the proceeds to be applied to district schools in Utah. The Perpetual Emigrating Company was also dissolved. Provisions of the act encouraged the successful prosecution of polygamy offenses, further restricted the Mormon voting rights, abolished woman suffrage and the Nauvoo Legion, and replaced the territorial superintendent of schools with a commissioner appointed by the Utah Supreme Court.

Church leaders (and several constitutional lawyers of national reputation) were of the opinion that many provisions of the act were unconstitutional and that they should make every effort to thwart enforcement of those provisions which would destroy the temporal power of the Church and end its mission. They felt only God had the power to revoke the principle of polygamy, and they refused to surrender the Church's financial resources. President Taylor and Church authorities planned to place Church properties in the hands of individuals and local congregations except for those they hoped the government receiver would find exempt, such as the temple block, the office of the president, the General Tithing Office, the historian's office, and the funds being used for charitable purposes.

Some Church properties were already held in secret trusts, some dating back to Brigham Young's administration. Since April 14, 1878, Robert and Maria Burton had held the deed to approximately two and a half acres of Block 88 (Main to State Streets, and South Temple to North Temple) upon which the General Tithing Office and grounds were located.

Church leaders organized separate nonprofit associations like the St. George, Logan, and Manti temple associations to hold certain real and personal property, and ward and stake ecclesiastical associations were given title to local meetinghouses, tithing houses, and granaries and to capital stock in community stock herds, general stores, irrigation projects, and other local enterprises in which the local or general Church had a financial interest. At first, they did not transfer the tithing receipts to the stake associations, but on or about February 28, 1887, after the Edmunds-Tucker Act was passed but before it became law, President Taylor ordered the personal property in the Church tithing offices transferred to the stake associations in which it was physically located. Thus, they transferred $270,000 out of the hands of the trustee-in-trust, President Taylor. About this same time, the Church sold its livestock to Mormon capitalists or the semipublic livestock associations which Robert T. Burton helped to organize in 1884. Also, it "sold" (actually transferred) certain properties and stocks to ZCMI, Zion's Savings Bank, Church officers, and syndicates of Mormon capitalists. These trust assignments were in the form of "sales" in which the trustee gave his personal note rather than a payment; and there is no evidence that the notes were ever presented for payment when they matured (Arrington 1958, 362–65).

The Edmunds-Tucker Act abolished the position of trustee-in-trust but allowed "that, all religious societies, sects and congregations shall have the right to have and to hold through trustees appointed by any court exercising Probate powers in a Territory, only on the nomination of the authorities of such society, sect or congregation, so much real property for the erection or use of houses of worship and for such parsonages and burial grounds as shall be necessary" (Deed 1887, 1). Therefore, at General Conference, on April 7, 1887, the authorities nominated the Presiding Bishopric to hold in trust for the unincorporated body of worshipers known as The Church of Jesus Christ of Latter-day Saints, the meetinghouses, parsonages, burial grounds and other properties belonging to that body, and filed the appropriate legal papers in the probate court on May 19, 1887, appointing William B. Preston, Robert T. Burton, and John R. Winder as trustees.

As a result of this action, on July 9, 1887, Robert and Maria deeded the property and buildings which they had held in secret trust since 1878 to these trustees to be held with other real property "for the use, benefit and behoof of that certain body of religious worshippers known and called the Church of Jesus Christ of Latter-day Saints, and to and for such use as such Church or its duly constituted authorities shall name, dictate and appoint" (Deed 1887, 3).[6]

Meeting clandestinely, Bishops Preston, Burton, and Winder worked to transfer the property which was not kept in their control and to maintain that which they held in trust. They worked at the General Tithing Office or president's office on occasion, but more often met at the stock farm or at safe homes, such as Charles Burton's, Lewis Hills's, or George Crismon's.

Once during the heat of July, Robert met Bishop Preston at the cabins near the granite quarries in Little Cottonwood Canyon, which were called Wasatch Resort. They invited family members and celebrated the Twenty-fourth, but also kept busy reading and writing. Virginia remembered traveling in the carriage with her father and Aunt Maria.

> We traveled in a white top with a team of horses. My brother Charles, Aunt Maria's son, did the driving, and his wife Julia, who was then an invalid, traveled with us. It took us almost all day to reach Wasatch. . . . It had a white canvas top and that's why it was called a "white top." It was sort of a heavy carriage, a cross between a lumber wagon and a light carriage, and was used for that kind of travel. It had curtains on it; and this time, I imagine, the curtains in the back were drawn, or were lowered, so that the back seat was pretty well covered. I rode in the back seat with father and Aunt Maria. The thing that I didn't know at that time was why I was taken along, but perhaps you can guess when I tell you that every time a carriage or a wagon came to pass us from the other direction father took me on his lap to hide his face and then when the wagon had passed, or the carriage or the man on a horse had passed, I sat down on the seat again. I might have told you that this period of my father's life was one of the hardest periods. . . . Well, he was sought by the marshall because he was a polygamist; and so, of course, that was the reason I was taken along so I could be a shield to him as we rode up the canyon (A. Cutler 1976, 180–81).

Robert rarely indicated in his journal the nature of the business which occupied the Presiding Bishopric and their clerks for so many hours. However, on February 16, 1888, before Virginia's trip to Wasatch, Robert recorded that he and Bishops Preston and Winder made some important appointments and suggestions about recommencing work on the Salt Lake Temple. Virginia thought they went to Wasatch to supervise work at the quarries because the rock for the temple was being cut at that time (A. Cutler 1976, 182).

The day after President John Taylor was buried, July 30, 1887, the federal government filed a suit in the Supreme Court of Utah Territory to recover all property held by the trustee-in-trust in excess of $50,000 acquired after 1862. The government contended that the Church had real estate subject to escheat valued at over $2 million and personal property amounting to over $1 million; it requested appointment of a receiver to hold all Church properties until the suit was settled. This was the beginning of nine years of litigation, during which time the Church leaders, most in exile, wrestled with the Utah Supreme Court, the receiver (U.S. Marshal Frank H. Dyer) appointed by that court, the U.S. Supreme Court, and Congress. The Utah Supreme Court, in October 1888, allowed the Church to keep only the temple block, to be used exclusively for religious worship. All other properties, real and personal, including the tithing turned over to the stake associations, came into the hands of the receiver. The General Tithing Office, the Church historian's office, the Gardo House, and the Church farm were all rented back to the Church (Arrington 1958, 365–69).

As the receiver's costs and mismanagement ate away at the funds and property which he controlled, Church authorities placed their hopes for financial salvation on the outcome of their major suit before the U.S. Supreme Court on the constitutionality of the Edmunds-Tucker Act. The principal questions of the suit argued in January 1889 were, first, whether Congress had the power to repeal the territorial charter by which the Church was incorporated, and second, whether Congress and the courts had the power to seize the property of the corporation and hold it for the purposes specified in the Edmunds-Tucker Act. Seventeen months later, the Court ruled that the act was constitutional and that Congress did have these powers. By this time, the receivership was in trouble due to the receiver's poor business management and exorbitant salary. The Church was also deeply in debt, having borrowed money to meet the obligations demanded by the receiver, cash expenses for legal fees, and the normal Church expenses for charity and education (Arrington 1958, 369–75).

During 1888, Robert left Salt Lake City twice. From March 21 to May 26, he returned to the Midwest on a cattle-buying trip, purchasing mainly Durham cattle for the Burton Stock Company established in 1887. The trip was marred by the death of his brother-in-law, Elijah Austin, on March 25, 1888. Elijah and his wife, Kate, had visited in Salt Lake in January, traveled to see their children in California, and returned to their farm in Sublette, Illinois, only a few weeks before Elijah's death. Robert received word of his death while in Abilene, Kansas. Business kept him from traveling directly to Sublette, but he spent three weeks there in April helping to settle Elijah's estate. From August 23 to October 3, Robert and his son William traveled through Colorado, Arizona, and California where they attended LDS conferences in settlements along the Little Colorado and Gila rivers and in Mesa. During both of these trips, Robert carried certificates signed by Wilford Woodruff identifying him as a missionary for the Church. He also suffered recurrences of poor health during each trip.

During the early summer of 1888, Frank J. Cannon, son of George Q. Cannon, was in Washington, D.C., negotiating a settlement of the difficulties between the government and the polygamists. He told President Cleveland that a "humane and just judicial policy" would bring from hiding many Mormon polygamists who were ready to go to prison for a short time rather than continue in their present circumstances (Lyman 1986, 99–100). Through Cannon's efforts, President Cleveland was persuaded to appoint Elliot F. Sandford as Chief Justice of Utah, replacing Charles Zane, whose four-year term of office ended in September 1888. Judge Sandford carried out a new administration policy of adjudication and his appointment "purged the third district court of the crusading spirit which had ignored the statute of limitations in polygamy trials and had bred the doctrine of segregation and other forms of harassment" (Larson 1971, 231). Sandford's judgments were consistently less severe and this encouraged the polygamists under indictment to come out of hiding, plead guilty in court, accept their punishment, and clear themselves of charges. George Q. Cannon was one of the first to do so, surrendering on September 17, 1888, and receiving judgment on two indictments totaling $500 and 175 days (Whitney 3:633–636; R. T. Burton 1856–1907, February 21, 1889). Although Judge Sandford was much criticized by the anti-Mormons, the number of convictions for unlawful cohabitation actually increased as more polygamists allowed themselves to be arrested or turned themselves in to the court. Sentences were reduced on an average by half, and fines were also reduced (Larson 1971, 231).

On March 12, 1889, Robert T. Burton wrote in his journal that he was "making arrangements to surrender myself to the Court for living with my family." Three days later, he and his older sons appeared in the courtroom of Judge Sandford, where Robert pleaded guilty to an indictment "for living with more than one wife between January 1, 1885 and September 1, 1886." His attorney, Franklin S. Richards, rose to speak before sentence was passed:

> I desire to call the court's attention to a few facts pertaining to the case. The defendant is over sixty-eight years of age. He married his last wife in 1856—six years before the passage of the first act of Congress forbidding the practice of polygamy or making it an offense. His families have at all times lived separate and apart. For several years prior to the finding of this indictment, I believe, he has lived with his first wife only. He is a man of good standing in the community, and has held important positions, which he at all times filled to the satisfaction of his constituents. In addition to the fact that this is his first offense, when he learned that witnesses against him were wanted, he instructed his sons to go before the grand jury and give that body all the information within their power (*Deseret News*, March 16, 1889).

He went on to describe Robert's health as so poor that "if imprisoned for any length of time, it would have a bad if not fatal affect." He then produced a statement signed by nine prominent non-Mormon residents of Utah testifying to Robert's "high character and excellent standing as a law abiding citizen with the exception of the present charge." Richards claimed that he could have secured a hundred more signatures (*Deseret News*, March 16, 1889).

After this, Judge Sandford and District Attorney George S. Peters, who did not know Robert T. Burton, conferred. Peters told Sandford that he had been told Robert was once appointed by President Lincoln as collector of internal revenue, and he knew the gentlemen on the statement as "men of highest standing."

Judge Sandford, satisfied that justice could be served without imprisonment, set a fine of $150, plus $8.50 in court costs. Looking down at the defendant, he concluded, "I hope we will not see you here again. If [we] do, the sentence will be heavier." Apparently Richards could not resist remarking, "It is quite possible, your honor, that you may see Mr. Burton in court again. His business frequently calls him into court, but when he comes again it will be in a different capacity" (*Deseret News*, March 16, 1889).

Robert Taylor Burton paid his fine and left the court a free man. Needless to say, there was a celebration that night at Haven Villa. "This evening my children came in & we had a time of rejoicing together," he wrote in his journal.

While Robert was free to attend to his business in public, to ride alone by horse or buggy, and to come and go openly with Maria, his relationships with Sarah and Susan were still forbidden. The family rejoiced because fear of arrest and imprisonment was past, but the plural wives and their children still suffered. Robert's anger toward this injustice is apparent in a letter written to his daughter Ada on April 18, just a few weeks after his surrender, while he was attending to tithing business in central Utah.

> I intended to have made you some little recognition of your 13th [birthday] anniversary in some way, but did not even have the chance to congratulate you or to say a word to you. Please acept my kind love and best wishes. Sometimes it makes me feel very bad that cruel unjust laws should be so interpreted as to prevent a father from seeing his own children at their home, but so it is at least for the present and I must bow in humble submission to the decree.

The first Sunday morning after surrendering, he had attended Sunday School at the Fifteenth Ward with Maria and some of their grandchildren. That afternoon, he took his daughters Mary and Florence from the city down to Farmers Ward (his son Henry was now the bishop), where they attended sacrament meeting together. Robert was the main speaker, addressing the congregation for over an hour. He once again attended funerals, programs, services in the Tabernacle, and entertainments at the theatre. He bought a new buggy for himself and sometimes took his younger children and grandchildren for rides.

Although spirits lifted as the Saints were once again able to see President Woodruff and listen to the apostles at general conferences in April and October of 1889, the problems of the Church were deepening.

The spring of 1890 brought four blows to the Saints which led to the issuance of what is called the Manifesto.

First, the U.S. Supreme Court affirmed the constitutionality of the Idaho Test Oath Law which disfranchised all Latter-day Saints in Idaho by requiring them to swear they were not even members of "any sect or organization which teaches, advises, or encourages the practice of bigamy or polygamy" (in CHC 6:213).

Second, the city election in Salt Lake City was stolen by the Liberal Party. "This is Election Day (City) & we have one of the most remarkable Elections. All the Courts, all the Commissions, and the Registrars in the Oposite Party with the most unscrupulous men as tools. Nothing hinders them *stealing* the City," Robert recorded in his journal the evening of February 10. People's Party representatives showed ample evidence of bias toward Liberal Party voters in registration practices, and charged election fraud like that which allowed the Liberals to take over Ogden's city government in February 1889 when non-Mormons from the mining camps and Wyoming railroad sections were brought to town just to vote the Liberal ticket (Lyman 1986, 111–18; CHC 6:203–209). Liberal control of Salt Lake City's administration quickly showed the Mormons how disastrous life can be for the majority when they cannot vote. The change to a non-Mormon government produced a real estate boom and property values and taxes doubled and tripled; new construction was begun but with little general planning or direction from the municipal authorities. Newspapers and clergymen charged leniency in law enforcement allowing an alarming increase in gambling, prostitution, and Sunday saloon activity.

The Liberal leaders began much needed improvements in sidewalks, waterworks and water quality, street sprinkling and paving, and sewer system extension—all projects requiring an increase in taxes. However, the taxes were much higher than expected because property evaluations were increased 400 percent by a unscrupulous assessor using inflated property values; he was allowed by city ordinance to keep 2.5 percent of all funds collected. Taxpayers from all classes complained at the county court and petitioned the city council without success to countermand the assessor's actions (Lyman 1986, 118–19).

Third, the new Cullum-Strebble Bill was introduced in Congress to disfranchise every Latter-day Saint in Utah, stating, "No person belonging to a church organization teaching or practicing polygamy shall be permitted to vote" (in Lyman 1986, 126). Patterned after the Idaho Test Oath and written by Utah Liberal Robert Baskin, he intended the law "to wrest from the hands of the priesthood the political power which it had so long wrongfully usurped and shamefully abused" (Baskin 1914, 184). The Liberals had fought all efforts aimed at statehood for Utah while they were the minority of voters but were expected to reverse this position if the Mormon majority was denied the right to vote.

Fourth, in May, the U.S. Supreme Court ruled that the Edmunds-Tucker Act was constitutional, and the Church faced the loss of all property held by the receivership.

Finally, in September, after "praying to the Lord and feeling inspired," President Woodruff acted "for the temporal salvation of the Church" by issuing the proclamation which told Church members that the Lord no longer required His people to contract any marriage forbidden by the law of the land (CHC 6:220–21). Both Robert and Maria mention this Manifesto in their diary entries for Sunday, October 6, when Orson F. Whitney read the text of the statement in general conference and the Saints voted "to accept [Woodruff's] declaration concerning plural marriage as authoritative and binding" (CHC 6:222). Opinions differed as to whether its restrictions applied only to future polygamous marriages or also to those already established. Questions about the course of polygamy continued in the community and the courts for some time, and the problems of the Church continued through the 1890s. However, the long-term effect of the Manifesto was to hasten the end of the anti-polygamy crusade and pave the path to statehood.

While the Manifesto had great political impact, it did not immediately affect the lives of Robert, his wives, and children. For example, until the summer of 1891, whenever Robert spent the night at the farm, he slept at Henry's or Alfred's, where they had built a room especially for him.

"Time was on the side of existing plural marriages," says a recent historian, "for with emotional subsidence came toleration, and gradually the Gentiles became willing to wink at long-established polygamous relations" (Larson 1971, 275). Until this time of toleration, Robert continued to follow the course of honor, outwardly obeying the laws of the land by living with only one wife, but without forsaking his other wives and their children as some thought necessary. In practice, he bound his families together economically, socially, and spiritually by righteous example, strong leadership, and tender love during the remaining years of his life.

Notes

1. This was also quarters for President George Q. Cannon and L. John Nuttall, secretary to the First Presidency, during the early months of the raid (Larson 1971, 115n).

2. The colonization of Juarez continued through the summer of 1886 in spite of rumors that the Saints had inadvertently settled on the old San Diego ranch instead of land owned by Senor del Campo. The rumors were confirmed in January 1887, and the town site moved two miles north into a rocky, narrow canyon, which seemed wholly unacceptable until an earthquake opened new fissures and springs of water all along the course of the Piedras Verdes river (Hatch 1954, 13–24).

3. A. H. Martin was found "not guilty" of the murder on November 17, 1887. Robert T. Burton's opinion written in his journal that day was that the verdict was contrary to all evidence in the case because the jury and/or the witnesses had been tampered with.

4. Rebecca's husband, Nathaniel Very Jones, died February 15, 1863 of pneumonia at age forty. He had been bishop of the Fifteenth Ward, a missionary to India and England, an officer in the Nauvoo Legion, and a member of the Iron Mission in southern Utah. He and Rebecca had eight children. He had five other children by three plural wives (Jenson 2:368–69).

5. Politics during these years were complicated, but very interesting. For more information see Edward Leo Lyman, *Political Deliverance: The Mormon Quest for Utah Statehood*, Urbana and Chicago: University of Illinois Press, 1986, and Gustive O. Larson, *The "Americanization" of Utah for Statehood*, San Marino, California: The Huntington Library, 1971.

6. The Utah Supreme Court annulled the transfer of this deed on October 9, 1888, ruling that it was executed without authority (Whitney 3:656–57).

The Aging Patriarch, 1890–1907

For over fifty years, Robert's life was woven into the historical fabric of both The Church of Jesus Christ of Latter-day Saints and the Territory of Utah. As the territory moved toward statehood and the nineteenth century drew to a close, his role changed, but his dedication continued. In 1890, Robert's once tall, strong body showed the wear of seventy years "in the saddle," and his hair and beard were silver gray. His final years reveal his determination to keep working for church and family as long as possible. "When I can't work here," he told his sons, "then I want to go some place else to work." That call came seventeen days after his eighty-sixth birthday, November 11, 1907.

Momentous changes were in store for the people of Utah as they moved into the decade of the 1890s. Forces were at work to "Americanize" the territorial institutions and political parties which would lead to statehood. Isolation was gone forever. National political and economic events affected Utahns more and more. The changing social and economic conditions were a source of concern to Robert Taylor Burton. As was his custom on New Year's Eve, Robert sat at his desk December 31,

1890 and penned a few thoughts about the past year. This time, they were bleak.

> Wed [December] 31 The wind up of the year 90 has been with important events. The enormous increase of crime in all parts of the world and more especially in our own land, together with the financial condition of the world [are] the signs of the times indicating very great changes in the near future. Utah has had an unusual prosperous year but closes with a general depression on all sides.
>
> Extravagance and want of economy is the rule. So ends the year. What will the year 1891 produce.

He had reason to worry about the economic circumstances of his own large family of sixty persons, including his wives, children and their spouses, and grandchildren. It had always been a tremendous challenge for large polygamist families to meet temporal needs, and the families suffered more than usual while their fathers were on the underground. The raid had come at an economic turning point in Utah's development. The population had outgrown the agricultural society: land and water were almost all appropriated, and new families could no longer find new land to settle.

As the Burton sons reached maturity, they had to decide whether to work within the family agricultural system or choose some other kind of work. The earlier woolen mill venture had given Willard and Charles their first jobs off the farm and started them in careers of merchandising and banking. William, John, and Walter also gained construction experience building for the family. Several sons helped with the surveying and construction of the Utah Eastern Railroad, while others worked at mining and mining engineering.

In an effort to expand the family resources, in 1887 they incorporated the Burton Stock Company with Robert T. Burton as president and LaFayette G. Burton as secretary. This company ran the 160-acre ranch near Peoa on the Upper Weber River in Summit County which Robert called the "Weber Ranch." William, his wife Eloise, and LaFayette owned fifty-four acres in the area and sold it to the stock company on April 7, 1888 (Summit County, Book F, 469–71.) The family probably leased other acreage. Several sons surveyed the property in the summer of 1887. During the spring of 1888, Robert purchased at least sixty head of Durham cattle in the Midwest. The cattle and some of the Burton horses were taken to the ranch each spring and brought back in the fall. Alfred and his bride, Lizzie, spent the first summer of their marriage living in a small cabin on the ranch. There Lizzie delivered a baby girl, Sarah Laurette, on August 8, 1889. Apparently the venture did not work out as planned, and they sold the fifty-four acres for $2500 (a $550 loss) on June 30, 1891 (Summit County, Book C. W.D. 248–49).

Robert also had reason to be concerned about the financial position of the Church in the aftermath of the anti-polygamy crusade. It had paid the receiver with borrowed funds; three years of judicial hearings would pass before what was left of the Church personal property would be returned on January 10, 1894, and five and a half years before the Church real estate, including the tithing office and church farm, was returned on June 8, 1896. However, the farm was rented back from the receivership, and some of the Church cattle remained part of Robert's stewardship during these years. He maintained the registrations of pedigree for prize animals in the Church herd as well as those now part of the Burton Stock Company.

Robert's problems were more than economic. In spite of improvements in medical care, there were at least ten deaths in the family between 1889 and 1907, including his daughter, Mary, two daughters-in-law, Julia Young Burton and Eloise Crismon Burton, and seven grandchildren. The children who no longer needed their father to sit by their sick beds all night now turned to him in times of mourning. He understood the pain of losing a loved one, but he also knew the comfort from gospel teachings of life after death though the resurrection of Jesus Christ. With love and empathy, he consoled William, Charles, Robert, Willard, Henry, Edward, their wives, Florence and her husband, and Mary's husband, Ezra T. Stevenson. Of Mary's death on July 26, 1897, he wrote, "At 7 AM today my daughter Mrs. Mary Burton Stevenson was taken very suddenly ill. . . . Three phisicians in attendance but she continued to grow worse and died at 9–15 tonight. This is a sorrowfull day for my family and myself as my daughter Mary was Joyous and full of life but 24 hours previous."

Charles's first wife, Julia, suffered for many years from an unnamed illness. Charles took her to New York City for diagnosis and treatment from September to December 1887, and to Birmingham, England, in the fall of 1889 for very difficult surgery. Charles wired his family that the "operation had been performed on Julia with a fair prospect of success" on November 27, but the next day, she died. Her funeral service was held December 16, 1889, in the Lion House because she was an adopted daughter of Brigham Young. Charles later married Josephine Young Beatie, June 1, 1893.

In the fall of 1890, Willard's children caught scarlet fever. Carl C. Burton remembered they were so sick their beds were brought to the living room to be near the coal stove and their mother bathed their feverish heads to reduce the fever (1969, 3). In spite of all she could do, two-year-old Earl died October 15, the day before their Uncle Walter's marriage. Robert performed the wedding as planned at the home of the bride, Lucy Ellen Brown, and the next morning the family gathered at Willard's residence on Second South for the toddler's funeral.

There were also family funerals for children of Robert, Henry, Edward, and Florence. Florence and her young physician husband, Edwin Wilcox, lost their first daughter, Mildred, at birth, and first son, Donald, before his first birthday. During his second summer their third child, Edwin, was vacationing at Wasatch Resort with his parents and grandmother, who thought the fresh canyon air would be good for him, when he died very suddenly on August 5, 1901. Robert received the news in Salt Lake City as a terrible shock; he arranged for Elder James E. Talmage to address the family at the funeral. Sadly, Florence and Edwin had no more children. Florence, a compassionate woman, frequently took care of others, including her mother Maria until her death. Edwin doctored many family members during illnesses and after accidents and was especially attentive to Robert T. Burton during his last years.

The death of William's second wife, Eloise, on October 5, 1904, was also a family tragedy. She left nine children, the youngest just six years old. They lived next door to Haven Villa, and Maria helped his older girls raise their younger brothers and sisters.

Robert also noted in his journal the deaths of his older sisters, Jane Leybourn, in Toledo, Ohio, October 19, 1881; Ann Shipley in Pultneyville, New York, June 3, 1893; and Mary White, in Beaver, Utah, December 3, 1894; his younger sister, Melissa C. Kimball, in Salt Lake City on September 21, 1903; his younger brother, Charles Edward Burton, in Mesa, Arizona, on July 26, 1896; and his sister-in-law, Elizabeth (Betsy) Oats Burton, widow of William Burton, at the age of ninety-one, on May 2, 1895. Robert outlived all of his thirteen brothers and sisters.

On the other hand, there were many happy family celebrations, such as birthdays, anniversaries, and weddings. All of Robert's children except George (Susan's son) and Ada May (Sarah's daughter) were married before his death, and in 1897, the grandchildren also began to marry. In 1888, LaFayette (Lafe or L.G.) married Ella Mitchell on October 17, in Salt Lake City, and the same day Alfred married Elizabeth Laurette (Lizzie) Peart in the Logan Temple. After the brides' parents had given separate wedding parties, on October 19, Robert and Maria hosted a supper party to honor of both young couples. The sixty guests were members of the Burton, Frederick Mitchell, and Jacob Peart families. The family had similar wedding parties when Lizzie, Mary, Florence, and Virginia married.[1] The names of Robert's children, their spouses, wedding dates, and children are listed in Appendices B, C, and D.

The spacious home of Lewis and Theresa Hills was the setting for the golden wedding party of Robert and Maria on December 17, 1895. Sixty guests received engraved cards bearing the inscription,

Mr. Robert T. Burton,
Miss Maria S. Haven,
Married,
Nauvoo, December eighteenth,
1845.
The impress of their virtues
on our hearts will long remain.

During the summers, members of the Burton family often retreated to the canyons above Salt Lake City to escape the heat. Sometimes Robert would take his children camping and fishing, but more often they went to Little Cottonwood Canyon, the Weber ranch, or the Hills's summer home in Parleys Canyon.

Several of the General Authorities and members of the Presiding Bishopric had cabins near the granite quarries in Little Cottonwood Canyon. They first used this location as a safe retreat for polygamists during the raid, but later it became a vacation resort, usually called Wasatch, but also known as Granite. Small tent cabins were built in the 1880s; and in 1893, Robert and Bishop Preston directed the building of a hotel. The Burtons had a set of three small cabins which all the family members used, although Maria was fonder of spending summers at Wasatch than some of the others. Virginia remembered it from a visit in 1887:

> Wasatch at that time was more beautiful than I have ever seen it. Our father's cabin was in a latticed enclosure with the other two members of the Presiding Bishopric. This lattice fence and the lattice gate made it quite a private, secluded place. My father's camp consisted of a bowery on a platform and a little old 10' by 12' lumber place where we had a little stove to do the cooking on and a tent to sleep in. . . .
>
> I will never forget the quaint picture Wasatch presented at this time. The worker's cottages were in an orderly row about 10 x 12 feet, unpainted, weathered gray, and gay bright flowers blooming in front of each cottage. A tiny stream of water was running past each cottage in a small wooden trough. (A. Cutler 1976, 181–82).

Another description comes from Carl C. Burton:

> I also have very pleasant childhood recollections of the summer
> cottages at Wasatch in Little Cottonwood. There being two small
> half tent houses and a cook house facing on a bowery and the small
> stream of water conveyed by wooden trough past each house . . .
> and also the large hotel which was located by the main stream and
> the small railroad train that would come up as I recall every day to
> bring mail, supplies and passengers. (C. Burton to T. M. Burton
> 1953, 1)

Sometimes several families gathered there to celebrate the Fourth or Twenty-fourth of July. A photograph taken at Wasatch in the late 1890s shows members of the family dressed for a party. This may have been a special outing for the young adult children, grandchildren, and cousins. The young people could have enjoyed hiking during the day, and singing and parlor games in the evening. Maria's sister and her husband, Eliza and Charles Westover, are also in the photo. (See photograph on p. 140.)

When Robert went to the Weber Ranch during the summer, he would stop en route at the summer home of the Hills family in Parley's Canyon. Sometimes he would find several grandchildren there, as Theresa often had her brothers' children join them at the cabin. The Hills also had property that Robert called Cottonwood, near 5300 South and 2600 East, where they first built a small cabin for summer outings and later their home, which they called Hillsden.

Three great events in 1893, 1896, and 1897 highlighted Robert's public life during the 1890s. First, the Salt Lake Temple was completed under direction of the Presiding Bishopric and dedicated on April 6, 1893, forty years after the laying of the cornerstones. Second, Utah became a state on January 6, 1896. Third, the Saints commemorated the fiftieth anniversary of the arrival of the pioneers with a jubilee celebration from July 20 to 24, 1897.

Although the Salt Lake Temple was started first, temples in St. George, Logan, and Manti were finished while construction on the Salt Lake Temple was at a standstill. However, in February 1888, the Presiding Bishopric appointed workers to resume work on the temple. These were dark days for Church leaders and in 1890, before the Manifesto was issued, the temples were almost lost to the government. However Bishops Preston, Burton, and especially Winder kept the construction going. Finally, the capstone was set in place in a dramatic ceremony on April 6, 1892. Robert was at the temple early that morning making sure that arrangements were complete. Forty thousand people thronged Temple Square and watched from nearby housetops or buildings. Bands led a procession, the choir and audience sang, then President Woodruff pressed an electric button that settled the stone in place, and Lorenzo Snow led the "Hosanna Shout." That day, Apostle Francis M. Lyman offered the following resolution, which was passed by the vast assemblage with a loud vocal "aye,": "Believing that the instructions of President Woodruff, respecting the early completion of the Salt Lake temple, is the word of the Lord unto us, I propose that this assemblage pledge themselves, collectively and individually, to furnish, as fast as it may be needed, all the money that may be required to complete the temple at the earliest time possible, so that the dedication may take place on April 6th, 1893" (CHC 6:232–35).

Accordingly, Robert wrote in his journal on April 11 that he had been with the First Presidency, some of the apostles, and the Presiding Bishopric that afternoon in the President's Office "to devise measures for the completion of the S. L. Temple." Robert was accepted the assignment to raise the funds and John R. Winder was assigned to oversee construction. After considering the great amount of work left and the financial straits of the church, they set aside Sunday, May 1, as a day for fasting and prayer to get the means to complete the temple.

Construction continued through the summer of 1892; and in October, the priesthood session of General Conference was held in the partly finished temple. Robert recorded that the most important business of the meeting was to collect funds to finish the building, and an astounding $50,000 was subscribed (October 10, 1892).

The temple was dedicated as planned on April 6, 1893, although the finishing touches of the interior had been completed only the previous afternoon. That evening, the temple was opened for a general inspection, and a thousand prominent non-Mormon men and women were invited to walk through.

Robert T. Burton arrived at the temple at 9:30 A.M. on April 6, with his wife, Maria, and daughters, Mary and Florence. Sarah and several of her children joined them in the temple, and they were witnesses to the first session in which President Woodruff offered the dedicatory prayer. Robert concluded his journal entry that day, "We had a glorious time. The spirit of the Lord is richly enjoyed by all present at both meetings."

Thousands of Church members had come to Salt Lake, and dedication services continued every day from April 6 to May 18, so that all could participate. Robert's homes were full of out-of-town guests, both relatives and old friends, whom he took to the temple. He loved the services and went to at least one session every day for nineteen days. He recorded on the twelfth day that the services were just as interesting as the first day; and after attending two meetings on the eighteenth day, he wrote, "We had a glorious meeting again today."

On April 19–20, the General Authorities held special priesthood sessions attended by stake presidents and other Church leaders. The first day, devoted to instruction, concluded with a "great union of feeling" according to Robert's journal entry. On the second day, the brethren joined in a prayer circle in the celestial room, which Robert noted "in all probability is the largest Circle ever formed since the days of Enoch." Robert helped Bishop Preston administer the sacrament to the 115 priesthood leaders in attendance.

For the next two days, the temple was open to Sunday School children who were not old enough for baptism, and Robert was there to witness the children passing through the temple "in great order and with much joy."

The temple opening gave the Burtons their first opportunity to provide the temple ordinances for their ancestors. Between

August and October 1893, Robert and his sisters Mary and Melissa and some of their children performed baptisms, endowments, and sealings for deceased family members. On October 10, 1893, they resealed Samuel and Hannah Burton and had their children sealed to them.[2] Samuel and Hannah had originally been sealed February 6, 1846, in the Nauvoo Temple just as the Saints were fleeing Nauvoo. Robert had been gathering genealogical information for over twenty years as he traveled in Ohio, New York, and England. He found it difficult to trace his family relationships and twice told family members at the reunion that they should make it easier for future generations to know their heritage by keeping good records. In 1886, the Burton Family Association appointed William S., Willard C., and Henry F. Burton as the Committee on Genealogy. At the family meeting, October 25, 1893, they reported that genealogical information on their grandparents and great-grandparents, plus collateral branches of the family, had been collected and systematically arranged.

> We have also with the assistance of Sister Mary [Burton] White and other members of the family, done considerable work in the Salt Lake Temple for those who are dead. Baptisms have been attended to for some seventy three persons, while many of these, and some others who received the Gospel while living but had not the privelige [sic] of working in a Temple for themselves, have been officiated for in the higher ordinances during the past Summer & Fall (Burton Family Association 1885–1953, October 24, 1893)

On May 9, 1895, Robert and Maria went to the temple to be sealed to their three oldest children, Theresa, William, and Charles, who were born before their parents were sealed, March 18, 1856. Sarah Garr Burton, her brother, Abel, and sisters, Nancy and Caroline, also compiled genealogical information on their parents and grandparents and took those names to the temple in May 1895 (May 9, 22–23, 1895).

Between the Manifesto in 1890 and Utah statehood in January 1896, there was a time of tumultuous political struggle in Utah and in Washington, D.C. After the Manifesto, non-Mormons feared that the Church authorities, particularly the

First Presidency, would continue to exercise political control over Church members and thus control the state. This fear kept the territory from statehood. To prove that Latter-day Saints were at liberty to vote their own political convictions and were not controlled by the priesthood leadership, the Church leaders realized that national political parties had to replace the traditional Mormon (Peoples) and non-Mormon (Liberal) division. Beginning in Ogden in February 1891 and extending to Salt Lake City the following May and June, leaders attempted to dissolve the local Peoples and Liberal parties and encouraged members to choose between the national parties. The Church and Peoples Party leaders dissolved their party in June 1891 (Larson 1971, 287–88), but the Liberals were somewhat slower to disband (CIIC 6.306–07, 313).

Utah had long been considered a Democratic state because the national Democratic Party had tried to restrain the extreme anti-polygamy legislation. It was a Republican Congress that enacted the Edmunds and Edmunds-Tucker bills, and a Republican president who appointed the crusading judges. However, in 1891, as the People's Party was being dissolved, some Mormon leaders encouraged the Saints to divide equally between the national parties. Those who were already of the Democratic persuasion were encouraged to remain so—quietly—while those without affiliation were to be proselyted by the Republican Party. Thus, some apostles promoted Republicanism openly, believing that the Republican Congress would be more likely to admit a territory with a strong Republican party. The new political alignments often pitted Church leaders against each other as they divided over such issues as free silver and protective tariffs. Former Mormon/gentile enemies found themselves working together for their national party (Lyman 1986, 150–62; Larson 1971, 283–90; Alexander 1986, 6–10).

Robert's political prominence ended when polygamists were disfranchised in 1885. However, he maintained great interest in political events and a strong loyalty to the Democratic Party, as did the other members of the Presiding Bishopric. Until amnesty was granted to polygamists in January 1893, Robert could not vote; but he attended party rallies and was pleased when the November 1892 election was a "general Democratic victory" in Utah and throughout the States. He wrote in his journal November 9, 1892, of the "great rejoicing all over the U.S. among the Democrats & in Utah especially" and participated in a great parade and Democratic meeting at the Salt Lake Theatre on the evening of November 10. Once permitted to register and vote again, Robert exercised that privilege in every election thereafter, voting for the last time just six days before his death.

The Democratic Congress in 1893 restored the Church's personal property. In July 1894, it also passed Utah's Enabling Act, which called for the election of delegates to a constitutional convention to convene in March 1895. President Grover Cleveland signed it into law on July 16, 1894.

Robert watched with great interest as the state constitution was written between March 4 and May 8, 1895, and as the parties nominated their candidates for state and national offices. His journal entries indicate approval of B. H. Roberts's candidacy on the Democratic ticket for representative to Congress. After a rally at the Salt Lake Theatre on November 1, 1895, he wrote, "Speakers [were] J. T. Caine and B. H. Roberts. The latter gentleman made one of the most eloquent speaches I most ever listened to." On November 5, he described the election as "very close and exciting" but made no comment about the victory of the Republican candidates over his personal choices. Soon he was involved as a member of the Committee on Inauguration in arranging activities for Statehood Day.

Snow covered the Salt Lake City streets and sleighs were the principal mode of transportation around the city on Saturday morning, January 4, 1896. Robert left his home just after 8 A.M. and had just arrived at the corner of Main and South Temple when the signal was given at 8:15 that President Cleveland had signed the proclamation admitting Utah as the forty-fifth state in the Union. Excited citizens fired cannons, blew horns, and rang sleigh bells. People gathered on the sidewalks and crowded into the streets in an impromptu parade (R. T. Burton 1856–1907, January 4, 1896).

The inaugural activities began Monday morning at 11:00 A.M. with a grand parade. Members of the large Burton family lined Main Street to cheer for their father and grandfather who headed the procession as marshal of the day (see photograph, p. 141). The procession moved through downtown Salt Lake streets, ending at the Temple Block. The new state officers were inaugurated in the Tabernacle, where a large star gleamed across the tall organ pipes, representing the addition Utah made to the United States flag. A chorus of a thousand sang "The Star Spangled Banner" and Evan Stephens's new state song, "Utah, We Love Thee." As each state officer took the oath of office, a cannon boomed on Capitol Hill. Finally, the new Republican governor, Heber M. Wells, delivered his inaugural address detailing Utah's struggle for statehood. That night, a grand ball was held at the Salt Lake Theatre. Robert, too weary from the lengthy preparations and events to celebrate into the early morning hours with the younger citizens of the state, stayed for just a short time.

The photograph of Robert as marshal of the day, sitting astride his beautiful bay horse in full dress uniform, is a family keepsake. His daughter, Virginia, expressed the family's admiration of their father on Statehood Day: "He did it so well we were awfully proud of him, that he could sit up as straight as he did because he was then what was considered an old man" (V. Cutler 1955, 3).

The well-known photograph of Robert in his Nauvoo Legion uniform was taken for his eightieth birthday in October 1901 (see photograph, p. 142). He had over thirty copies made in various poses and sizes and gave them to his children, close friends, and relatives. A large copy of the portrait and the uniform he wore are part of the exhibit at the Daughters of the Utah Pioneers Museum on North Main Street in Salt Lake City.

Eighteen months after statehood, the citizens of Utah united for a five-day celebration of the Jubilee or fiftieth anniversary of the arrival of the pioneers. B. H. Roberts described this as an "era of good feeling" with "Gentile, Jew, and 'Mormon' entering into a generous spirit of emulation to show honor to the life, labor, sacrifices and achievements of the Utah Pioneers" (CHC 6:349). Out-of-town friends and relatives filled the Burton homes for the Jubilee week. Salt Lake City was thronging with visitors, and Robert described it as a time of "bustle and hurry."

On July 20, Wilford Woodruff dedicated the Brigham Young monument at the head of Main Street at South Temple. The members of the Presiding Bishopric directed placement of the granite shaft the week before, and Robert occupied a place on the stand at the unveiling and dedication.

The next four days were marked with a variety of parades. On the first day the military paraded, and Robert, dressed in his uniform, rode with his old military friends representing the Nauvoo Legion. The second day was Children's Day, with the Sunday Schools marching in the morning and a special illuminated parade of "Great Salt Lake, Real and Fanciful" moving down Main Street at night. Robert brought his family from the farm to see the evening parade, reportedly the greatest ever witnessed in Salt Lake City. "Main Street was a mass of moving light, while the electrical decorations were magnificent" (CHC 6:350–51). On "County Day," Robert was on the grandstand to witness the floats representing the counties of Utah. Finally, on the Twenty-fourth of July a great parade moved through the city featuring all the floats and marching groups of the earlier parades and the pioneers of 1847. Robert rode with the representatives of the Nauvoo Legion, among the federal and state military troops. The celebration ended with a display of fireworks on Capitol Hill.

After 1897, Robert organized many other processions, usually for the funerals of great pioneer leaders such as Wilford Woodruff, Lorenzo Snow, and Brigham Young, Jr. In 1903, after Young's funeral, Robert wrote in his journal, "I am quite unused to horseback riding but got along nicely." We do not know how many times Robert was responsible for a parade or procession through downtown Salt Lake, although it seems it was for every such occasion until he could no longer mount his horse.

Between 1891 and 1896, Robert reviewed the manuscripts of Orson F. Whitney's three-volume *History of Utah*. Other members of the special review committee included Church historian Franklin D. Richards, John Jacques, and A. M. Musser. In the preface to Volume 2, Whitney expressed appreciation for the committee's "intelligent discussion and patient deliberation over the contents of the volume." Robert purchased a number of sets of the history for his children. One of these sets passed through three generations of Henry F. Burton's descendants and into the author's hands where it has been a valuable resource for this biography. Robert also took a great interest in a genealogical project undertaken by John C. Garr, a distant cousin of his wife Sarah Garr Burton. Garr visited Salt Lake City in December 1892, where he was entertained by Robert and Sarah. Robert purchased a number of copies of his book, *The Garr Genealogy*, published in 1894, and gave them to his children.

During the early 1900s Robert enlisted the aid of his sons, William and Charles, to prepare evidence from the military papers of the Nauvoo Legion in support of legislation recognizing the veterans of the Utah Indian Wars. In 1912–13, the Utah legislature finally awarded medals of honor and $50,000 for the veterans (CHC 5:157).

As Robert moved into old age, he was plagued with aches and illnesses. He often wrote of not feeling well and not being able to sleep at night. He mentioned pleurisy, rheumatism, colds, sick headaches, bowel and kidney trouble. However, he did not contract smallpox, scarlet fever, and other epidemics which quarantined his children and grandchildren at their homes. Robert often called upon his sons for priesthood blessings during these years, and he joined with them in administering to other family members, placing great faith in the power of the Lord to heal. His sons Henry, Alfred, and Theodore, and his daughters Theresa and Florence recovered from very serious illnesses after constant medical care and many priesthood administrations.

Robert rarely allowed poor health to keep him away from the Presiding Bishop's office, but he gave up traveling long distances for the Church. Bishop William B. Preston, ten years younger than Robert and John R. Winder, assumed the greater responsibility for travel to the outlying stakes during the 1890s. When Preston was not in Salt Lake, Robert made an extra effort to go to the office even if he was not feeling well. After he turned eighty in 1901, some of his sons said, "Now father, it's time for you to quit and you mustn't go to the office any more." But Robert replied, "No, when I can't work here then I want to go some place else to work" (V. Cutler 1955, 3). He did his best to fulfill this resolve.

During the 1890s, the Church undertook a number of financial enterprises, hoping to recover from the debts incurred under the Edmunds-Tucker Act and to finance increased educational and welfare expenses. Tithing receipts were down drastically during the late 1880s and early 1890s, because Church members hesitated to pay tithing if the government was going to get it. A June 28, 1893 journal entry reveals Robert's concern: "We [speaking collectively of the Church and community] are now having a very serious time financially." Unfortunately, these enterprises led the Church into greater debt, and outside banks and businessmen became it's creditors.

According to Robert's journal, shortly after Lorenzo Snow became president of the Church in the fall of 1898, the Presiding Bishopric began meeting with the First Presidency to discuss the financial problems of the Church (October 27 and November 23, 1898). President Snow first directed the issuance of $1.5 million in 6-percent bonds to replace many short-term loans. The first issue of $500,000 was offered on January 1, 1899; the second on January 4, 1899; the third was not needed. Nearly all the bonds were purchased by Mormons and Mormon financial institutions and were to be redeemed by paying $50,000 per year, plus $30,000 in interest, from tithing funds. Next, President Snow moved to get the Church out of some business enterprises by closing or selling mining, milling, and railroad ventures. Finally, he told the Saints that the Church would get out of debt and Zion be redeemed if they would observe the Lord's law of tithing. He reached these decisions in important council meetings during the winter of 1898–99. In May 1899, Bishop Preston accompanied President Snow to the now-famous conference in St. George, where he promised the Lord would open "the windows of heaven" if the Saints would pay their tithes.

In every meeting President Snow addressed thereafter he stressed tithing. At a solemn assembly in the Salt Lake Temple on July 2, 1899, the General Authorities of the Church and the priesthood leaders of the forty stakes, the 478 wards, and the auxiliary organizations recommitted themselves to accepting the doctrine of tithing as the word and will of the Lord (CHC 6:357–60). Robert described the meeting in his journal: "Fast Day and the Solemn Assembly at the Temple. I came to the Temple at 9–30 and the meeting opened at 10. Present all the leading authorities of the Church, some 700 in all and some 16 or 17 speakers. We had a glorious time. The Sacrament was administered. Bishop Preston and I officiated. Meeting continued in session until after 7 P.M. A day long to be remembered."

For twenty-five years, Robert had been a steward over the tithing funds of the Church, and he rejoiced at the renewal of the doctrine. He welcomed the increase in activity at the General Tithing Office, where the day after the solemn assembly was "a very busy day indeed as there [are] so many Brethren from all parts of the country calling all day in regard to tithing affairs of the stake" (July 3, 1899). Over the next eight years, Robert observed the increase in tithing receipts as the Saints responded to President Snow's admonitions. In just one year—1900—tithes increased from $800,000 to $1.3 million (in Alexander 1985, 6), thus allowing the first issue of bonds to be paid off by 1903. In 1907, the second issue was redeemed, and the Church was once again out of debt (Arrington 1958, 403).

President Snow did not live to see that day. He died October 10, 1901. Joseph F. Smith was chosen president on October 17, and sustained in a special general conference on November 10, 1901. President Smith called John R. Winder, second counselor to Bishop Preston, as his first counselor, and Anthon H. Lund as his second counselor. Of John Winder's new call, Robert wrote, "This removes from our Quorum our very dear friend and fellow laborer" (October 17, 1901).[3] This new presidency continued the course begun by President Snow after he thought the financial affairs were properly adjusted, which was to take the message of the restored gospel to the world (CHC 6:375–80).

Robert T. Burton served in the Presiding Bishopric for six more years under President Joseph F. Smith until his death. His twenty-two years as a counselor in the Presiding Bishopric spanned the administrations of five Church presidents. Because he had shared missionary experiences with Joseph F. Smith in England in 1874–75, Robert was as well acquainted with the new, much younger president as he had been with Brigham Young, John Taylor, Wilford Woodruff, and Lorenzo Snow.

Robert's journal during his declining years reflects an "enduring to the end" attitude. He had no intention of retiring from either the Presiding Bishopric or his farm. When he went to the farm, he did not go just to watch. He introduced new equipment and inventions for the farming and for Sarah's convenience in the house. During 1902, he helped install a new system of drains and ditches, cut down many of the old poplar trees, and planted new shade trees around the farm house. He hired men for specific tasks, but supervised the farming operations and helped with chores when he was able. Because weather conditions usually influenced decisions on planting, harvesting, breeding, spraying, and pruning, he faithfully kept track of each day's weather. He became very interested in his orchards and his strawberry patch, spending both time and money to made them productive. Each spring, he added new strawberry plants, making an excursion to Mill Creek for the starts.

During these years, many of his intimate friends and military comrades died. Like Robert, they were men and women in their seventies and eighties who had pioneered the mountain valleys, raised large families, and endured persecution and privation. He specifically mentioned the deaths of Joseph Pollard (February 25, 1890), Daniel H. Wells (March 24, 1891), John

Sharp (December 23, 1891), Lot Smith (June 21, 1892), Abraham O. Smoot (March 6, 1895), Joseph M. Benedict (July 25, 1896), Theodore McKean (July 9, 1897), Elias Morris (March 17, 1898), Sarah M. Kimball (December 1, 1898), George Q. Cannon (April 12, 1901), and Brigham Young, Jr. (April 11, 1903). Robert commented on their deaths and funeral services, but recorded no words of grief. Instead, he rejoiced for lives well lived. At the conclusion of many pioneer funerals, members of the congregation were given the opportunity to speak. In this way, Robert frequently made remarks at the funerals he attended, although he also spoke by request on many, many occasions.

Robert T. Burton celebrated his eighty-sixth birthday and the Burton Family Association held its twenty-second annual meeting on October 25, 1907. It was the first family meeting that Robert did not conduct, and the second meeting held at the Burton farm instead of Haven Villa. Although Robert was physically weak, his mind was still clear. He spent the morning of his birthday at the Presiding Bishopric's office and then allowed his grandson Harold Hills to take him, Maria, his great-niece from Ohio Mary (Minnie) Blanchard, and his granddaughter Eloise to the farm in his automobile. One hundred and thirty-eight family members attended the reunion. At many earlier gatherings, Robert had reminded them that he did not organize the family to bring honor to himself, but rather to keep the members close. "These gatherings are to give the children and grandchildren an opportunity to become acquainted with each other. . . . I have tried myself to keep the family together by these means" (Burton Family Association 1885–1953, October 25, 1902). He always described these family gatherings as the greatest pleasure and happiest days of his life.

Two weeks later, Robert suffered a general collapse while at the farm where he was confined to bed on Thursday morning, November 7. At his bedside were many tender scenes. He asked for Maria on Friday afternoon and Edwin and Florence brought her to the farm where she stayed at his side all night, even though encouraged to go home and rest. "Had a pleasant time," she wrote in her journal. "He expressed himself as being much pleased at my staying. He said, 'I am glad you staid. I wanted you." Two days later, he smiled and told her, "My old troubles have come back to me." On Monday morning, Maria wrote "Mr. Burton is still with us with his intelect bright. He knows everyone and shakes hands. All of his family have seen [him] except Lafe (he is at Newhouse)" (November 8, 10, 11, 1907).

When Robert realized his death was near, he called for William, Willard, and Henry, who were the oldest sons of each family. He gave them these instructions as a guide for the members of the family: "Never disgrace the name of Burton. Be faithful to the Church. Keep the family together. Be kind to the poor" (C. Burton 1969, 18).

He died at the farm Monday afternoon, November 11, 1907, at 1:30 P.M. in the presence of his wives and twenty-one of his children.

The *Deseret Evening News* had prepared a lengthy article to report his illness and inserted the bulletin announcing his death just before press time on November 11:

> **GEN. R. T. BURTON ENDS HIS CAREER. . . . Bulletin—**
> **Gen. Burton died at 1:30 o'clock this afternoon, surrounded**
> **by members of his family. His ailment was a general col-**
> **lapse, following a life which remained active to the end of**
> **his 86 years.**
>
> After living for more than eight-six years, fifty-nine of which have been spent in Utah, and only a few weeks of which have been spent in bed from any physical ailment, General Robert T. Burton is now seriously ill at his country home, 2406 South State street. General Burton is suffering from no particular ailment, but from a general collapse which commenced several days ago. . . . He is still able to recognize friends, but is unable to speak, and most of the members of his large family have spent this morning at the home (November 11, 1907, p. 1).

Wednesday, November 13, his body lay in state at Haven Villa, where friends and family gathered in the evening. Later that night, while walking from Haven Villa to his home, William S. Burton saw smoke and flames coming from the Redman Van and Storage buildings immediately to the west. He quickly sounded the alarm and began rounding up men to fight the fire. The Redman buildings included storage warehouses and barns for the horses which pulled their vans. Within a short time, the entire complex, including 100 tons of hay, was on fire. The sounds of the horses kicking to get loose and screaming as they burned filled the entire block.

Since the Burton cow barn overlapped the Redman horse barn, boys and men from the family took up stations on the barn roof, spraying water from their hoses to keep their property from burning. Helen Burton Raybould, William's youngest daughter, then eleven, still remembers the terror of that night and how worried she was that the Burton homes and buildings might catch on fire (Raybould 1978).

B. F. Redman lost an estimated $250,000. The buildings and their contents—including pianos, personal belongings, wagons, and an electric automobile—burned to the ground. However, Redman considered his greatest loss the thirty-seven horses, particularly his own fine riding horse. The Burtons, who also admired those horses, mourned their loss and mingled memories of this tragedy with their memories of Robert's death and funeral.

At 9:30 A.M. Thursday, a horse-drawn hearse and the vehicles bearing the Burton family left the corner of First South and Second West. As the hearse approached Temple Square, survivors of Utah's Indian Wars stood in double rank to salute their one-time commander. Mostly silver-haired, still they stood with "martial bearing that was suggestive of their former leader" (*Deseret News*, November 15, 1907).

Six of Robert's sons, LaFayette, Hosea, Heber, Austin, Walter, and Hardy, bore his casket into the filled Assembly Hall. The organ, stand, and railings of the hall were adorned in white, with living potted palm trees and ferns and masses of cut flowers in arrangements which had been given in tribute by the organizations with which Robert had been affiliated. The most visible was a large tri-color arrangement from the military veterans set upon a large American flag draped over the organ.

To fill Robert's request for a special musical service, his funeral opened with an organ solo by J. J. McClellan, followed by the Tabernacle Choir, conducted by Evan Stephens, singing "When First the Glorious Light of Truth." After Orson F. Whitney's invocation, the choir sang, "O My Father." Later in the services, Horace S. Ensign sang "Unanswered Yet," and Lizzie Thomas Edward, "Sometime We Will Understand" (*Deseret News*, November 15, 1907).

Leading men of the Church, each of whom had known Robert from the time he entered the Salt Lake Valley, delivered sermons stressing that Robert's life was one to emulate. Bishop Orrin P. Miller spoke of learning to love him for "his genial nature, his generalship and charity." He admonished his family to emulate his example and keep the commandments of God as he had kept them. President John R. Winder said that he and Robert had been like twin brothers for sixty years, coming to the valley together, then serving in the Indian wars, the departments of national and city government, and finally in the Church Tithing Office as members of the Presiding Bishopric. Since he was just forty-seven days younger than Robert, he said it would be no surprise if he were one of the first to join him on the other side of the veil, and he rejoiced in the prospect of being associated with him there for an even longer period of time (*Deseret News*, November 15, 1907).

President Anthon H. Lund testified of Robert's integrity, love, honor, and fullness of years filled with good works. Elder Francis M. Lyman described him as a "general in the army of right, in the army of truth and of love." Yet, he said, "he was tender-hearted, sympathetic and worthy of our confidence and love." Elder John Henry Smith implored his surviving family to live in his footsteps.

President Joseph F. Smith was the concluding speaker.

> Perhaps there are hundreds here who could speak fervently of the excellent life of Bishop Burton, and if the time would permit we should be delighted to hear their testimonies of his work and life. I know that there are thousands who are not here who could do so.

He knew the Prophet Joseph Smith and when he testified to the divinity of his mission on earth he knew what he was saying, and he knew it was true. No man ever lived more consistently to his profession of faith in this work than he. I have known him all my life it seems to me. I cannot recall the time I was not familiar with him. I crossed the plains the same year. All my life in Utah he has been a prominent figure in life before my eyes. . . . I was with him on a two year's mission in Great Britain and was directly in his company all of that time, 1874–1875. It was while there that I had every opportunity to become familiar with his noble traits. He was never false to God, to himself or to his fellow-man, friend or foe (*Deseret News*, November 15, 1907).

President Smith further discussed the principles of celestial marriage, "concerning the association of men and women in the capacity of husbands and wives, of which the world knows little."

What gives me supremest joy is the fact that Bishop Burton has delved into these principles. He has received them in his heart and has obeyed them and carried them out in his life. He has put himself in a position to receive the gift of the priesthood, the gift of wives and children, which are the gifts of God to him. They are as eternal as the immortal soul and death, man nor anything else can put them asunder. These blessings have been sealed upon him and the promise that he shall come forth in the morning of the first resurrection has also been sealed upon him.

He concluded by imploring the family, "Honor your father, walk in his footsteps and emulate his example. Your exaltation will be sure. May the Lord bless the bereaved family in their hour of sorrow."

A long cortege moved from Temple Square to the city cemetery where the body was interred shortly after noon. Francis M. Lyman dedicated the grave, and the Pyper-Whitney-Spencer-Ensign quartet sang, "I Need Thee Every Hour."

Robert T. Burton was buried near the graves of his deceased children in the family burial plot, high on the avenues overlooking Salt Lake City. The family association cemetery committee had been responsible for upkeep of this area. They graded the site in 1890, placed a coping around the lots in 1891, and set headstones to mark the graves in 1893 or 1894. In more recent years, a tall monument has been placed by the family honoring Robert, his three wives, and twenty-seven children. It is today a sacred spot for his more than 2,000 descendants.

Robert Taylor Burton's influence continues strong among his posterity more than eighty years after his death. Many of his deeds have become bedtime stories, two-and-a-half minute talks, Twenty-fourth of July addresses and skits, and inspirational letters to missionaries. His grandchildren to the fourth, fifth, and sixth generations have been drawn together in distant areas of the United States and the world, through missionary service, attendance at Latter-day Saint services, or in less expected ways. One missionary grandson, Ralph Garr Cutler, served during the 1920s under President Hugh J. Cannon, an admirer of Robert Taylor Burton (see A. Cutler 1976, 489). Elder Cutler, eldest son of Robert's daughter Virginia, wrote home:

I am more associated with Pres. Cannon than heretofore and it is wonderful to feel of his power and influence. He told me a great deal about Grandfather Burton and it has awakened a desire to learn more of him. . . . I have a feeling he has turned his interest to us and is pleased if we are doing the right thing. I have resolved that I am going to be like him if I can.

Notes

Edward Leo Lyman describes the struggle leading to statehood in *Political Deliverance*, and Thomas G. Alexander discusses many of the political and spiritual changes required by the events of the 1880s and 1890s in *Mormonism in Transition: A History of the Latter-day Saints, 1890–1930*, both published by the University of Illinois Press in 1986.

1. Virginia's wedding party is described in the biography of her husband, entitled *Ralph Cutler* (A. Cutler 1976, 158–63).

2. All children were sealed except for Charles Edward Burton who was living in Mesa, Arizona, at that time. His sealing was performed by his family members in the Arizona Temple, November 29, 1951.

3. Orrin P. Miller replaced Winder as second counselor in the Presiding Bishopric.

Epilogue

In the fall of 1838, as a seventeen-year-old Canadian farm boy, Robert Taylor Burton received "convincing evidence" of the truth of the restored gospel of Jesus Christ. Over the next sixty-nine years, that experience led him from an obscure village to the great cities of the United States and Europe and to a position of power and influence in his church and community. Robert truly fits the title coined by modern Mormon historians of "supporting saint." He belongs with "those Latter-day Saints who gave of their energies at a Church level once removed from certain of their contemporaries who, because of their assigned stations, have often received the greater recognition through the years. . . . those individuals who were very literally the spokes which made the greater wheel of Zion go around (Cannon and Whittaker 1985, xi).

While his life was an example of kindness, unselfishness, and fatherly love, he was remembered after his death for his courage in fighting the enemies of the Church, his role as a builder of the state, and his service as a bishop, missionary, and member of the Presiding Bishopric.

John R. Young left this description of Robert and his military associates: "I knew Personally Porter Rockwell, Howard Egan, Lot Smith, Ephraim Hanks, Robt. T. Burton, Price Nelson & Warren Snow. They were all strong, fearless men—who like Levi the Son of Aaron, had the nerve and zeal to sweep cess Pools of Iniquity from the Camps of Israel, and as Levi acted upon the impulse of the moment, so these noble men acted in cases of emergency upon their own Judgement, and I am thankfull that we had such men. They have been a Blessing to the Church, and to the world" (1928-30, 88).

Robert's life was summarized in a newspaper series entitled "Our Gallery of Pioneers":

> One of the most conspicuous military men in Utah history; one of the community's most energetic officials in city, county and territorial affairs; one of the earliest and most persistent of home man-

ufacturers; and for many years preceding his death known everywhere throughout the intermountain country as one of the presiding bishopric of the Church, Robert Taylor Burton will always occupy a prominent place in the gallery where are inscribed the names and deeds of the builders of the state.

President Joseph F. Smith said of Robert at his funeral: "His lips are sealed, but I sincerely hope that the example of his life and his testimony of the truth he has borne will not perish, but live throughout this generation and generations to come."

Appendix A

Genealogy of Samuel and Hannah Burton

HUSBAND Samuel BURTON

		LDS ORDINANCE DATA	
BORN: 12 JUN 1783	PLACE: Garthorpe, Lincolnshire, England	BAP.:	4 DEC 1837
CHR.:	PLACE:	END.:	6 FEB 1846 NV
MARR.: 12 JUN 1804	PLACE: Luddington, Lincolnshire, England	SEAL.:	6 FEB 1846 NV
DIED: 21 JAN 1852	PLACE: Suttersville, Sacramento, California	SP:	29 JUN 1932 SL
BUR.: JAN 1852	PLACE: Suttersville, Sacramento, California		

Father: Samuel BURTON
Mother: Mary JOHNSON
OTHER WIVES: Louisa CHAPIN

WIFE Hannah SHIPLEY

		LDS ORDINANCE DATA	
BORN: 12 OCT 1786	PLACE: Gilberdyke, Yorkshire, England	BAP.:	4 DEC 1937
CHR.:	PLACE:	END.:	24 DEC 1845 NV
DIED: 26 JUL 1847	PLACE: Austen Township, Atchison, Missouri	SP:	29 JUN 1932 SL
BUR.:	PLACE: Atchison, Missouri		

Father: William SHIPLEY
Mother: Jane TAYLOR
OTHER HUSBANDS:

SEX M/F	CHILDREN LIST EACH CHILD (LIVING OR DEAD) IN ORDER OF BIRTH	LDS ORDINANCE DATA FOR CHILDREN	
1.	NAME: Mary BURTON		
F	BORN: 12 NOV 1804 PLACE: Luddington, Lincolnshire, England	BAP.:	CHILD
	MARR.: PLACE:	END.:	
	DIED: 29 JAN 1811 PLACE: Luddington, Lincolnshire, England	SP:	10 OCT 1893 SL
	SPOUSE:		

SPOUSE: (1)John LEYBOURN (2)Anthony LEYBOURN

2.
F

NAME:	Jane BURTON		
BORN:	3 FEB 1806	PLACE: Luddington, Lincolnshire, England	BAP.: 1843
MARR:	30 SEP 1823	PLACE: Mersea, Essex, Ontario, Canada	END.: 21 SEP 1893 SL
DIED:	19 OCT 1881	PLACE: Tremainsville, Lucas, Ohio	SP.: 10 OCT 1893 SL

3.
M

NAME:	Samuel BURTON	SPOUSE:	
BORN:	6 NOV 1807	PLACE: Luddington, Lincolnshire, England	BAP.: CHILD
MARR:			END.:
DIED:	28 JUL 1809	PLACE: Garthorpe, Lincolnshire, England	SP.: 10 OCT 1893 SL

4.
M

NAME:	William BURTON	SPOUSE: Elizabeth OATS	
BORN:	3 OCT 1809	PLACE: Garthorpe, Lincolnshire, England	BAP.: 9 DEC 1837
MARR:	28 JUL 1834	PLACE: Mersea, Essex, Ontario, Canada	END.: 16 DEC 1845 NV
DIED:	17 MAR 1851	PLACE: Edinburgh, Scotland	SP.: 10 OCT 1893 SL

5.
F

NAME:	Betsy BURTON	SPOUSE: Joseph ROOP	
BORN:	6 SEP 1811	PLACE: Garthorpe, Lincolnshire, England	BAP.: 15 AUG 1893 SL
MARR:	8 SEP 1829	PLACE: Port Lawrence, Lucas, Ohio	END.: 23 AUG 1893 SL
DIED:	6 MAR 1847	PLACE: Sylvania, Lucas, Ohio	SP.: 10 OCT 1893 SL

6.
M

NAME:	Samuel BURTON	SPOUSE:	
BORN:	21 SEP 1813	PLACE: Garthorpe, Lincolnshire, England	BAP.: CHILD
MARR:		PLACE:	END.:
DIED:	3 DEC 1814	PLACE: Garthorpe, Lincolnshire, England	SP.: 10 OCT 1893 SL

7.
F

NAME:	Ann BURTON	SPOUSE: Waters SHIPLEY	
BORN:	29 OCT 1815	PLACE: Hull, Yorkshire, England	BAP.: 23 JUN 1931 SL
MARR:	24 SEP 1841	PLACE: Toledo, Lucas, Ohio	END.: 26 JUN 1931 SL
DIED:	3 JUN 1893	PLACE: Pultneyville, Ontario, New York	SP.: 10 OCT 1893 SL

8.
F

NAME:	Mary Hannah BURTON	SPOUSE: Samuel Dennis WHITE	
BORN:	31 AUG 1818	PLACE: Pultneyville, Ontario, New York	BAP.: 7 MAY 1838
MARR:	24 OCT 1841	PLACE: Walnut Grove, Knox, Illinois	END.: 12 JAN 184 NV
DIED:	2 DEC 1894	PLACE: Beaver, Beaver, Utah	SP.: 10 OCT 1893 SL

9. NAME: John Shipley BURTON SPOUSE:
   M
   - BORN: 21 AUG 1820 PLACE: Essex, Ontario, Canada BAP:
   - MARR: PLACE: END:
   - DIED: 18 OCT 1820 PLACE: Essex, Ontario, Canada SP: CHILD 10 OCT 1893 SL

10. NAME: Robert Taylor BURTON SPOUSE: (1)Maria Susan HAVEN (2)Sarah Anna GARR (3)Susan Ellen McBRIDE
    M
    - BORN: 25 OCT 1821 PLACE: Amherstburg, Essex, Ontario, Canada BAP: 23 OCT 1838
    - MARR: 18 DEC 1845 PLACE: Nauvoo, Hancock, Illinois END: 15 DEC 1845 NV
    - DIED: 11 NOV 1907 PLACE: Salt Lake City, Salt Lake, Utah SP: 10 OCT 1893 SL

11. NAME: Sarah BURTON SPOUSE: Elijah AUSTIN
    F
    - BORN: 16 NOV 1823 PLACE: Mersea, Essex, Ontario, Canada BAP: 1838
    - MARR: 16 MAR 1843 PLACE: Walnut Grove, Knox, Illinois END: 21 SEP 1893 SL
    - DIED: 9 MAR 1859 PLACE: Sublette, Lee, Illinois SP: 10 OCT 1893 SL

12. NAME: Rebecca Maria BURTON SPOUSE: Nathaniel Very JONES
    F
    - BORN: 16 FEB 1826 PLACE: Mersea, Essex, Ontario, Canada BAP: 23 DEC 1837
    - MARR: 13 MAR 1845 PLACE: Nauvoo, Hancock, Illinois END: 3 FEB 1846 NV
    - DIED: 19 NOV 1888 PLACE: Salt Lake City, Salt Lake, Utah SP: 10 OCT 1893 SL

13. NAME: Melissa BURTON SPOUSE: (1)William CORAY (2)William Henry KIMBALL
    F
    - BORN: 2 MAR 1828 PLACE: Mersea, Essex, Ontario, Canada BAP: 23 DEC 1837
    - MARR: 22 JUN 1846 PLACE: Mount Pisgah, Union, Iowa END: 24 DEC 1845 NV
    - DIED: 21 SEP 1903 PLACE: Salt Lake City, Salt Lake, Utah SP: 10 OCT 1893 SL

14. NAME: Charles Edward BURTON SPOUSE: Harriet Maria MINER
    M
    - BORN: 4 JUN 1830 PLACE: Adrian, Lenawee, Michigan BAP: 5 MAR 1872
    - MARR: 20 MAR 1860 PLACE: Toledo, Lucas, Ohio END: 23 FEB 1944 IF
    - DIED: 26 JUL 1896 PLACE: Mesa, Maricopa, Arizona SP: 1 DEC 1960 IF

Samuel and Mary Burton

HUSBAND Samuel BURTON

			LDS ORDINANCE DATA
BORN:		PLACE:	
CHR.:	14 OCT 1744	PLACE: Hatfield, Yorkshire, England	BAP.: 15 AUG 1893 SL
MARR:	30 DEC 1766	PLACE: Garthorpe, Lincolnshire, England	END.: 16 AUG 1893 SL
DIED:		PLACE:	SEAL.: 16 AUG 1893 SL
BUR.:	7 SEP 1789	PLACE: Garthorpe, Lincolnshire, England	SP: 23 JUL 1963 SL
Father:	John BURTON		
Mother:	Sarah PARISH		
OTHER WIVES:			

WIFE Mary JOHNSON

			LDS ORDINANCE DATA
BORN:	1745	PLACE: Garthorpe, Lincolnshire, England	BAP.: 15 AUG 1893 SL
CHR.:		PLACE:	END.: 16 AUG 1893 SL
DIED:	15 JUL 1809	PLACE:	SP: 23 AUG 1893 SL
BUR.:	17 JUL 1809	PLACE:	
Father:	John JOHNSON		
Mother:	Anne GODFREY		
OTHER HUSBANDS:			

SEX M/F	CHILDREN LIST EACH CHILD (LIVING OR DEAD) IN ORDER OF BIRTH		LDS ORDINANCE DATA FOR CHILDREN
1.	NAME: John BURTON	SPOUSE:	
	CHR.: 19 SEP 1767	PLACE: Garthorpe, Lincolnshire, England	BAP.: 22 AUG 1893 SL
M	MARR:	PLACE:	END.: 19 MAY 1897 SL
	DIED: 27 AUG 1789	PLACE:	SP: 29 JUN 1932 SL

2.	NAME:	Sarah BURTON	SPOUSE:	
F	CHR.:	13 DEC 1769	PLACE: Garthorpe, Lincolnshire, England	BAP.: 15 AUG 1893 SL
	MARR:		PLACE:	END.: 17 AUG 1893 SL
	DIED:	10 MAR 1789	PLACE:	SP.: 29 JUN 1932 SL
3.	NAME:	Ann BURTON	SPOUSE: William Oliver GREENSIDES	
F	CHR.:	13 JAN 1772	PLACE: Garthorpe, Lincolnshire, England	BAP.: 15 AUG 1893 SL
	MARR:		PLACE:	END.: 23 AUG 1893 SL
	DIED:	15 FEB 1848	PLACE:	SP.: 29 JUN 1932 SL
4.	NAME:	Mary BURTON	SPOUSE:	
F	CHR.:	15 SEP 1774	PLACE: Garthorpe, Lincolnshire, England	BAP.: 15 AUG 1893 SL
	MARR:		PLACE:	END.: 17 AUG 1893 SL
	DIED:	9 APR 1790	PLACE:	SP.: 29 JUN 1932 SL
5.	NAME:	Elizabeth BURTON	SPOUSE: Joseph PINDER	
F	CHR.:	28 FEB 1778	PLACE: Garthorpe, Lincolnshire, England	BAP.: 15 AUG 1893 SL
	MARR:		PLACE:	END.: 17 AUG 1893 SL
	DIED:	10 MAR 1818	PLACE:	SP.: 29 JUN 1932 SL
6.	NAME:	Jenny BURTON	SPOUSE:	
F	CHR.:	15 DEC 1781	PLACE: Garthorpe, Lincolnshire, England	BAP.: CHILD
	MARR:		PLACE:	END.:
	DIED:	23 APR 1782	PLACE:	SP.: 29 JUN 1932 SL
7.	NAME:	Samuel BURTON	SPOUSE: (1)Hannah SHIPLEY	
M	BORN:	12 JUN 1783	PLACE: Garthorpe, Lincolnshire, England	BAP.: 4 DEC 1837
	MARR:	12 JUN 1804	PLACE: Luddington, Lincolnshire, England	END.: 6 FEB 1846 NV
	DIED:	21 JAN 1852	PLACE: Suttersville, Sacramento, California	SP.: 29 JUN 1932 SL

427

William and Jane Shipley

HUSBAND William SHIPLEY

		LDS ORDINANCE DATA	
BORN:	19 MAR 1755	PLACE: Reedness, Whitgift, Yorkshire, England	BAP.: 22 AUG 1893 SL
CHR.:		PLACE:	END.: 30 AUG 1893 SL
MARR.:		PLACE: , , England	SEAL.: 30 AUG 1893 SL
DIED:	5 JAN 1818	PLACE: Gilberdike, Yorkshire, England	SP: 25 OCT 1932 SL
BUR.:		PLACE:	

Father: John SHIPLEY
Mother: Hannah IBBOTSON
OTHER WIVES: Elizabeth EDLINGTON

WIFE Jane TAYLOR

		LDS ORDINANCE DATA	
BORN:	20 JUN 1757	PLACE: Skelton, Yorkshire, England	BAP.: 15 AUG 1893 SL
CHR.:		PLACE:	END.: 17 AUG 1893 SL
DIED:	11 APR 1792	PLACE: Gilberdyke, Yorkshire, England	SP: 14 OCT 1969 SL
BUR.:		PLACE:	

Father: Robert TAYLOR
Mother: Mary HORNSEY
OTHER HUSBANDS:

SEX M/F	CHILDREN	LIST EACH CHILD (LIVING OR DEAD) IN ORDER OF BIRTH	LDS ORDINANCE DATA FOR CHILDREN

1.
NAME: Mary SHIPLEY   SPOUSE: Charles HAIRSINE

F	BORN: 11 OCT 1781	PLACE: Gilberdyke, Yorkshire, England	BAP.: 22 AUG 189 SL
	MARR.:	PLACE:	END.: 31 AUG 1893 SL
	DIED: 27 JAN 1837	PLACE:	SP: 29 JUN 1932 SL

	NAME:		SPOUSE: Elizabeth WATERS		
2.	William SHIPLEY				
	BORN: 17 OCT 1785	PLACE: Gilberdyke, Yorkshire, England		BAP.: 22 AUG 1893	SL
M	MARR:	PLACE:		END.: 29 MAY 1896	SL
	DIED: 27 JUL 1859	PLACE: Pultneyville, Ontario, New York		SP: 29 JUN 1932	SL

	NAME:		SPOUSE: Samuel Burton		
3.	Hannah SHIPLEY				
	BORN: 12 OCT 1786	PLACE: Gilberdyke, Yorkshire, England		BAP.: 4 DEC 1837	
F	MARR: 12 JUN 1804	PLACE: Luddington, Lincolnshire, England		END.: 24 DEC 1845	NV
	DIED: 26 JUL 1847	PLACE: Austen Township, Atchison, Missouri		SP: 29 JUN 1932	SL

	NAME:		SPOUSE:		
4.	John SHIPLEY				
	BORN: 13 MAR 1790	PLACE: Gilberdyke, Yorkshire, England		BAP.:	CHILD
M	MARR:	PLACE:		END.:	
	DIED: 14 MAR 1790	PLACE: Gilberdyke, Yorkshire, England		SP:	

Appendix B
Maria Susan Haven Burton

Maria Susan Haven was born April 10, 1826, in Holliston, Middlesex County, Massachusetts. She was the first of two daughters born to John Haven (1774-1853) and his second wife, Judith Woodbury Temple (1798-1891). Her sister, Eliza Ann, was born May 15, 1829.

John Haven was a prominent citizen of Holliston, owning "a large farm, farming land, pasture, hay-land, and a good many cows" (Westover 1918, 1). "My father was a farmer and had a good education and taught in the district school where he lived several winters," wrote his daughter from his first marriage, Elizabeth Haven Barlow, "He was a man of excellent morals and strove diligently by example and precept to instill into the minds of his children the principals of virtue, integrety and honor. He taught us to venerate our Father in Heaven and Jesus Christ our Savior, which caused me to be a great lover of the Scriptures" (in Barlow 1968, 139). He was a deacon in the First Congregational Church for forty years and raised his nine children very strictly, especially to reverence the Sabbath Day. On the Sabbath, family members attended church and read the Bible or other good books. No other activities were permitted, not even visiting friends (Barlow 1968, 139).

His first wife was Elizabeth (Betsy) Howe, sister to Abigail Howe Young, mother of Brigham Young. They had seven children born between 1802 and 1817: Pamela, Mary, Nancy, John, Elizabeth, Jesse, and Phinehas Brigham. Elizabeth Howe Haven died March 31, 1821. John married Judith Temple on February 9, 1823.

Nancy and Elizabeth Haven were the first family members to accept the restored gospel as taught by The Church of Jesus Christ of Latter-day Saints. Their cousins Brigham Young and Willard Richards came preaching in the summer of 1837 and gave Elizabeth a copy of the Book of Mormon. She read it attentively, and "The Spirit of God rested on me and I felt convinced to say in my heart 'This is the way I long have sought and mourned because I found it not' " (in Barlow 1968, 141). She and Nancy were baptized by Parley P. Pratt in September 1837. At first, John Haven greatly opposed his children's interest in the new religion. However, he was impressed that his nephew Brigham Young could look him in the face and say he was a Mormon. John Haven explained this at a family meeting in Nauvoo, January 8, 1845:

> . . . I found that he had the courage to say that he was [a Mormon]—I wanted to know what they said and then I took the Bible to see if it was true—I found they were the only sect that kept to the Bible in all its purity (in Arrington 1985, 55).

Before Elizabeth left Massachusetts in May 1838 to join the Latter-day Saints in Far West, Missouri, she bore a strong testimony to her father of the true and everlasting gospel of Christ and told him he would be convinced. She was right. John and Judith were baptized later that year. In the spring of 1841, John sold the farm he had lived on for over sixty years and took Judith, Maria, and Eliza to Nauvoo. Maria had not been converted and she did not want to leave her friends in Holliston. However, she was only fifteen, and her mother told her she had to leave, but could return when she was eighteen if she still wanted to. After she got to Nauvoo and heard the prophet Joseph Smith speak, she was converted (Raybould 1978). Maria and Eliza were baptized on May 2, 1842, by Brigham Young (R. T. Burton n.d.^{c}).

John Haven purchased a lot from his son-in-law, Israel Barlow, Sr., who had married Elizabeth on February 23, 1840. The lot was three-fourths of a mile east of the temple on Mulholland Street. The Havens and Barlows were neighbors in Nauvoo and later in Salt Lake City. On an 1844 Nauvoo valuation report by assessor Jonathan Hale, John Haven is listed as owning "Lot 70 B2 value [$]200" (in Barlow 1968, 186). Judith trained her daughters to weave straw hats, and they sold hats to customers from their home (Raybould 1978).

John Haven and his family participated in one of the first family meetings in the LDS Church. The Young, Richards, and Haven families met in the Seventies Hall on January 8, 1845. Phinehas Richards presided and John Haven spoke on the "History and Character of Their Ancestors." Although he was a relative by marriage, he spoke with authority about Phinehas Howe and Susannah Goddard, the common ancestors of the Youngs, the Richards, and his own children (Barlow 1968, 210-11).

Maria Susan Haven and Robert Taylor Burton were married on December 18, 1845, by Brigham Young in a ceremony at her father's home. She was nineteen years old. (They were sealed by Brigham Young in the Endowment House on March 18, 1856). Robert and Maria left Nauvoo in February, 1846; John, Judith, and Eliza Haven followed in May; and they were reunited at Mt. Pisgah in June. The Havens lived with the Burtons in Missouri from August 1846 to May 1848, and they crossed the plains in the same company arriving in Salt Lake City in September 1848. John Haven and Robert T. Burton built a log cabin in the South Fort in which the Havens lived during their first winter in Salt Lake City (Westover 1918, 2).

John Haven was assigned Lot 6 in Block 36, which is on Fifth South, one lot east of Second East. The corner lot (#5) was assigned to Israel Barlow, Sr. In the spring of 1849, Robert helped the Havens move their cabin from the fort to this lot (Westover 1918, 2). On January 18, 1852, Brigham Young visited John and Judith Haven and sealed John to his wives. John Haven and Elizabeth Howe were sealed first with Judith acting as proxy. Then, Judith was sealed to John (Barlow 1968, 277). He died March 16, 1853, at the age of seventy-nine.

Judith T. Haven lived to be ninety-two. In 1881, Maria described her to her great-granddaughters: "Your great-grandmother is living now, 82 years old last December 18, a remarkable bright, active woman, does all her own work, has a very pretty flower garden which she attends to herself" (M. Burton to her granddaughters 1881, 1).

Eliza Ann Haven married Charles Westover in Salt Lake City on October 14, 1848. They moved to southern Utah, living at St. George, Pinto, and finally Washington. They were parents of eleven children. Charles and Eliza are in the photographs on pages 139 and 140, and a photograph of Maria and Eliza with their aged mother is on page 129.

Maria, who was small of stature with very fine facial features, dark eyes, and brunette hair, was photographed with Robert and their children Theresa and William about 1851 and with seven of her children about 1869. (See pp. 117 and 126.)

Robert and Maria settled on a lot at the corner of First South and Second West on August 16, 1849. They lived in their wagon while working together to build an adobe home. That home was replaced in 1878 by Haven Villa, in which Maria lived until about 1910. After a family reunion in 1904, the *Deseret News* reported:

> Mrs. Burton is only a few years younger than her husband and yet she still enjoys the wonderful health that was "bred in the bone" of the plains people, who spent their young years overcoming the western desert. She sat in perfect comfort last night, beside her husband. . . . "It seems good," she said "to think back over our long lives in the light of the comforts around us now. . . . We came west across the plains together with the Saints, and arrived in this valley Sept. 23, 1848. We moved on this lot the next spring and I guess we are now the only family who still live on the original holdings taken by all of those who came in the first year of the emigration" (October 27, 1904).

Maria did beautiful sewing and knitting. She writes in her diary in the 1880s of having a seamstress come to help her, but for many years she did all the family's sewing. She also believed it important to teach her daughters and granddaughters to sew. Helen Raybould, William's youngest daughter, remembers "Grandma thought that we should learn to sew and she had a sewing class every Thursday afternoon and we went. First we made patch-work doll quilts and then we learned other stitches." Maria invited Sarah's and Susan's granddaughters as well as her own, so there would be quite a group of cousins for these classes. Helen also recalls Maria gathering the children together

on the back porch to watch her make candles, soap, and dough-
nuts:

> This was after electricity. She wanted us to know how these things
> were done. We also quilted and learned to knit, but I'm sorry I
> never did learn to knit as grandma did. She did beautiful fine knit-
> ting, little sweaters for babies that were beautiful pieces. When I
> used to come and sit with grandma in the evening and listen to her
> stories, she nearly always said, "Now I want you to have a pair of
> these baby booties," and when she died I had sixteen pair of booties
> that she had given to me (Raybould 1978).

After Robert's death in 1907, William's daughter Eloise lived
with her grandmother Maria in Haven Villa until about 1910.
When her daughter and son-in-law, Florence and Edwin Wilcox,
built a new home at 531 Third Avenue right next door to her
son Heber, Maria agreed to live with Florence if William and
his family would also moved to the avenues, which they did.
She lived there until her death, March 30, 1920, just a few days
before her ninety-fourth birthday.

Robert and Maria were parents of ten children, all of them
born in Salt Lake City except the first daughter:

1. *Theresa Hannah Burton* was born March 26, 1848, in
Austen Township, Atchison County Missouri, a few miles south
of Hamburg, Iowa. She married Lewis Samuel Hills on October 17, 1866. They were the parents of six children: Lewis Burton,
Maria Theresa, Edgar Samuel, Eugene Temple, Herbert Thayer,
and Harold Haven. She died April 9, 1924.

2. *William Shipley Burton* was born September 27, 1850.
He married Julia Maria Horne on March 6, 1872. She died in
childbirth on November 26, 1872, and their infant daughter,
Julia, died October 24, 1873. He married Eloise Crismon on
June 11, 1879. They were parents of nine children: Evadna,
Leone, Theresa, Eloise, Vernico, Florence, Ralph Shipley, Helen
Crismon, and George Crismon. He died November 8, 1931.

3. *Robert Taylor Burton Jr.* was born March 20, 1853. He
married Rosalia Maria Salisbury on April 21, 1873. They were
parents of ten children: Robert Taylor III, John Franklin, Ray
Shipley, Don Carlos, Ivie Rosalia, Theresa Louisa, Mary

Salisbury, Charles LaFayette, Clara Salisbury, and Fredrick Holder. He died January 10, 1926.

4. *Charles Samuel Burton* was born May 18, 1855. He married Julia Young on May 7, 1878. She died in England, November 29, 1889. He married Josephine Young Beatie on June 1, 1893. They were parents of three children: Richard Wells, Julian Young, and Josephine Lou. He died December 19, 1923.

5. *John Haven Burton* was born May 28, 1857. He married Kathleen or Katherine (Kate) Ferguson on January 10, 1883. They were parents of two children: Charles Haven and Phyllis Hardy. He was killed May 29, 1887 (see Chapter 19).

6. *LaFayette Grant Burton* was born January 22, 1860. He married Ella Mitchell on October 17, 1888. They were parents of two children: Margaret Mitchell and Clarence Mitchell. He died on July 28, 1934.

7. *Albert Temple Burton* was born January 29, 1862, and died as an infant, August 31, 1863.

8. *Florence May Burton* was born May 9, 1864. She married Edwin E. Wilcox on June 6, 1895. They were parents of three children, all who died in infancy: Mildred Burton, Donald, and Edwin Burton. She died March 20, 1944.

9. *Mary Amelia Burton* was born August 11, 1866. She married Ezra T. Stevenson on June 22, 1893. They were parents of a son, Edward Burton, who died at birth. Mary died July 26, 1897. Ezra married Rhoda Richards in 1901 and they were parents of five children: Mary, Ralph, Ezra, Rhoda, and Amelia.

10. *Heber Kimball Burton* was born January 7, 1871. He married Clara Louisa Herman on August 7, 1895. They were parents of three children: Maud, Inez May, and Herman Wilcox. He died September 15, 1949.

Maria kept a daily journal from 1875 to 1919. It is not introspective, but does record the activities of her household and her family members. During these years, Maria often had boarders living in her home. She gave them board and room in exchange for cash which helped meet household expenses or their help with chores. The boarders were usually cousins or friends of the family from northern or southern Utah, such as

Hyrum A. Campbell from Cache Valley who lived there in 1884-85 while attending the University of Deseret. Hyrum shared a room with Abe Knowlton through the winter; he later married Caroline Garr, Sarah's niece (Campbell 1954, 1, 9). Will White, a nephew from Beaver, and nieces Eliza and Hattie Westover from St. George also lived at Haven Villa (Raybould 1978) as did Sarah's son Lyman while he worked at Deseret National Bank in the early 1890s (A. Cutler 1976, 189).

Maria's journals reveal many acts of service performed for family, friends, and neighbors for over forty years. The original has been donated to the LDS Historical Department Archives where it can be read by interested family members and scholars.

Maria is remembered as a wonderful woman of great strength and character who was a true matriarch in keeping the three families close together. She quietly and contentedly served within her sphere of influence, but her husband always came first (M. Cram to the author, December 29, 1987).

In 1881, Maria wrote a letter to two of her granddaughters, Maria Hills and Evadna Burton which was placed in a box with those of other Relief Society sisters and sealed for fifty years. That letter concludes with the "prayer" of a faithful woman for her posterity:

> My dear granddaughters, when you open this, I hope it will find you happy wives, and mothers, yes, grandmothers, faithful women in God's work, for that is the desire of my heart, that my posterity may be good and faithful, and have a part in the First Resurrection.
>
> Is the prayer of your grandmother.
>
> Maria S. Burton

Appendix C
Sarah Anna Garr Burton

Sarah Anna Garr was born September 24, 1838, in Richmond, Wayne County, Indiana. Her parents were Fielding Garr (originally *Gaar*) (1794-1855) and Paulina Turner (1805-44). Fielding was a veteran of the War of 1812 and a land owner in Wayne County, having purchased eighty acres in 1821 from his father, Abraham Gaar, who was one of Wayne County's first settlers (G. Garr n.d., 1)

Sarah was the ninth of eleven children and fourth of five daughters. Her brothers were Richard Rue, John Turner, Abraham (died in infancy), William Henry, Abel Weaver, and Benjamin Franklin. Her sisters were Eliza Jane, Nancy, Caroline Martin, and Mary Virginia. Her oldest sister, Eliza Jane, was married to James Davidson in 1839 and did not move west with the pioneers.

In 1840, Paulina was baptized into The Church of Jesus Christ of Latter-day Saints, followed in early 1842 by her husband Fielding. In April 1842, they sold their land in Indiana for $1500 and moved to Hancock County, Illinois (G. Garr n.d., 2). They purchased a 186-acre farm about twenty miles east of Nauvoo from Stephen and Sarah Munn for $500 on July 6, 1842, and later sold it for $500 to Lewis Long on February 9, 1846, as the Saints were being driven from Illinois (Deed Books, Book L, 288-89 and Book O, 417, Hancock County Courthouse, Carthage, Illinois).

There were both happy occasions and tragedies during nearly four years in Hancock County where the Garrs lived only two miles northwest of the Mormon community of Ramus. Sarah's youngest brother, Benjamin Franklin, was born on the farm, May 21, 1843. He was just 18 months old when his mother, Paulina Turner Garr, died in November of 1844 (J. Garr 1894, 578-79). On her deathbed, Fielding promised Paulina to keep the children in the Church. Twenty-year-old Richard Rue, the oldest son, died the following year on September 29, 1845, of consumption ("Early Church" 1938, 143).[1]

Fielding Garr brought his family across the plains during the summer of 1847. Nancy Garr had married Rodney Badger on March 9, 1845, and their first child Nancy Marie was born February 27, 1846. Rodney went west with the pioneer company under Brigham Young in April from Winter Quarters. Fielding Garr, with Nancy, her daughter Nancy Marie, and his other seven children, ages twenty to four, left Winter Quarters about May 1, and were organized into Jedediah M. Grant's company. They were the last company of westward bound Saints in 1847, and met Brigham Young's party returning to Winter Quarters September 9 on the Sweetwater River. It had already snowed once, and while they were camped together, fifty head of horses were stolen by Indians in the night. The loss materially weakened both companies (CHC 3:298). Sarah, who walked most of the thousand miles, celebrated her ninth birthday on September 24, two and a half weeks before they reached the valley on October 10.

The Garrs spent the first winter in the pioneer fort where the children found that the hardships of that winter were worse than those endured on the plains. The hastily built mud and log huts in the fort had flat roofs which leaked badly. Food was very scarce and they ate thistle and sego roots. However, it was the story of making and eating cowhide soup that Sarah repeated to her children and grandchildren years later. Her father brought home the belly part of a cowhide, removed the hair, and then boiled it for hours until a "little more tender," and made the soup (W. Burton n.d.[a], 7). It is no wonder they were frantic when the crickets descended on their new fields of grain in May of 1848. Sarah helped drive the crickets into City Creek and rejoiced when the seagulls came and helped them save their crops (Campbell 1954, 3). Sarah was baptized on May 15, 1851, by Bishop Nathaniel V. Jones.

When lots were assigned, Fielding Garr and Rodney Badger received adjoining lots on the west side of Second West between South Temple and First South (Lots 7 and 8 in Block 79). Sarah said that in 1848 her father built the first adobe house erected in Salt Lake City outside the Old Fort (W. Burton n.d.[a], 7). However, Fielding Garr did not live in it very long. He moved in 1849 to Antelope Island in the Great Salt Lake where he was hired by Captain Howard Stansbury to take care of his stock near a small supply depot on the island. Fielding took his horses and his own herd of cattle with him, and also became caretaker of the Church's livestock as well as the personal herds of Brigham Young and Heber C. Kimball. Antelope Island was a natural herd ground, needing no fences, quite safe from raiding Indians, and accessible by a shallow ford. There were 31 fresh water springs and an abundance of good grass.[2]

In 1849, Fielding Garr began constructing a home out of materials found on the island. It's thick adobe brick walls enclose five rooms, three with fireplaces. Although Fielding Garr died in 1855, the ranch house was used for 130 years and was the oldest continually occupied structure in Utah in 1981 when the state purchased the ranch and the island became a state park (Pederson 1977, C1). (A recent photograph is on p. 119.) Fielding Garr raised his children on the island from 1849-55; his sons became dependable herdsmen and his daughters learned to milk, make butter, cook, and run a household.

Before Fielding's death, his son-in-law, Rodney Badger, drowned in the Weber River April 29, 1853, while trying to save a woman and her six children (Wadley 1976, 8W). Only twenty-nine years old, he left Nancy with four small children to raise.

Fielding Garr died June 15, 1855, on Antelope Island and was likely buried there. His son, Abel, in a biographical sketch for *The Garr Genealogy* (J. Garr 1894, 578-79), wrote this tribute:

> Fielding Garr was of an excellent disposition, and was a lover of society. At this time—a very early day in Utah—the young people were always around where he was. Young boys were more taken up with his society than they were with those of their own age. He always took delight in instructing the young. He was a very robust, large, square-framed man, weighing 225 pounds, with a mild, open

countenance. He had a very mild, fascinating voice—nothing gruff or uncouth. He was one that was never in trouble. He never borrowed trouble, never had a lawsuit, and never was sued. He always had friends and plenty of them, and always took a liking in entertaining them. . . .

At the time of his death, Fielding Garr was sixty-one years of age. He was a good neighbor, and a kind, loving, and affectionate father.

After their father's death, Sarah, Caroline, and Mary Garr went to live with Nancy and her children on Second West in Salt Lake City. On October 9, 1857, Caroline became the plural wife of Nathaniel V. Jones. After Jones's death, she married John Reed Jamison, on December 22, 1869. Mary married Nathaniel Ashby on February 13, 1858. On December 14, 1858, Nancy Garr Badger became the plural wife of Briant Stringham. He had been associated with her brothers, John, Willaim, Abel, and Benjamin, in opening Cache Valley for ranching in July and August 1855. The Garr boys worked on the Elk Horn Ranch, but later moved into Millville in 1860 and were prominent in Cache Valley for many years (J. Garr 1894, 259–60; Campbell 1954, 4–8).

Sarah was seventeen years old when she became the second wife of Robert Taylor Burton on February 7, 1856. A photograph of her in her wedding dress showing her dark hair and eyes is on page 119. Their marriage was sealed by Brigham Young in the Endowment House on March 18, 1856. She lived in downtown Salt Lake in Maria and Robert's home for eight years. Robert and his older sons built a house on the farm during 1868 and Sarah with her five sons and a daughter moved there in the spring of 1869. Sarah is shown in a photograph from this time period on page 124. Maria and Sarah had a very close relationship, and Maria often came to the farm to visit or to help with the delivery of Sarah's children or when someone was sick.

A large brick home was built on the farm in 1889 (see Chapter 18). Family gatherings were often held on the farm, especially in the summer when the families could picnic in the shady grove north of the house. The farm home was landscaped by Maxwell the florist and had a deep circular drive from State Street lined with trees, a grove on the north, and an orchard on the south (J. Burton, December 21, 1987).

The farm was important in supporting Robert's families and Sarah worked as hard at her responsibilities as the men and boys did. Her youngest daughter Virginia wrote of her mother and life on the farm:

> The largest herd of cows must have been kept when Ed and Theodore were growing up. At that time the milk was sold to a dairy but at other times mother made butter. At one time she took a prize of $25.00 for the best 25 pounds of home made butter at the State Fair. . . . When I think back on those days, I wonder how mother was able to do all she did. Until after she had six children, all the sewing was done by hand. All the stockings were hand knit. After going to the farm to live she took care of the chickens and milk and made butter for herself and she used to furnish butter and eggs to the other two families as well. . . .
>
> I had to wash dishes, scour the knives (unpolished steel) with brick dust. My mother never let us [girls] learn how to milk cows because she had to milk cows on Antelope Island while the men folk stayed in the house and she was determined that her daughters would not ever milk cows. . . . One of the hardest tasks at this period of time was to take mother's butter and eggs and sometimes dressed chickens to her customers on Saturday. For this purpose I had to drive a horse hitched to a buggy. I dreaded Saturday to come.
>
> Instead of this attitude I should have been proud to do this when my mother worked so hard to earn something to assist in supplying our needs in the home (in A. Cutler 1976, 186-87).

Several years after Robert's death, a smaller brick home was built for Sarah and her unmarried daughter Ada, north and east of the large farm home, next to Hardy Burton's house on State Street. Many of the grandchildren and great-grandchildren recall visits to see Sarah at her home on Sunday afternoon. Her grandson Jacob recalls doing chores for Sarah about 1905-15: "As a child I cut the lawn, cleaned the chicken coops, milked the cows, and worked many days with Grandma in the barnyard and orchard as a 'little dandy boy.' Always with Grandma. She had a horse named Dexter and a dump cart

12

to haul garbage, leaves, trash, straw for the coops, etc. Grandma never, never spoke cross to me. She always paid well" (J. Burton, December 21, 1987).

Robert and Sarah were parents of twelve children, all of them born in Salt Lake City.

1. *Henry Fielding Burton* was born February 21, 1858. He married Anna Eliza Gibby on January 11, 1883. They were parents of twelve children: Henry Fielding Jr., Alice Maria, Anna Gibby, Julia, Grover Garr, Harvey Leon, Roberta, Edna, Shipley Davis, Mildred, Louise, and Sarah Anna. He died February 16, 1920.

2. *Franklin Garr Burton* was born January 19, 1860. He was ordained an Elder October 17, 1876, and received his endowments October 20, 1876, at the very young age of sixteen. He died eighteen months later on April 30, 1878. He was unmarried.

3. *Alfred Jones Burton* was born March 21, 1862. He married Elizabeth L. Peart on October 17, 1888. They were the parents of nine children: Sarah Laurette, Franklin Lebron, Margaret Gray, Clifford Peart, Marelda, Jacob Peart, Fielding Garr, Lloyd Taylor, and Ruth. He died May 9, 1928.

4. *Alice Maria Burton* was born April 23, 1864. She died as a child of six on August 21, 1870.

5. *Lyman Wells Burton* was born August 14, 1866. He married Ella C. Comings on June 17, 1903. They were parents of five children: Melvin Comings, Dorothy Comings, Linda Comings, Edith Comings, and Clara Comings. He died February 20, 1915.

6. *Elbert Turner Burton* was born December 19, 1868. He married Ida Larson on September 17, 1902. They were parents of six children: Elbert Neil, Lillian, Raymond Toyn, Wallace Larson, Roy, and Roma. He died November 16, 1934.

7. *Edward Leon Burton* was born June 24, 1871. He married Isabella Armstrong on March 26, 1896. They were parents of six children: Isabella Armstrong, Sarah, Leah, Edward Leon Jr., Frances Armstrong, and Robert Harold. He died January 17, 1953.

8. *Theodore Taylor Burton* was born January 21, 1873. He married Florence Moyle on November 15, 1899. They were parents of three sons: Theodore Moyle, Wilford Moyle, and Kenneth Moyle. He died September 8, 1937.

9. *Ada May Burton* was born April 23, 1876. She did not marry, but devoted her life to her parents and family. She assisted her father in the completion of his journal and biography and took care of her mother until her death in 1927. Ada died December 15, 1961.

10. *Virginia Louise Burton* was born December 2, 1878. She married Ralph Cutler on September 24, 1902. They were parents of eight children: Ralph Garr, Douglas Burton, Geneve, Lenore, Roberta, Louise, Alice May, and Ivan Burton. She died June 8, 1970.

11. *Austin Garr Burton* was born November 26, 1881. He married Leonora McMillan on December 21, 1904. They were parents of eight children: Austin McMillan, Leon McMillan, Lawrence Neil, Ellis McMillan, Janet, Paul Garr, Anna, and Virginia. He died November 16, 1940.

12. *Hardy Garr Burton* was born July 11, 1884. He married Florence Self on October 9, 1907. They were the parents of three children: Sylvia, Herbert Self, and Lyman Self. He died March 26, 1941.

Sarah died at home at the age of seventy-eight after a long illness on April 20, 1927. On April 21, the *Deseret News* wrote: "Mrs. Burton was one of the early pioneers of 1847 and lived in the first house built outside of the Old Fort. . . . She also had the distinction of living in Utah for 80 years without having once crossed over the state line during that time. . . . She was the mother of 12 children and devoted her life to their upbringing, but finding time to devote to Church duties." She was survived by eight living children, fifty-seven grandchildren, and forty-seven great-grandchildren. The Salt Lake City Commission, of which her son T. T. Burton was a member, passed a resolution stating in part, "Be it resolved that the board does express appreciation of the noble character and long service to humanity of Mrs. Sarah Ann Garr Burton, who was a pioneer and builder in this community."

Notes

1. The location of graves for Paulina and Richard has been attempted by family members visiting in Nauvoo. In the old Pioneer Cemetery, two miles east of Nauvoo, Theodore C. Walker, a great-grandson of Sarah Garr Burton, discovered a gravestone marked, "P.G. 40 years old." This could be Paulina Garr's grave.

2. The history of Antelope Island is the subject of Barbara Jacobs, "The Lure of Antelope Island," *Improvement Era* 67 (July 1964) 584-86, 602; and *East of Antelope Island* by the Davis County Daughter of Utah Pioneers.

Appendix D

Susan Ellen McBride Burton

Susan Ellen McBride was born in Waynesville, Warren County, Ohio, on July 29, 1836, the third daughter of William McBride (1807-95) and Elizabeth Harris Ball Boram (or Booram) (1812-98). They had seven daughters and two sons; five children lived to adulthood.

William and Elizabeth McBride were early converts to the Church in Ohio and were both acquainted with the Prophet Joseph Smith when they moved to Nauvoo (Stohl 1987, 1). William was baptized October 1, 1842, by Henry Elliott (Patriarch Information, Member Services, Historical Department Library). Susan was baptized at the age of eight in July 1844 by Milton Peck (R. Burton n.d.ᶜ). The McBrides moved to Nauvoo in 1845, and William and Elizabeth were sealed in the Nauvoo Temple on January 24, 1846. William left Nauvoo shortly thereafter in the vanguard of the exodus. Returning later in the summer to get his family, he helped defend Nauvoo at the last battle with the "mob-posse" of Thomas Brockman before leaving with his family (*Deseret News*, March 13, 1895, 6).

On July 9, 1848, William and Elizabeth McBride and four children were organized into Willard Richards's company for crossing the plains. William McBride was one of the captains of ten under Franklin D. Richards, captain of hundred, according to Robert Campbell, company historian (JH, July 9, 1848, 1). The wagon train included a large group of Mississippi Saints and there were a total of 502 whites and 24 Negroes (JH, July 9, 1848, 2). Susan McBride celebrated her twelfth birthday as she walked to the Salt Lake valley. The company left the Elkhorn River on July 10 and arrived in the Great Salt Lake City on October 19, 1848.

The McBrides lived first in the Old Fort with all the other pioneers. Susan's mother, after arriving at the fort, took the wagon cover that sheltered them while crossing the plains and made dresses for her daughters, Susan and Rebecca. William

McBride was assigned Lot 7 in Block 96 on First North between First and Second West where he built his home and a blacksmith shop, reportedly the first in the valley. In June 1850, the *Deseret News* contained his advertisement:

> BLACK SMITHING. EMIGRANTS LOOK HERE. Horses & Oxen-Shod on the shortest notice, and all kind of work in my line, Prices reasonable. MY SHOP Is in the 17th ward, a little west of the Council House, and a few rods west of Messrs Livingston and Kinkade's store. ALL MY FRIENDS Who want blacksmithing, can be accommodated, on the shortest notice and on reasonable terms. Wm. McBRIDE.

At a conference of elders on August 28 and 29, 1852, William McBride was appointed to serve a mission in the Sandwich Isles (now Hawaii) with eight other elders: Benjamin F. Johnson, Ephraim Green, Thomas Kairnes, James Lawson, Reddick N. Allred, Reddin A. Allred, Edgerton Snyder, and Nathan Tanner (JH, August 18, 1852, 5). William McBride described their trip from Salt Lake City to Honolulu:

> We started from Salt Lake City, October 22, 1852. We went to San Bernardino, thence to San Pedro and on board the brig "Freemont", under Captain Hastings, sailed to San Francisco, where we rented a room and stayed until we obtained sufficient means to pay our passage. . . .
>
> It was decided by the brethren that Brother B. F. Johnson and I should go down to the shipping and secure a passage for the Sandwich Islands Mission. We found James S. Lambert, captain and owner of the ship "Huntress" bound for the Islands. With him we engaged our passage with first class fare. While in San Francisco I was called into the office of Samuel Brannon. He asked me where I was going and what was my business, etc. I replied—"On the same business you were upon the first time I ever saw you, and under similar circumstances." . . . I told him that we should go as soon as we had sufficient means to defray our expenses. He said, "You need not trouble about means, I will pay your passage and fill your trunk with clothing to suit the climate, and put it aboard the ship "Huntress" in care of Captain Lambert."
>
> When we left, I called to bid him farewell, and he gave me a fine seven dollar hat, a fifty dollar gold piece and a certificate for my trunk (W. McBride n.d., 6)).

During their voyage on the "Huntress," the missionaries were favorably treated by the captain, fed at his table, and permitted to preach and sing Mormon hymns.

They arrived in Honolulu February 17, 1853. William was sent to labor on the island of Maui where George Q. Cannon was engaged in translating the *Book of Mormon* into the Hawaiian language (JH, October 13, 1852 and March 9, 1853). William wrote in his journal:

> At a conference in the fall of 1863 . . . the question came up relative to publishing the Book of Mormon in the Hawaiian language. Whether to have 5,000 copies printed, or purchase a press, type, paper and ink, and do the work ourselves as we had printers of our own,—was the subject of discussion.
>
> It was decided that we purchase the materials and print the books ourselves. The money was raised by subscription and loan, and I was appointed to go to San Francisco and make the purchase. My trunk was packed and put on board the brig "De Jonival", but I had not a dollar to pay my passage. I told the brethren to exercise all the faith they could, and I called on Cody and Co., ship agents of the line, and asked them to take my note of hand, payable in San Francisco, and give me a certificate, which they did, although they were no friends of ours (W. McBride n.d., 8).

On board the "De Jonival," William found that all the berths were taken. The captain allowed him to sleep on a lounge in the after cabin until a man named Perkins, an agent of the whaling fleet, found out he was a Mormon and objected to his presence in the lounge. Thereafter he slept in the steerage on sacks of grain. William continued:

> The first night after my bed was moved a heavy storm arose, and drove us off our course to the north. The weather turned very cold, raining, hailing, and blowing a hurricane.
>
> After the storm slacked a little, I came out of the hatchway and sat on the side, holding on while the ship tumbled from side to side amid the waves. Mr. Perkins called out, "Look at that d——d 'Mormon', he has not sense enough to be frightened."
>
> Then the first mate came, and . . . said, "Mr. McBride, did you not enter for San Francisco? What would you think if we should land you among the rocks of Oregon?"

> I replied: "It makes but little difference with me, only so I land among the human family—my mission is to all the world."
>
> Soon after, the captain came beside me. . . . At this time the storm had increased to a heavy gale, and the captain, throwing himself suddenly into his seat in the cabin exclaimed: "I can do nothing more!"
>
> I said to him: "We shall all go into San Francisco and not a hair of our heads shall be lost, but we shall have to be helped in" (W. McBride n.d., 8-9).

When the storm ceased, the ship was 400 miles north of its course, but the crew set the sails and the voyage continued without incident until they were in sight of San Francisco.

> At this point the indomitable Perkins imagined anchorage already secure, and exultingly said: "We are going in without help and that "Mormon" has told one d——d lie."
>
> Before we came to the mouth of the gate, however, a strong wind arose and drove us back. The captain signalled for a tug—we were drifting toward the rocks, but the tug hooked us just in time to save us (W. McBride n.d., 9).

William could not purchase an suitable printing press in San Francisco and had to order one shipped from the East Coast. He stayed in the San Francisco-San Jose area as a missionary until the spring of 1855. Parley P. Pratt was presiding over the San Francisco Conference at this time and William served with him. His journal, describing his labors in California and his return to Salt Lake as captain of the spring emigration from the San Francisco Conference, records a great many spiritual experiences while serving with Apostle Pratt (W. McBride 1854-55).

William McBride entered into polygamy February 7, 1856, when he married Helen Jeanette Murray Cushing, widow of his neighbor Hosea Cushing. They had one child, Lucretia. He was also sealed in the 1870s to Majory Stiles, Sarah Ann Shepherd, Regina Maria Hudson, and Mary Grace Booty. During 1856, he moved to Grantsville, Tooele County, but left there during the exodus south when the Utah Expedition was entering Salt Lake City. He located in Santaquin and remained there through the 1860s where he served as bishop (*Deseret News*, March 13,

1895, 13), agent for the Deseret Manufacturing and Agricultural Society (JH, August 27, 1862, 1; August 8, 1864, 1), and major in the Nauvoo Legion (JH, July 4, 1867, 7).

William and Elizabeth moved to Richfield before 1871 where Robert visited them a number of times during his travels. William was ordained a patriarch by Brigham Young on July 26, 1875, and served as Richfield Stake patriarch. About 1880, he and his wife moved to Pima, Arizona, with their son James Andrew McBride and his family; William served as St. Joseph Stake patriarch. In October 1890, William and Elizabeth were persuaded to return to Salt Lake because of William's failing health. Susan took care of her parents in her home on Second West until their deaths.

William McBride died March 8, 1895. Robert recorded in his journal details of William's funeral and burial: "Sun [March] 10 . . . At 12-15 we assembled at Susans & conveyed the remains of her Father Patriarch McBride to the 15th Ward Assembly Room where his funeral is held. Comforting remarks was made by A. M. Musser, C. W. Penrose & myself and at 2 P.M. we repaired to the Cemetary and deposited the mortal remains of Father McBride on my old Cemetary lot near the graves of Wm Burton and N. V. Jones. At the ripe old age of 88, he and his wife have lived hapily together 64 years."

Elizabeth Boram McBride died at Susan's home on October 1, 1898. Her funeral was also held in the 15th Ward with Charles W. Penrose as speaker. She was buried at her husband's side in the Salt Lake Cemetery (R. T. Burton 1856-1907, October 1-4, 1898).

Susan Ellen McBride was betrothed to Hosea Cushing whose home was across the street from her parents, but he unexpectedly died on May 6, 1854. In 1856, when Brigham Young approved Robert's plural marriage to Sarah, he asked him to take Susan as his third wife. Robert and Susan were married at her father's home February 7, 1857. Temple Index Bureau records indicate that same day Susan was sealed to Hosea Cushing and her father was married for time to Hosea's widow, Helen Jeanette Murray Cushing (Stohl 1987, 1).

For a few years, all Robert's wives and children shared the adobe home on the corner of First South and Second West. However, in the early 1860s, Robert built a two-story adobe home for Susan and her young family on Second South just west of Second West (C. Burton 1953). Robert eventually owned most of the east half of this block and had his barns and garden between the two homes. A new home was built for Susan on Second West which she occupied on January 2, 1878. In this home, called "the redwood house" by family members, she took care of many people. Her daughter-in-law, Mary Jane (Mollie), lived with her while Willard served a mission in North Carolina the first two years of their marriage. George, who never married, lived with Susan during the 1890s and early 1900s.

Susan's photograph is reproduced is on page 131. She and her mother are in the photograph on page 139 taken at the 1891 Burton Family Association meeting.

Susan lived in the redwood house until shortly after Robert's death in November 1907. The night before his funeral, fire destroyed the Redman Van & Storage warehouse and barns west of Susan's house. The sounds of horses screaming as they burned and the fear of the fire spreading to the Burton buildings were terrifying to the family members and soon after Susan suffered a general nervous breakdown. She did not return to live in her house, but moved to a home at 611 East Ninth South where she died July 24, 1911, five days before her seventy-fifth birthday. Her funeral was held in the Fourteenth Ward and she was buried in the Burton Section of the Salt Lake Cemetery.

She and Robert T. Burton were parents to four sons and a daughter, all born in Salt Lake City:

1. *Willard Cushing Burton* was born December 1, 1856. He married Mary Jane Gardner on January 6, 1881. They were the parents of seven children: Willard Gardner, Carl Cushing, Arthur Taylor, Earl Gardner, Hazel Gardner, Alma Gardner, and Mabel Gardner. He died June 12, 1949.

2. *Hosea McBride Burton* was born October 7, 1858. He married Annie Moore on December 20, 1899. They had no children and were later divorced. His nephew, Carl Burton,

remembered him: "I also recall Hosea Burton who organized and operated a small circus known as the Dom Bartholemew Circus. Hosea was a trapeze artist and a real showman. I recall enjoying going to the circus with my grandmother and Aunt Lizzie" (1969, 14) He died in December 1920.

3. *George Washington Burton* was born September 29, 1860 and died September 24, 1916. He never married. He was a mining engineer who worked in Tintic and Park City.

4. *Walter James Burton* was born February 15, 1865. He married Lucy Ellen Brown, October 16, 1890. They were the parents of four children: Lucile, Walter Brown, Sarah, and Rebecca. He died August 2, 1943.

5. *Sarah Elizabeth (Lizzie) Burton* was born February 29, 1869. She married Robert Alfred Fenton on February 15, 1893. They were parents of five children: Robert Alfred Jr., Harris, Lee Combs, Ellen Clarissa, and Burton Thomas. She died November 2, 1958.

At the time of Susan's death, the *Deseret News* reported: "Mrs. Burton was a prominent and active worker in Church circles for many years and only retired from active service when compelled to by ill health. She had a wide acquaintance and many friends who will mourn her loss. . . . Because of her many sterling attributes of character, Mrs. Burton was loved, honored and respected by all who associated with her. At all times, she was a consistent believer in the principles of the Church, which she had adopted in early days" (July 25, 1911).

Notes

1. Hosea Cushing was a member of the first pioneer company in 1847 and a stalwart member of the Church. His death in 1854 was attributed to consumption (Jenson 4:638).

Bibliography

Note: In quotations from original sources (journals, letters, etc.), the original spelling and capitalization has been kept; punctuation has been changed or added only to make the meaning more clear. Historical Department Archives, Historical Department Library, or Genealogical Library refer to those of The Church of Jesus Christ of Latter-day Saints, Salt Lake City, Utah. Utah State Archives and Utah State Historical Society are also in Salt Lake City.

Alexander, E. B., to officers in his regiment. October 8, 1857. House Exec. Doc. No. 71, U.S. Congress 35th, 1st Session, pp. 38-40.

Alexander, Thomas G. "Federal Authority Versus Polygamic Theocracy: James B. McKean and the Mormons 1870-75." *Dialogue* 1 (Autumn 1966): 85-100.

_____. *Mormonism in Transition: A History of the Latter-day Saints, 1890-1930*. Urbana: University of Illinois Press, 1986.

Anderson, C. LeRoy. *For Christ Will Come Tomorrow: The Saga of the Morrisites*. Logan: Utah State University Press, 1981.

Anderson, C. LeRoy, and Larry J. Halford. "The Mormons and the Morrisite War." *Montana: The Magazine of Western History* 24 (Autumn 1974): 42-53.

Arrington, Leonard J. "Utah's Coal Road in the Age of Unregulated Competition." *Utah Historical Quarterly* 23 (January 1955): 35-63.

_____. "Taxable Income in Utah, 1862-72." *Utah Historical Quarterly* 24 (January 1956): 21-47.

_____. *Great Basin Kingdom: An Economic History of the Latter-day Saints 1830-1900*. Cambridge, Mass.: Harvard University Press, 1958.

_____. *Charles C. Rich: Mormon General and Western Frontiersman*. Provo: BYU Press, 1974.

_____. *Brigham Young: American Moses*. New York: Alfred A. Knopf, 1985.

Barlow, Ora H. *The Israel Barlow Story and Mormon Mores*. The Israel Barlow Family Association, 1968.

Baskin, Robert N. *Reminiscences of Early Utah*. Salt Lake City, 1914.

Bean, George Washington. *Autobiography of George Washington Bean; A Utah Pioneer of 1847 and His Family Records*. Ed., Flora Diana Bean Horne. Salt Lake City: Utah Printing Co., 1945.

Biographical Record of Salt Lake City and Vicinity. Chicago: National Historical Record Co., 1902.

Brooks, Juanita, ed. *On the Mormon Frontier: The Diary of Hosea Stout. 1844-1861*. 2 vols. Salt Lake City: University of Utah Press/Utah State Historical Society, 1964.

Burton, Carl C., to Theodore M. Burton, November 9, 1953. Photocopy of typescript in my possession.

———. *Autobiography of Carl Cushing Burton and Ella Christopherson Burton.* Pamphlet. Salt Lake City: Carl C. Burton, 1969.

Burton Family Association. Minutes, 1885-1953. Holograph in Robert Taylor Burton Family Association Files. Photocopy in my possession.

Burton, Jacob P., to Janet B. Seegmiller, December 21, 1987.

Burton, Maria S. Untitled note, n.d. Photocopy of holograph in my possession.

———. "Memoranda," 1845-46. Photograph of holograph in my possession.

———. Diaries, 1875-1919. 43 vols. Holograph in Historical Department Archives.

———, to her granddaughters, Evadne Burton and Maria Hills, March 13, 1881. Photocopy of typescript in my possession.

Burton, Robert T.. Autobiography, n.d.[a] Holograph. Written by his children, William S. Burton and Ada M. Burton as Robert dictated from his notes. Location of original unknown. Photocopy of typescript, Historical Department Archives. Photocopy of holograph in my possession.

———. Notes on appointments. n.d.[b] Holograph in my possession.

———. "Family Record of Robert Taylor Burton," n.d.[c] Holograph in Robert Taylor Burton Family Association files. Photocopy in my possession.

———. Journal, 1843-69. Titled "Journal on his First Mission 1843 and other items of his History untill 1856" and "Robt T. Burton's Mission to the Eastern States 1869." Holograph. An unidentified transcriber, most probably Ada M. Burton, copied it by hand from the original. Location of original unknown. Photocopy of Ada's copy in my possession.

———, to Mariah [sic] S. Burton, January 3, 1847. Photocopy of typescript in my possession.

———. Diaries, 1856-1907. Holographs in Historical Department Archives. I have used a handwritten copy now in my possession made from the originals by Rebecca Burton Upham about 1975. Includes relief camp journal for the rescue of the handcart pioneers, October 7-November 30, 1856.

———, to Maria [S. Burton] and Family, June 28, 1858. Photocopy of holograph in my possession.

———, to Maria [S. Burton], November 3, 1865. Photocopy of holograph in my possession.

———, to Franklin D. Richards, June 10, 1866. Holograph in my possession. I received this letter anonymously during a Robert Taylor Burton Association meeting in October 1983; it had probably been kept in the Richards family for over 117 years.

———, to Daniel H. Wells, June 14 and July 7, 1866. Holographs in Utah State Archives; microfilm at Genealogical Society, items 884 and 897, reel 2, Nauvoo Legion Correspondence.

———, to Joseph F. Smith, February 8, 1875. JH, February 8, 1875, p. 2.

———, to Joseph F. Smith, March 31, 1875. JH, March 31, 1875, pp. 2-3.

———, to Heber K. Burton, April 21, 1875. Photocopy of holograph in my possession.

———, to Edward Hanham, June 8, 1875. JH, June 8, 1875, p. 2.

_____, to Joseph F. Smith, June 17, 1875. JH, June 17, 1875, p. 2.

_____, to Ada & Jeny [Ada M. and Virginia Burton], January 19, 1886. Holograph. Typescript copy in my possession.

_____, to Ada [M. Burton], April 19, 1886. Holograph. Typescript copy in my possession.

_____, to Geny [Virginia] and Austin [Burton], April 19, 1886. Holograph. Typescript copy in my possession.

_____, to Ada, Geny, and Austin [Burton], May 30, 1886. Holograph. Typescript copy in my possession.

_____, to Ada [M. Burton], April 18, 1889. Holograph. Typescript copy in my possession.

_____, to Theodore T. Burton, summer 1898. Photocopy of typescript in my possession.

_____. "Dates of the Ordination of Presiding Bishopric," March 5, 1900. Holograph in my possession.

_____. "Address of Bishop R. T. Burton, October 25, 1903." Photocopy of typescript in my possession.

_____. "Statement on Succession," July 28, 1905. Photocopy of typescript. Historical Department Archives.

_____, to Members of the Hand Cart Association, October 1, 1907. Letter. Photocopy of typescript in my possession.

Burton, Robert T., and William B. Pace, to Brigham Young, August 14, 1867. Holograph in Utah State Archives; microfilm of holograph at Genealogical Society, item 1035, reel 2, Nauvoo Legion Correspondence.

Burton, Samuel, to Anthony and Jane Leybourn, November 29, 1846. Original in Daughters of Utah Pioneers Library, Salt Lake City. Reprinted in Kate B. Carter, ed., *Heart Throbs of the West*. Salt Lake City: DUP, 5:387-89.

Burton, Samuel, and Hannah Burton, to Elijah and Sarah Austin, July 11, 1847. Carbon copy of typescript in my possession.

Burton, Sarah, to Robert T. Burton, February 5, 1842. Photocopy of typescript in my possession.

Burton, William. Autobiography, n.d. Holograph. Historical Department Archives.

_____. Papers, c1837-51. Holograph and typescript. Historical Department Archives.

_____. Diaries, 1839-51. Typescript. Historical Department Archives.

_____, to Robert T. Burton, July 2, 1847. Photocopy of typescript in my possession.

_____, to Elizabeth Burton, July 5, 1850. Carbon copy of typescript in my possession.

_____, to Anthony and Jane Leybourn, August 13, 1850. Carbon copy of typescript in my possession.

_____, to Elijah and Sarah Austin, October 22, 1850. Photocopy of typescript in my possession.

Burton, William and Elizabeth, to Elijah and Sarah Austin, February 26, 1847. Photocopy of typescript in my possession.

Burton, William S. "A Partial Record of the Family and decendants [sic] of Samuel Burton," n.d.[a] Holograph in files of Mildred B. Cram. Photocopy in my possession.

_____. "A Sketch of the Life of General Robert Taylor Burton," n.d.[b] Photocopy of typescript in my possession.

_____. "Some of the things or hapenings [sic] that I remember," n.d.[c] Holograph in files of Helen B. Raybold. Photocopy in my possession.

_____. "A Biographical Sketch and Some Things I Remember," 1931. Photocopy of typescript in my possession.

Bush, Lester E., Jr. "Brigham Young in Life and Death: A Medical Overview." *Journal of Mormon History* 5 (1978): 92-103.

Campbell, Robert, to Robert T. Burton. Letter of appointment to City Council of Great Salt Lake City, June 28, 1858. Holograph in my possession.

Campbell, Hyrum A. Interviewed by Theodore M. Burton, February 14, 1954. Transcript in my possession.

Canning, Ray R., and Beverly Beeton, eds. *The Genteel Gentile: Letters of Elizabeth Cumming, 1857-1858*. Salt Lake City: University of Utah Library, 1977.

Cannon, Donald Q., and David J. Whittaker, eds. *Supporting Saints: Life Stories of Nineteenth-Century Mormons*. Provo: Religious Studies Center, Brigham Young University, 1985.

Chamberlain, Ralph V. *The University of Utah, A History of Its First Hundred Years*. Salt Lake City: University of Utah, 1960.

CHC. B. H. Roberts, *A Comprehensive History of The Church of Jesus Christ of Latter-day Saints, Century I*. 6 vols. 1930; rpt.ed., Provo: BYU, 1965.

Clive, Clifford S. Story of his great-grandmother, [first name not known] Thompson, related orally to Janet B. Seegmiller, 1980.

Compiled Laws of the Territory of Utah. Salt Lake City: Printed by the Deseret News Steam Printing Establishment for the Territory of Utah, 1876.

Compiled Laws of Utah. Salt Lake City: Herbert Pembroke for the Territory of Utah, 1888.

Cornwall, Rebecca, and Leonard J. Arrington. *Rescue of the 1856 Handcart Companies*. Charles Redd Monographs in Western History No. 11. Provo: BYU Press, 1981.

Craig, Gerald M. *Upper Canada: The Formative Years 1784-1841*. London and New York: McClelland and Stewart Limited, 1963.

Cram, Mildred B., to Janet B. Seegmiller, December 29, 1987. Mildred is a daughter of Theresa Burton Brown, who kept many of the papers and letters of her father, William S. Burton.

Cutler, Alice May. *Ralph Cutler*. Ralph Cutler Family Association, 1976.

Cutler, Alice May, to Janet B. Seegmiller, November 13, 1977.

Cutler, Virginia Burton. Talk given at Robert Taylor Burton Family Reunion, October 21, 1955. Photocopy of typescript in my possession.

Deed, 1887. Robert T. Burton, Maria S. Burton to Wm. B. Preston, Presiding Bishop of the Church, and Robert T. Burton and John R. Winder

Counsellors, Recorded July 9, 1887, at 5 p.m. in Book "2F" of Deeds and Transfers, pages 188-90. Typescript. Historical Department Archives.

Dewey, Richard Lloyd. *Porter Rockwell: A Biography*. 3rd ed. New York: Paramount Books, 1986.

Eady, Ronald J. "Anti-American Sentiment in Essex County in the Wake of the Rebellions of 1837," *Ontario History* 61 (March 1969): 1-5.

"Early Church Vital Records, Cont." *Utah Genealogical and History Magazine* 29 (July 1938): 143.

"Eighty years ago . . . ," *Toledo Blade*, undated clipping, c1905. Photocopy of untitled and undated typescript in my possession.

Encyclopedia International. 20 vols. New York: Grolier Inc., 1966.

Fisher, Margaret. *Utah and the Civil War*. Salt Lake City: Deseret Book, 1929.

Flanders, Robert Bruce. *Nauvoo: Kingdom on the Mississippi*. Urbana: University of Illinois Press, 1965.

Furniss, Norman F. *The Mormon Conflict, 1850-1859*. New Haven: Yale University Press, 1960.

Garr, Glen. "Fielding Garr," n.d. Unpublished paper. Photocopy of typescript in my possession.

Garr, John C. *The Garr Genealogy: Genealogy of the Descendants of John Gar, or more particularly of his son, Andreas Gaar*. Cincinnati, Ohio: John C. Garr, 1894.

Gazetteer of the British Isles. Edinburgh: John Bartholomew & Son Ltd., 1966.

Goodman, Jack. "One-time Basque Haven, Hotel Now Shelters Antique Gallery." *Salt Lake Tribune*, July 19, 1876, E-5.

Grant, George D., to Brigham Young. *Deseret News*, November 19, 1856.

Grow, Stewart L. "Development of Political Parties in Utah." Ph.D. diss., University of Utah, 1954.

Gunderson, Lenore C. "Grandfather's Part in the Rescue of the Handcart Companies of 1856." Skit for Robert Taylor Burton Family Reunion, October 25, 1956. Photocopy of typescript in my possession.

Hafen, LeRoy R. *The Overland Mail*. 1926; rpt. ed., Lawrence, Mass.: Quarterman Publications, Inc., 1976.

Hafen, LeRoy R., and Ann W. Hafen. *The Utah Expedition, 1857-58*. Glendale, California: Arthur H. Clark Company, 1958.

_____. *Handcarts to Zion*. Glendale, California: Arthur H. Clark Company, 1960.

Hanks, Sidney A., and Ephraim K. Hanks. *Scouting for the Mormons on the Great Frontier*. Salt Lake City: Deseret News Press, 1948.

Hansen, Klaus J. *Quest for Empire: The Political Kingdom of God and the Council of Fifty in Mormon History*. East Lansing, Mich.: Michigan State University Press, 1967.

Hartley, William G. "Edward Hunter, Pioneer Presiding Bishop." In Donald Q. Cannon and David J. Whittaker, eds., 175-304. *Supporting Saints: Life Stories of Nineteenth-Century Mormons*. Provo: Religious Studies Center, Brigham Young University, 1985.

Hatch, Nelle. *Colonia Juarez*. Salt Lake City: Deseret Book, 1954.

Haven, Judith T., and Eliza Ann Haven, to Maria S. Burton, May 3, 1846. Photocopy of typescript in my possession.

HC. Joseph Smith, Jr., *History of the Church of Jesus Christ of Latter-day Saints.* B. H. Roberts, ed. 2d. ed. rev. 7 vols. Salt Lake City: Deseret Book Company, 1978.

Hill, Donna. *Joseph Smith: The First Mormon.* Garden City, New York: Doubleday, 1977.

History of the Relief Society, 1842-1966. Salt Lake City: The General Board of Relief Society, 1966.

Holley, H. Orvil. *The History and Effect of Apostasy on a Small Mormon Community.* M.A. thesis, Brigham Young University, 1966.

Howard, G. M. "Men, Motives, and Misunderstandings: A New Look at the Morrisite War of 1862." *Utah Historical Quarterly,* 44 (Spring 1976): 112-32.

Irving, Gordon. "Railroad Missionaries." 1974a. Unpublished paper. Photocopy in my possession.

Irving, Gordon. "The U. S. Missionary Effort of 1869-70." 1975b. Unpublished paper. Photocopy in my possession.

JD. *Journal of Discourses.* 26 vols. Liverpool and London: Latter-day Saints' Book Depot, 1855-86.

Jenson, Andrew. *Latter-day Saint Biographical Encyclopedia.* 4 vols. Salt Lake City: Andrew Jenson History Company, 1901-30.

JH. *Journal History.* Microfilm of scrapbook. Historical Department Archives.

Jones, Daniel W. *Forty Years Among the Indians.* 1890; rpt. ed., Salt Lake City: Bookcraft, 1960.

Jones, Nathaniel Very. Diary, 1846-47. Typescript. Historical Department Archives.

Kimball, Solomon F. "Our Pioneer Boys." *Improvement Era* 11 (July 1908): 668-80.

_____. "Belated Emigrants of 1856." 4 pts. *Improvement Era* 17 (November 1913): 4-15; (December 1913): 108-117; (January 1914); (February 1914): 286-99.

Kimball, Stanley B. "The Iowa Trek of 1846." *Ensign* 2 (June 1972): 36-45.

Kimball, William H., to Col. Robt T. Burton. August 13, 1857. Photocopy of holograph in my possession.

Klemgard, E. N. *Peter, James & John: Pacific Northwest Pioneers.* Chicago: E. N. Klemgard, 1977.

Knapp, John I., and R. I. Bonner. *Illustrated History and Biographical Record of Lenawee County, Michigan.* Adrian, Mich.: Times Printing Co., 1903.

Larson, Gustive O. "The Mormon Reformation." *Utah Historical Quarterly* 26 (January 1958): 45-63.

_____. *The "Americanization" of Utah for Statehood.* San Marino, Calif.: The Huntington Library, 1971.

Lyman, Edward Leo. *Political Deliverance: The Mormon Quest for Utah Statehood.* Urbana: University of Illinois Press, 1986.

McKell, Charles R. "The Utah State Hospital, A Study in the Care of the Mentally Ill." *Utah Historical Quarterly* 23 (October 1955): 297-327.

McBride, William. " 'Missionary Incidents': a leaf from the private journal of the Patriarch William McBride," n.d. Transcribed by E. R. Snow. From the family papers of Delsa McBride, Pima, Arizona. Photocopy of typescript in my possession.

————. Journal, 1854-55. Holograph. Historical Department Archives.

Miller, David E., and Miller, Della S. *Nauvoo: The City of Joseph.* Santa Barbara and Salt Lake City: Peregrine Smith, Inc., 1974.

"Minutes of a Special Meeting of the 15th Ward F. R. Society and the Ward teachers held in Society Hall, Thursday, Nov. 23rd, 1876." Relief Society Minutes, Fifteenth Ward, Riverside Stake, 1868-76. Historical Department Archives.

Mulvay, Jill C. " 'The Liberal Shall be Blessed': Sarah M. Kimball." *Utah Historical Quarterly* 44 (Summer 1976): 205-22.

Nauvoo Legion. Orders issued by General Robert T. Burton. April 28, 1866. Holograph in Utah State Archives; microfilm in Genealogical Society, item 842, reel 2, Nauvoo Legion Correspondence.

Neal, Frederick. *The Township of Sandwich.* Sandwich, Ont.: Frederick Neal, 1909.

Nibley, Preston. *Brigham Young: The Man and His Work.* 2nd ed. Salt Lake City: Deseret News Press, 1937.

"Our Gallery of Pioneers: Gen. Robert T. Burton," undated newspaper clipping in my possession.

Palmer, William R. "Francis Webster." *Men You Should Know: Biographical Sketches.* Radio Series. April 25, 1943. Typescript. William R. Palmer Collection, SUSC Special Collections, Cedar City, Utah.

Pedersen, Rose Mary. "Antelope Island—Beyond the Ranch's Fence." *Deseret News,* February 7, 1977, C-1.

Pratt, Parley P. *Autobiography of Parley Parker Pratt.* 7th ed. Salt Lake City: Deseret Book, 1968.

Pulsipher, Zerah. *Reminiscences of Zerah Pulsipher,* n.d. Holograph. Historical Department Archives.

Purdy, William E. "They Marched Their Way West: The Nauvoo Brass Band." *Ensign* 10 (July 1980): 20-23

Quinn, D. Michael. "The Mormon Succession Crisis of 1844." *BYU Studies* 16 (Winter 1976): 187-233.

————. "The Council of Fifty and Its Members, 1844-1945." *BYU Studies* 20 (Winter 1980): 163-97.

Raybould, Helen B. Interviewed by Janet B. Seegmiller, April 13, 1978. Helen is a granddaughter of Robert T. and Maria Burton who grew up in the house next door to Haven Villa. In 1910, her father, William S. Burton, moved his family to the avenues when Maria went to live on Third Avenue with her daughter Florence. While keeping her grandmother company when Florence and Edwin were away from home, Helen listened to her tell stories about her life. Tapes and transcript in my possession.

Register of Baptisms in the Parish of Amherstburg. Christ Church Parish Records, Amherstburg, Ontario, Vol. 2, 1829-72. Microfilm at Genealogical Society.

Relief Society Minutes, Fifteenth Ward, Riverside Stake, 1868-76. Historical Department Archives.

Russell, William D. "King James Strang: Joseph Smith Successor?" In F. Mark McKiernan, Alma R. Blair, and Paul M. Edwards, eds., 231-56. *The Restoration Movement: Essays in Mormon History*. Lawrence, Kansas: Coronado Press, 1973.

Schindler, Harold. *Orrin Porter Rockwell: Man of God, Son of Thunder*. Salt Lake City: University of Utah Press, 1966.

Schoenfeld, Elizabeth. "Brigham Young: He Died 100 Years Ago Today." *Deseret News*, August 29, 1977, C-1.

Seifrit, William C. "Charles Henry Wilcken, an Undervalued Saint." *Utah Historical Quarterly*, 55 (Fall 1987): 308-21.

Snow, Lorenzo, to Robert T. Burton. May 13, 1873. Photocopy of holograph in my possession.

Sonne, Conway B. *Saints on the Seas: A Maritime History of Mormon Migration 1830-1890*. Salt Lake City: University of Utah Press, 1983.

Stegner, Wallace. "Ordeal by Handcart," *Collier's* 138 (July 6, 1956): 78-85.

Stenhouse, T. B. H. *The Rocky Mountain Saints*. New York: D. Appleton and Company, 1878.

Stuart, Mark E. *Joseph Morris and the Morrisites*. B.A. thesis, Weber State College, Ogden, Utah, 1975. Photocopy of draft in my possession.

Stuart, Mark E., to Janet B. Seegmiller, April 16, 1982.

Stohl, Betty Burton. Untitled history of Susan Ellen McBride, prepared 1987. Typescript. Original in my possession.

Summit County. Miscellaneous Records. County Recorder, Summit County Courthouse, Coalville, Utah.

Talmage, John R. *The Talmage Story*. Salt Lake City: Bookcraft, 1972.

Taylor, John, to Robert T. Burton, October 10, 1878. Letter of election to Zion's Board of Trade and appointment as one of the Executive Committee. Holograph in my possession.

"Trunk Factory Burned." *Salt Lake Herald*, December 25, 1877.

Tullidge, Edward W. *The History of Salt Lake City and its Founders*. Salt Lake City: Edward W. Tullidge, c1886.

United States of America vs. James Bridger. Bench Warrant. August 17, 1853. Criminal Court Cases, July 1853, 737 thru 748, First District Court. Utah State Archives.

University of Illinois. *History of Knox County*. Chas. C. Chapman & Co., 1878.

Van Tassel, Charles Sumner. *Story of the Maumee Valley, Toledo and the Sandusky Region*. Chicago: S. J. Clarke, 1929.

Vetterli, Richard. *Mormonism, Americanism and Politics*. Salt Lake City: Ensign Publications, 1961.

Wadley, Carma. "Gravestone Rubbings: Tracing Our Pioneer Past." *Deseret News*, July 24, 1976, 8-W.

Waldroup, William. "New Mexico During the Civil War." *New Mexico Historical Review* 27 (1953): 163-67.

Wells, Daniel H., to Robert T. Burton, October 5 and October 18, 1857. Photocopies of holographs in my possession.

Wells, Daniel H. "Special Orders No. 15," April 9, 1858. Photocopy of holograph in my possession.

Westover, Eliza Ann, to Lewis Westover, July 2, 1918. Photocopy of typescript in my possession.

Whitney, Orson F. *History of Utah*. 4 vols. Salt Lake City: George Q. Cannon, 1892-98.

WW. Woodruff, Wilford. *Wilford Woodruff's Journal*. 1833-1898. Typescript. Ed., Scott G. Kenney. 9 vols. Midvale, Utah: Signature Books, 1983-85.

Young, John R. Scrapbook, 1928-30. Historical Department Archives.

Young, Brigham. "Citizens of Utah," broadside proclamation, August 8, 1857. Historical Department Archives.

Young, Brigham. *Diary of Brigham Young, 1857*. Ed., Everett L. Cooley. Salt Lake City: University of Utah Library, 1980.

Young, Brigham. to Robert T. Burton. November 26, 1856. Photocopy of holograph in my possession.

Index

(Pages of photographs are italicized.)

This book designed by
Bailey-Montague & Associates
printed by Publishers Press
and bound by
Mountain States Bindery